REA

P9-AFY-187

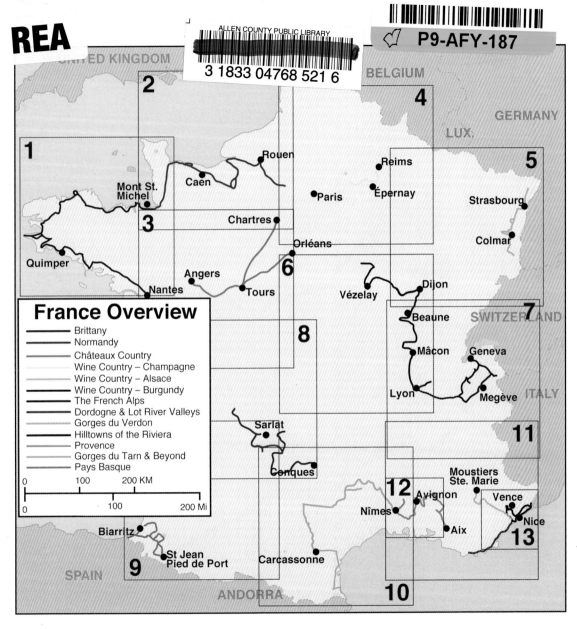

UNITED KINGDOM

BELGIUM

LUX.

GERMANY

2

4

1

5

Rouen

Reims

Caen

Paris

Épernay

Mont St. Michel

Strasbourg

3

Chartres

Colmar

Orléans

Quimper

6

Angers

Vézelay

Dijon

Nantes

Tours

Beaune

SWITZERLAND

7

France Overview

———	Brittany
———	Normandy
———	Châteaux Country
———	Wine Country – Champagne
———	Wine Country – Alsace
———	Wine Country – Burgundy
———	The French Alps
———	Dordogne & Lot River Valleys
———	Gorges du Verdon
———	Hilltowns of the Riviera
———	Provence
———	Gorges du Tarn & Beyond
———	Pays Basque

8

Mâcon

Geneva

Lyon

Megève

ITALY

0   100   200 KM

0   100   200 Mi

Sarlat

11

Conques

Moustiers Ste. Marie

12

Vence

Biarritz

Avignon

Nîmes

Nice

13

St Jean Pied de Port

Carcassonne

Aix

9

SPAIN

10

ANDORRA

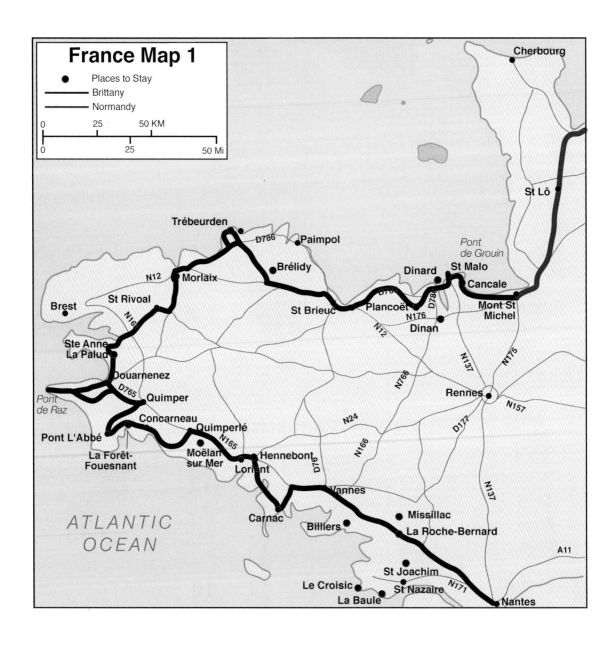

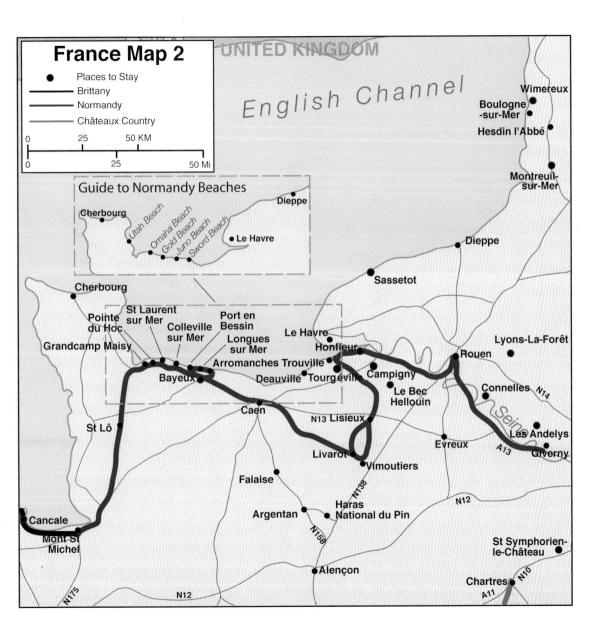

France Map 2

- ● Places to Stay
- —— Brittany
- —— Normandy
- —— Châteaux Country

0   25   50 KM

0   25   50 Mi

UNITED KINGDOM

English Channel

Guide to Normandy Beaches

Cherbourg

Utah Beach

Omaha Beach

Gold Beach

Juno Beach

Sword Beach

Dieppe

● Le Havre

Wimereux

Boulogne -sur-Mer

Hesdin l'Abbé

Montreuil- sur-Mer

Dieppe

Sassetot

Cherbourg

Pointe du Hoc

St Laurent sur Mer

Colleville sur Mer

Port en Bessin

Longues sur Mer

Grandcamp Maisy

Arromanches

Le Havre

Honfleur

Trouville

Deauville

Tourgéville

Campigny

Rouen

Lyons-La-Forêt

Bayeux

Connelles

N14

Seine

Le Bec Hellouin

Les Andelys

Caen

N13

Lisieux

St Lô

Evreux

A13

Giverny

Livarot

Vimoutiers

Falaise

N13B

Argentan

Haras National du Pin

N12

N158

Cancale

Mont St Michel

Alençon

Chartres

St Symphorien- le-Château

N10

A11

N175

N12

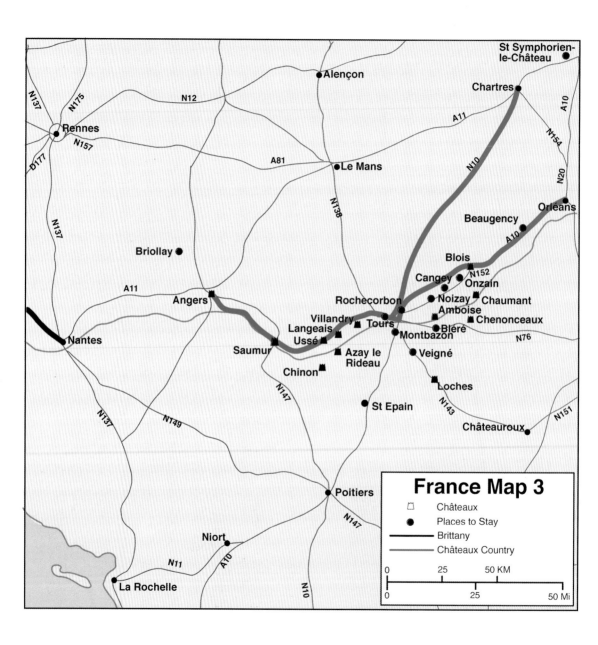

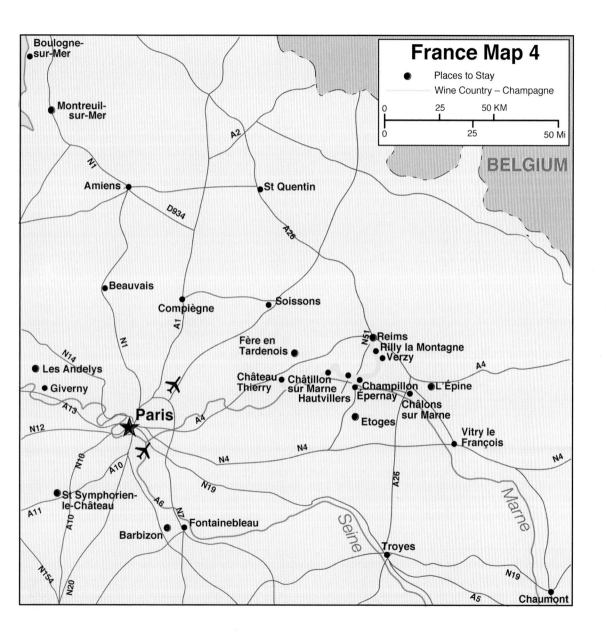

France Map 4

- ● Places to Stay
- — Wine Country – Champagne

0 25 50 KM
0 25 50 Mi

BELGIUM

Boulogne-sur-Mer

Montreuil-sur-Mer

Amiens

St Quentin

A2

N1

D934

A26

Beauvais

Compiègne

Soissons

A1

N14

N1

Fère en Tardenois

Reims

N51

Rilly la Montagne

Verzy

A4

Les Andelys

Giverny

Château Thierry

Châtillon sur Marne

Champillon

Hautvillers

Épernay

L'Épine

A13

Paris

A4

Châlons sur Marne

N12

Etoges

Vitry le François

N4

N4

N4

A26

N10

A10

N19

A6

A26

Marne

St Symphorien-le-Château

N7

Fontainebleau

A11

A10

Seine

Barbizon

Troyes

N19

N154

N20

A5

Chaumont

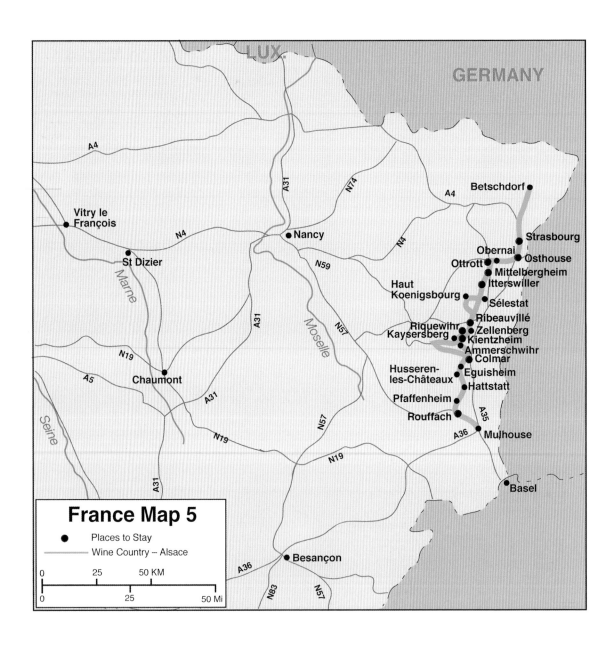

France Map 5

- ● Places to Stay
- ── Wine Country -- Alsace

| 0 | 25 | 50 KM |
| 0 | 25 | 50 Mi |

LUX.

GERMANY

A4

A31

N74

A4

Betschdorf ●

Vitry le
François ●

N4

● Nancy

N4

Strasbourg ●

Obernai ●
Ottrott ●

Osthouse ●

St Dizier ●

N59

Mittelbergheim ●
Itterswiller ●

Marne

Haut
Koenigsbourg ●

Sélestat ●

Moselle

N57

Ribeauvillé ●

Riquewihr ●

Zellenberg ●

Kaysersberg ●

Kientzheim ●
Ammerschwihr ●

A31

N19

Colmar ●

A5

Chaumont ●

A31

Husseren-
les-Châteaux ●

Eguisheim ●
Hattstatt ●

Seine

Pfaffenheim ●

N57

A35

Rouffach ●

N19

A36

Mulhouse ●

N19

A31

Basel ●

A36

● Besançon

N83

N57

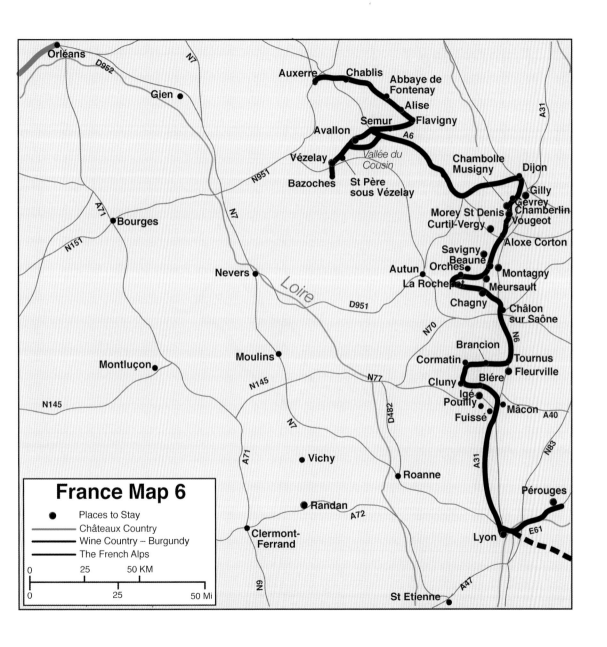

France Map 6

- ● Places to Stay
- ── Châteaux Country
- ━ Wine Country -- Burgundy
- ━ The French Alps

0   25   50 KM

0   25   50 Mi

Orléans

Gien

Auxerre

Chablis

Abbaye de Fontenay

Alise

Semur

Flavigny

Avallon

Vézelay

Vallée du Cousin

Bazoches

St Père sous Vézelay

Chambolle Musigny

Dijon

Gilly

Gevrey Chamberlin

Morey St Denis

Vougeot

Curtil-Vergy

Aloxe Corton

Bourges

Savigny

Beaune

Orches

Montagny

Autun

Meursault

La Rochepot

Nevers

Chagny

Châlon sur Saône

Brancion

Tournus

Cormatin

Fleurville

Moulins

Blére

Cluny

Montluçon

Igé

Pouilly

Mâcon

Fuissé

Vichy

Pérouges

Roanne

Lyon

Randan

Clermont-Ferrand

St Etienne

Loire

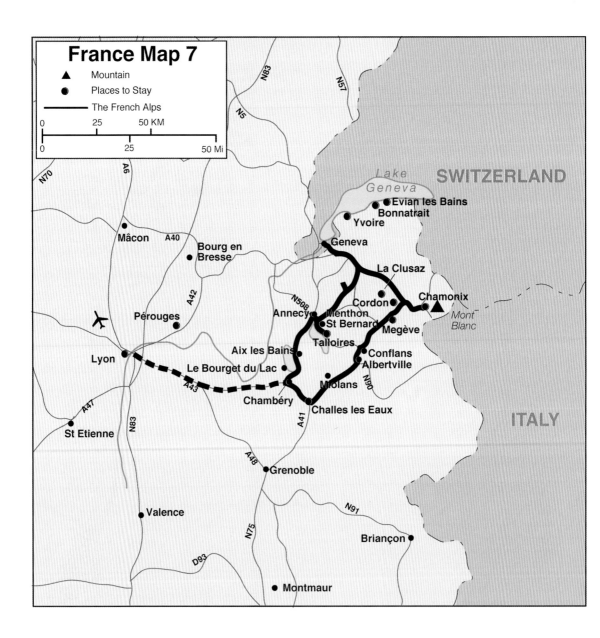

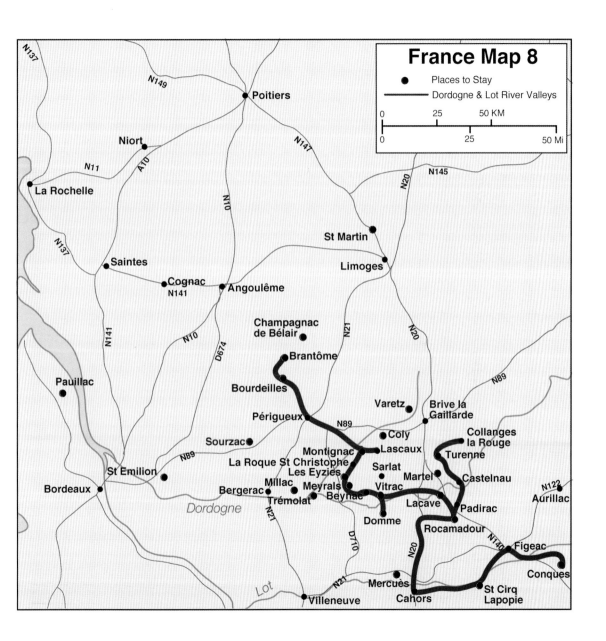

France Map 8

● Places to Stay

— Dordogne & Lot River Valleys

0   25   50 KM

0   25   50 Mi

N137

N149

Poitiers

N147

Niort

A10

N11

N10

St Martin

N145

N20

La Rochelle

N137

Saintes

Cognac
N141

Angoulême

Limoges

N141

N10

D674

Champagnac
de Bélair

N21

N20

Brantôme

Bourdeilles

Pauillac

Varetz

Brive la
Gaillarde

N89

Périgueux

N89

Coly

Collanges
la Rouge

Sourzac

Montignac

Lascaux

Turenne

La Roque St Christophe

Sarlat

Martel

Castelnau

N89

Les Eyzies

St Emilion

Millac

Meyrals

Vitrac

N122

Bergerac

Beynac

Lacave

Aurillac

Bordeaux

Trémolat

N21

Dordogne

Padirac

Domme

Rocamadour

N140

Figeac

D710

N20

Conques

Lot

N21

Mercuès

St Cirq
Lapopie

Villeneuve

Cahors

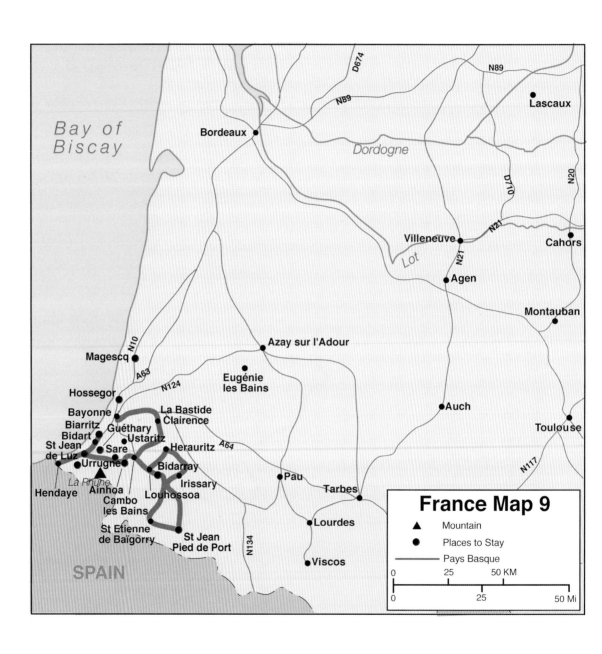

Bay of
Biscay

Bordeaux

Dordogne

Lascaux

N89

N89

D674

Villeneuve

Lot

N21

Cahors

D710

N20

Agen

Montauban

N21

Azay sur l'Adour

N10

Magescq

A63

Eugénie
les Bains

N124

Auch

Hossegor

Bayonne

La Bastide
Clairence

Biarritz
Bidart
St Jean
de Luz

Guéthary
Ustaritz

Sare

Herauritz

A64

Toulouse

Urrugne

Bidarray

N117

La Rhune

Irissary

Pau

Hendaye

Ainhoa

Louhossoa

Cambo
les Bains

Tarbes

St Etienne
de Baïgorry

St Jean
Pied de Port

N134

Lourdes

SPAIN

Viscos

France Map 9

▲   Mountain

●   Places to Stay

━   Pays Basque

0   25   50 KM

0   25   50 Mi

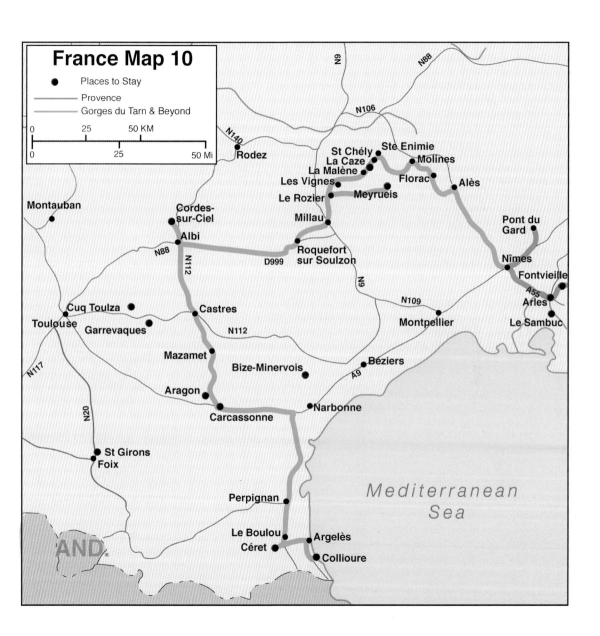

France Map 10

- ● Places to Stay
- Provence
- Gorges du Tarn & Beyond

0   25   50 KM

0   25   50 Mi

N9

N88

N106

N140

Rodez

St Chély
La Caze
La Malène
Les Vignes
Le Rozier
Meyrueis
Ste Enimie
Molines
Florac
Alès

Montauban

Cordes-
sur-Ciel
Albi

Millau

Pont du
Gard

N88

N112

Roquefort
sur Soulzon

D999

Nîmes

N9

Fontvieille

A55

Arles

Cuq Toulza

Castres

N112

N109

Le Sambuc

Toulouse

Garrevaques

Montpellier

N117

Mazamet

Bize-Minervois

Béziers

A9

N20

Aragon

Carcassonne

Narbonne

St Girons
Foix

Mediterranean
Sea

Perpignan

AND.

Le Boulou
Céret

Argelès

Collioure

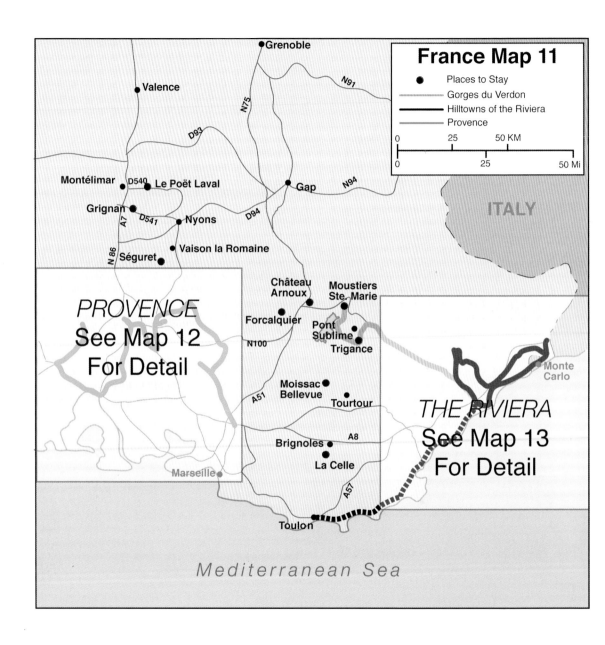

France Map 11

- ● Places to Stay
- ┄┄┄ Gorges du Verdon
- ━━━ Hilltowns of the Riviera
- ━━━ Provence

| 0 | 25 | 50 KM |
| 0 | 25 | 50 Mi |

Grenoble

Valence

N91

N75

D93

N94

Montélimar

D540

Le Poët Laval

Gap

ITALY

Grignan

D541

Nyons

D94

A7

N 86

Séguret

Vaison la Romaine

PROVENCE
See Map 12
For Detail

Château Arnoux

Moustiers Ste. Marie

Forcalquier

Pont Sublime

N100

Trigance

A51

Moissac Bellevue

Tourtour

Monte Carlo

THE RIVIERA
See Map 13
For Detail

Brignoles

A8

La Celle

Marseille

A57

Toulon

Mediterranean Sea

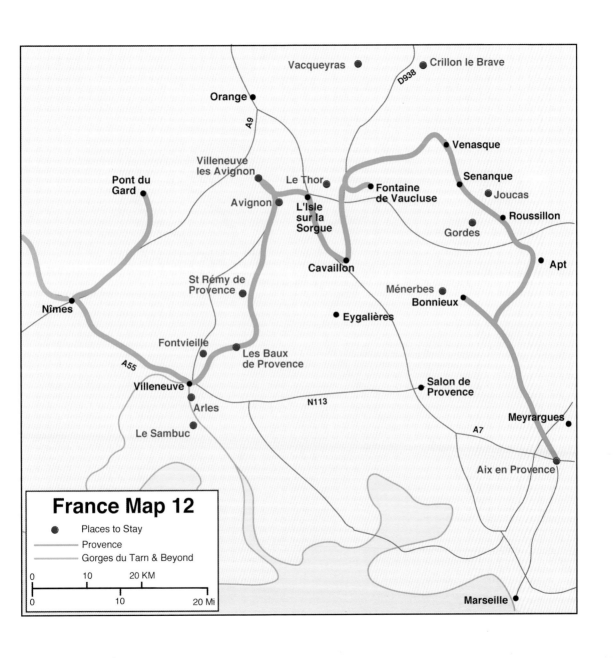

France Map 12

● Places to Stay
— Provence
— Gorges du Tarn & Beyond

0   10   20 KM
0   10   20 Mi

Vacqueyras ●

D938

● Crillon le Brave

Orange ●

A9

Villeneuve les Avignon ●

Le Thor ●

● Venasque

● Senanque

Fontaine de Vaucluse ●

● Joucas

Avignon ●

L'Isle sur la Sorgue ●

● Roussillon

Gordes ●

● Apt

Pont du Gard ●

Cavaillon ●

St Rémy de Provence ●

Ménerbes ●

Bonnieux ●

Eygalières ●

Nîmes ●

Fontvieille ●

Les Baux de Provence ●

A55

Villeneuve ●

Arles ●

N113

Salon de Provence ●

Meyrargues ●

A7

Le Sambuc ●

Aix en Provence ●

Marseille ●

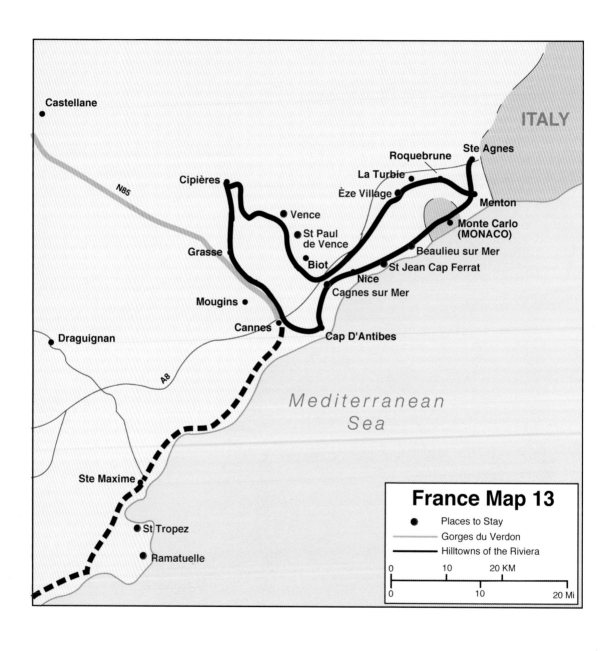

Castellane

ITALY

Cipières

Ste Agnes

Roquebrune

La Turbie

Èze Village

Menton

Vence

Monte Carlo
(MONACO)

St Paul
de Vence

Grasse

Beaulieu sur Mer

Biot

St Jean Cap Ferrat

Nice

Mougins

Cagnes sur Mer

Draguignan

Cannes

Cap D'Antibes

N85

A8

Mediterranean
Sea

Ste Maxime

St Tropez

Ramatuelle

France Map 13

●   Places to Stay

     Gorges du Verdon

━━━   Hilltowns of the Riviera

0	10	20 KM
0	10	20 Mi

Karen Brown's
FRANCE
2006

Contents

In memory of our wonderful Nancy,
who adored France and loved to travel.
Thank you for your company over all those miles,
for your friendship and love.
You will always live on in our hearts.

2006 Cover Painting: Château de Maulmont, Randan

Authors: Karen Brown and Clare Brown.

Contributing Author: Marie Collins Ksstentini.

Editors: Anthony Brown, Clare Brown, Karen Brown, June Eveleigh Brown, Courtney Gaviorno, Yvonne Sartain, Debbie Tokumoto.

Illustrations: Barbara Maclurcan Tapp.

Color photo: Conques.

Cover painting: Jann Pollard.

Maps: Michael Fiegel.

Technical support: Michael Fiegel, Gary Meisner.

Distributed by National Book Network, 15200 NBN Way, Blue Ridge Summit, PA 17214, USA. Tel: 717-794-3800 or 1-800-462-6420, Fax: 1-800-338-4500, Email: custserv@nbnbooks.com

A catalog record for this book is available from the British Library.

ISSN 1535-735X

Introduction

Yes, you can fly to Paris, eat hamburgers, stay in a generic chain hotel, and return home with stacks of snapshots or you can follow our regional itineraries and venture into the ever-changing French countryside. You can eat, sleep, and drink France, enjoy lovely scenery and unusual sights, mingle with the French, and return home with special memories as well as snapshots to recall them. To further tempt you, we have selected magnificent places to lay your head each night: elegant châteaux, cozy inns, scenic mills, and refined manors owned and managed by warm and fascinating people. Many of these were designed and built centuries ago as private residences and are set in beautiful surroundings. As travelers, you can take full advantage of this opportunity to live France every minute, twenty-four hours a day.

PURPOSE OF THIS GUIDE

This guide is written with two main objectives: to describe the most charming, beguiling lodgings throughout France and to "tie" them together with itineraries to enable travelers to plan their own holiday. The aim is not simply to inform you of the fact that these places exist, but to encourage you to go and see for yourself: explore towns and villages not emphasized on tours and stay at hotels that truly reflect the French lifestyle. This book contains all of the necessary ingredients to assist you with your travel arrangements: easy-to-follow driving itineraries that take you deep into the lovely French countryside, and, most importantly, a selective listing of hotels that we have seen and enjoy. It might be an elegant château dominating a bank of the River Loire or a cozy mill tucked into the landscape of the Dordogne Valley, but there is a common denominator—they all have charm, an enticing location, and comfort. Our theory is that where you stay each night matters: your hotels should add the touch of perfection that makes your holiday very special. The memories you bring home should be of more than just museums, landmarks, and palace tours. Such sights are important, but with this guide you can add a romantic element to your trip: traveling the enchanting back roads of France and staying in picturesque hideaways.

If you also enjoy traveling the "bed and breakfast way," we suggest you refer to our companion guide, *France: Bed & Breakfasts & Itineraries*. Bed and breakfasts, reasonably priced, are a fantastic value and offer charming accommodation with a more intimate experience—you are a guest in a private château or romantic farmhouse and often have the opportunity to dine with your hosts. An itinerary incorporating stays at bed and breakfasts as well as country inns can result in a wonderful and memorable trip.

We encourage you to buy new editions of our guide as in each new edition we add new discoveries, update prices, phone and fax numbers, and delete places that no longer meet our standards. This title on France is the flagship of the series and it is now over a quarter of a century that it has been in print. This eighteenth edition proudly boasts 215 hotel recommendations and thirteen wonderful driving itineraries that weave a journey through the landscape of the French countryside.

AIRFARE

Karen Brown's Guides have long recommended Auto Europe for their excellent car rental services. Their air travel division, Destination Europe, an airline broker working with major American and European carriers, offers deeply discounted coach- and business-class fares to over 200 European gateway cities. It also gives Karen Brown travelers an additional 5% discount off its already highly competitive prices (cannot be combined with any other offers or promotions). We recommend making reservations by phone at (800) 223-5555. When phoning, be sure to use the Karen Brown ID number 99006187 to secure your discount.

CAR RENTAL

Readers frequently ask our advice on car rental companies. We always use Auto Europe, a car rental broker that works with the major car rental companies to find the lowest possible price. They also offer motor homes and chauffeur services. Auto Europe's toll-free phone service from every European country connects you to their U.S.-based, 24-hour reservation center (ask for the European Phone Number Card to be sent to you). Auto Europe offers our readers a discount, and occasionally free upgrades. Be sure to use the Karen Brown ID number 99006187 to receive your discount and any special offers.

You can also make your own reservations online via our website, *www.karenbrown.com* (select *Auto Europe* from the home page), or by telephone (800-223-5555).

CELLPHONES

Cellphones are wonderful to have, especially at the smaller hotels and inns that do not have direct-dial phones in the guestrooms. Also, cellphones are enormously convenient when you are on the road and want to call for directions, advise of a changed arrival time, or simply make sure that someone is home—especially since public phones in France are no longer coin-operated but require that you purchase a phone card.

Cellphones can be rented through your car rental company, at the airport or train stations, or you can purchase an international phone once you are overseas. If you are considering taking your cellphone from home, check with your carrier to make sure that your phone even has international capability. Sometimes it is necessary to make arrangements before you depart to activate a special service. We would also recommend getting international phone access numbers and inquiring about international charges.

CHILDREN

Places to stay that have advised us that their establishment is appropriate for children have the symbol 🛏️ in the description details. While legally children cannot be refused accommodation, as parents, we really want to stay where our children are genuinely welcome.

CLOTHING

France stretches some 1,200 kilometers from Calais on the north coast to Nice on the Riviera in the south, so there is a great range of weather conditions, regardless of the season. For winter bring warm coats, sweaters, gloves, snug hats, and boots. The rest of the year a layered effect will equip you for any kind of weather: skirts or trousers combined with blouses or shirts that can be "built upon" with layers of sweaters depending upon the chill of the day. A raincoat is a necessity, along with a folding umbrella. Sturdy, comfortable walking shoes are recommended not only for roaming the countryside and mountain trails, but also for negotiating cobbled streets. Daytime dress is casual, but in the evening it is courteous to dress up for dinner at your hotel.

CREDIT CARDS

Whether or not an establishment accepts credit cards is indicated in the list of icons at the bottom of each description by the symbol ▣. We have also indicated the specific cards accepted using the following codes: AX–American Express, MC–MasterCard, VS–Visa, or simply, all major. *Note:* Even if an inn does not accept credit card payment, it will perhaps request your account number as a guarantee of arrival.

Also, conveniently and wonderfully, credit cards are now widely accepted at most gas stations and can be used for paying tolls on the autoroutes. (Previously it was necessary to ensure that you always had enough cash in hand to pay for gas and toll, both French currency guzzlers!)

CURRENCY–EURO

All pricing, including room rates, is quoted in euros, using the "€" symbol. The euro is now the official currency of most European Union countries, including France, having completely replaced national currencies as of February 2002. Visit our website (*www.karenbrown.com*) for an easy-to-use online currency converter.

When traveling, an increasingly popular and convenient way to obtain foreign currency is simply to use your bankcard at an ATM machine. You pay a fixed fee for this but, depending on the amount you withdraw, it is usually less than the percentage-based fee charged to exchange currency or travelers' checks. Be sure to check with your bank or credit card company about fees and necessary pin numbers prior to departure.

DRIVING

BELTS: It is mandatory and strictly enforced in France that every passenger wears a seat belt. Children under ten years of age must sit in the back seat.

DRIVER'S LICENSE: A valid driver's license from your home country is accepted in France if your stay does not exceed one year. The minimum driving age is 18.

GASOLINE: Americans are shocked by the high price of gasoline in Europe, especially when they realize published prices are for liters—only one fourth of a gallon. At some self-service stations you must pay in advance, before using the pumps (credit cards such as MasterCard and Visa are now often accepted). "Fill her up, please" translates as *"Faîtes le plein, s'il vous plaît."*

PARKING: It is illegal to park a car in the same place for more than 24 hours. In larger towns it is often customary that on the first 15 days of a month parking is permitted on the side of the road whose building addresses are odd numbers, and from the 16th to the end of the month on the even-numbered side of the road. Parking is prohibited in front of hospitals, police stations, and post offices. Blue Zones restrict parking to just one hour and require that you place a disc in your car window on Monday to Saturday from 9 am to 12:30 pm and again from 2:30 to 7 pm. Discs can be purchased at police stations and tobacco shops. Gray Zones are metered zones and a fee must be paid between the hours of 9 am and 7 pm.

ROADS: The French highway network consists of *autoroutes* (freeways or motorways), *péages* (autoroutes on which a toll is charged), and secondary roads (also excellent highways). Charges on toll roads are assessed according to the distance traveled. A travel ticket is issued on entry and you pay the toll on leaving the autoroute. The ticket will outline costs for distance traveled for various types of vehicles. It is expensive to travel on toll roads, so weigh carefully the advantage of time versus cost. If you have unlimited time and a limited budget, you may prefer the smaller highways and country roads. A suggestion would be to use the autoroutes to navigate in and out of, or bypass large cities and then return to the country roads. Credit cards are now accepted at tollbooths.

SPEED: Posted speed limits are strictly enforced and fines are hefty. Traffic moves fast on the autoroutes and toll roads with speed limits of 130 kph (81 mph). On the secondary highways the speed limit is 90 kph (56 mph). The speed limit within city and town boundaries is usually 60 kph (38 mph). Keep a lookout for the *gendarmes*!

ELECTRICAL CURRENT

If you are taking any electrical appliances made for use in the United States, you will need a transformer plus a two-pin adapter. A voltage of 220 AC current at 50 cycles per second is almost countrywide, though in remote areas you may encounter 120V. The voltage is often displayed on the socket. Even though we recommend that you purchase appliances with dual-voltage options whenever possible, it will still be necessary to have the appropriate socket adapter. Also, be especially careful with expensive equipment such as computers—verify with the manufacturer the adapter/converter capabilities and requirements.

HOTELS

HOTEL DESCRIPTIONS: Following the itinerary section, the second half of this guide is devoted to hotel descriptions. The selective listing of hotels are divided into two parts: Paris Hotels and Countryside Places to Stay. The first part of this section focuses on Paris and these hotels are alphabetically sequenced within their arrondissement (or district). A Paris map and key proceed the descriptions to provide a general idea as to the hotels' locations within the city. Paris hotels are followed by descriptions of places to stay in the countryside and these properties are referenced alphabetically by town. The location of the countryside hotels are pinpointed on the color maps found at the front of the book.

Every property recommended has been personally visited by us. It is impossible to revisit every hotel on a research trip as there are always new hotels to investigate, but we try to check up on as many as possible. We also rely on feedback from readers, follow up on any complaints, and eliminate hotels that do not maintain their quality of service, accommodation, and welcome. People who seek personal experiences and unforgettable accommodation rather than predictable motel-like rooms will appreciate our recommendations—we include château-hotels, hostelleries, hotels, old mills, manors, country inns, and restaurants with rooms. As the accommodation varies from luxurious to country-cozy, we have tried provide an honest written appraisal of what each hotel has to offer so that you can make a choice to suit your preferences. However, no matter how careful we are, sometimes we misjudge a hotel's merits, or the ownership changes, or unfortunately sometimes hotels just do not maintain their standards. If you find a hotel is not as we have indicated, we would greatly appreciate your comments.

HOTEL DIRECTIONS: Many of the places we recommend are located outside the town or village under which they are listed and are often difficult to find. To make finding your destination easier, we most definitely recommend that you purchase detailed, regional maps (see paragraph on maps). We do provide driving instructions with each description but in many cases they are general directions and not extensively detailed. In some cases, it would honestly take an entire page, compromising the description, to adequately address all you need to know in order to actually locate a specific property. We strongly recommend that you ask the property for detailed directions and a map when making your reservation, or go to *www.karenbrown.com* and link through to the property's own website, where in many cases detailed directions and maps are available and can be printed out for future reference. An added suggestion: Always plan to arrive at your destination before nightfall since road signs are difficult to see after dark.

HOTEL MEMBERSHIP AFFILIATIONS: A number of properties recommended in our guides also belong to private membership organizations. These associations impose their own criteria for selection and membership standards and have established a reputation for the particular type of property they include.

One affiliation that is very well recognized throughout the world is Relais & Châteaux and a number of properties that we recommend are members. Another, representing only properties in France, is Châteaux & Hôtels de France. Privately owned by one man, Pierre Traversac, there are also a number of châteaux-hôtels referred to as members of Grandes Étapes Françaises. We are familiar with the selection process, criteria, and membership standards of the various organizations and we feel comfortable in recommending them to our readers. If a property that we recommend is also a member of Relais & Châteaux, Châteaux & Hôtels de France or Grandes Étapes Françaises we note that in the bottom description details. Each organization has a central reservations center.

HOTEL RATES: We quote high-season, 2006 rates as provided by the hotels. The rates given are for the least expensive to the most expensive rooms or suites, inclusive of tax, for two persons. If breakfast is included in the room rate, it will be indicated in the list of icons at the bottom of the description by the symbol 🛏. If breakfast is not included it is priced per person. Please always check prices when making reservations. Prices can vary according to season, local special events, and additional features such as sitting rooms, balconies, and views. Remember that we show the rate for the high season (which is usually April through October), so if you travel off peak, you can frequently save money.

HOTEL RESERVATIONS & CANCELLATIONS: Whether or not you opt to secure reservations in advance depends on how flexible you want to be, how tight your schedule is, during which season you are traveling, and how disappointed you would be if your first choice were unavailable. Reservations are confining and usually must be guaranteed by a deposit. Refunds are difficult should you change your plans—especially at the last minute. In France a hotel is not required by law to refund a deposit, regardless of the cancellation notice given. Although reservations can be restrictive, it is nice not to spend a part of your vacation day searching for available accommodation, particularly during the peak summer months and holiday periods.

Should you decide to secure reservations in advance, several options are discussed on the following page. However, in each case, when making a reservation be sure to state clearly and exactly what you want, how many people are in your party, how many rooms you require, the category of room you prefer (standard, superior, deluxe), and your dates of arrival and departure. Inquire also about rates—which might have changed from those given in the book—and deposit requirements. In any written correspondence be sure to **spell out the month** since Europeans reverse the numerical month/day order—to them 9/6 means June 9th, not September 6th as interpreted in the USA. It is also wise to advise them of your anticipated arrival time; discuss dining options if so desired; and ask for a confirmation letter with brochure and map to be sent to you.

When making your reservations be sure to identify yourself as a "Karen Brown traveler." We hear over and over again that the people who use our guides are such wonderful guests. The hoteliers appreciate your visit, value their inclusion in our guide, and frequently tell us they take special care of our readers. In addition, many offer special rates to Karen Brown Club members (visit our website at *www.karenbrown.com*).

EMAIL: This is our preferred way of making a reservation. All properties featured on the Karen Brown website that also have e-mail addresses have those addresses listed on their web pages (this information is constantly kept updated and correct). You can link directly to a property from its page on our website using its email hyperlink.

FAX: Faxing is a very quick way to reach a hotel. If the hotel has a fax, we have included the number in its listing. As you are communicating with a machine, you also don't have to concern yourself with the time of day or worry about disturbing someone's sleep.

LETTER: Although most hotels can understand a letter written in English, for ease of communicating, on the following page is a template of a reservation request letter in French and English.

TELEPHONE: A very efficient way of making reservations is by telephone—the cost is minimal and you have your answer immediately—so if space is not available, you can then choose an alternative hotel. If calling from the United States, allow for the time difference. (France is five hours ahead of New York) so that you can call during their business day. Dial 011 (the international code), 33 (France's code), and then only the last nine digits of the ten-digit number. The '0' in the regional prefixes is dropped (it is used only when dialing from within France).

Introduction

SAMPLE RESERVATION REQUEST LETTER

Madame/Monsieur:

Nous souhaiterions réserver/ We would like to reserve

_____ *chambre(s) à deux lits simples/* (number) room(s) with twin beds

_____ *chambre(s) avec un grand lit/* (number) room(s) with double bed

_____ *chambre(s) avec un lit supplémentaire/* (number) room(s) with an extra bed

___ *avec toilette et baignoire ou douche privée./* with a private toilet & bathtub or shower.

Pour _____ *nuits,* / for (number) of nights,

du _____ *au* _____/ from (arrival date) to (departure date) inclusive,

au nom de M ou Mme _____/ under the name of Mr. or Mrs. (your last name).

Note: For clarity, spell out date (month and day) or use day/month/year order with numbers.

Merci de nous confirmer cette réservation en nous communicant le prix de la (des) chambre(s), et le montant des arrhes que vous souhaitez./ Please confirm the reservation, rate of room (s) and deposit required.

Dans l'attente de votre réponse nous vous prions d'agréer, Madame, Monsieur, l'expression de nos salutations distinguées.
Please advise availability, rate of room and deposit needed. We will be waiting for your confirmation and send our kindest regards.

Your name & address

HOTEL RESTAURANTS: French cuisine is incomparable in creativity and price—it is not uncommon to pay more for dinner than for a room. We do not discuss restaurants in depth but we note whether a hotel has a restaurant. Some of France's most charming hotels are actually "restaurants with rooms," principally restaurants that offer rooms to patrons of their restaurant. Restaurants often have a tourist menu or menu of the day. Set meals, which usually include specialties of the house, are good value for money and offer a meal where the courses complement one another. Restaurants known for their gourmet cuisine often offer a *menu dégustation* (tasting menu) so that on one visit you can sample a selection of the chef's many artful creations. Many hotels prefer overnight guests to dine at their restaurant. To avoid misunderstandings, inquire about a hotel's dining policy when making your room reservation. If a recommended property does have a restaurant and serves meals to non-guests, we have indicated this with the symbol ¶ in the list of icons at the bottom of the description.

ICONS

Icons allow us to provide additional information about our recommended properties. When using our website to supplement the guides, positioning the cursor over an icon will in many cases give you further details. For easy reference an icon key can be found on the last page of the book.

We have introduced these icons in the guidebooks and there are more on our website, *www.karenbrown.com.* ❁ Air conditioning in rooms, ⊥ Beach nearby, ☙ Breakfast included in room rate, ↗ Children welcome, ♨ Cooking classes offered, ▥ Credit cards accepted, ☎ Direct-dial telephone in room, ⌂ Dogs by special request, ⊞ Elevator, ⊀ Exercise room, ⟁ Mini-refrigerator in rooms, ⊛ Some non-smoking rooms, P Parking available, ¶ Restaurant, ⚘ Spa, ⚲ Swimming pool, ⊀ Tennis, ▣ Television with English channels, ♋ Wedding facilities, ♿ Wheelchair friendly, ⟆ Golf course nearby, ⋀ Hiking trails nearby, ⋔ Horseback riding nearby, ⚔ Skiing nearby, ⚓ Water sports nearby, ♟ Wineries nearby.

INFORMATION

Syndicat d'Initiative is the name for the tourist offices (symbolized by a large "I") found in all larger towns and resorts in France. Tourist offices are pleased to give advice on local events and timetables for local trains, buses and boats, and they often have maps and brochures on the region's points of interest. They can also help with location and availability of local hotels and bed and breakfasts. The offices often close for two hours for lunch in the middle of the day.

In Paris the main tourist office is located at 127, Avenue Champs Élysées, near the George V Métro stop. (*Open all year, 9 am to 8 pm.*) They also have a website: *www.paris_touristoffice.com.*

There are also 45 regional *Accueil de France* (French Welcome) offices that will make reservations at hotels in their area no more than eight days in advance. A list of regional offices is available through the French Government Tourist Office.

You can obtain assistance, information, and free brochures before you leave the United States for France by calling the hotline "France on Call" at (410) 286-8310 from 9 am to 7 pm EST. You can also visit their website at *www.franceguide.com* to obtain contact information for all the individual, regional tourist offices throughout France.

FRENCH GOVERNMENT TOURIST OFFICES

USA: 444 Madison Ave., 16th Floor, New York, NY 10022-6903, tel: (212) 838-7800

USA: 9454 Wilshire Blvd., Suite 715, Beverly Hills, CA 90212-2967, tel: (310) 271-6665

USA: 676 N. Michigan Ave., Suite 3214, Chicago, IL 60611, tel: (312) 327-0290

UK: 178 Piccadilly, London W1V 9AL, England, tel: (020) 7399 3500

CA: 1981 Ave., McGill College, Ste 490, Montreal, Quebec H3A 2W9, tel: (514) 288-4264

ITINERARIES

Thirteen driving itineraries are included in this guide to help you map a route through the various regions of France. New to this edition is a wonderful itinerary that originates across the Swiss border in Geneva and explores the beautiful and breathtaking region of the French Alps. Depending on your time and interests, you might want to patchwork together a trip encompassing a couple of itineraries.

An overview map that shows all 13 itineraries is found on page 17. At the beginning of each itinerary we suggest our recommended pacing to help you decide the amount of time to allocate to each region.

MAPS

Each itinerary is preceded by a map showing the suggested route and sightseeing town locations. At the front of the book, in the Color Map section, the maps reference the location of every town where we recommend a bed and breakfast as well as an outline of the various countryside itineraries. All maps included in this guide are intended to provide a general impression of a region and itinerary route, and an approximate location of the towns where recommended places are found. These maps were drawn by an artist and are not intended to replace accurate commercial maps.

Detailed maps are essential for identifying, navigating, and exploring all the wonderful country roads and finding secluded countryside properties, and we recommend purchasing them in advance of your trip, both to aid in the planning of your journey and to avoid spending vacation time searching for the appropriate maps. We find Michelin maps are good and dependable and we refer to them in this book for bed and breakfast locations. Since we ourselves often had difficulty finding all the maps we wanted from one source, for our readers' convenience we stock a full inventory of the Michelin maps referenced in our guides, in addition to other Michelin products. You can easily order maps online through our website, *www.karenbrown.com*, and we will ship them out immediately.

POST OFFICES

Post offices are open in most towns from 8 am to 7 pm Monday to Friday and from 8 am to midday on Saturdays. There is a post office in Paris—at 52, Rue du Louvre, 75001—that is open 24 hours a day. In addition to the standard services typically provided by post offices, domestic and international telephone calls can be made there, efficiently and relatively inexpensively.

TRAINS

France does have an excellent train system serving major towns and cities, but it is often necessary to supplement your travel arrangements with either a taxi or car rental to reach small countryside towns and isolated inns. If you plan to use trains in France, you can research schedules and fares and even purchase tickets and passes online. (Note that many special fares and passes are available only if purchased in the United States.) For information and the best possible fares, and to book tickets online, visit our website, *www.karenbrown.com*.

TRIP CANCELLATION INSURANCE

Because unexpected medical or personal emergencies—or other situations beyond our control—sometimes result in the need to alter or cancel travel plans, we strongly recommend travel insurance. Prepaid travel expenses such as airline tickets, car rentals, and train fares are not always refundable and most hotels will expect payment of some, if not all of your booking, even in an emergency. While the owners might be sympathetic, many of the properties in our guides have relatively few rooms, so it is difficult for them to absorb the cost of a cancellation. We recommend insurance to cover these types of additional expenses arising from cancellation due to unforeseen circumstances. A link on our website (*www.karenbrown.com*) will connect you to a variety of insurance policies that can be purchased online.

WEBSITE

Please visit the Karen Brown website (*www.karenbrown.com*) in conjunction with this book. It provides information about the Karen Brown Club, comments and discoveries from you, our readers, information on our latest finds, post-press updates, the opportunity to purchase goods and services that we recommend (rail tickets, car rental, travel insurance), and one-stop shopping for our guides and associated maps. Most of our favorite places to stay are featured on our website (their web addresses are on their description pages in this book) with color photos and, through direct links to their own websites, even more information. For the properties that do not have their own online booking program, you can e-mail them directly, making reservations a breeze.

WHEELCHAIR ACCESSIBILITY

If an inn has *at least* one guestroom that is accessible by wheelchair, it is noted with the symbol ♿. This is not the same as saying it meets full disability standards. In reality, it can be anything from a basic ground-floor room to a fully equipped facility. Please discuss your requirements when you call your chosen place to stay to determine if they have accommodation that suits your needs and preference.

Itinerary Overview

Rouen

Champagne

Reims

Mont St.
Michel

Caen

Épernay

Alsace

Strasbourg

St. Malo

Normandy

Colmar

Brittany

Rennes

PARIS

Quimper

Angers

Vézelay

Tours

Orléans

Dijon

Nantes

Châteaux Country

Burgundy

Beaune

Geneva

The
French
Alps

Annecy

Brantôme

Dordogne & Lot
River Valleys

Lyon

Megève

Les Eyzies

Sarlat

Gorges
du Verdon

Conques

Moustiers
Ste. Marie

Pays Basque

Cahors

Trigance

Biarritz

Cordes

Millau

Ste. Enimie

Avignon

Vence

Cambo
les Bains

Nîmes

Gordes

Grasse

Nice

St Jean
de Luz

Gorges du Tarn
& Beyond

Arles

Aix

Sare

Carcassonne

Hilltowns of
the Riviera

St Jean
Pied de Port

Perpignan

Provence

Collioure

17

Normandy

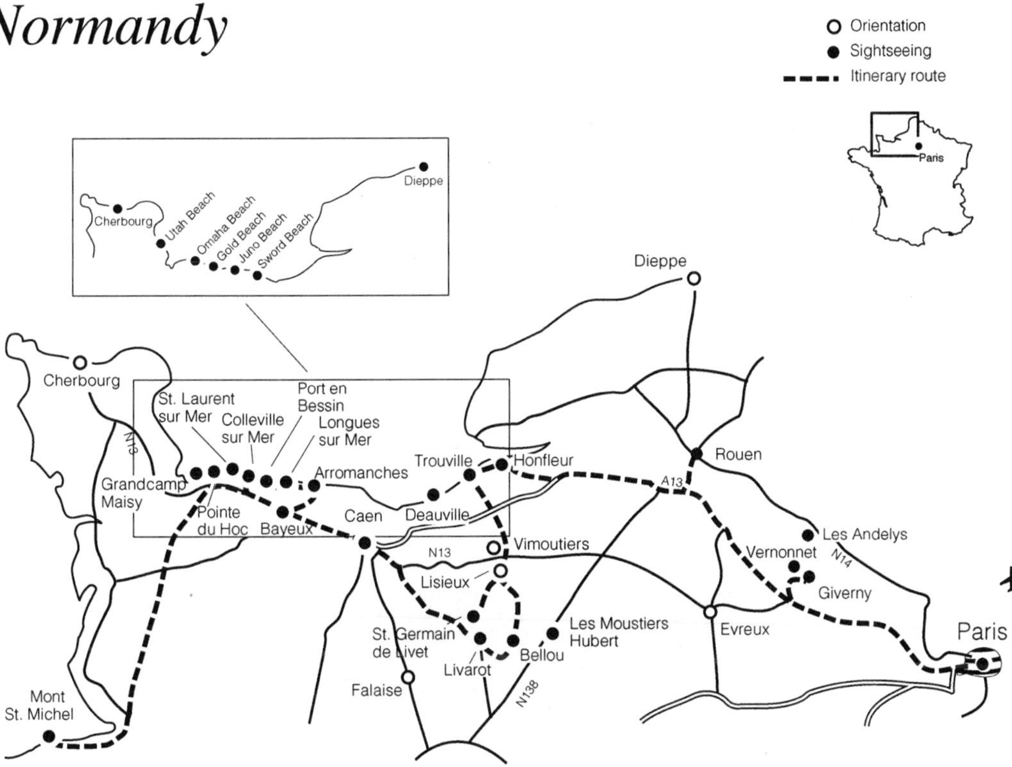

Legend:
- ○ Orientation
- ● Sightseeing
- ▪▪▪ Itinerary route

Inset map (beaches):
Cherbourg • Utah Beach • Omaha Beach • Gold Beach • Juno Beach • Sword Beach • Dieppe

Main map labels:
Dieppe
Cherbourg
St. Laurent sur Mer
Colleville sur Mer
Port en Bessin
Longues sur Mer
Arromanches
Trouville
Honfleur
Rouen
Les Andelys
Vernonnet
Giverny
Grandcamp Maisy
Pointe du Hoc
Bayeux
Caen
Deauville
N13
Vimoutiers
Lisieux
Les Moustiers Hubert
Evreux
Paris
St. Germain de Livet
Livarot
Bellou
Falaise
Mont St. Michel
N138
A13
N14
N13

Normandy

This itinerary heads north from Paris to Monet's wonderful gardens at Giverny, includes a detour to the historic city of Rouen, continues on to the coast with the picturesque port of Honfleur, and to the world-famous D-Day beaches and the Normandy coastline where on June 6, 1944 the Allies made their major offensive, reinforcing the turnaround in World War II. Decades have passed but abandoned pillboxes remain, the floating harbor endures, and museums document the events of the war. Turning inland, you visit historic Bayeux to marvel at its almost-thousand-year-old tapestry and the hinterland of Normandy with rolling farmland and villages of half-timbered houses—an area famous for its cheese. We conclude this itinerary, and begin the Brittany itinerary, with Normandy's famous Mont Saint Michel, a sightseeing venue that has attracted legions of visitors for hundreds of years.

Recommended Pacing: While you can use Honfleur as a base for this itinerary (except for visiting Mont Saint Michel), our preference is to spend at least one night near Giverny, possibly a night in Rouen, a night in Honfleur, and a minimum of two nights at the heart of Normandy to visit Bayeux, explore the D-Day beaches, and allow a day to follow the scenic roads through the lush countryside.

Follow the Seine north out of Paris (Porte d'Auteuil) on the A13 and exit at Bonnières sur Seine. Travel a scenic route following the N15 north along the Seine to Vernon. As you cross the Seine with the village of **Vernonette** sitting at the crossroads, you see the remains of a picturesque 12th-century bridge and an ancient timbered dungeon (a great picnic spot!). Just a few kilometers upstream lies the village of **Giverny**, a name synonymous worldwide with artist Claude Monet who came to live in the village in 1883.

Monet converted the barn into his studio, where he loved to paint, smoke, and reflect on his work. Now it's a visitors' center and gift shop selling all things Monet from posters of his masterpieces to key-rings. The walls are hung with reproductions of some of his larger canvases and photos of the famous artist at work. Monet's sun-washed peach stucco home with green shutters is decorated much as it was when he lived there—the walls hung with Japanese-style paintings and family pictures. From the striking blue-and-yellow dining room with its matching china, through his bedroom, to the cozy tiled kitchen, you get a feeling for the home life of this famous artist.

The magic of a visit to Giverny is the gardens, a multicolored tapestry of flowers, meandering paths shaded by trellises of roses, and the enchanting oasis of the water garden, whose green waters are covered with lily pads and crossed by Japanese bridges hung with white and mauve wisteria. Monet loved to paint outdoors and it is memorable to search out just the spot where he stood and painted a masterpiece. There is only one problem: you are not alone in your endeavors—Giverny attracts a multitude of pilgrims. However, the influx of tourists also means that this tiny village has a surprising number of facilities, including cafés, restaurants, and gift stores. (*Open Apr to Oct, closed Mon.*)

Another wonderful highlight and attraction, just a couple of hundred yards from Giverny, is the **Musée d'Art Américan**, which is dedicated to the appreciation of American art, focusing on the historical connection between French and American artists throughout the Impressionist and other 19th- and 20th-century periods. During the time of Claude Monet many American artists made pilgrimages to France to partake of the cultural and artistic fever of the time and be inspired by the beauty of the French countryside. If you desire a private tour, it can be scheduled directly through the museum: Musée d'Art Américan, 99, Rue Claude Monet, 27620 Giverny, tel: 02.32.51.94.65, fax: 02.32.51.94.67. (*Open Apr to Oct, closed Mon.*)

From Giverny, we recommend venturing farther on in the direction of Rouen and the coast. You can either go directly to Rouen by first returning to Vernon from Giverny and from there following signposts for that historic city, or consider a short detour to the scenic town of **Les Andelys.** Les Andelys is located on the banks of the Seine. It was once the hub of Franco-English relations during the Middle Ages and one can visit the ruins of the **Château Gaillard** whose hillside location affords a wonderful view of the path of the Seine as it loops north in the direction of Rouen. To reach Les Andelys, from Giverny, return to Vernonette and then follow the D313 (approximately 22 km) as it makes a scenic journey along the banks of the Seine. To continue on to Rouen from Les Andelys, cross the river to the south of town and follow the D135 to intersect with Autoroute and follow direction Rouen.

Rich in history, **Rouen** is termed the "museum city," but it is also famous for its magnificent cathedral and its connection with **Joan of Arc** and the Dauphin. Don't let the size of the city or its industrial outskirts intimidate you—it is easy to navigate to the charming heart of the old city and parking garages are well signed and convenient for exploring the historic pedestrian district.

Captured near Compiègne, Joan of Arc was brought to Rouen for judgment, charged with heresy, and sentenced to be burned at the stake. Before English authorities, church officials, and the masses, on May 30, 1431, she was burned alive at the Old Market Square. You can walk the square; visit the Tour de la Purcelle, the tower of the fortress where she was held prisoner; visit the neighboring Tour Jeanne d'Arc, the tower where she was threatened with torture before officials backed down, fearful of her religious demeanor; visit the Saint Ouén cemetery behind the town hall, where she was taken to renounce her sins; tour the Archevéché, the ecclesiastical court where the verdict was cast; and walk across the Pont Jeanne d'Arc which spans the river where her ashes and unburnt heart were cast into the water.

Rouen is also famous for its 11th-century **cathedral** with its striking Norman tower and 14th-century embellishments which was captured on canvas in every mood and light by Monet. Monet moved here to be with his brother in 1872 and at the peak of the Impressionist period painted the cathedral, the river, the factories—all acclaimed paintings, many of which now hang in the Musée Marmottan in Paris. Many other masters (Caravaggio, Velasquez, Fragonard, Géricault, and Sisley) were also inspired by the city and Rouen's **Musée des Beaux-Arts** has a wealth of their art on display. Rouen's many attractions include two 15th-century churches, a palace of justice, a big clock, and the 16th-century Bourgtheroulde Mansion.

From Rouen, continue the journey on to the coast by following signs to Caen along the A13. Exit the autoroute at Beuzeville and travel north on the D22 and then west on the D180 to Honfleur. **Honfleur** is a gem, its narrow, 17th-century harbor filled with tall-masted boats and lined with tall, slender, pastel-washed houses. Narrow cobbled streets lined with ancient timbered houses lead up from the harbor. Cafés and restaurants set up tables and umbrellas outside so that customers can enjoy the sun and the picturesque location. Small wonder that this pretty port has inspired artists, writers, and musicians. Markets are held every Saturday on Saint Catherine's Square with its unusual wooden belfry, a tall bell-tower and bell-ringer's home, standing apart from the nearby church. Just off the square, farther up the hillside, on Rue de l'Homme de Bois, is the interesting **Eugène Boudin Museum** with its impressive collection of pre-Impressionist and contemporary paintings by Norman artists: Boudin, Dubourg, Dufy, Monet, Friesz, and Gernez. There are also displays of Norman costumes and paintings depicting life in 18th- and 19th-century Normandy. (*Closed Tues, tel: 02.31.89.54.00.*)

Just by the harbor, in a former church, the **Musée Marine** traces the history of the port of Honfleur. Nearby, the ancient timbered prison is now the **Musée d'Art Populaire**, consisting of 12 rooms depicting the interiors of Norman houses including a weaver's workshop and a manor-house dining room. (*Closed Mondays, tel: 02.31.89.14.12.*) In addition to having quaint shops and inviting fish restaurants, Honfleur is a haven for artists and there are a number of galleries to visit.

Our advice is that if you visit Honfleur, stay for the night because this will give you the opportunity to enjoy this scenic town without the hordes of daytime visitors.

For a contrast to the quaintness of Honfleur you may choose to visit her two famous neighbors, Trouville and Deauville. **Trouville** has set the pace on the Côte Fleurie since 1852. A stretch of water divides it from its very close neighbor, **Deauville**, a much ritzier resort where row upon row of beach cabanas line the sands and well-heeled folks parade the streets. The casinos are a hub of activity, and if you visit in the late summer, you will

Honfleur

experience the excitement and sophistication of a major summer playground for the rich and famous. For a few weeks each August there is the allure of the racetracks, polo fields, glamorous luncheons, and black-tie dinners. Celebrities and the wealthy international set come here to cheer on their prize thoroughbreds.

From Honfleur dip south into a region of Normandy referred to as the **Pays d'Auge**, a lush region sandwiched between the Risle and Dives rivers. Here quaint villages of timbered and some thatched houses cluster on rolling green hillsides grazed by cows or planted with apple orchards. It is a region to experience by driving along its quiet country roads. The drive we suggest is a leisurely half-day outing beginning at **Lisieux**, the region's commercial center. If you are fortunate enough to arrive on Saturday, enjoy the town's colorful farmers' market where stalls offer everything from live chickens, vegetables, and cheese to underwear and shoes.

Leave Lisieux in the direction of Vimoutiers (D579), travel for just a few kilometers, and take a left turn down a country lane to **Saint Germain de Livet**, a hamlet at the bottom of the valley. Here you see a picture-postcard timbered farm, a couple of cottages, a church, and the adorable 15th-century **Château Saint Germain de Livet**. This whimsical little château with pepper-pot turrets and pretty pink-and-white-checkerboard façade sits in geometric gardens behind a high wall. The interior contains some attractive furniture and some paintings and frescoes. (*Closed Tues, tel: 02.31.31.00.03.*) Leaving the château, follow signposts for Vimoutiers (D268) till you reach the D47, which you follow into Fervaques, a picturesque village in a green valley. Drive past its château, a vast 16th-century stone building, to the village with its timbered cottages set round a quiet square. Here you pick up signposts for **Route de Fromage**, a tourist route that guides you through this lush and scenic cheese-producing region.

Follow the well-signposted Route de Fromage into **Les Moutiers Hubert**, a hamlet of farms along the road, up to **Bellou** with its large brown timbered manor house, and on to Lisores with its little church, ivy-covered houses, and farms in the valley. Regain the main road heading towards Livarot (D579) and travel for a few kilometers before being directed right by the Route de Fromage onto a back road that brings you by a more scenic route into the heart of the attractive old town of **Livarot**, home of the cheese that bears the same name. On the edge of town (driving in the direction of Caen), it is worth a stop to see the **Musée du Fromage** in the basement of one of the town's grand old homes. Here you watch a video on the production of Livarot, Pont l'Évêque, and Camembert cheeses, and tour a replica of an old dairy farm with its traditional cheese-making shop and old-fashioned dairy. (*Open all year, tel: 02.31.48.20.10.*)

As you continue on to Caen (40 kilometers), the countryside is pancake-flat. **Caen**, a large port situated on the banks of the Orne and one of Normandy's largest cities, lost nearly all of its 10,000 buildings in the Allied invasion of 1944. It is also the city that William the Conqueror made his seat of government. Your destination in Caen is the **Memorial** (Memorial to Peace). The museum is well signposted and has its own exit off the autoroute (exit 7 off the Caen ring road). Displays, films, tapes, and photos cover the events that led up to the outbreak of World War II, the invasion of France, total war, D-Day, the Battle of Normandy, and hope for lasting world peace. A good look round takes several hours, an in-depth visit all day. (*Closed Dec 25, Jan 1 to 15, tel: 02.31.06.06.44.*)

A 15-minute drive down the N13 brings you to **Bayeux**, a lovely old town where inviting shops and honey-colored stone houses line narrow streets. **Saint Patrice** square is filled with colorful market stalls on Saturday and Wednesday mornings. There has been a town on this site since Roman times: it was invaded by the Bretons, the Saxons, and the Vikings, but thankfully escaped the Allied bombers. It's a great place for shopping and serves as a convenient base for visiting the landing beaches.

Apart from the town itself, your premier destination in Bayeux is the **Musée de la Tapisserie**, which displays the famous tapestry that Odo, Bishop of Bayeux, had the English embroider following the conquest of England by his half-brother William the Conqueror in 1066. The color and richness of the tapestry make the little stick figures look as if they were stitched just yesterday, not over 900 years ago. With the aid of earphones the intricately embroidered scenes come alive. We found we needed to go past it twice—once quickly to appreciate its enormous proportions and the second time to hear the story it tells. (*Open all year, tel: 02.31.51.25.50.*)

Bayeux Tapestry

Next to the cathedral, the **Musée Baron Gérard** has some lovely examples of porcelain and lace manufactured in Bayeux. (*Open all year, tel: 02.31.92.14.21.*)

With World War II still recent history, for those who witnessed and experienced the Normandy Invasion, a trip to this region is a sentimental and poignant journey. Towns have been restored; but abandoned fortifications on the beaches as well as in the water, numerous museums, memorials, and cemeteries hauntingly remain as testaments and reminders of that heroic and tragic battle. There are eight itineraries that are well signposted and offer the traveler a trail based on the chronological sequence of events of this incredible battle. One could easily spend weeks here following the individual itineraries and the historical trail of each military force and mission. (The eight itineraries are signed on the roadways as follows: Overlord—The Assault or *Overlord—L'Assaut*; D-Day—The Onslaught or *D-Day—LeChoc*; Objective—A Port or *Objectif—Un Port;* The Confrontation or *L'Affrontement;* Cobra—The Breakout or *Cobra—La Percée*; The Counter Attack or *La Contre-Attaque*; The Encirclement or *L'Encerclement*; The Outcome or *Le Denouement.*) However, for the purposes of this itinerary, we propose a route that serves as an introduction to the major events and battles that so greatly influenced the outcome of the Second World War.

Bayeux was the first French town to be liberated and it seems appropriate to begin our D-Day journey here. On the main ring road around the old town is the **1944 Battle of Normandy Museum** with its exhibitions of tanks, guns, and armored vehicles used in the battle. (*Open all year, tel: 02.31.30.47.60.*) On the other side of the ring road, opposite the museum, is the **British Cemetery and Memorial**, honoring the memory of 1,837 missing servicemen.

From Bayeux, in search of the D-Day landmarks and beaches you will travel a scenic route that follows the coast, through the seaside villages that lay exposed to the battle, which took place on five principal landing beaches—Sword (farthest to the east), Juno, Gold, Omaha, and Utah (to the northwest). You will also weave through little gray-stone villages whose tall walled farmhouses and barns form their own little fortifications scattered around the fields. Although different route numbers identify various segments, there is basically one road that hugs the coastline.

To reach the coast, travel approximately 10 kilometers northeast of Bayeux to Gold Beach and **Arromanches**. Arromanches is a lively seaside town whose broad crescent of golden sand was one of the D-Day landing beaches dominated by the British troops. In June, 1944 a huge floating harbor was erected in a gigantic U in the bay. Designed by British engineers, the harbor was comprised of massive concrete blocks, floating pier-heads, and 10 kilometers of floating pier "roads." It was towed across the Channel and erected here, enabling the Allies to unload half-a-million tons of materials in a three-month period. After nearly 60 years of Atlantic storms much of the harbor is still in place and you can get an up-close look at several enormous sections marooned on the beach. Beside the beach is the **D-Day Museum** with its displays of models, photographs, and films of the military operations of June, 1944. (*Closed Jan, tel: 02.31.22.34.31.*) On the hillside above town is **Arromanches 360**, where an 18-minute production, *The Price of Freedom*, is dramatically shown on nine screens of this theater in the round. (*Closed Jan, tel: 02.31.22.30.30.*)

If time allows, you might want to continue east to explore the beaches of **Juno** and **Sword**, but for the purposes of this itinerary we direct you west along the coast from Arromanches to the village of **Longues sur Mer**. A country road from Longues sur Mer dead-ends on the bluffs at an open-air museum where you can walk along a path that weaves through the wheatfields to abandoned gun emplacements, overlooking the stretch of coastline that the German artillery so fiercely guarded. Longues sur Mer is the only naval artillery battery on the Normandy coast that still has its guns. *(Open all year, tel: 02.31.06.06.44)*

On the coast just 5 kilometers away, tucked on an inlet, is the small, charming port and fishing village of **Port en Bessin**, not far from our starting point, Bayeux. Port en Bessin has a museum with a collection of remains found on the sunken warships. *(Open Apr to Oct, tel: 02.31.21.17.06.)*

The road travels inland from the water's edge from Port en Bessin to **Colleville sur Mer**, where a road takes you out to the **American Cemetery** and an expansive 170-acre plot overlooking Omaha Beach. A dignified tribute to those who gave their lives in battle, 9,387 white crosses stand in perfect alignment on acreage that looks out to a backdrop of sand and ocean. The memory of this gorgeous setting, the beautiful paths that weave along the bluffs, the chapel, and the dramatic memorial will linger. *(Open all year, tel: 02.31.51.62.00.)*

Continue along the length of Omaha Beach to the town of **Saint Laurent sur Mer**. This town hosts a museum just yards from the sand, **Musée Omaha**, which boasts a collection of vehicles, weapons, uniforms, and insignia found on the sandy battlefield. *(Open Feb 15 to Nov 20, tel: 02.31.21.97.44.)* Both **Omaha Beach** and **Utah Beach** to the northwest are where the American army landed under the direction of General Bradley.

Follow the coast around Pointe et Raz de la Percée to the dramatic vantage point of **Pointe du Hoc**. As you stand on this rugged stretch of coastline, pockmarked by bombs, on the ruins of the German fortifications, it is hard to comprehend the courage of the American soldiers who braved the cliffs and blindly stormed the enemy believing this was a strategic stronghold. From here it is approximately 5 kilometers on to **Grandcamp Maisy**. Here the **Musée des Rangers** focuses on the specially-trained American unit and the capture of Pointe du Hoc.

From here you can easily travel the stretch north along the coast to Utah Beach or leave the coast and travel south via St. Lô to Mont Saint Michel where this itinerary concludes. Straddling the border of Brittany and Normandy, **Mont Saint Michel** is France's most visited tourist attraction. Joined to the mainland by a narrow strip of roadway, Mont Saint Michel, initially a place of pilgrimage, then a fortress, and in the 19th century a prison, clings to a rock island and towers 150 meters above sea level. Depending on the tide, it is either almost surrounded by water or by marshes and quicksand. Wander up the narrow cobblestoned streets to the crowning 12th-century abbey and visit the remarkable Gothic and Romanesque complex, culminating in the glories of the *Merveille* (Marvel) — the group of buildings on the north side of the mount. Saint Michael, the militant archangel, is the saint for the beaches you have just seen.

From Mont Saint Michel you can return to Paris, join the *Châteaux Country* itinerary, or continue on the following itinerary into Brittany.

Breton Women in Traditional Dress

Normandy

Brittany

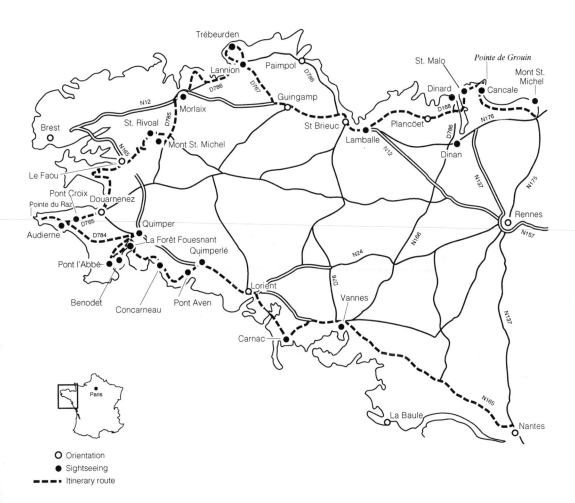

Trébeurden

Lannion
Paimpol
D786

St. Malo
Pointe de Grouin

Dinard
Cancale
Mont St.
Michel

D786
D767

Guingamp
D168

Morlaix
N12

St. Rivoal
Mont St. Michel
St Brieuc
Plancöet
D786

Brest
Lamballe
N12
Dinan

Le Faou
N165

Pont Croix
Douarnenez

Pointe du Raz
N137
N175

D765
Rennes

Audierne
D784
Quimper
N157

La Forêt Fouesnant
Quimperlé
N186

Pont l'Abbé
Pont Aven

Benodet
Concarneau
Lorient
N24
Vannes

D76

Carnac

N137

Paris

N165

La Baule
Nantes

○ Orientation
● Sightseeing
▪▪▪ Itinerary route

31

Brittany

Brittany is a rugged region of beautiful forests bounded by nearly 1,000 kilometers of coastline. This peninsula, jutting out from the northwest side of France, was for many years isolated from the rest of the country and regarded by Bretons as a separate country. The regional language is Breton and you see signposts in both French and Breton. Most of the houses are fresh white stucco with angled blue-gray roofs. *Crêpes* filled with butter, sugar, chocolate, or jam, *galettes* (wheat crêpes) enhanced with cheese, ham, onions, or mushrooms, and cider are Brittany's culinary specialties. This itinerary begins on Brittany's border at Mont Saint Michel and explores the coast before it ventures into the forested interior, culminating on the southern coast at Vannes with its charming old walled town.

Breton Coastal Village

Brittany

Recommended Pacing: Select a location in northern Brittany for the northern portion of the itinerary and one on the southwestern coast for the southern portion. Two nights in each spot should give you ample time to explore the peninsula.

While **Mont Saint Michel** is technically in Normandy, it is geographically in Brittany. Mont Saint Michel is France's premier tourist attraction, and although it is wonderful, we think it best to warn our readers that in high season, the effort of pushing your way uphill through teeming crowds, past souvenir shops, to reach the abbey at the summit is not enjoyable. The appearance of the town is that of a child's sand castle, with narrow, cobblestoned streets winding up to the 12th-century abbey and lovely Romanesque church, dedicated to Archangel Michael. Depending on the tide, the mount is either almost surrounded by water or by marshland and quicksand. Drive across the paved causeway that joins the mount to the mainland, park in the car park, and explore on foot.

Leaving Mont Saint Michel, take the D976 to Dol. Follow signposts for Saint Malo across the flat farmland to **Cancale** whose beachside port is full of lobsters, mussels, oysters, and clams, and whose attractive little town is nestled on the cliffs above. Follow signposts for *Saint Malo par la Côte* to Pointe du Grouin, a windswept headland and promontory. Rounding the point, you are rewarded by vistas of coastline stretching into the far distance.

Saint Malo corsairs, who menaced British seafarers during the 16th century, were pirates with royal permission to take foreign ships. With its tall 13th- and 14th-century ramparts facing the sea and enormous harbor (the terminal of ferries from Portsmouth and the Channel Islands), the town is almost surrounded by water. Within the walls are narrow streets lined with interesting shops and small restaurants. Much was destroyed in battle between Germans and Americans in 1944 but it has all been magnificently restored. Walk round the walls (stairs by Saint Vincent's gate), visit the courtyard of the 14th-century castle (now the town hall), and sample *crêpes* or *galettes*.

Following the D168, cross the *barrière* (low pontoon bridge) over the bay to **Dinard**, a popular beach resort. Once a sleepy fishing village, its confusion of one-way streets and seafront hotels (blocking views) discourage you from leaving the main highway.

Approximately 25 kilometers south of Dinard is the wonderful walled town of **Dinan**. Embraced by medieval ramparts, it is a charming city with cobbled streets, half-timbered houses, a historic convent, and castle ruins. It is a great place to spend an afternoon exploring the maze of streets, from its picturesque port to the encircling ramparts. Known as "the city of art history," Dinan has intriguing stores, a multitude of art galleries, and inviting sidewalk cafés.

A 45-kilometer drive through Plancoët brings you to **Lamballe**. At the heart of Lamballe's industrial sprawl are some fine old houses on the Place du Martrai, including the executioner's house, which is now the tourist office. The traffic is congested.

Join the N12 bypassing Saint Brieuc and Guigamp (the town where gingham was first woven) and take the D767 northwest to Lannion. **Lannion** is an attractive town beside the fast-flowing River Léguer with some fine medieval houses at its center, near the Place Général Leclerc. Follow signposts for Perros Guirec then **Trébeurden**, an attractive seaside resort with a small sheltered harbor separated from a curve of sandy beach by a wooded peninsula. Make your way back to Lannion along the beautiful stretch of coast and take the D786 towards Morlaix. At Saint Michel the road traces a vast sandy curve of beach and exposes vistas of succeeding headlands. Just as the road leaves the bay, turn right following signposts for *Morlaix par la Côte,* which gives you the opportunity to sample another small stretch of very attractive coastline. At Locquirec turn inland through Guimaéc and Lanmeur to regain the D786 to Morlaix.

Morlaix is a central market town whose quays shelter boats that travel the passage inland from the sea. You do not have to deal with city traffic as you follow the N12 (signposted Brest) around the town for a short distance to the D785 (signposted Pleyben Christ), which leads you into the **Regional Parc d'Amorique**. After the very gray little towns of Pleyben Christ and Plounéour Ménez the scenery becomes more interesting as the road leads you up onto moorlands where rock escarpments jut out from the highest hill. A narrow road winds up to the little chapel high atop **Mont Saint Michel** (an isolated windswept spot very different from its famous namesake). Return to the D785 for a short distance taking the first right turn to **Saint Rivoal**, which has a **Maison Cornic**, a small park with an interesting collection of old Breton houses.

Following signposts for Le Faou, you travel up the escarpment to be rewarded by sky-wide views of the distant coast. Travel through Forêt du Cranou with its majestic oak trees to Le Faou where you continue straight (signposted Crozon). The route hugs the Aulne estuary and offers lovely vistas of houses dotting the far shore, then gives way to wooded fjords before crossing a high bridge and turning away from the coast. At Tar-ar-Groas make an almost 180-degree turn in the center of the village and continue the very pleasant drive following signposts for Douarnenez, a large fishing port that you skirt on the D765 following signposts for Audierne. **Pont Croix** is built on terraces up from the River Goyen. Leading to the bridge, its photogenic narrow streets are lined with old houses. **Audierne** is a pretty fishing port on the estuary of the Goyen where fishing boats bring in their harvest of lobsters, crayfish, and tunny.

Your destination is **Pointe du Raz**, the Land's End of France. Thankfully it is less commercial than England's, but it is certainly not isolated. Uniformly sized white holiday cottages dot the landscape and a large café and enormous museum lie at road's end. If you can ignore the commercialism, you will find the views across the windswept headlands spectacular. This journey is not recommended in the height of summer when roads are congested.

An hour's drive (60 kilometers on the D784) brings you to the large town of **Quimper**, set where the Odet and Steir rivers meet. Park by the river, wander the town's pleasant streets and visit the **Musée de la Faïence** with its displays of attractive regional pottery. *(Open mid-Apr to end-Oct, closed Sundays, tel: 02.98.90.12.72.)* If the name of Quimper pottery is not familiar, it is, however, likely that you will immediately recognize the endearing figures painted in warm washes of predominantly blues and yellows that are now appreciated and recognized worldwide. The paintings on the pottery depict country folk in the old traditional dress and costume of Brittany.

This itinerary now explores Brittany's southern coast. The individual towns are very attractive but we were disappointed not to find more scenic countryside between them. Your first stop is **Pont l'Abbé**, set deep in a sheltered estuary. The squat castle contains a museum, **Musée Bigoudin**, of costume and furniture, with some fine examples of the tall white lace coifs that Breton women wear on their heads for festivals. (*Open Mar to end-*

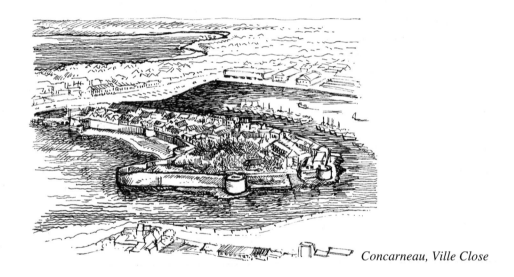

Concarneau, Ville Close

Sep) A pleasant park borders the river and the town square has a large covered market. Cross the high bridge that spans the River Odet and catch a panoramic view of **Benodet**. If you go into its crowded streets, follow signs for the port, which bring you to its yacht harbor—from here the coast road weaves past sandy bays and holiday hotels to the casino. In summer do not tackle the crowded streets; we recommend that you just admire the town from the bridge.

Ten kilometers away lies **Fouesnant**, a traditional center for cider production. Its pretty port, **La Forêt Fouesnant**, with its harbor full of yachts and small arc of golden sand, lies just a few kilometers away. Leaving the village, follow signs for *Concarneau par la Côte*, which quickly take you on a scenic back road into town.

Ignore **Concarneau's** bustling town and park by the harbor as close as possible to **Ville Close**, the 14th-century walled town sitting amidst a vast harbor of colorful boats varying from sleek yachts to commercial fishing trawlers. The old town, with its narrow streets and old houses full of crêperies and gift shops, is fun to explore. Visit the interesting **Musée de la Pêche**, which covers all things nautical inside and has three old fishing boats tied up outside of what was once the town's arsenal. (*Open all year, tel: 02.98.97.10.20.*) Climbing the walls gives you good views of the inner harbor where fishing boats unload their catch.

From Concarneau the D783 brings you to **Pont Aven**, a pretty resort by the River Aven made famous by Gauguin and his school of artists who moved here in the 1890s. Gauguin with his bohemian ways was not popular with the locals and he soon moved on. There are a great many galleries and in summer it's a colorful and crowded spot.

Turning inland, the D783 brings you to **Quimperlé** (20 kilometers) where the rivers Ellé and Isole converge to form the Lafta. One of the town's central streets is cobbled and lined with old houses. From here head through the large town of Hennebont for the 27-kilometer (D9 and D781) drive to the rather dull seaside town of **Carnac**. In the windswept fields on the edge of town are over 2,700 standing stones (*menhirs*) arranged in lines (*alignements*). The stones, believed to have been erected between 4,000 and 2,000 B.C., consist of three groups each arranged in patterns of 10 to 13 rows. The area is somewhat divided by country roads but the site is large enough that you can meander around and enjoy the groupings unhindered by the milling crowds and ticket barriers that impede your enjoyment of the British counterpart, Stonehenge. The **Musée de la Préhistoire** will help you interpret the stones. (*Open all year, tel: 02.97.52.22.04.*)

Leaving Carnac, follow signposts to **Vannes**, the region's largest city, complete with all the traffic and navigation headaches that plague so many downtown areas. The old walled town surrounding **Saint Peter's Cathedral** is delightful. The cathedral was built between the 13th and 19th centuries and has a great mixture of styles. The nearby parliament building has been converted to a covered market for artists, leather workers, metalworkers, and crêperies. There is a maze of old streets with beautiful timbered and gabled houses. Market days are Wednesdays and Saturdays on the Place des Lices.

This section of Brittany with its rocky promontories serves as a dramatic and wonderful base from which to explore Brittany's rugged south coast before leaving the region.

From Vannes the N165 whisks you around Nantes and onto the A11, which brings you to Angers, a convenient point to join our *Châteaux Country* itinerary.

Carnac

Châteaux Country

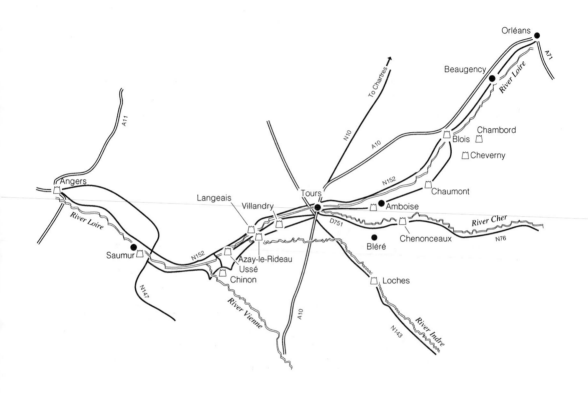

Paris

○ Orientation
● Sightseeing
⌂ Châteaux

39

Châteaux Country

A highlight of any holiday in France is a visit to the elegant châteaux of the Loire river valley. This itinerary suggests a route for visiting the châteaux based on a logical sequence assuming you either begin or end your trip in Paris. There are over 1,000 châteaux along the River Loire between Nantes and Orléans, and over 100 are open to the public. For the purposes of this itinerary, the Châteaux Country stretches from Angers to Orléans. Most of the châteaux were built for love, not war, and they range from traditional castles and grandiose homes to romantic ruins: we try to paint a picture of what you will see when you tour each château. In our opinion the best are Azay-le-Rideau and Chenonceaux. Be forewarned that in July and August you will be caught up in a crush of visitors.

Chambord

Recommended Pacing: Any hotel from Map 3 makes an ideal base for exploring the châteaux country. If you are going to spend just a few days and visit the most famous châteaux, select a place to stay at the heart of the region. If you plan an extensive visit to the valley and numerous châteaux, you might want to consider first stopping en route from Paris along the river to the northeast, then settle at its heart and, finally, continue on to its western outskirts. This region has a wealth of marvelous places to stay and they vary from small country farmhouses or inns to elegant, regal châteaux. In terms of how to pace your sightseeing—please do not try to visit all the châteaux we describe—it would be just too many for one trip. Rather, read our descriptions and choose those that appeal most to you. As we do not tell you how to get from château to château, we recommend Michelin maps 518 and 519 for outlining your route. Three nights in the region should give you all the time you need—one can visit only so many castles. Allow more if you are an avid fan of French furniture, French gardens, or the like, and want to explore properties in depth.

Many visitors spend time in Paris before coming to the Loire Valley and an excellent sightseeing venue on the way is **Chartres**, about an hour and a half southwest of Paris (97 kilometers). **Chartres Cathedral** towers high above the town and stands proud on the horizon. Light from three 13th-century stained-glass windows dapple the inside of the church with color. It's a magnificent edifice and the old city surrounding the cathedral has been lovingly restored. It's delightful to explore its old winding streets.

From Chartres the N10 takes you to Tours (130 kilometers, about a 2-hour drive). Located at the junction of the Cher and Loire rivers, Tours is a convenient starting point for our itinerary.

Begin your adventures in the Loire Valley by a visit to **Langeais**, one of the region's smaller châteaux. Remarkably, it has not been altered since it was built between 1465 and 1471 for Louis XI as a defense against Bretons. It is beautifully furnished and wax figurines commemorate the royal wedding of Charles VIII and Anne of Brittany, which took place on a cold December morning in 1491. On a nearby ridge are the ruins of a

10th-century stone *donjon* or keep, one of Europe's first. This was a stronghold of the notorious Fulk Nerra the Black, Count of Anjou. (*Open all year, tel: 02.47.96.72.60.*)

Angers was the former capital of the Dukes of Anjou and is now a city full of factories with an old town and its 13th-century fortress at its heart. During the 16th century many of the 17 massive towers were dismantled, on royal command, to the level of the wall-walk. The castle has some spectacular displays of tapestries, including the Apocalypse Tapestry, the longest ever woven in France, displayed in a special gallery. It was originally 164 meters long but during the Revolution it was thrown over the walls into the street and citizens snipped bits off. In 1843 the bishop managed to repiece two-thirds of it and about 100 meters are on display. (*Open all year, tel: 02.41.87.43.47.*)

Saumur lies on the edge of the River Loire. Rising from the town are the walls of Saumur castle, a 14th-century fortification built atop a sheer cliff. The castle is closed through 2006 for remodeling. (*Tel: 02.41.40.24.40.*) For horse enthusiasts, on the outskirts of the city is an internationally acclaimed equestrian center, *L'École Nationale d'Équitation*, and school for the famous riders and horses of the *Cadre Noir*. It is possible to take guided tours of the facility and observe the training. Riding events and staged performances are seasonal. (*Open Apr 1 to Sep 30, Tues through Sat, tel: 02.41.53.50.60.*)

Chinon is a huge crumbling fortress set high above the River Vienne, with a medieval town and tree-lined boulevard at its feet. Henry II of England died here, his son Richard the Lionheart owned it, King John lost it to the French, and Joan of Arc came here to plead with Charles VII for an army. It is an interesting walk around the skeleton of this fortification, but be prepared to fill in large chunks of the interior with your imagination. There is an interesting museum celebrating Joan of Arc. (*Open all year, tel: 02.47.93.13.45.*)

Ussé overlooks the River Indre and is everything you expect a château to be, with turrets, towers, chimneys, dormers, and enchantment. The house is completely furnished in period style, illustrating the way things were in the 16th and 17th centuries, complete with wax figurines dressed in period costume. Magnificent Flemish tapestries grace the Great Gallery and while you are waiting for your guided tour (narrated in French with English description sheets), you can climb the tower whose turret rooms are furnished with scenes from *Sleeping Beauty*. Conjecture has it that Ussé was the château that inspired Perault to write the famous fairy tale. (*Closed Nov to mid-Feb, tel: 02.47.95.54.05.*)

Azay-le-Rideau and its elegant Renaissance château are not far from Ussé. Azay-le-Rideau's graceful façade is framed by wispy trees and is reflected in its lake and the River Indre, from whose banks it rises on one side. It was built by Gilles Berthelot, the treasurer to Francis I between 1518 and 1527. Francis accused Gilles of fiddling the nation's books and confiscated this ornate château. It was not until the 19th century that it was completed. You can accompany a knowledgeable guide on a detailed tour or explore on your own, walking from one showpiece room to the next, admiring the fine furniture and tapestries. This is one of our favorite châteaux. (*Open all year, tel: 02.47.45.42.04.*)

Villandry is known for its formal, geometric French gardens—even the paths are raked into designs. While you can tour the house, the real reason for visiting Villandry is to spend time in the gardens wandering along the little paths between the neatly clipped box hedges. Even the vegetable garden has been planted to produce geometric patterns. Be sure to capture the bird's-eye view of this colorful quilt of a garden from the upper terrace. (*Gardens open all year, house open mid-Feb to mid-Nov, tel: 02.47.50.02.09.*)

Southeast of Montbazon is the town of **Loches**, found in the hills along the banks of the Indre, and referred to as the "City of Kings." The ancient castle is the "Acropolis of the Loire;" the buildings around it form what is called *Haute Ville*. It was a favorite retreat of King Charles VII and here you will find a copy of the proceedings of Joan of Arc's trial. The king's mistress, Agnes Sorel, is buried in the tower and her portrait is in one of the rooms. (*Open all year, tel: 02.47.59.07.86.*)

Chenonceaux almost spans the River Cher and is without a doubt one of the loveliest of the Loire's châteaux. This château owes a great deal to each of its six female occupants. Catherine Briconnet built Chenonceaux as a home, not a fortification, and sexy Diane de

Chenonceaux

Poitiers, the mistress of Henry II, added a garden and the bridge between the house and the banks of the River Cher. When Henry died, his jealous wife, Catherine de Medici, took Chenonceaux back and consigned Diane to Château de Chaumont. Catherine had the gallery built on the bridge, laid out the park, and held decadent parties. She bequeathed her home to Louise de Lorraine, her daughter-in-law who, after her husband's death, retired here and went into mourning for the rest of her life. In 1733 it passed to Monsieur Dupin whose intellectual wife was so beloved by the locals that it escaped the Revolution unscathed. In 1864 it was bought by Madame Peolouze who made it her life's work to restore her home. The château is now the home of the Menier family. Chenonceaux merits a leisurely visit: you want to allocate at least two hours for wandering through the park, gardens, and its elegant interior. The grounds also contain a wax museum with scenes from the château's history. (*Open all year, tel: 02.47.23.90.07.*)

Just a few kilometers north of Chenonceaux is the striking castle of **Amboise**. A tour of this large property will fill you with tales of grandeur, intrigue, and gruesome history. Francis I loved to party, reveling in grand balls, masquerades, festivals, and tournaments. He invited Leonardo da Vinci here and the artist spent his last years at the neighboring manor **Clos Lucé**. You can see his bedroom, models of machines he invented, and copies of his drawings. Catherine de Medici brought her young son Francis II and his young bride Mary, later Queen of Scots, to Amboise when the Protestants rose up after the Saint Bartholomew massacre. The Amboise Conspiracy of 1560 involved a group of Protestant reformers who followed the royal court from Blois to Amboise under the pretense of asking the king for permission to practice their religion. However, their plot was betrayed to the powerful Duke of Guise (Scarface) and upon arrival they were tortured, hung from the battlements, and left twisting in pain for days—the court and the royal family would come out to watch them. (*Open all year, fax: 02.47.57.62.88.*)

From Amboise follow the Loire to **Chaumont**, a château that has more appeal viewed from across the river than up close. Catherine de Medici was reputedly living here when her husband Henry II was killed and she became regent. She supposedly bought the château so that she could swap it with Diane de Poitiers (her husband's mistress) for Chenonceaux. Diane found it did not match up to Chenonceaux and left—you can understand why. Later Benjamin Franklin paid a visit to sit for an Italian sculptor who had set up his headquarters in the stables. Approached across a drawbridge, the château has three wings—the fourth side was pulled down in 1739—opening up to a fine view of the Loire Valley. You can tour the apartments and the stables. (*Open all year, tel: 02.54.51.26.26.*)

Blois sits on the north bank of the River Loire. The Chamber of the States General and part of a tower are all that remain of the 13th-century fortification that occupied this site. Much of the magnificent edifice you see today is due to Francis I's trying to keep his brother Gaston d'Orléans (who was always conspiring against him) out of trouble. In 1662 he banished him to Blois and gave him the project of restoring the château. Gaston hired the famous architect Mansart. The château has its stories of love, intrigue, and politicking, but its most famous is the murder of the Duke of Guise. In 1688 the powerful Henri de Guise called the States General here with the intention of deposing Henry III and making himself king. Henry found out about the plot and murdered the Duke. Who did what and where is explained in great detail on the tour. The most interesting room on the tour is Catherine de Medici's bedchamber with its many secret wall panels, used in the true Medici tradition to hide jewels, documents, and poisons. (*Open all year, tel: 02.54.90.33.33.*)

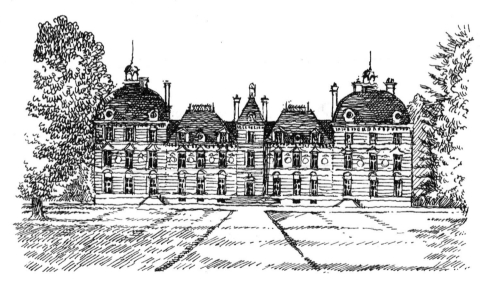

Cheverny

Ten kilometers from Blois lies **Cheverny**, a château built in 1634 for the Hurault family. It is smaller than Blois and Chambord and more interesting to tour because it still has its 17th-century decorations and furnishings. The Hurault family has carefully preserved their inheritance with its exquisite painted woodwork, tapestries, and furniture—in fact Cheverny is one of the most magnificently furnished châteaux in the Loire. One can also tour the acres of park by electric cart or by boat traveling the canals. Cheverny is also famous for its kennels. The grounds are home to 70 hounds and watching them patiently line up for dinner is a popular event. (*Feedings: Apr to mid-Sep except Sat and Sun 5 pm, otherwise 3 pm except Tues and weekends.*) In another outbuilding is a collection of 2,000 deer antlers, the family's hunting trophies. (*Open all year, tel: 02.54.79.96.29.*)

Standing on a grassy expanse amidst vast acres of forest, **Chambord** is enormous. Francis I built Chambord as a hunting lodge, but he believed that bigger was better so the vast edifice has 440 rooms and 80 staircases. Francis spent only 40 days at his huge home, which now has far less furniture than many other properties and is owned by the state. Apart from its impressive size and isolated location, Chambord's most interesting feature is the double-spiral staircase in the center of the building. (*Open all year, tel: 08.25.82.60.88.*)

The last stretch along the Loire takes you to the lovely old town of **Beaugency** with its historic church, **Nôtre Dame**. A magnificent bridge with 22 arches spans the river. The French blew it apart in 1940 to delay the Germans, but it has been completely restored (the central arches are original) and provides an ideal viewpoint for looking at the river and this delightful little town with its narrow medieval streets.

Orléans is a modern town rebuilt after the destruction of World War II. This was the scene of Joan of Arc's greatest triumph, when she successfully drove the English from France in 1429. There is little left for Joan of Arc fans to visit except her statue in Place Martoi.

From Orléans it is a 120-kilometer drive on the autoroute A10 back to Paris.

Azay le Rideau

Châteaux Country

Dordogne & Lot
River Valleys

O Orientation
● Sightseeing
■ ■ ■ Itinerary route

Paris

River Dronne

Brantôme
Bourdeilles
Périgueux

D939

N89

N21

D67

Vézère River

to Brive ↑

Noailles
N20
D158

Monplaisir

D38

Collonges-la-Rouge

D8

Turenne

D20

Turenne-Gare

Dordogne River

St.-Laurent-les-Tours

D20

Castelnau

D30

St. Céré

Carennac

Montal

La Poujade

D118

D135

Loubressac

La Roque
St. Christophe

Lascaux II

N20

Les Eyzies

D704

D706

Combarelles
Font de Gaume

Gouffre
de Padirac

Autoire

D38

Le Boutel

Campagne

Sarlat

Lacave

D90

Padirac

St. Cyprien

Beynac

D703

Montfort

Le Roque
Gageac

Domme

Rocamadour

D673

N140

Figeac

D42

D901

Conques

N20

Grotte du
Pech Mere

Cabrerets

N140

Decazeville

St Pierre Toirac

Montbrun

Bouzies

Calvignac

Cahors

D662

St. Cirq
Lapopie

Lot River

49

Dordogne & Lot River Valleys

The lazy Dordogne and Lot rivers wind gracefully through some of France's most picturesque countryside past villages dressed with grand castles, through peaceful meadows dotted with farms, beneath towering cliffs, and into pretty woodlands. However, this itinerary is more than just traveling along river valleys, for the region is France's prehistoric capital: the Cro-Magnon skull was discovered at Les Eyzies; colorful 15,000-year-old paintings decorate the Lascaux, Font de Gaume, and Les Combarelles caves; and man occupied the terraces on the cliffside of La Roque Saint Christophe as long ago as 70,000 B.C. Visit Rocamadour, an ancient village that tumbles down a rocky canyon, and Conques, a medieval village on a dramatic hillside site.

View of the Dordogne River from Domme

Recommended Pacing: You could happily spend a couple of weeks in the Dordogne, venturing along the river valley then adding unscheduled meanderings up little side roads to country villages. For the purposes of this itinerary, an efficient pacing would be to base yourself a night or two in the northern region, two to three nights close to the river itself (more if you make reservations at several of the caves), a night near Rocamdour, one night to the north of the river in the village of Turenne (or use Rocamdour as a base for another night and make the journey to Turenne for a daytrip loop), and then continue south to the River Lot where you will need two nights to explore this lovely river valley and include a visit to the hillside village of Conques at its eastern boundary.

In the northern region of the Dordogne, **Brantôme** is a delightful little town on the banks of the River Dronne with narrow winding streets and a riverside park that leads you across the famous 16th-century elbow bridge to the old abbey, nestled at the foot of a rocky cliff. Founded by Charlemagne in 769, the abbey was reconstructed in the 11th century after it was ransacked by the Normans. The church and adjoining buildings were constructed and modified between the 14th and 18th centuries.

Follow the River Dronne for 10 kilometers on the D78 into the very pretty village of **Bourdeilles**. A little bridge takes you across the river to its 12th-century castle which the English and French squabbled about for years. From Bourdeilles country roads direct you to the D939 and on to Périgueux.

Périgueux changed allies twice in the 100 Years' War, eventually opting for France. It's a pleasant, large market town with an interesting domed cathedral resplendent with little turrets. From Périgueux follow signposts towards Brive (D47) and at Thenon take the D67 to Montignac (40 kilometers).

Montignac is a popular tourist town because on its outskirts are the wondrous **Lascaux Caves** with their magnificent 15,000-year-old paintings. In 1963 these caves were closed to the public because the paintings were being damaged by the rise and fall in temperature as hordes of visitors came and went. It took ten years to construct an exact replica—**Lascaux II**. Except for the even, non-slip floor you will not know that you are not in the real Lascaux. The bulls, bison, and stags appear to be moving around the cave—so skillfully did the artists utilize every feature of the rocks that bumps appear as humps, cheekbones, and haunches. In July and August the quota of 2,000 tickets a day go on sale at 9 am at the *Syndicat d'Initiative* (Tourist Office) in Montignac. Tickets are not available in advance. For the rest of the year tickets are sold at the site on a first come, first served basis, so you may arrive at 11 am and find that you are offered a 4 pm tour. Tours are given in English and French.

Leaving Lascaux II, watch for signs that will direct you to Le Thot along the D65. The admission ticket for Lascaux includes admission to **Le Thot** where you can see a film of the building of Lascaux II and displays of large photos of the many prehistoric paintings found in caves in the valley. The grounds also have a park and a re-creation of a prehistoric village.

Leaving Le Thot, follow signposts for **La Roque Saint Christophe**. As the road winds by the river, a sheer cliff rises to a deep natural terrace before continuing upwards. As long ago as 70,000 B.C. man took advantage of this natural terrace for shelter and by medieval times it was home to over 1,000 people. The thousands of niches that you see today were used to hold up supporting beams for the houses and the rings you see carved into the rock were used to hang lamps and to tether animals. (*Open all year, tel: 05.53.50.70.45.*)

Following the winding River Vézère, the D706 brings you into **Les Eyzies de Tayac**. The caves in the cliff that towers above the town were home to prehistoric man who took shelter here during the second Ice Age. People lived here for tens of thousands of years. Archaeologists have uncovered flints, pottery, jewelry, and skeletons that have been identified as those of Cro-Magnon man found in the cave behind the hotel of the same name. Visit the **Musée National de la Préhistoire** in the 11th-century castle set high on the cliff beneath the overhanging rock, guarded by the gigantic sculpture of Cro-Magnon man. (*Open all year, tel: 05.53.06.45.45.*)

Nearby, the **Font de Gaume** cave has prehistoric wall paintings of horses, bison, mammoths, and reindeer with colors still so rich that it is hard to comprehend the actual passage of time. The caves are a bit damp and dark and entail a steep 400-meter climb to reach the entrance. The grotto is deep, winding, and narrow in parts. There are some 230 drawings, of which about 30 are presented and discussed. Displayed in three tiers, some drawings are marred by graffiti, others are not clearly visible as the walls tower above the floor of the cave. Entrance is limited to 200 people per day but you can make reservations in advance by calling the tourist office in Les Eyzies (*tel: 05.53.06.97.05, fax: 05.53.06.90.79*). There is a small additional charge for advance booking. With the closure of more caves each year, it is uncertain how much longer the opportunity to visit Font de Gaume will continue. (*Open all year.*)

A short distance from Font de Guam is **Les Combarelles**, a cave discovered in 1901. The entrance is about a 100-meter (level) walk from the car park. The cave is a winding passage with engravings of mammoth, ibex, bears, reindeer, bison, and horses—and man in the last 70 meters. Entrance is limited to 140 visitors per day and the cave is closed every Wednesday. Advance booking and hours of opening are identical to Font de Gaume.

From Les Eyzies follow the scenic D706 to **Campagne** with its abandoned château sitting behind padlocked gates. From Campagne take the pretty D35 to **Saint Cyprien**, an attractive town just a short distance from the Dordogne. It has more shops and cafés than most small towns in the valley, making it an appealing and interesting place to break your journey.

Through pretty countryside follow the Dordogne river valley, just out of sight of the river. As you approach **Beynac**, you are presented with a lovely picture of a small village huddled beneath a cliff crowned by a 12th-century fortress before a broad sweep of the Dordogne. The castle, while its furnishings are sparse, is well worth visiting for the spectacular views. (*Open all year.*) On the water's edge is **Hôtel Bonnet**, recommended not for its accommodation, but as a scenic and excellent choice for lunch under vine-covered trellises.

Have your cameras ready as you approach **La Roque Gageac**. The town, clinging to the hillside above the River Dordogne and framed by lacy trees, is a photographer's dream. There's a grassy area on the riverbank with a few picnic tables and an inviting path, following the curves of the river, tempts you farther.

Just upstream, cross the bridge and climb the hill to **Domme**, a medieval walled village that has for centuries stood guard high above the river and commanded a magnificent panorama. The town itself is enchanting, with ramparts that date from the 13th century and narrow streets that wind through its old quarter and past a lovely 14th-century **Hôtel de Ville**. At the town center under the old market place, you find access to some interesting stalactite and stalagmite grottos. However, most visitors come to Domme for its spectacular views—the best vantage point is from the **Terrasse de la Barre**.

Château de Montfort

Because it is more scenic on the north side of the river, retrace your steps across the bridge and continue downriver on the D703 to **Château de Montfort**, a majestic castle shadowing a wide loop in the river. Built by one of the region's most powerful barons, this intimate, restored castle, furnished like a private residence, rises out of a rocky ledge. The **Cingle de Montfort** offers some delightful views of the river. When the D703 intersects with the D704, take a short detour north to the city of **Sarlat**. Sarlat has a delightful old quarter with narrow cobbled streets that wind through a maze of magnificent gourmet shops. The church and the Episcopal palace create a roomy space along the narrow bustling streets. Sarlat bustles with activity and color on market day.

After visiting Sarlat, return to the banks of the Dordogne and continue east once again along its shore, this time in the direction of **Souillac**. When the D703 reaches this lovely riverside town, travel south following the N20 in the direction of Cahors. As you leave houses behind you, turn left on the D43 (rather than crossing the river) and begin a very picturesque stretch of the valley. As you cross a single-lane wooden bridge spanning the Dordogne, take note of the picture-postcard **Château de la Treyne**, one of our favorite hotels in the region, perched above the riverbank. **Lacave** is also known for some spectacular geological formations in its caves, which you can tour on a diminutive train. As you climb out of Lacave towards Rocamadour, the fields are filled with bustling geese being fattened for *foie gras* and you get a picturesque view of a castle sitting high above the distant Dordogne. A scenic country road winds to where the ground disappears into an abyss and the village of **Rocamadour** tumbles down the narrow canyon.

Our preference is to park in the large car park adjacent to the castle, but if it is full, head for the valley floor and park in one of the grassy car parks. A stairway leads down, from beside the castle to the chapels, houses, and narrow streets that cling precipitously to the rock face, to the little chapels and the large basilica that incorporates the cliff face as one wall of the building. From the 12th century onwards Rocamadour was a popular pilgrimage site. There are lots of tourist shops and, thankfully, cafés providing a spot to sit and rest after climbing up and down the staircases. If steep climbs are not for you, buy a ticket on the elevator that goes up and down the hillside. From Rocamadour you can either travel directly on to the Lot river valley to the south or take a scenic detour of approximately 100 kilometers north to some enchanting and picturesque villages.

For a scenic loop north from Rocamadour travel east on D673 for just 4 kilometers, cross the N140, continue on D673 as it winds through the village of Alvignac, and then travel on to Padirac.

Château de la Treyne

At Padirac, detour off on the D90 to **Gouffre de Padirac**. A gouffre is a great opening in the ground, and this wide circular chimney of Padirac was formed by the roof of a cave falling in. This impressive grotto leads over 100 meters underground to a mysterious river where the visitor can negotiate a stretch of some 500 meters by boat to discover the sparkling Lac de la Pluie (Lake of Rain) and its huge stalactite in the immense Great Dome room with its vault rising up 90 meters. The roof lies quite near the surface and it is almost inevitable that it too will one day collapse to form another chasm. (*Open Apr to Oct. Allow approximately 1½ hours for a guided tour, tel: 05.65.33.64.56.*)

Retrace your trail back to Padirac and then wind along the D38 traveling east and then north in the direction of Autoire. This scenic drive winds down a hill to reveal the beautiful village of **Autoire** set in a rich green valley shadowed by majestic, towering limestone cliffs. Autoire is lovely with its old stone houses topped with slate roofs clustering together along the narrow alleyways. Windowboxes overflow with flowers to provide a profusion of color against the mellowed stone of the buildings.

From Autoire, travel the few short kilometers to the picturesque village of **Loubressac**. Crowning the mountaintop, Loubressac appears dramatically on the horizon—another charming village, with a picturesque main square.

From Loubressac you enjoy gorgeous views across the river valley to the medieval fortress of **Castelnau** on the opposite bank in the town of **Bretenoux**. Impressive from a distance, the long façade of the fortress dominates the village skyline. Colored in the rusty red of the regional rock, the castle is remarkably preserved and impressive from the massive wooden portal to splendid interior furnishings. (*Open all year, closed Tues Oct to Mar, tel: 05.65.10.98.00.*) Crossing back to Loubressac, wind down to the river and then detour east to the Renaissance Château de Montal, which is beautifully furnished and definitely worth a visit. (*Open Easter to Nov, closed Sat, tel: 05.65.38.13.72.*)

From the Château de Montal, it is a short distance farther on to the pretty market town of **Saint Céré** whose square comes alive and is particularly colorful when the commodity for sale is livestock. Worthy of a visit on the outskirts of Saint Céré in **Le Tours de Saint Laurent** is a tapestry museum, the **Atelier Musée Jean Lurçat**. (*Open mid-Jul to Oct, telephone number for the tourist office in Saint Céré: 05.65.38.11.85.*)

From Saint Céré journey back along the D30, once again following the path of the Dordogne to the pretty village of **Carennac**, set just above the river. This idyllic little village is even more picturesque because of the river that weaves through it, in the shadow of the lovely old timbered homes and a handsome church sheltered behind an arched entry.

From Carennac, cross the river and travel north to **Turenne**. This is a charming, picturesque village is surrounded by a patchwork of farmland. Narrow, cobbled streets wind steeply up to a crowning church and castle. (*Open Apr to Oct.*) Views from the top of the castle are very peaceful and pretty, and both the town and the inn offer a quiet setting for a night's repose.

From Turenne, according to the map, there is a road that appears to cross almost directly over to **Collonges la Rouge** (the D150 to connect with the D38, just 5 kilometers west of

Saint Cirq Lapopie

Collonges) but it is extremely difficult to find—I never discovered how to access it from Turenne. It might prove easier, as I found, to detour north on the D8 to just north of Monplaisir and then turn east on the D38 and on to Collonges la Rouge, a lovely village favored by local artisans, with cobbled streets winding through a maze of stone buildings all rich in a hue of burnt red. Probably the regional town most geared for tourists, it has a number of interesting craft shops to tempt you indoors. Collonges la Rouge is most beautiful on a clear day when the sun washes the stone in a rich, warm red against a backdrop of blue.

From Collonges la Rouge, return west on the D38 in the direction of Brive; and then just past Maranzat, jog south on the D8 and then almost immediately west on the D158 to Noailles and the junction of N20. Traveling south on the N20 at the town of Payrac, you will pass the junction of D673 which travels the rocky valley east to Rocamadour where you begin this scenic northern loop. From Payrac it is another 50 kilometers on to Cahors and the magical Lot River Valley.

Although it appears to be a large city, **Cahors**, in reality, is an enchanting, medieval city set on the bend of the River Lot. I would definitely recommend that you take time to venture into the city. Embraced by the banks of the river the city is famous for its architectural richness: the dramatic **Pont Valentré** bridge built in the 14th century, the Arc de Diane, a remnant of a vast Gallo-Roman thermal establishment, the Saint Etienne Cathedral from the 11th and 12th centuries, the tower of Pope John XXII, and the Saint Barthelemy Church. Not to be missed at the heart of the city is the old core with its houses, mansions, gates, lanes and squares. There are lots of restaurants, sidewalk cafes and interesting shops. With lots of character and a quiet pace, this is a city to explore on foot, or take advantage of the bike paths that follow the banks of the river Lot. Cahors serves as an excellent focal point for exploring the region and sampling its wonderful wines.

A destination in its own right, and dramatic in terms of a landmark, just a few kilometers west from Cahors, towering over the river is a magnificent château-hotel, the **Château de Mercuès**.

From the outskirts of Cahors travel east, following signposts for Figeac along the north bank of the river. This portion of the **Lot River Valley** can be driven in half a day on roads that wind along a riverbank that is narrower and quieter than that of the Dordogne. The River Lot winds along the curves of the wide canyon, cutting into its chalky walls. At some stretches the route follows the level of the river and at others it straddles the clifftops. Vistas are dramatic at every turn although the restricting narrow roads will frustrate the eye of any photographer because there is rarely a place to stop.

Cross the river at **Bouzies** and take a moment to look back across the bridge and see the medieval buildings constructed into the walls of the canyon above the small tunnel. This is also the departure point for many boat trips as evidenced by the many tethered rental boats. Just outside Bouzies, the road (D40) climbs and winds precipitously to the top of the cliff and rounding a bend, you find **Saint Cirq Lapopie** clinging precipitously to the sheer canyon walls and cascading back down towards the river. Drive around the village to one of the car parks and walk back up the hill to explore. Many of the buildings have been restored and only a few of the houses are lived in. It's most enjoyable to wander the quiet streets without being overwhelmed by tourist shops.

Travel down to the Lot and cross to its northernmost bank. As the river guides you farther, it presents a number of lovely towns and with each turn reveals another angle and view of the valley. **La Toulzanie** is a small, pretty village nestled into a bend of the river, interesting because of its houses built into the limestone cliffs. Calvignac is an ancient village clinging to the top of the cliff on the opposite bank. At Cajarc be careful to keep to the river road (D662). A short drive brings you to the village of **Montbrun**, a village that rises in tiers on jutting rock by steep cliffs. It looks down on the Lot, up at its ruined castle, and across the river to *Saut de la Mounine* (Jump of the Monkey). Legend recalls that to punish his daughter for falling in love with the son of a rival baron, a father ordered daughter to be thrown from the cliffs. A monkey was dressed in her clothes and thrown to its death instead. Father, regretting his harsh judgment, was overcome with joy when he discovered the substitution. Set on a plateau, the **Château de Larroque Toirac** is open to visitors and makes an impressive silhouette against the chalky cliffs and the village of **Saint Pierre Toirac**.

Less than 10 kilometers to the north of the Lot on the River Célé is the larger market town of **Figeac**. A wonderful example of 12th-century architecture, Figeac is an attractive river town and it is fun to explore the shops along its cobbled streets and alleyways.

Continue on to Conques, a bonus to this itinerary that requires that you journey farther along the winding Lot (on the N140 signposted Decazeville and then D963 and D42 signposted Entraygues). The route weaves through some beautiful farmland and attractive little villages. At La Vinzelle leave the Lot river valley and climb up the D901 to **Conques**, a tiny medieval town on a dramatic hillside site. Tucked a considerable distance off the beaten track, it is a delightful, unspoiled village that was once an important pilgrimage stop on the way to Santiago de Compostela in Spain.

Conques's pride is its 11th-century **Abbaye Sainte Foy** whose simple rounded arches give it the look of a Gothic cathedral. The carving of the Last Judgment in a semi-circle over the central door shows 124 characters—the grimacing devils and tortured souls are far more amusing than the somber few who are selected to go to heaven. The abbey's treasure is the 10th-century Sainte Foy reliquary, a statue sheathed in gold leaf and decorated with precious stones.

If time allows, linger in the town into early evening, when evening light plays on the wonderful old stone and cobbled streets. It is magical to hear the melodious bells as their sound echoes through the town.

Conques

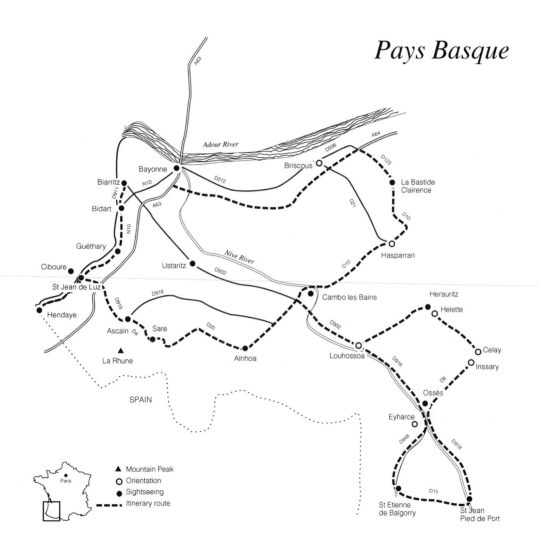

Pays Basque

Adour River

Bayonne

Biarritz

Bidart

Guéthary

Ciboure

St Jean de Luz

Hendaye

Ascain

Sare

Aïnhoa

La Rhune

SPAIN

Ustaritz

Nive River

Briscous

La Bastide
Clairence

Hasparran

Cambo les Bains

Louhossoa

Herauritz

Helette

Celay

Irissary

Ossès

Eyharce

St Etienne
de Baïgorry

St Jean
Pied de Port

▲ Mountain Peak
○ Orientation
● Sightseeing
▬ ▬ Itinerary route

Paris

63

Pays Basque

This itinerary traces a path through Pays Basque (Basque Country), a region of France that has always fiercely guarded and preserved its unique character. Seven Basque provinces straddle the western border between France and Spain; three in France: Labourd, Basse-Navarre, and Soule, and four in Spain: Biscaye, Guipuzcoa, Navarre, and Alava. Concerning the seven there is a saying, "*zazpiak bat*," which means "seven equals one." The local language, called Euskara, considered one of the oldest in Europe, and the traditions associated with the Basque style of life are found throughout the region. The area, stretching from the Atlantic Ocean to the start of the Pyrenees, abounds with beautiful landscapes—sandy beaches, old whaling villages, picturesque ports, beautiful valleys sliced by winding rivers, rolling green hills, and snow-capped mountains. The landscape is enhanced by distinctive architecture, which varies from province to province.

Saint Jean Pied de Port

The Basque people, with their strong sense of tradition, add their own color to this fascinating region with their local festivals and in their dress—they often wear traditional costume and are never without a beret or espadrilles.

This itinerary takes you to two of the French Basque provinces, exploring the coast and hilltowns of Labourd and then weaving deeper into the countryside to the heart of Basse-Navarre. Labourd, with its beaches, port towns, and green foothills, is the province with the most diverse landscape. Basse-Navarre is rich with lush countryside, rolling green pastures, a scenic valley cut by the path of the River Nive, and small farming communities that have become famous for their ewes' cheese.

Diverse in their landscape, the provinces are just as distinctive in architecture, influenced by both setting and tradition. Especially charming are the colorful, red-roofed, timbered houses of Labourd, which are intentionally built with their backs to the sea, with one side more richly decorated, and also strategically positioned east to face the rising sun and a new day. These houses are painted in the national red and green colors of Basque and it is fascinating to learn that ox blood was actually once used to stain the timbers red! Traditionally, Labourd homes are passed down to the oldest child and many have been in the same family for hundreds of years. To weather the more rugged climate, the homes of Basse-Navarre are built from the locally quarried stone and have distinctive circular balconies. The ground floor and entryway of Basque homes used to house the animals, with the family living above and drying hay serving to insulate the roof. You will notice in Labourd homes that one side of the roof extends further than the other—this gave the family the opportunity to expand the living quarters under the existing roof when financially able.

As well as being rich in tradition, landscape, and architecture, the region also offers a wealth of food specialties. To fully appreciate their culture, be sure to sample the rich ewes' cheeses, delicious macaroons, a complex fish soup often referred to as *ttoro*, a butter tart filled with delicious black cherry filling (*gâteau basque*), the salty, dried ham (*jamon de Bayonne*), and a side dish called *piperade*, which is a compote of cooked tomatoes, onions, eggplant, garlic, and pimentos (the origin of its name). The vineyards of Irouleguy produce a red and a rosé and there is said to be a secret recipe with ingredients cultivated from over 20 regional plants to produce the two varieties of *Izarra*, a green or yellow liquor.

Recommended Pacing: Biarritz and Bayonne, on the coast, are both logical and convenient cities from which to begin and conclude a circle trip of these gorgeous and diverse districts of Pays Basque. Plan to spend at least two nights on the coast in order to explore the beaches, charming towns, and fishing villages with either Biarritz or Saint Jean de Luz as a base, a night in the hilltown village of either of Sare or Aïnhoa, and continue on into the heart of Basse-Navarre, overnighting in Saint Etienne de Baïgorry or Saint Jean Pied de Port. Continue back to the coast and the capital city of Bayonne, including a stop in the picturesque village of La Bastide-Clairence.

Biarritz is a wonderful introduction to the style and life of Pays Basque. Once a whaling station, it is now recognized as a seaside resort of international renown. Don't let its size intimidate you—as the residents will tell you, this is still a small town in heart and soul—locals claim not even to lock their cars! Biarritz is captivating and charming and the center of the old town is very easy to explore on foot. Its central stretch of beach is flanked by a promenade and a few casinos, the most spectacular of which, the **Hôtel du Palais**, is also a hotel and an historic landmark, dating back to the days of the Spanish Countess, Eugenie of Montijo who married the Emperor Napoleon III. Being fond of Biarritz, she had the Hôtel du Palais (originally referred to as Villa Eugenie) built as a holiday home, hosted European aristocracy, and introduced them to the charms and festivities of the town. The Countess is fondly referred to as the "godmother" of the town. The nightlife is perhaps a bit more tame than in her time, but people are still attracted to Biarritz for the casinos, racecourses, nightclubs, and special events including the surf festival, pelota tournament, and numerous golf tournaments. While exploring Biarritz, be sure to visit the **Marine Museum** located in front of the Rocher de la Vierge (Virgin Rock) for its display of marine fauna and aquariums; the **Historical Museum**, which features fishing and agricultural influences through costumes, paintings, artifacts, and documents; and, for gourmands, the **Chocolate Museum**, whose sculptures are a delicious and interesting testament to the fact that chocolate originated in the Basque Country during the reign of Louis XIV.

With its absolutely gorgeous setting, Biarritz also inspires you to spend some time outdoors. Include a visit to the **Biarritz Lighthouse**, dating back to 1831, which towers 73 meters above the sea and (after a climb of 248 steps) offers an exceptional view of the town and Basque coastline. From the lighthouse follow the headland to the **Côte des Basque** beach with its dramatic offshore rocks of the Basta, the Madonna, and the Atalaye Plateau and most definitely include a walk along the Port des Pêcheurs, the old fishing village now referred to as the **Port Vieux** or Old Port. This is an enchanting path to walk at sunset: taking you from the beach around the old harbor, along its breakwater, which protects its active fishing fleet and intimate seafood restaurants, to a picturesque point and then wrapping around the other side of Biarritz below an exclusive residential district. It was from the old harbor where whaling ships used to sail out to the Bay of Biscaye.

Traditional Labourd Home

There are several charming villages that hug the coast south from Biarritz in a span of just 108 kilometers to the Spanish border. A few roads run parallel down the coast: we left Biarritz on the D911 and then opted for the smallest road, the N10, which wasn't the most direct but ribboned through the center of each of the villages. **Bidart**—with its quaint main square banded by timbered houses and its nearby church, which is characteristic of the fortress-style churches of the 16th century—is a typical Basque village in the Labourd style and was also once a bustling whaling and fishing port. For another wonderful view of the Basque coast, turn right off the square on the narrow street that leads to the cliffs, to the site of the Sainte-Madeline Chapel, dedicated to Basque mariners.

From Bidart's lovely beach, the road winds up through the coastal hills to **Guéthary**, the coast's smallest village, nestled in the hills above the beautiful expanse of blue ocean. Guéthary derives its name from the Latin word "to observe" as its setting provided a wonderful vantage point from which to spot whales. Its numerous villas, many of them lovely red-and-green timbered and shuttered houses, are a testament to its days as a very popular and wealthy seaside community. Don't leave without visiting its picturesque port and driving by the charming cliff-top railway station. Like Bidart, Guéthary boasts some lovely neighboring beaches (quite popular with surfers) and interesting shops.

Farther south is the larger town of **Saint Jean de Luz**, separated by a bridge and the mouth of the River Nivelle from the equally picturesque town of Ciboure. With its lovely expanse of beach, sheltered harbor, grassy beach promenade, distinctive regional architecture, quaint town square, outdoor cafés, and local artists, it is easy to understand the enduring popularity of this enchanting town. To complement its beauty it also has a rich and colorful history—the lavish homes are evidence of the wealth acquired by whalers-turned-pirates (the French—*corsaires*—sounds more dignified!) who sailed under the blessing of the French King. The town reached its peak of dignity and glory in 1660 with the arranged political union of Louis XIV of France and Marie-Thérèse of Spain. Still standing on either side of the town's main square are the two houses where they each awaited their marriage. (The Louis XIV House can be visited in summer months.) Also interesting to visit is the Church of St. John the Baptist, whose doorway was walled up immediately after the couple's departure so that no one else could cross the royal threshold. The interior is worth a visit for its simple architecture, high altar, and classic wooden Basque balconies. Although a popular tourist town, Saint Jean de Luz still has an active fishing industry, with anchovies, tuna, and sardines playing a vital role in its commercial success.

With a beautiful setting banded by ocean and hillside, **Ciboure** has always been considered an extension of Saint Jean de Luz; but because it is across the river, it became a comfortable refuge for the Bohemian set and remains a community of fishermen, artists, and musicians.

From Ciboure it is just a short distance traveling along the Corniche Basque following the D912 to the lovely town of **Hendaye** with its gorgeous 3-kilometer stretch of sandy beach (considered the region's safest beach for swimming). Right on the Spanish border, Hendaye has played an important historical role as a frontier town.

From Hendaye, cut east over to the N10, travel north back to the outskirts of Saint Jean de Luz, and then leave the coast and head inland on the D918. The scenery changes almost immediately as you leave the ocean behind and the road follows a picturesque sweep of the River Nivelle with a gorgeous backdrop of verdant mountain. The D918 travels across the river and passes right through the center of **Ascain**, a charming town nestled amongst fields of sheep and cattle. After Ascain take the D4, a road that winds a scenic route up from the town, and on its outskirts at the Col de St. Ignace, a number of parked cars will draw your attention to a little rack railway that climbs 905 meters up to the highest peak in Pays Basque, **La Rhune**, on the Spanish border. From La Rhune you enjoy spectacular vistas looking over the Pyrenees and to the distant coastline. The train trip takes approximately 30 minutes and at the top there are a few souvenir shops and places to eat. You can return to the bottom on foot, if you prefer. (*Mid-Mar to Nov 02, first departure 9:30 am, tel: 05.59.54.20.26, fax: 05.59.47.50.76, www.rhune.com.*)

Soon after you leave La Rhune a tree-lined drive winds down to the valley and the quiet, endearing village of **Sare**. I will always have fond memories of Sare that date to my early research years (now a quarter of a century ago!); memories of a typical timbered Labourd village whose central square at the time of my first visit was a stage for a colorful local festival with traditionally costumed dancers and musicians.

Historically, Sare, so close to the Spanish border, has played a dominant role in smuggling goods across the frontier—termed "night work" by the locals!

Although not on sightseeing maps, close to Sare there is a completely non-commercial, storybook-perfect hamlet of timbered homes that is worth a quick drive-by. To step back into this world of yesterday and visit a single-street village that was once a 16th-century farm, leave the center of Sare in the direction of Cambo les Bains and just on Sare's outskirts, at the roundabout, make a detour left, up the tree-lined road.

Return to the roundabout, take the D4 in the direction of Saint Pée, cross over a small bridge and travel through farmland, first on the D4 then the D305, a narrow road and lush, scenic route. The road jogs onto the D20 and brings you to Aïnhao. Located halfway between Sare and Cambo les Bains, **Aïnhoa** is one of France's most beautiful villages, traditional and typically Basque. Dating back to the Middle Ages, Aïnhao, just 2 kilometers from the Spanish border, served as a convenient stopover for pilgrims making their journey to Santiago de Compostella. Although almost totally destroyed by the Spanish in 1629, it was rebuilt in the 17th and 18th centuries and its one main street lined by timbered and shuttered homes represents the essence of Pays Basque. All the typical, essential, and fundamental elements in a traditional Basque village are present in Aïnhoa: the town hall, the church, and the *fronton* (the rounded wall used for playing the classic Basque game of pelota).

From Aïnhao return to the main road, following the D20 in the direction of Espelette and then the D918 in the direction of Bayonne, to the larger town of Cambo les Bains.

Proudly distinguished as a *ville fleurie* ("flowering village" is an award recognizing towns with dramatic flower displays), **Cambo les Bains**, with its pretty setting and mild climate, became a popular tourist spot because of the two thermal springs found in the village. The oldest homes are located in Bas Cambo down from the town on the other side of the river. You can also visit **Arnaga**, Edmond Rostand's magnificent château-home and gardens. Now a national monument, it is also a museum dedicated to this much-celebrated author of *Cyrano de Bergerac*. (*Open Apr to Nov, tel: 05.59.29.70.25.*)

Following the path of the River Nive from Cambo les Bains, it is a pretty drive on the D918 through lush countryside to the heart of Basse-Navarre and two wonderful towns, Saint Etienne de Baïgorry and Saint Jean Pied du Port. You will want to overnight in the area in order to explore the region and towns. I would select Saint Etienne de Baïgorry if you want a quieter setting, and Saint Jean Pied du Port if you want stay in one of France's most beautiful walled villages. The D918 goes directly to Saint Jean Pied de Port, but to reach Saint Etienne de Baïgorry, you leave the D918 on the D948 at Saint Martin d'Arrossa. From Saint Etienne de Baïgorry you can then drive 11 kilometers on the D15 to Saint Jean Pied de Port.

With the mountains as a dramatic backdrop, **Saint Etienne de Baïgorry** enjoys a beautiful, serene setting in the valley of the Aldudes, nestled among the vineyards of the Irouléguy. Now a sportsman's paradise (hiking, rafting, rock climbing), this rugged terrain was, for those who tended the land, hard to work and many of the summer festivals and the famous "Force Basque Games" are based on the old farming chores and challenges of mountain life.

The capital of Basse-Navarre and a border crossing into Spain, the fortified town of **Saint Jean Pied de Port** enjoys a strategic location at the base of the mountains and straddling the Nive River. The name Pied de Port translates to "foot of the pass" and refers to the famous Roncevaux Pass where Charlemagne was defeated by the Basques. This pass was also used by the Romans and by the pilgrims en route to the tomb of St. James at Santiago de Compostella—the scallop shell used as an emblem by the pilgrims of St. James appears as a carved decoration on many of the town's homes.

You can drive to the summit (1032 meters) of Roncevaux Pass and of interest, just after the summit, is a 13th-century Gothic church, cloister, and small chapel housing the tomb of the Basque King Sancho VII, the Strong of Navarre.

Saint Jean Pied de Port is pretty and distinctive, with many of its houses constructed in rose-colored granite. A picturesque medieval bridge spanning the Nive connects the two sections of town and cobbled, narrow streets wind up to the crowning citadel. It is a fun town with lots of outdoor cafés and shops selling regional goods, and is the principal market town for the region (*market day Mon*).

From Saint Jean Pied de Port you can drive directly back to the coast following the D918 or, if time allows for a scenic detour, leave the D918 at Eyharce and take the D8, crossing the river at Ossès, a cute town whose church has a distinctively striped steeple, on to Irissary. Here you pick up the D22 at Celay traveling north to the neighboring villages of Helette and Herauritz. This is definitely farm country and the drive is picturesque as it cuts a path right through the rich pastures and dairy farms, a route often appropriately signed *Route du Fromage* (Cheese Road). If you want to stop and sample the regional ewes' cheese, the tasting room of Fromage de Brebis, just past Herauritz, is well signed along this charming country road.

From Herauritz, take the D119 and travel back to Louhossoa and the junction of D918. The D918 will take you back to the outskirts of Cambo les Bains. Here you can continue on the D918, which becomes the D932 past Cambo les Bains, to Bayonne.

But for another rewarding detour, travel the D10 through Cambo les Bains to Hasparren and then the lovely Basque village of **La Bastide Clairence**. This is a sweet village made up entirely of timbered homes and, with the honor of being designated one of France's most beautiful villages, it serves as a wonderful last countryside stop before you continue back to the coast and the larger port city of Bayonne.

The regional capital, **Bayonne**, has played an important role in history as a strategic commercial port city located at the junction of two rivers, the Nive and the Adour, on the constantly challenged border between France and Spain. It is a relatively easy city to navigate in and out of and is most definitely well worth the effort. Travel to the heart of this captivating port city, which was once a Roman garrison and was ruled at different times by both the French and English crowns. Shaded by old, leaning timbered buildings, cobbled streets wind up from the river that cuts a path through its center. Bayonne flourished during the 300-year English reign of Eleanor of Aquitaine and Henry Plantagenet. Their son Richard the Lionheart found his bride here — a Basque princess from Navarre. The town was penetrated by canals until the 17th century and you can still see the unusual arcades that once housed merchants serving the seamen.

To walk the streets of this river town, still protected behind its old stone walls, is to discover a lovely city of pedestrian passages, quaysides, and wonderful stone and half-timbered houses. Visit **St. Mary's Cathedral**, built in the 13th and 14th centuries, and the **medieval cellars** — in fact, medieval shops — that are found under the upper and older part of the town surrounding the cathedral. Bayonne is home to the **Bonnat Museum**, which houses a fine collection of art, considered one of the most prestigious collections outside Paris, including works by Goya, Raphael, Delacroix, Michelangelo, and Constable. For an in-depth study and presentation of the history of Bayonne as well as Basque culture, you might also want to visit the **Basque Museum**.

Before leaving Basque allow yourself to be tempted into one of the many tea rooms that specialize in a regional decadence. Basque is intensely proud of its claim of introducing hot chocolate to the world.

In South America, Christopher Columbus came upon this strange concoction that was used by the Indians not for barter but as the necessary ingredient for a rich, strong drink. The explorers returned home with the distinctive bean and shared the secret technique for turning cacao into chocolate. The Jews became experts in its production and brought it to the southwest of France when fleeing the Inquisitions. It is said that Bayonne became the first town to taste this delicious new beverage. The church at first disapproved of it, claiming it to be an aphrodisiac! However, the threatened wrath of the church was quickly ignored for something so delicious and chocolate became one of Bayonne's most famous exports. Don't leave Basque without sampling some of this "devil's brew"!

Gorges du Tarn
& Beyond

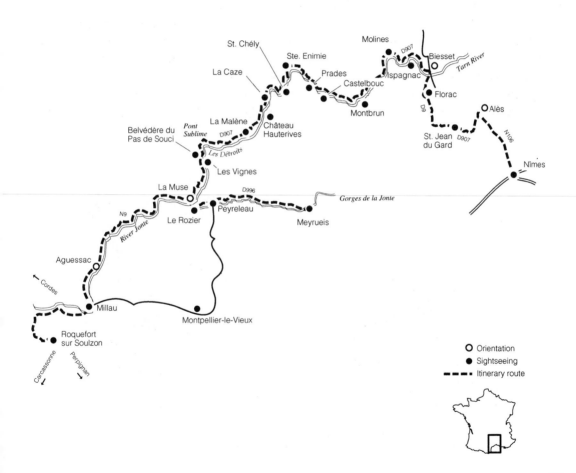

St. Chély
Ste. Enimie
Molines
Biesset
D907
Tarn River
La Caze
Prades
Ispagnac
Castelbouc
Florac
Montbrun
D9
Alès
La Malène
Château
Hauterives
Pont
Sublime
St. Jean
du Gard
D907
N106
Belvédère du
Pas de Souci
D907
Les Détroits
Nîmes
Les Vignes
La Muse
D996
Le Rozier
Peyreleau
Gorges de la Jonte
Meyrueis
N9
River Jonte
Aguessac
Cordes
Millau
Roquefort
sur Soulzon
Montpellier-le-Vieux
Carcassonne
Perpignan

○ Orientation
● Sightseeing
▪▪▪ Itinerary route

75

Gorges du Tarn & Beyond

This itinerary follows the truly spectacular River Tarn as it winds back and forth along the Tarn Canyon or *Gorges du Tarn*. With each turn the drive becomes more beautiful, never monotonous. The road cuts through the canyon, hugging its walls, always in sight of the peaceful waters of the Tarn and its picturesque villages, clusters of warm stone buildings that nestle above its shore. Encased in deep limestone cliffs, the river canyon is at its most glorious in early autumn—a perfect time to visit. In the fall the traffic has subsided and nature's colors contrast beautifully with the canyon walls: grass carpets the mountains, making hillsides lush in all shades of green, and the trees blaze gold, red, and orange in the sunlight. But whatever time of year, the Gorges du Tarn is lovely.

Recommended Pacing: This itinerary covers approximately 220 kilometers and can be driven in about 4 hours. The stretch along the canyon from Florac to Millau, about 75 kilometers, is sometimes crowded, often narrows to two lanes, and there are no short cuts once you're following the river. If you plan to cover the distance in a day's journey, get an early start. We suggest that you overnight near the river and give yourself two full days to drive, walk, picnic, and even float your way through the Tarn Canyon. At its conclusion, since this is relatively a short itinerary and based on the assumption that you will want to extend your trip into other regions of France, there are two suggestions for continuing your journey. Both suggestions incorporate a trip to the walled town of Carcassonne, one heads further west to visit the lovely cities of Albi and Toulouse, and the medieval, hill-town of Cordes; while the other recommends that once you leave Carcassonne, you efficiently span the distance, traveling the autoroutes, to the geographic, southwest corner where France neighbors Spain and overlooks the beautiful Mediterranean Sea.

With either **Avignon** or **Nîmes** on the western edge of Provence as a point of reference, travel northwest in the direction of Alès. Using a good map to plan the best route depending on your origin, travel southwest of Alès to the D907, going north in the direction of Saint Jean du Gard. **Saint Jean du Gard** is a very scenic village, located just before the **Corniche des Cevennes**. Just outside Saint Jean du Gard you are faced with the option of traveling the corniche along the canyon's south or north rim. This itinerary travels the D9, which follows the north rim and is the more scenic and better of the two roads. The drive is lovely, traveling through and above the forests of the region. At the northern tip of the corniche the road number changes from D9 to D983 and travels 6 kilometers to the junction of D907. Follow the D907 north just over 5 kilometers to **Florac** and then join the N106, continuing north in the direction of Mende, but at the tiny village of Biesset veer off and head west on the D907 bis. It is here that your true journey of the Tarn Canyon begins.

To appreciate the region you need to simply travel it: each turn affords a lovely vista or breathtakingly beautiful portrait of a hillside village. Opportunities to stop along the roadside are limited and will frustrate most photographers, but drive it leisurely and stop when possible to explore the little hamlets. The following is an overview of the river and its path, and some of its most picturesque highlights. With a good map in hand, enjoy its scenic journey.

The **Ispagnac Basin**, located at the entrance to the canyon, is filled with fruit trees, vineyards, and strawberries. Here towns are scattered artistically about; châteaux and ruins appear often enough to add enchantment. A lovely wide bridge spans the river at **Ispagnac** and farther along at **Molines**, set in the bend of the river, the canyon boasts a picturesque mill and castle. As the road hugs the hillside, the pretty town of **Montbrun** blends into the hillside on the opposite side of the river. The road then narrows and winds along the base of the canyon, looking up to rugged canyon walls and down to stretches of green along the river's edge. **Castelbouc**, on the other side of the river, is idyllically nestled on the hillside and is spectacular when illuminated on summer evenings. Just a short distance beyond Castelbouc the road carves a path to the north, providing a scenic overlook of the neighboring castle of **Prades**. One of the larger settlements in the region, **Sainte Énimie** is a charming village caught in the bend of the canyon where an old attractive bridge arches across the river and a church wedged into the mountainside piques the curiosity. From Sainte Énimie the road tunnels into the canyon walls colored in orange, gold, and green. **Saint Chély du Tarn** is nestled on the sides of the canyon wall and is illuminated in a spectacle of sound and light. A short distance south of Saint Chély, majestically positioned above the Tarn, is a fairy-tale castle offering accommodation, the **Château de la Caze**.

From the spectacular setting of La Caze, the road follows the river as it bends past the **Château Hauterives** and then passes through the lovely and probably most active village on the riverbank, **La Malène**. Many companies offer raft, kayak, and canoe trips departing from La Malène. From the river you have a better view of some of the old medieval towns and a section of the Tarn referred to as **Les Détroits**, the Straits, not visible from the road. Here the river is only a few meters wide, towered by canyon cliffs rising more than 300 meters straight above. From La Malène the road winds through the canyon rock and a cluster of buildings appears huddled on the other bank, just at the entrance to Les Détroits. Farther on, numerous buses stop at **Belvédère du Pas de Souci** and you can join the crowds to climb the steep metal stairway to views of the pools below (for an admission fee). From Pas de Souci, the river widens and the canyon walls turn to gentle slopes at the little village of **Les Vignes**. From Les Vignes it is worth a short detour following signs to **Point Sublime**. It is a steep climb up to one of the most impressive viewpoints of the canyon, 400 meters above the river.

Cross the river at La Muse to the village of **Le Rozier**, which enjoys a pretty setting at the junction of the Tarn and Jonte rivers. From Le Rozier you have a couple of options to extend your visit in this lovely region and explore another river canyon before continuing along the D907 the last 20 kilometers along the Tarn to Millau.

To extend your visit, venture east from Le Rozier, crossing the bridge, to the neighboring, picturesque village of **Peyreleau**. Straddling both sides of the river, buildings huddle on the narrow river ledges as mountain and canyon walls rise from this narrow stretch of the valley. As common as postcards in most towns, walking sticks are for sale at every shop and suggest that you should park your car and take time to explore the region on foot. If nothing else, cross the narrow bridge that spans the river and make the climb up the narrow streets to Peyreleau's dramatic castle.

From Peyreleau you can continue traveling the D996, a narrow, often roughly paved road following the dramatic and rugged **Gorges de la Jonte**. Overpowered by the towering Jonte canyon walls, this is a gorgeous drive and establishing an endpoint of the scenic journey is the picturesque village of **Meyrueis.** A charming village, located approximately 21 kilometers east of Le Rozier, the handsome buildings of Meyrueis huddle together along the banks of the Jonte. There are numerous outdoor restaurants that take advantage of the views and setting.

Another option from Peyreleau, rather than continuing east, exploring the Gorges de la Jonte, there is a narrow, winding road that travels 10 kilometers south to **Montpellier le Vieux**—a landscape of intriguing rock formations. There is an admission charge for driving through this complex of rock and then from here one continues another twisting stretch of almost 20 kilometers on to Millau. **Millau** is a lovely, large city located at the junction of two rivers, the Tarn and the Dourbie, known for its leather goods, particularly gloves. Millau marks the end of the canyon.

Because a visit of the Gorges du Tarn can be achieved in a few days time, we assume you will want to extend your trip and continue your journey into other regions of France. It would be easy to circle back to Provence; make the journey west to the Dordogne and Lot River Valleys, or travel west and then south to region Basque. However, the following are a couple of suggestions for some sightseeing that would necessitate just a few days in terms of an appendage to your itinerary.

SUGGESTION ONE: From Millau it is feasible to follow an itinerary loop that journeys southwest in the direction of Carcassonne, with the suggestion that you incorporate stops in Roquefort sur Soulzon, Albi, and the hilltown of Cordes-sur-Ciel (a short detour) and then circle back to the walled fortress of Carcassonne. **Roquefort sur Soulzon** is home to the distinctive Roquefort cheese: if this regional specialty appeals, you might enjoy a tour of one of the cheese cellars. **Albi**, a large city, is about a two-hour drive through farmland from Roquefort. With its cathedral dominating the entire city, Albi, mostly built of brick, is also referred to as "Albi the red." The **Musée Toulouse Lautrec** is one of its more interesting attractions. From Albi it is another half-hour drive to the medieval town of **Cordes-sur-Ciel**, also known as "Cordes in the Heavens," above the Cerou Valley. This is an enchanting hilltop village, a treasure that will prove a highlight of any itinerary. Known for its leather goods and hand-woven fabrics, Cordes-sur-Ciel offers many *ateliers* (craft shops) along its cobblestoned streets.

Retracing your path back to Albi, it is an undemanding drive south along the N112 and the D118 to Carcassonne. Europe's largest medieval fortress, **Carcassonne** is a highlight of any visit to France and a wonderful grand finale to this itinerary; Vieux Carcassonne rises above the vineyards at the foot of the Cevennes and Pyrenees.

The massive protecting walls of Carcassonne were first raised by the Romans in the 1st century B.C. Though never conquered in battle, the mighty city was lost to nature's weathering elements and has since been restored so that it looks as it did when constructed centuries ago. Stroll through the powerful gates along its winding cobbled streets and wander back into history. The walled city boasts numerous touristy shops and delightful restaurants and hotels.

MAP OF SUGGESTION ONE:

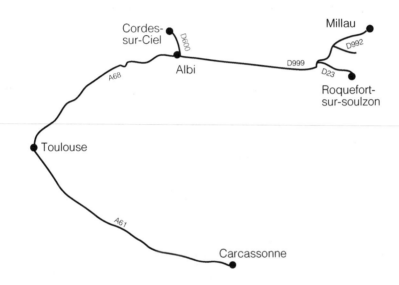

SUGGESTION TWO: This suggestion would be to head directly southwest to Carcassonne, visit the walled city and from there, make use of the Autoroutes to efficiently cover the distance to the southwest corner of France on the Spanish border.

Travel first on Autoroute 61 west to Narbonne and then connect with Autoroute 9 south, following the Mediterranean coast in the direction of Perpignan and the Spanish border.

Your goal is a very distinctive and enchanting region of France—one I have only just begun to discover and intend to explore in greater depth in the near future. Referred to as **Terre Catalane**, it is a region strongly influenced by its neighbor in its ambiance, flavor and the easy-going and relaxed style and warmth of the people who live here.

To begin your journey, exit the Autoroute at Le Boulou and travel approximately 10 km southwest to **Céret,** a charming hillside town of stucco buildings and tiled roofs. Home to many artists, Céret's seemingly greatest renown is for its *cerises* (cherries) as evidenced in the late spring and early summer by the many stands, banners and festivals. Céret is also the address of a wonderful museum, **Musée d'Art Moderne.** *(tel: 04.68.87.27.76, www.musee-ceret.com)*

From Céret, now chart a course east along the D618 to Argelès and then south on the D114 to the idyllic port town of **Collioure**. Reminiscent of Italy with pastel-colored stucco buildings and tile roofs against a backdrop of the deep Mediterranean sea, Collioure has long lured artists in appreciation of its beauty and setting. The heart of the port boasts narrow passageways that weave through a multitude of shops and restaurants, as well as access to a pretty little beach right in the town, protected and embraced by the breakwater. Center stage is **Château Royal,** which in its time served as both a strategic meeting point of the Mediterranean Sea and the Pyrenees mountains as well as a fortress. It was home to the Kings of Mallorca in the 13th and 14th centuries and was converted to a citadel in the 16th and 17th centuries.

From Collioure, travel the N114 that continues along the contours of the coast, possibly detouring out to the lighthouse and point of Port Vendres, and then on to **Banyuls**. Just north of the Spanish border, Banyuls warrants a trip because of its marvelous museum honoring one of France's most acclaimed sculpturers, the **Musée Maillol** *(Open all year, tel: 04.68.88.57.11)*. It is also the impressive site of the cellars of **Cellier des Templiers** where you can enjoy a free, guided tour, sample wines from a region that has been producing wines for over seven centuries, and enjoy panoramic views of the surrounding, terraced vineyards. *(Open all year, tel: 04.68.98.36.92)*

Unless you want to continue south to Spain, from Banyuls I would recommend retracing your path back north to **Perpignan,** where you will find both train and planes convenient options for continuing your travels.

MAP OF SUGGESTION TWO:

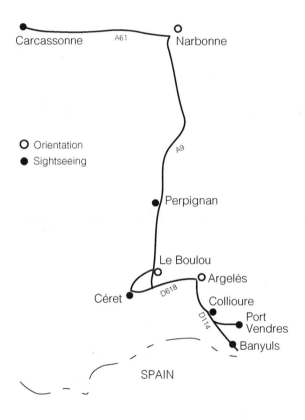

Walled City of Carcassonne

Provence

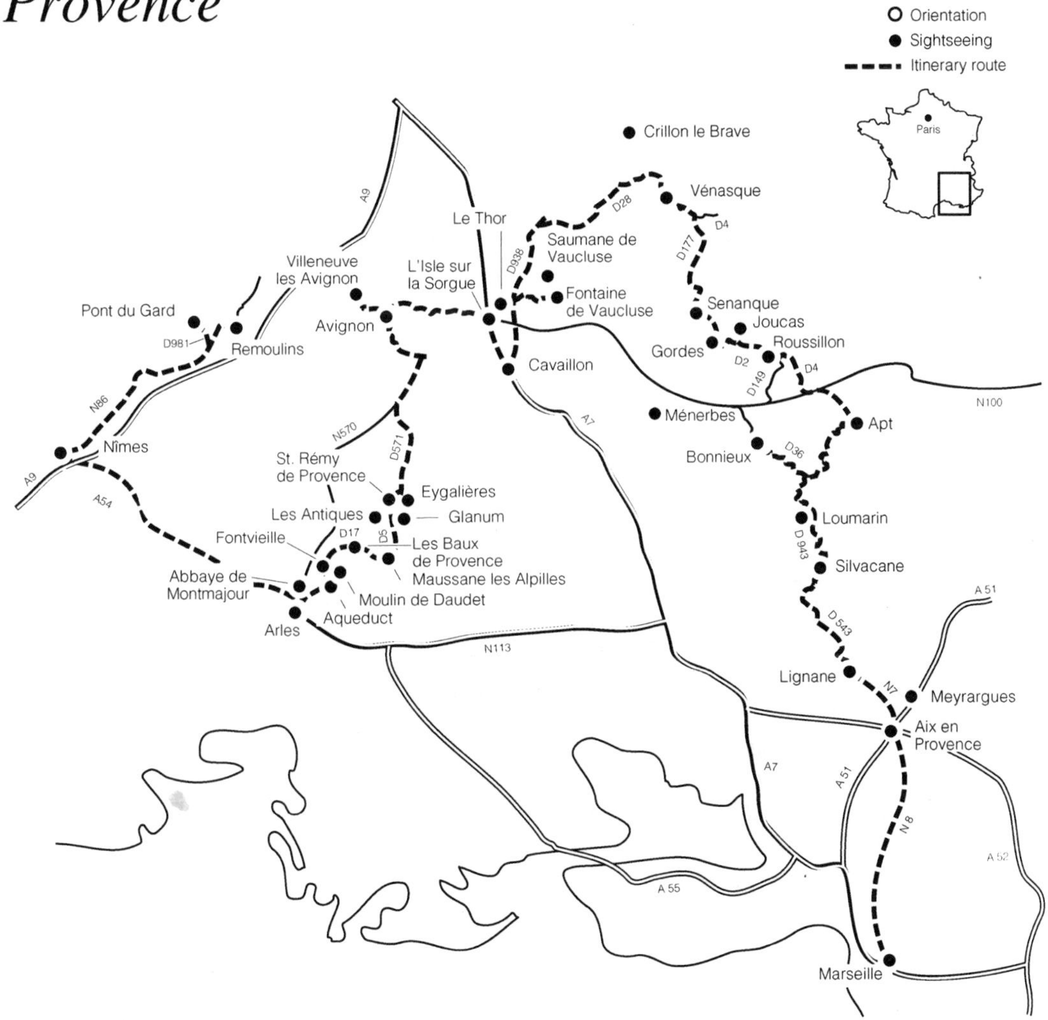
Orientation
Sightseeing
Itinerary route
Paris
Crillon le Brave
Vénasque
Le Thor
Saumane de Vaucluse
Villeneuve les Avignon
L'Isle sur la Sorgue
Fontaine de Vaucluse
Senanque
Joucas
Pont du Gard
Avignon
Gordes
Roussillon
D981
Remoulins
Cavaillon
Ménerbes
Apt
Nîmes
Bonnieux
St. Rémy de Provence
Eygalières
Les Antiques
Glanum
Loumarin
Fontvieille
Les Baux de Provence
Maussane les Alpilles
Abbaye de Montmajour
Silvacane
Moulin de Daudet
Aqueduct
Arles
Lignane
Meyrargues
Aix en Provence
Marseille
A9
N86
A54
N570
D571
D17
D5
N113
A7
D938
D28
D4
D177
D2
D149
N100
D36
D 943
D 543
N7
A 51
N 8
A 52
A 55

Provence

Provence, settled by the Romans around 120 B.C., is a region of contrasts and colors. This delightful region of the French *Midi* (the South) is associated with warm breezes, a mild climate, and rolling hillsides covered in the gray washes of olive trees and lavender. Its rich soil in the bath of the warm southern sun produces a bounty of produce that is incorporated into its regional cuisine. Some of the world's most popular wines are produced here and complement the delicious local dishes. The romance and beauty of Provence has inspired artists and writers for generations.

Pont du Gard

Recommended Pacing: This itinerary assumes the large port city of Marseille as a starting point, winds north to the beautiful university city of Aix en Provence, into the hilltowns of Haute Provence, and then circles back to the heart of the region and the lovely towns set in its valley. It is possible to see Provence in just a few days, but the countryside calls for you to linger, to settle and absorb the climate, the beauty, and the landscape. Our ideal would be a night in Aix en Provence, one to two nights in one of the hilltowns of Haute Provence, and at least three nights at the heart of Provence.

Marseille is the second-largest city in France. Settled as a Phoenician colony, this major Mediterranean port is where our Provence itinerary begins. Apart from the Roman docks and fortified church of Saint Victor, there are few monuments to its past within the city. However, you must see **La Canebière**, a major boulevard that captures the activity, gaiety, and pace of Marseille. The old port has a number of museums to draw your interest; the **Musée Grobet-Labadie** has a beautiful collection of tapestries, furniture, paintings, musical instruments, pottery, and sculpture. (*Open daily 10 am to 5 pm, Sun noon to 7 pm.*)

From Marseille drive north following either the N8 or the Autoroute 51 to the southern periphery of **Aix en Provence**, an elegant city that deserves an overnight stay. Aix achieved fame when "Good King René," count of Provence, and his wife chose it as their preferred residence in the 1450s. Upon his death Aix fell under the rule of the French crown and was made the seat of parliament. The city flourished in the 17th and 18th centuries and became one of the most prosperous metropolises of the region. Much of Aix's elegant architecture is attributed to this period of affluence. Today it is predominantly a university town, home to some 40,000 students who represent almost a third of the city's population. Numerous fountains adorn the elegant tree-lined Cours Mirabeau, edged by aristocratic residences and numerous cafés. The Cours Mirabeau separates the Quartier Mazarin to the south from the Quartier Ancien on the north. The Quartier Mazarin attracted dignitaries and many lovely parliamentary homes still stand in this neighborhood. By contrast, the Quartier Ancien is the heart of the city, with a bustle of activity along its charming little back streets lined with numerous cafés and restaurants.

Aix is an enchanting, beautiful and aristocratic city to explore. The beckoning cobblestoned streets of its **Old Quarter** are intriguing to wander along at night and the illuminated tree-lined Cours Mirabeau is enchanting—a bit reminiscent of Paris with its many sidewalk cafés. Nineteen 17th-century tapestries from Beauvois are on display in the **Museum of Tapestries**. Another fifteen Flemish tapestries can be found in the **Cathedral Saint Sauveur**. (*Closed noon to 2:00 pm and all day Tues.*) Aix is also the birthplace of Paul Cézanne who was born here in 1839 but left to join his colleagues and the impressionistic fever that prevailed in Paris. He returned to his hometown in 1870 and settled here until his death in 1906. You can visit the studio he built, **Atelier Paul Cézanne**, set behind a little wooden gate just north of the old quarter. Paul Cézanne studied in Aix with Émile Zola and the distant Mont Saint Victoire, which inspired much of his work, can be seen from various vantage points in the city. (*Closed noon to 2 pm except in summer–noon to 2:30 pm, and all day Tues.*)

From Aix en Provence you travel north on country roads through groves of olive trees and acres of vineyards to the hilltowns of Haute Provence. Less traveled, the medieval hillside perched villages of this region are intriguing to explore.

From Aix follow the N7 northwest in the direction of Saint Cannat. Turn north 6 kilometers out of Aix at Lignane, following the D543 north across the Chaîne de la Tréversse, to Silvacane on the waters of the River Durance and the Canal de Marseille. Cross the river and the D543 becomes the D943, traveling first to Cadenet and then on to **Loumarin**, the capital of this region of Luberon. Loumarin is a small city surrounded by the bounty of the region: fruit trees, flowers, and produce. The château on the outskirts of town is a school for artists.

From Loumarin, the D943 enjoys the beautiful path of the Aigue Brun for 6 kilometers and then you take the D36 just a few kilometers farther west to the hillside village of **Bonnieux**. From Bonnieux you can wind a course northeast to the thriving city of **Apt**, known for its crystallized fruits and preserves, truffles, lavender perfume, and old Sainte Anne Cathedral, which is still the site of an annual pilgrimage. From Apt follow the N100 west for 4½ kilometers to the D4 north to the turnoff west to Roussillon. Another

Gordes

option is to navigate a course directly north to Roussillon, an exploration along countryside roads.

Whichever the route, **Roussillon** is worth the effort to find. This lovely village is a maze of narrow streets, small shops, and restaurants that climb to the town's summit. In various shades of ochres, Roussillon is an enchanting village, especially on a clear day when the sun warms and intensifies the colors.

From Roussillon travel first north on the D105 and then west on the D2 to the neighboring village of **Gordes**, perched at one end of the Vaucluse Plateau and dominating the Imergue Valley. Bathed in tones of gray, this is a wonderful place. Off its main square are some inviting cafés, restaurants, and shops selling Provence's wonderful bounties: lavender, olive oils, wines, regional dolls (*santons*), and garments in the charming local fabrics. Gordes is also known for the ancient village of 20 restored *bories,* or dry-stone huts, that lie in its shadow. Unusual in their round or rectangular shapes, these intriguing buildings (many of which accommodate 20th-century comforts) are thought to date from the 17th century.

Across from Gordes, **Joucas** is a perfectly preserved jewel of a village perched above the Luberon Valley.

Just four kilometers to the north of Gordes is **Senanque**, a 12th-century Cistercian abbey standing dramatically isolated at the edge of the mountainside surrounded by lavender and oak trees. Vacated by the monks in 1869 and accessible on foot by a 2-kilometer path up from the car park, the abbey is now a religious cultural center and hosts concerts in the summer months.

A Restaurant Housed in a Borie

From Senanque follow the small country road (D177) north to connect with the D4 and then travel west through the dense Forest of Vénasque to the beautiful and striking hilltop village of **Vénasque**. Charmingly untouched by civilization, this village is tucked in a dense forest cupped between two steep hills and is notable for its 6th-century **Église de Notre Dame** and the 17th-century **Chapelle Notre Dame de Vie**. The town comes to life during the early summer when it is the market center for the region's cherry crop. Near Vénasque is another lovely hilltop village, **Crillon le Brave**.

90   *Provence*

From Vénasque weave a course south in the direction of the market town of **Cavaillon**. Known for its melon fields, Cavaillon is another village to include on your itinerary if your schedule permits. On the outskirts of Cavaillon, detour east to the amazing **Fontaine de Vaucluse**, fed by rainwater that seeps through the Vaucluse Plateau. In the late afternoon as the sun begins its descent, walk around this celebrated natural fountain: at certain times of the year the shooting water is so powerful that it becomes dangerous and the fountain is closed to observers. The most dramatic seasons to visit the spewing fountain are winter and spring. Over a million tourists travel to Vaucluse each year to see the fountain, but few venture the 4 kilometers farther to the idyllic perched village of **Saumane de Vaucluse** whose hillside location affords an idyllic spot from which to watch the sun bathe the countryside in the soft hues so characteristic of Provence.

Retrace a path back in the direction of Cavaillon from Fontaine de Vaucluse and take the N100 southwest in the direction of Avignon. A wonderful place to stop en route, especially if you like antiques, is the country town of **L'Isle sur la Sorgue**, known for its many shops.

Considered a gateway to Provence, **Avignon** is one of France's most interesting and beautiful cities. Easy to navigate, its medieval encasement is encircled by one main boulevard and various gates allow entry into the walled city. The Porte de l'Oulle on the northwestern perimeter has parking just outside the wall and a small tourist booth with maps and information, and provides convenient access into the heart of the old city. The Porte de la Republique on the south side is opposite the train station and opens onto the Cour Jean Jaures, the location of the main tourist office. The Cour Jean Jaures becomes the Rue de la République and leads straight to the Place du Palais on the city's northern border. You might want to inquire at the tourist office about the miniature train that travels the city, highlighting the key points of interest, and the excellent guide service that conducts either full- or half-day walking tours of the city. Avignon is fun to explore—a wonderful selection of shops line its streets, a festive air prevails with numerous street performers, and the historical attractions are monumental.

Avignon was the papal residency from 1309 to 1377 and the **Palais des Papes** is a highlight of a visit to this lovely city—if only to stand on the main square and look up at the long, soft-yellow stone structure that dominates the city skyline, stretching the length of the square and towering against the blue skies of Provence. If time permits, enter the papal city through the Porte des Chapeaux into the Grande Cour. A little shop just off the entrance provides maps, information, and admission into the palace. Just off the entry, the impressive inner courtyard and beginning point for a palace tour is often a stage for the open-air theater performances of the popular summer festival.

Allow approximately an hour to explore the palace effectively, noting the distinction between the old palace, built by Pope Benedict XII from 1334 to 1342, and the new palace commissioned by his successor, Pope Clement VI, and finished in 1348. The tour will take you down the Hall of the Consistory (*Aile du Consistoire*), hung with portraits of popes who resided in Avignon, to the upstairs banqueting hall (*Grand Tinel*), to the impressive Deer Room (*Chambre du Cerf*), whose walls display a beautifully painted fresco by Giovanetti depicting the decadent life of leisure led by the papal court in the 14th century, on to the Audience Hall (*Aile de Grande Audience*), elaborate with its star-studded ceiling, and the magnificent Saint Martial Chapel *(open only on Sun for church service, tel: 04.90.27.50.00)*

Devote the majority of your time to visiting this feudal structure, but don't miss the two lovely churches, **Cathédral de Notre Dame des Doms** and **L'Église Saint Didier**. Just off the Rue Joseph Vernet is the **Musée Calvet**, named for the doctor who bequeathed his personal collection of art and funds to launch it. The museum displays a rich collection of work from artists of the French and Avignon schools of painting and sculpture: Delacroix, Corot, and Manet are some of the impressive masters represented. (*Closed 1 to 2 pm and all day Tues.*)

Although only four of its original twenty-two arches still stand, the **Pont Saint Bénezet** is an impressive sight. A small chapel still sits on one of its piers and shadows the waters of the encircling River Rhône. This is the bridge referred to in the song familiar to all French children, "*Sur le pont d'Avignon, on y dance, on y dance.*" Even if all the arches still stood, passage would be difficult by modern-day transportation as the bridge was constructed at the end of the 12th century with pedestrians and horses in mind.

Villeneuve les Avignon is separated from Avignon by the Rhône. (Cross the river by following the N100 west of the city and then turn immediately on D900 in the direction of Villeneuve.) Villeneuve flourished when the pope held residence in Avignon and a number of cardinals chose it for their magnificent estates. Today it presents a lovely setting on the river, enjoys magnificent views of its neighbor, and yet benefits from a quieter setting and pace. A stronghold that once guarded the frontier of France when Avignon was allied to the Holy Roman Empire, it has towering on its skyline **Fort Saint André** whose vantage point commands a magnificent view across the Rhône to Avignon and the Popes' Palace. Another military structure still standing is the **Philippe le Bel Tower** and the curator is often on hand to provide all the historical facts. The Saturday morning antique and flea market is a popular attraction.

From Avignon it is a very pleasant drive south along a lazy, tree-lined road, the D571, to **Saint Rémy de Provence**, a pretty, sleepy town, nestled in the shade of its plane trees. Of interest in the town are a Romanesque church, Renaissance houses, and a busy public square.

On the outskirts of Saint Rémy, following the D5 south in the direction of Les Baux de Provence, you can visit the **Clinique de Saint Paul** where Van Gogh was nursed back to health after slicing off his earlobe; **Les Antiques**, an impressive arch and mausoleum commissioned by Augustus; and **Glanum**, a thriving point of commerce during the Gallo-Greek years that was virtually destroyed in the 3rd century.

From Saint Rémy it is a beautiful drive along the D5 as it winds through the chalky gray hills referred to as *Les Alpilles* and then turns off to cover the short distance across the valley to the charming Provençal village of **Les Baux de Provence**. (The mineral bauxite was discovered here and derives its name from the town.)

The village appears to be a continuation of the rocky spur from which it rises. This site has been occupied for the past 5,000 years, and is now visited by more than a million visitors every year. A number of craft shops, inviting crêperies, and ice cream vendors are tucked away along the village streets. From Les Baux you have splendid views of the area.

En route to the lovely Roman city of Arles from Les Baux, the D17 travels first to the small roadside town of **Fontvieille**. Fontvieille is home to a wonderful hotel and restaurant, **La Régalido**, and is also worth a stop to visit the **Moulin de Daudet**, an abandoned mill set on the hillside above town, reputedly where Daudet wrote *Letters from My Windmill*.

Continuing on the back road from Fontvieille, the D33, as it travels beyond the mill, passes the ruins of an old **Roman Aqueduct** that stands unceremoniously in a field just off the road at the intersection of the D82. Head west from the aqueduct along the D82 to connect with the D17 and travel once again in the direction of Arles. On the approach to

Les Baux de Provence

the city, surrounded by fields, stand the ruins of **Abbaye de Montmajour**, which was built in the 10th century by Benedictine monks.

The skyline of **Arles** can be seen as you approach the city. Abounding in character, this is a truly lovely city whose growth is governed by the banks and curves of the Rhône. It has fierce ties to its Roman past when it thrived as a strong port city and gateway. Arles is glorified because of its magnificent Gallo-Roman arenas and theaters in the heart of the old city. This is a city to explore on foot: it is fun to wander through the narrow maze of winding streets that weave through the old section. Bullfights and festivals are still staged in the magnificent **Amphithéâtre**, or arena, able to accommodate in its prime more than 20,000 spectators. (*Open Jun to Sep all day, Oct to May seasonal hours.*)

The **Théâtre Antique**, although apparently a ruin by day, becomes a lovely stage on summer nights under the soft lights of the Festival d'Arles. (*Same hours as the Amphithéâtre.*) The Place du Forum is bordered by cafés and is a social spot to settle in the afternoons and into the balmy evenings of Provence. Just a block from the Place du Forum, the **Muséon Arlaten** was conceived and funded by the town's poet, Frédéric Mistral, from the money he received for winning the Nobel Prize in literature, to honor all that is Provençal. The museum is rich in its portrayal of the culture and fierce traditions of Provence. (*Closed noon to 2 pm and all day Mon in winter.*) Another fascinating museum in Arles is the **Musée de l'Arles Antique**, just south of the Nouveau Pont, which you can reach by walking along the ramparts on the edge of the Rhône. Large and open, the museum houses a dramatic display of sarcophagi, mosaics, statuary, models, and replicas depicting the dramatic arenas and theaters, as well as jewelry, tools, and pottery that lend a glimpse of life in ancient Arles. It is built on a site overlooking the ruins of the Roman hippodrome and from the rooftop of the museum you can see the outline of the track, which in time they hope to restore to its original dimensions. (*Open Apr to Oct, 9 am to 7 pm daily; rest of year 10 am to 6 pm, closed Tues.*)

At the gateway to the Camargue and nestled at the heart of Provence, Arles is a wonderful base from which to experience the region.

Nîmes lies approximately 35 kilometers west of Arles. A Gaelic capital, it was also popular with the Romans who built its monuments. Without fail see the **Amphithéâtre** that once held 21,000 spectators, the **Arénas**, **Maison Carrée**, the best-preserved Roman temple in the world, and the magnificent **fountain gardens**.

As a final destination, journey just another 20 kilometers or so north of Nîmes (N86 Remoulins, D981) to the spectacular **Pont du Gard**, an aqueduct that impressively bridges the River Gard. Still intact, three tiers of stone arches tower more than 36 meters across the valley. Built by Roman engineers about 20 B.C. as part of a 50-kilometer-long system bringing water from Uzès to Nîmes, the aqueduct remains one of the world's marvels. Park in the car park amid the tourist stalls and food stands and walk a pedestrian road to the span of river that thankfully lies uncluttered, dominated only by the impact and shadow of the towering structure.

From Pont du Gard, you can easily return to Nîmes or complete the circle back to Avignon.

Palais des Papes, Avignon

Provence

Gorges du Verdon

○ Orientation
● Sightseeing
■ ■ ■ ■ Itinerary route

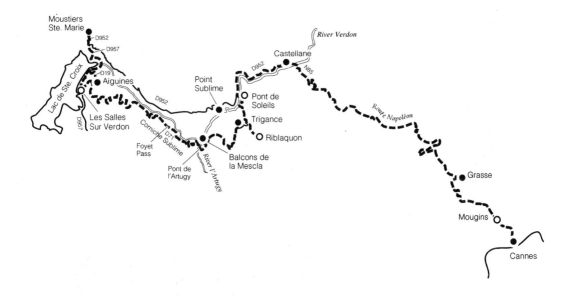

97

Gorges du Verdon

The Gorges du Verdon is the French equivalent of the Grand Canyon. The striking blue-green water of the Verdon is dramatic in its intensity as it carves through and contrasts with the magnificent limestone plateau. The river then plunges into the spectacular trench-like Gorges du Verdon and is enclosed within its steep jagged walls. When you are traveling between the Riviera and central Provence, the Gorges du Verdon makes for a wonderful detour, and a few days spent in this region will prove memorable.

Gorges du Verdon

Recommended Pacing: This itinerary extends from Castellane to the delightful village of Moustiers Sainte Marie just to the north of Lac de Sainte Croix. The total distance covered is only about 40 kilometers, including the dramatic 20-kilometer span of the canyon from the Pont de Soleils to the town of Aiguines. The most logical access from the Riviera is to follow the N85, a lovely forested road that winds from Grasse northwest along the Route Napoléon to Castellane, a town set on the banks of the Verdon. You can include a visit to the canyon and cover the distance between the Riviera and Provence in one day, but it would require a very early start and make for an exceptionally long day. We recommend an overnight on the edge of the canyon at the Château de Trigance in the small hillside village of Trigance. Breaking the journey here gives you time to enjoy an unhurried drive along the dramatic canyon rim and then a leisurely next day to explore Moustiers Sainte Marie. We would also recommend including an overnight in Moustiers Sainte Marie — as we are certain the town and its setting will captivate you as it has us — before continuing your journey on to Provence.

Castellane is a natural starting point for an exploration of the canyon. It enjoys a lovely setting on the banks of the River Verdon and is famous for its crowning rock that towers above the town, crested by the **Nôtre Dame du Roc Chapel**. Traveling the D952 west following the path of the Verdon, at Pont de Soleils you can either choose to follow the south bank or the north bank of the canyon. (If time and enthusiasm allow, it is also possible to make one grand circle journey traveling both sides of the canyon.) For the purposes of this itinerary, the suggested routing follows the south bank, the *Corniche Sublime*, as it affords spectacular vistas of the canyon and also conveniently passes the enchanting medieval village of Trigance whose thick stone walls guard a wonderful hotel and restaurant, the Château de Trigance. To reach Trigance from Pont de Soleils, travel first south 16 kilometers on the D955 and just before the village of Riblaquon, cross over the Jabron river to the medieval town of **Trigance** on the opposite hillside.

Following the road round the back of Trigance, the D90 travels a short distance (6 kilometers) before it ends at the D71. Turn north on the D71 and you will soon be rewarded with a spectacular vista of the dramatic Verdon at the **Balcons de la Mescla**.

You can pull off here, and there are terraced points from which you can look down at the dramatic loop in the path of the river some 760 meters below. (There is also a small café where you can purchase snacks and postcards.) From Mescla the road winds through sparse vegetation of boxwood and then crosses over a dramatic span, the **Pont de l'Artugy**, a concrete, one-arch bridge that rises precariously high above the waters below. From the bridge, the drive is constantly spectacular in its drama and scenery. It rises and falls above the canyon walls, winding in and out of tunnels impressively cut into its rock face. From Artuby the road climbs on the fringe of the ravine to the **Fayet**

Gorges du Verdon

Pass. Here a tunnel carves through the rock and square openings through the thick tunnel walls create windows that afford glimpses of the river's dramatic passage. Every second of the drive following the jagged mouth of the Verdon Canyon is spectacular. The canyon is almost overpowering: the river forges a path through narrow stretches where the canyon sides plunge down to depths far below, and then slows and calms in wider sections, pausing to create glistening, dark-green pools.

The road periodically veers away from the edge of the canyon and rolls past beautiful green meadows dotted by a few mountain cabins and hamlets. In spring, wildflowers bloom everywhere. As the ruggedness and fierceness of the canyon wanes, the road gradually returns to the valley, opening up to vistas of the brilliant blue waters of **Lac de Sainte Croix** where you see **Aiguines**, a rosy-hued village silhouetted against the backdrop of the lake. The numerous docks hint at what a paradise the lake is for sportsmen in summer months. At the water's edge, the road (now numbered D957), travels in the direction of Moustiers Sainte Marie, crossing over the Verdon as it flows into the lake. Be sure to take a moment and park just before the bridge, as it is a beautiful sight looking back up the narrow canyon and if you are fortunate, you might see kayakers at the conclusion of their journey.

Moustiers Sainte Marie is a grand finale to this itinerary. Famous for its pottery, it is a wonderful village whose cluster of buildings with their patchwork of red-tiled roofs hugs the hillside and crawls back into the protection of a sheltered mountain alcove. Monks came here in 433, took shelter in caves dug into the mountainside, and founded the monastery **Nôtre Dame de Beauvoir**, which towers over the village. The church was rebuilt during the 12th century and enlarged in the 16th. You can reach the sanctuary by a winding footpath paved with round stones leading up from the heart of the village.

This is a beautiful Provençal hilltown whose narrow, winding streets offer a wealth of stores displaying the famous Moustiers pottery. As early as 1678, the first master potter created a pattern that originated the style associated with the village. Today, some 15 master potters offer high-quality handmade and hand-decorated products, and pottery is the principal industry in the area. You can actually come to Moustiers and commission a personalized pattern in one of the workshops. Considering the size of the village and its seemingly remote location, it is hard to believe that the workshops of Moustiers Sainte Marie fulfill requests from all over the world for their hand-painted *faïence*.

From Moustiers Sainte Marie, it is a 1½-hour drive to Aix en Provence where you can join our *Provence* itinerary.

Moustiers Sainte Marie

Gorges du Verdon

Hilltowns of the
French Riviera

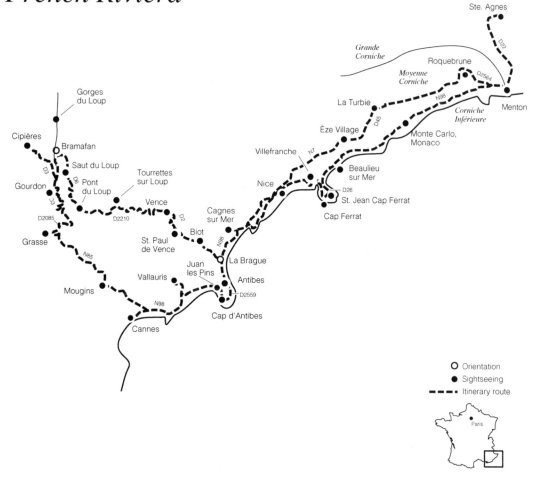

Ste. Agnes

Grande Corniche

Roquebrune

Moyenne Corniche

D2564

La Turbie

N98

Corniche Inférieure

Menton

D45

Èze Village

Monte Carlo, Monaco

Villefranche

N7

Beaulieu sur Mer

Nice

D26

St. Jean Cap Ferrat

Cap Ferrat

Gorges du Loup

Cipières

Bramafan

Saut du Loup

Tourrettes sur Loup

D3

D6

Pont du Loup

Gourdon

33

Vence

Cagnes sur Mer

D2085

D2210

D2

Biot

Grasse

St. Paul de Vence

N98

N85

Juan les Pins

La Brague

Vallauris

Antibes

Mougins

N98

D2559

Cannes

Cap d'Antibes

○ Orientation
● Sightseeing
■ ■ ■ Itinerary route

Paris

103

Hilltowns of the French Riviera

People in the hundreds of thousands flock to the Riviera for its sun and dazzling blue waters. When planning your trip, be aware that most of these sun-worshipers congregate during the spring and summer with the coastal towns as their base and during this time the coastside is a constant hub of activity and excitement. The Riviera attracts an international group, jet-setters here to see and be seen. In the mountains overlooking the Mediterranean are a number of smaller, "hillside-perched" towns, removed from the continuous activity of the Riviera and offering a beautiful setting and escape.

View from Eze Village

Recommended Pacing: We suggest at least three full days to explore the coastal and hilltowns of the French Riviera. Assuming your time is going to be devoted to the Riviera, this itinerary traces a routing that both begins and ends in Nice. Keep in perspective that distances between destinations are short (Nice and Menton are just 23 kilometers apart), and although you can make a circle trip staying at one or two places, it would also be feasible to select one hotel as a base from which to explore the entire region. Remember that during peak summer months the Riviera is crowded with tourists—it is difficult to find places to stay and dine, negotiate the roads, find parking, and visit museums, so you must incorporate more time into your itinerary to do so. Our suggestion would be to avoid summer on the Riviera and, alternatively, escape up into the hills above the coastal towns.

The French Riviera, or the Côte d'Azur, is the area between Menton and Nice. Its inhabitants are a breed apart: even the French themselves say the *Niçoise* are not typically French—warmed and subdued by the climate, they are more gentle and agreeable. We recommend that you begin your explorations in the region's capital, Nice, "Queen of the Riviera." France's wonderful express trains service the Nice train station and convenient connections can be made from many cities within Europe into the Nice airport (the second busiest in France). Equally appealing, both the train station and airport are small and easy to get around, and car rental agencies are represented at both.

Nice is a large city whose population of 400,000 has carpeted the land with apartments and condominiums bounded only by the ocean and the surrounding hills. Along the waterfront, the **Promenade des Anglais** takes a grand sweep from the city's western edge along the Baie des Anges and the new city to the edge of the picturesque old quarter. The new district of Nice is a mecca for tourists with the promenade along the seashore lined with elegant hotels and casinos. Lighted at night, the promenade is a romantic place for strolling. Just off this majestic promenade is the **Musée International d'Art Naïf** (Avenue Val Marie), which boasts an inventory of over 6,000 paintings from all over the world. (*Open all year, tel: 04.93.71.78.33.*) The **Musée des Beaux-Arts Jules Cheret** (33, Avenue des Baumettes) focuses on a wealth of paintings from the 19th century. (*Open all year, tel: 04.92.15.28.28.*) A landmark of the promenade is the stately **Hôtel Negresco** whose terrace is a wonderful place to settle and enjoy a café or ice cream, a tradition to be equated with tea at Harrods. Just a little farther on, the Jardin Albert 1 is dressed with fountains and a bandstand that hosts numerous rock concerts. From the Jardin a mini-train departs every 20 minutes to tour the old town, the flower market, and castle gardens. The lovely **Place Masséna** stands proud on the promenade with its dramatic fountains and fronts the area's principal shopping district along the Avenue Jean Médecin. Also leading off the Place Masséna, the Rue Masséna and the Rue de France are charmingly restricted to pedestrian traffic, and banked by cafés, boutiques, and restaurants.

On the other side of the River Paillon is the old quarter of Nice, **La Vieille Ville**, full of character and ambiance. Narrow alleys wind through this district of cobbled streets shaded by towering buildings. The district is colored with flowerboxes and upward glimpses of sky are crisscrossed by banners of laundry. The flower market is very picturesque—a display of color all day and every day on the Cours Saleya, except on Mondays when a flea market of antiques and collectibles invades its space. A bountiful fish market is set out every morning (except Mondays) on the Place Saint François. From the Cours Saleya it is possible to climb the hill, known as the Château (by stairs, a lift, or by strolling up the Rue Ségurane), to some spectacular views of the Baie des Anges. "Château" refers to the château that last stood between the harbor and the old town some 300 years ago. The harbor with its colorful mix of fishing boats and neighboring yachts is fun to explore.

The territory mapped out and referred to as **Cimiez** is where the Romans constructed Cemenelum, a town to rival the then existing Greek town of Nikaia (Nice) in the 1st century B.C. The renovated Roman amphitheater hosts a famous jazz festival that takes place every July. Cimiez also flourishes in March during the *Festival des Cougourdons*, and in May, Sundays are an offering of dances, picnics, and folklore presentations during the *Fêtes des Mais*. Cimiez is also worth the journey to visit the **Musée d'Archéologie**, 160 Avenue des Arènes (*Closed Tuesdays, tel: 04.93.81.59.57*), the **Musée Chagall** at the corner of Boulevard de Cimiez and Avenue Dr Ménard (*Closed Tuesdays, tel: 04.93.53.87.20*), and the **Musée Matisse** in the Villa des Arènes (*Closed Tuesdays, tel: 04.93.81.08.08*). The Musée Chagall houses the largest single collection of the master's work, while the Musée Matisse honors its namesake, who made Nice his home for 20 years, through presentation of the artist's paintings, drawings, and figurines.

Leaving Nice in the direction of Menton, you have a choice of three roads that all run somewhat parallel to each other following the contours of the coast. The **Grande Corniche** or "high" road was built by Napoleon and passes through picturesque *villages perchés*. The **Moyenne Corniche** or "middle" road is a lovely, wide, modern road. The **Corniche Inférieure** or "low" road was built in the 18th century by the Prince of Monaco and enables you to visit the wealthy coastal communities and the principality of Monaco. Each road offers a uniquely appealing route. A suggestion would be to loop in one direction on the Corniche Inférieure to enjoy the water and the coastal towns (this is the busiest road during the summer months), and return via a combination of both the Grande and Moyenne Corniches.

From Nice the Corniche Inférieure, the N98, hugs the contours of the coast and the lovely inlet of **Villefranche sur Mer** whose gentle waters are home to numerous yachts and fishing boats. Round the bay from Villefranche and follow the D26 through the exclusive residential district and peninsula of **Cap Ferrat**.

Sometimes only glimpses are possible of the million-dollar mansions, home to many celebrities, which stand proud behind towering hedges and security gates along this 10-kilometer drive. It is possible to visit the former residence of the Baroness Ephrussi de Rothschild, who commissioned the Italian-style palace to house her personal art collection. It is now owned by the state and open to the public as a museum—the gardens and setting alone merit a visit. Traveling along the peninsula, climb the steps of the lighthouse for a wonderful view. Farther out on the tip is a tower that housed prisoners in the 18th century.

Saint Jean Cap Ferrat is nestled on the other side of the peninsula from Villefranche, enjoying a picturesque setting and a quiet ambiance, with just a few homes, restaurants, and hotels tucked into the hillside. It has lovely views across the towering masts of yachts that grace its waters. From Saint Jean Cap Ferrat, the road winds back to the N98 through another wealthy enclave of homes and luxurious hotels enjoying the protected climate, the town of **Beaulieu sur Mer**.

Saint Jean Cap Ferrat

As the N98 leaves Beaulieu sur Mer, the road hugs the mountain and tunnels through the cliff face just above the Mediterranean, through Cap d'Ail, and into the principality of **Monaco**. First-class hotels and excellent restaurants are numerous in **Monte Carlo**, catering to the millions of annual visitors who come to play in its casino and hope to catch a glimpse of the royal family or resident international celebrities. Monaco is independent of French rule, and an exclusive tax haven for a privileged few. Step inside the **Palais du Casino**, fronted by beautifully manicured gardens. To experience gambling fever, step inside the private salons where high stakes are an everyday agenda.

Beyond Monaco the N98 merges with the N7 and continues on to the graceful city of **Menton**, on the Italian border. Menton boasts streets shaded by fruit trees and stretches of sandy beach in addition to a colorful harbor, casino, and an endless array of shops. At the heart of the old town, Rue Saint Michel is a charming shopping street restricted to foot traffic. The nearby Place aux Herbes and Place du Marché are picturesque with their covered stalls and flower displays. Menton is also known for its gardens, the most famous being the **Jardin des Colombières** (Rue Ferdinand Bac), located on the hill above the town and enjoying lovely views through pines and cypress trees to the waters of the Mediterranean.

From Menton, a 10-kilometer detour into the hills brings you to the picturesque walled town of **Sainte Agnes**. The D22, often just a single lane, winds precariously up into the hills to this attractive mountain village of cobbled streets, a few restaurants, shops, and unsurpassed views of the coastline. (Although the hillside town of **Gorbio** is often recommended in connection with Sainte Agnes, the drive is even more demanding. Sainte Agnes is a little larger and very similar, with better views.)

Returning in the direction of Nice with Menton and the Italian border at your back, follow signs to Roquebrune Cap Martin and you find yourself traveling on the D2564 and the Grande Corniche. **Roquebrune** is divided into two districts: the new town on the water and a medieval village on the hillside dating from the dynasty of Charlemagne. Very picturesque on the approach, the medieval Roquebrune is well worth a detour and some time for exploration. Park on the main square and follow its maze of narrow, cobbled streets to the 13th-century keep, protected at the core of the medieval village.

From Roquebrune, the Grande Corniche continues along a very scenic stretch affording beautiful views of the principality of Monaco stretched out below. Just past the charming hillside town of **La Turbie**, watch for the D45, a short connector to the Moyenne Corniche and the idyllic village of Èze.

Like Roquebrune, there are two divisions of Èze, **Èze Village**, the medieval village perched on the hillside above the Riviera, and **Èze Bord de la Mer**, a modern town on the water's edge. Of all the perched villages along the Riviera, Èze Village, a quaint medieval enclave with cobblestoned streets overlooking the sea, remains a favorite: park your car below the village and explore it on foot. This is a village whose residences have for more than a thousand years soaked up the sun and looked down upon the beautiful blue water associated with the magnificent Côte d'Azur.

Èze Village

From Èze, the Moyenne Corniche follows a beautiful route, the N7, which winds back into Nice. Once in Nice you can either follow the Promenade des Anglais along its waterfront, the N98 in the direction of Cannes, or circumvent the city and traffic by taking the Autoroute A8, exiting at Cagnes Est and following signs to Haut de Cagnes. (If you opt for the N98, take the D18 at Cros de Cagnes and follow signs away from the coast in the direction of Haut de Cagnes.)

Cagnes sur Mer is on the waterfront, a port town struggling to resemble the other coastal centers. **Haut de Cagnes**, however, is an old section located on the hill, with an abundance of charm and character. Follow narrow, steep, cobbled streets to the heart of the old village. Opt for the underground parking just on the approach to the village crest—you might find space on the street, but it takes a brave soul to negotiate a spot, and unless you find a generous section, the streets are so narrow, it's never certain that there is enough room left for passing vehicles.

The most visited site in Haut de Cagnes, the **Château Grimaldi** was originally built as a fortress in 1309, commissioned by Raynier Grimaldi, Lord of Monaco and Admiral of France. A citadel was built a year later and then, in the 17th century, Henri Grimaldi had the citadel refurbished into very spacious accommodations. His descendent, Gaspard Grimaldi, was forced to abandon the castle at the time of the French Revolution. During the reign of the Grimaldis, the residents within the walls of this medieval enclave prospered by cultivating wheat, wine, and olives. Mules were used to haul the bounty of produce from the neighboring hillsides and a wealth of seafood from the coast.

On the other side of Cagnes sur Mer from Haut de Cagnes, and definitely worth the hassle of its congested streets, is the absolutely wonderful **Musée Renoir**. (*Closed Oct 20 to Nov 9, and Tues.*) Advised to move to a warmer climate because of ill health, Renoir relocated to the coast and lived his last years in this sun-washed villa above the town. Surrounded by a sprawling, peaceful garden graced with olive trees, rhododendrons, iris, geraniums, and stretches of lawn, you can almost sense the peace and quiet that he must have experienced and the environment that inspired him to paint— artists today frequent the gardens seeking their own inspiration. The town of Cagnes purchased the home, which displays many of Renoir's works, photos, and personal and family memoirs. Especially moving is the sentimental staging in his studio: Renoir's wheelchair is parked in front of the easel, dried flowers rest on the easel's side, and a day bed which enabled Renoir to rest between his efforts is set up nearby. When you study the photo of Renoir during his later years, he appears so old and yet determined to give the world his last ounce of creativity.

Return to the water from Haut de Cagnes and follow the N7 or the N98 along the Baie des Anges in the direction of Antibes. At La Brague detour just a few kilometers off the coastal road following the D4 to the hillside village of **Biot**. Biot, where glassware has been made for just under three decades, has won high acclaim. A visit to a glass factory to see the assortment of styles and types of glassware available is very interesting. Bottles vary from the usual types to the Provençal *calères* or *ponons-bouteilles* that have two long necks and are used for drinking. This medieval village of small narrow streets, lovely little squares, and a maze of galleries and shops is a gem.

After retracing your path back to the coastside, continue to **Antibes**—allow at least half a day for exploring this waterfront fortress. **Fort Carré**, not to be confused with the Château de Grimaldi, is closed to the public and located on the south entrance of town. The fort guards the waters of Antibes, which is home to thousands of yachts berthed in the modern Port Vauban Yacht Harbor. The rectangular towers and battlements of the **Château de Grimaldi** can be seen beyond the fort, within the ramparts of the medieval village. At the heart of the village, the château commands some of the town's best views and now houses some of Picasso's work in the **Musée Picasso**. Picasso resided at the château just after the war in 1946 and, in appreciation of his stay, left much of his work to the town. Spacious and uncluttered, open, bright rooms in the château admirably display his work and photographs of the master when he resided here in addition to contemporary works by Léger, Magnelli, and Max Ernst. Entry to the museum also gives you some of Antibes' most beautiful views of the Mediterranean framed through the thick medieval walls. (*Closed Mon.*) The town with its cobbled streets is charming.

From Antibes a scenic drive follows the D2559 around the peninsula to its point, **Cap d'Antibes**, another exclusive residential community with gorgeous homes, exclusive hotels, and lovely sandy beaches. On the other side of the peninsula from Antibes is the pretty resort town of **Juan les Pins**, which is popular for its lovely stretch of white-sand beach and whose sparkling harbor shelters many attractive boats.

As the N98 hugs the bay of Golfe Juan and before it stretches to **Pointe de la Croisette** in Cannes, you can detour into the hills just up from the town of Golfe Juan to **Vallauris**. Picasso settled in Vallauris after his time in Antibes and tested his skill at the potter's wheel, producing thousands of pieces of pottery using the Madoura pottery shop as his *atelier*. He restored the craft and brought fame to the village and in gratitude the town made him an honorary citizen. He, in turn, showed his appreciation by crafting a life-size bronze statue, which stands on Place Paul Isnard outside the church. A museum, **Musée de Vallauris**, displaying Picasso's work is housed in the château, originally a 13th-century priory rebuilt in the 16th century. There are numerous workshops in Vallauris, now considered the ceramic capital of France—the **Galerie Madoura** remains one of the best, and stores sell a vast assortment of styles and qualities. (*Closed Nov, Sat and Sun, tel: 04.93.64.66.39.*) Over 200 craftsmen reside in Vallauris, creating original designs and copying patterns made famous by Picasso.

From Vallauris, return to the coast and continue on to the cosmopolitan city of Cannes. Located on the Golfe de Napoule, **Cannes** is the center for many festivals, the most famous being the Cannes Film Festival held annually in May. The **Boulevard de la Croisette** is a wide street bordered by palm trees separating the beach from the elaborate grand hotels and apartment buildings. La Croissette is congested with stop-and-go traffic in the summer, and the lovely beaches that it borders are dotted with parasols and covered with tanning bodies. The **old port** (*Vieux Port*) is a melange of fishing boats and sleek luxury craft. You find the flower market, Fortville, along the Allées de la Liberté and the bounty displayed at the covered market is set up every morning except Mondays. The picturesque pedestrian street of Rue Meynadier is worth seeking out for delicious picnic supplies such as cheeses, bread, and paté. Rising above the port at the western end of the popular Boulevard de la Croisette is **Le Suquet**, the old quarter of Cannes, which has a superior view of the colorful port.

It is easy to escape the bustle of the cosmopolitan fever of Cannes by traveling just a few short miles directly north out of the city along the N85 to the hilltown village of **Mougins**. This charming village achieved gastronomic fame when Roger Vergé converted a 16th-century olive mill into an internationally famous restaurant. Other notable chefs have been attracted to the village and Michelin has awarded the village and its restaurants in total four gourmet stars. The fortified town of Mougins is characteristic of many of the medieval towns that are accessible only to pedestrian traffic, which luckily preserves the atmosphere that horns and traffic congestion all too often obliterate. Located in the center of Mougins is a small courtyard decorated with a fountain and flowers and shaded by trees. Here you will discover a few small cafés where locals meet to gossip about society, life, and politics.

Continuing into the coastal hills, you come to a region of lavender, roses, carnations, violets, jasmine, olives, and oranges. Approximately 12 kilometers north of Mougins in the heart of this region is **Grasse**. Grasse's initial industry was the tanning of imported sheepskins from Provence and Italy. It was Catherine de Medicis who introduced the concept of perfume when she commissioned scented gloves from the town in a trade agreement with Tuscany. When gloves fell out of fashion and their sales dwindled, the town refocused on the perfume industry. The town is constantly growing, but the old section is fun to wander through. Interesting tours of perfume factories are given in English by **Fragonard** (at 20 Boulevard Fragonard and at Les 4 Chemins), **Molinard** (60 Boulevard Victor-Hugo), and **Gallimard** (73 Route de Cannes).

Leave Grasse to the northeast on the D2085 and travel for 6 kilometers to the D3, which travels north and winds back and forth along a steep ascent to the beautiful village of Gourdon. Endeared as one of France's most beautiful villages, **Gourdon** is an unspoiled gem that commands an absolutely spectacular setting as it hugs and clings to the walls of the steep hillside. Vistas from the village look north down the Loup Canyon or southeast over the countryside dotted with villages of sun-washed stucco and tiled roofs to the glistening water of the distant Riviera. On clear days you can see from Nice to the Italian border. The village's cobbled streets are lined with delightful, untouristy shops and a handful of restaurants. **Le Nid d'Aigle** on the Place Victoria is a restaurant whose terraces step daringly down the hillside.

From Gourdon, the D3 hugs the hillside and affords glimpses of the twisting River Loup far below. As the road winds down to a lower altitude, you can either drive north on the D603 to the medieval village of **Cipières** and cross the river at a more northerly point or continue on the D3 and cross the Loup on the Pont de Bramafan. After crossing the river, just before Bramafan, follow the D8 south in the direction of Pont du Loup. This 6-kilometer stretch of road winds through the **Gorges du Loup**. The canyon's beauty and its high granite walls beckon you into the ever-narrowing gorge. The River Loup flows far below, only visible to the passenger who might chance a peek over the edge. The road passes through some jaggedly carved tunnels—pathways blasted through sheer rock, which open to glorious vistas of the canyon, trees, and rock. Pull off the road at **Saut du Loup**. The stop requires no more than 15 minutes and, for a fee, you can walk down a short, steep flight of steps to a terrace overlooking magnificent waterfalls and pools. The small riverside village of **Pont du Loup** is situated at the mouth of the canyon, on a bend in the river shadowed by the ruins of a towering bridge. It is a pretty town and a lovely end to the Loup Canyon.

Beyond Pont du Loup, traveling east along the D2210 in the direction of Vence, you pass through a few more towns, each consisting of a cluster of medieval buildings and winding, narrow streets that, without exception, encircle a towering church and its steeple. **Tourrettes sur Loup** is an especially lovely town whose medieval core of clustered rosy-golden-stone houses enjoys a backdrop of the three small towers that give the town its name. Every March the hillsides of Tourettes sur Loup are a mass of violets and the village is dressed with fragrant bouquets for the *Fête des Violettes*. After World War II the town revived its long-abandoned textile production and is one of the world's top *tissage à main* (hand-weaving) centers. The workshops are open to the public.

The D2210 continues from Tourrettes sur Loup and approaches the wonderful old town of **Vence** from the west. Located just 10 kilometers above the coast and Riviera, the hillsides surrounding Vence afford a lovely coastal panorama and are dotted with palatial homes and villas. Entering through the gates into the old village, you find dozens of tiny streets with interesting shops and little cafés where you can enjoy scrumptious pastries.

The Place du Peyra was once the Roman forum and it's now the colorful town marketplace. In 1941 Matisse moved here and, in gratitude for being nursed back to health by the Dominican Sisters, he constructed and decorated the simple **Chapelle du Rosaire**. (Follow the Avenue des Poilus to the Route de Saint Jeannet La Gaude.) (*Closed Sundays, tel: 04.93.58.03.26.*) Vence makes a wonderful base from which to explore the coast and the hilltowns, and its location affords spectacular views across the hills to the blue waters.

A few kilometers beyond Vence (D2 in the direction of Cagnes sur Mer) is the picturesque mountain stronghold of **Saint Paul de Vence**, which once guarded the ancient Var Frontier. Cars are forbidden inside the walls of the old town whose cobbled streets are lined with galleries and tourist shops. From the encircling ramparts you get panoramic views of the hilltowns of the Riviera. Located outside the walled town in the woods along the Cagnes road, the **Foundation Maeght**, a private museum that sponsors and hosts numerous collections of works of some of the world's finest contemporary artists, is one of the principal attractions of Saint Paul de Vence. (*Open Oct to Jun.*) Saint Paul de Vence is also a convenient base from which to explore the Riviera and we recommend a number of places both within its fortified walls on its outskirts. From Saint Paul de Vence it is a short drive back to Nice.

From Nice you can join our *Provence* itinerary by taking the scenic autoroute through the mountains, bridging the distance with our *Gorges du Verdon* itinerary. Or you can follow the coastline, referred to as the Corniche d'Or, between La Napoule (just outside Cannes) and Saint Raphaël, which offers spectacular views: fire-red mountains contrasting dramatically with the dark-blue sea. Saint Raphaël is a small commercial port with a pleasant, tourist-thronged beach. Continuing on, Saint Tropez is easily the most enchanting of the dozens of small ports and beaches that you'll pass. If you choose to continue along the coastal road, take the Corniche des Maures, which hugs the waterfront at the base of the Massif des Maures. At Hyères the scenery wanes, and we suggest you take the A50 to the A8-E80, which travels west to Aix en Provence.

Wine Country – Burgundy

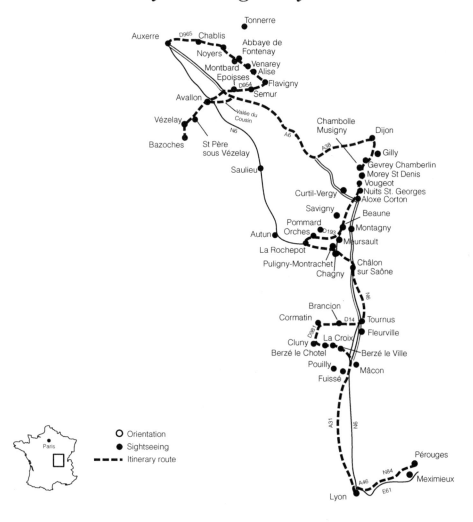

Tonnerre

Auxerre — D965 — Chablis

Abbaye de Fontenay

Noyers

Venarey Alise

Montbard

Epoisses

D954 — Flavigny

Semur

Avallon

Valée du Cousin

Vézelay

Bazoches

St Père sous Vézelay

N6

A6

Chambolle Musigny

Dijon

Gilly

A38

Gevrey Chamberlin

Morey St Denis

Vougeot

Saulieu

Curtil-Vergy

Nuits St. Georges

Aloxe Corton

Savigny

Beaune

Pommard

Montagny

Orches

D193

Autun

Meursault

La Rochepot

Puligny-Montrachet

Châlon sur Saône

Chagny

N6

Brancion

Cormatin — D14 — Tournus

Fleurville

D981

La Croix

Cluny

Berzé le Chotel

Berzé le Ville

Pouilly

Mâcon

Fuissé

A31

N6

Pérouges

N84

Meximieux

A46

E61

Lyon

Paris

O Orientation
● Sightseeing
- - - Itinerary route

117

Wine Country–Burgundy

Burgundy, which lies to the southeast of Paris, is a name used to designate a geographic region of France as well as a reference synonymous with some of the world's finest wines. Vineyards dress the landscape and stretch from one enchanting, steepled village to the next. In terms of wine, Burgundy is distinguished by five different areas, each with its own special characteristics. The backbone of this itinerary follows the Côte d'Or from Chablis in the north to the Côte de Nuits, which travels from Dijon to beyond Nuits Saint Georges, and on to the Côte de Beaune whose vineyards spider web the countryside around the magical wine town of Beaune. It then continues south from Chagny into the region of the Côte de Chalonnaise and concludes in the wine district of Mâconnais with Mâcon as its southern boundary.

Vézelay

In addition to a focus on wine, this itinerary weaves a path through some enchanting and historic towns and monuments. In the vicinity of Chablis is the memorable Abbaye de Fontenay that was declared a World Heritage site by UNESCO in 1981, the seemingly undiscovered ruins of Alise Sainte Reine, and the enchanting village of Flavigny sur Ozerain whose claim to fame is the movie *Chocolat*. Before heading south to the capital wine town of Beaune, the trail sweeps west to include Vézelay, an idyllic medieval village sitting high atop a hill and the scenic Vallée du Cousin and then journey along the Route des Grands Crus. Exploring the area is like traveling through a wine list, for the region covers half the famous names in French wine.

Recommended Pacing: Spend at least two nights in northern Burgundy with the magnificent town of Vézelay as the recommended base; two nights in the neighborhood of Beaune so that you have time to spontaneously explore the narrow roads that spoke off the main roads and weave through the vineyards, and a night in southern Burgundy with a possible conclusion in the grand city of Lyon or the hilltown village of Pérouges.

Before you embark on this itinerary—since wine is the underlying attraction—it seems best to provide you with some basic information to enhance your understanding and appreciation of the region's bounty that you will sample. From Chablis in the north to Mâcon in the south, 25,000 hectares of vineyards represent Burgundy's five wine districts which boast an incredible diversity, evidenced by the amazing 98 distinct appellations. Grouped into four categories, the appellations, Regional, Communal, Premiers Crus and Grands Crus, define the quality and origin of the grape. The general rule is the higher the quality, the more precisely identified the origin of the grape.

Four key factors influence the quality of great wines: The soil, the grape, the climate and the talent of the vintner. Because Burgundy is a tapestry of different soil types that distinguish the wines, vineyards are often sectioned off by stone walls from one soil variation to the next and are referred to as *terroirs*. Understandably the variety of grape or *cépage* selected is based on which best compliments the soil. In spite of the diversity of soil, with a few minor exceptions, the wines of Burgundy are from two supreme varietals: Chardonnay for the white wines and Pinot Noir for the red grape. So conveniently close to Paris, it is puzzling that Burgundy is not considered a year-round destination until one experiences the cold, dry winters that influence the wine.

Leave Paris to the southeast and take the A6 autoroute for the 1½-hour drive to the *Auxerre Sud* exit where you take the D965 for the 12-kilometer drive into **Chablis**, a busy little town synonymous with the elegant, dry white wine of Burgundy. (Note: You might also want to consider taking the TGV to Dijon and beginning your journey at the heart of the region.) Chablis wine roads travel into the surrounding hills, with the finest vineyards being found just northeast of the town. Cross the River Serein and turn left on the D91, a small road that leads you to the region's seven *grand crus*, which lie side by side: Bougros, Les Preuses, Vaudésir, Les Clos, Grenouilles, Valmur, and Blanchot. Vineyards cover over 1,300 hectares with the principal grape being the Chardonnay.

Returning to Chablis, take the D45 and follow the Serein upstream to **Noyers**, a charming little walled town of timbered houses. From Noyers take the D956 east 21 km to the junction of D905 and then south 10 km to **Montbard**. From Montbard it is just a few kilometers further to one of France's most wonderful monuments and attractions, **L'Abbaye de Fontenay**. Set against a backdrop of forest, this beautiful abbaye, its fountains and gardens will prove a highlight of your trip. (*Tel: 03.80.92.15.00, www.abbayedefontenay.com.*) Founded in 1118 by St Bernard this is a perfect example of a Cistercian abbey. It has endured dramatic changes with each century. It became the Royal Abbey in 1269, was pillaged by Edward III in 1553, during the French Revolution saw the last eight monks leave in 1790, and then was sold by the revolutionaries to an industrialist who installed a paper mill. It was then purchased by the Montgolfier family whose descendent in 1906 decided to dismantle the industrial buildings and bring the abbey back to its original medieval glory. You can tour—on your own or with a guide—and visit everything from the bakery to the dormitory and the Cloister, which remains one of the most wonderful examples of Romanesque architecture. (*Open all year, tel: 03.80.92.15.00.*)

Abbaye de Fontenay

Returning to Montbard, it is just a short journey south on the D905 to Venarey les Laumes. From here a circle detour on the D103 will take you to **Alise Sainte Reine**, a quiet hilltown with Roman ties. This fortified town is the scene of the last stand of the Gauls against Caesar. Follow signs to Mont Auxois which is located above the village and was the site of Caesar's final victory over the heroic Gaulic chieftain Vercingetorix in 52 B.C. after a six-week siege. The first excavations were undertaken in the mid 19th century, and they uncovered the remains of a thriving Gallo-Roman town, Alise, complete with a theater, forum, and a well-laid street plan. The Musée Alise has a collection of artifacts, jewelry, and bronze figures from the site.

From Alise continue the journey on to the picturesque village of **Flavigny sur Ozerain**, whose most recent fame is due to the fact it was used as the stage set for the film *Chocolat*. With its ancient narrow streets, fortified gates and religious and architectural heritage this is a wonderful old city to explore on foot. It is also famous for the production of anise balls and sweets made by the Abbaye since 1591. They accept visitors each day from 8:30 to 10:30 am. You might also want to plan a meal at La Grange les Quatre Heures where local farmers offer an à la carte menu featuring their own produce. (*Open July through August every day except Mondays, 12:30 to 5:00, tel: 03 80 96 20 62.*)

From Flavigny traveling the D954 west it is a pretty drive to the medieval town of **Semur en Auxois**. Nestled on the loop of the river Armançon, this is a very picturesque walled village with its massive stone towers, numerous bridges, church or Notre Dame and maze of houses all straddling the river on either side of the rocky spur.

Continuing east from Semur it is a beautiful drive through farmland past the Château at **Epoisses** and then on to connect with the N6 where you will turn north in the direction of Avallon. With its narrow cobbled streets **Avallon** is a larger town with cozy old houses at its center. Journey down through the old city, following signs to Pontaubert and then continue on to the magical pilgrimage site of **Vézelay.** Sitting high on its hilltop above the surrounding countryside and for many people the highlight of a visit to Burgundy, this little town of Vézelay is full of narrow streets lined with old houses with sculptured doorways and mullioned windows leading up to the 12th-century **Basilica Sainte Madeleine**, the enormous building that sits above the village. This extraordinarily long church is beautiful in its simplicity with its soaring columns and paved floor and when religious pilgrimages were the fashion, it was an important stop on the pilgrimage route to Santiago de Compostela in Spain. Take note of the brass coquille saint Jacques, the pilgrimage sign of welcome and hospitality that are still embedded in the cobbled streets. From Vézelay retrace your path to Pontaubert where you will cross the river, and turn immediately right, signposted **Vallée du Cousin.**

This is a very scenic drive on a country road that follows the picturesque, narrow, wooded valley of the rushing River Cousin and will deliver you back to Avallon. From Avallon follow signposts for the autoroute A6, which you take to the A38 towards Dijon.

Note: If time allows or if you use **Vézelay** as a base, be sure to travel the 10 km south on the D958 to a wonderful privately owned 12th century château, it is gorgeous in its furnishings and regal setting. The medieval stronghold of **Château Bazoches-du-Morvan** enjoys a bucolic setting on the site of a former Roman base and makes for a delightful and interesting excursion. (*Open all year, Nov 6 to Mar 24 by reservation only, tel: 03.86.22.10.22.*)

Semur

If you like bustling cities, follow the A38 all the way to **Dijon** where sprawling suburbs hide a historic core. Rue des Forges is the most outstanding of the old streets. Even if you are not a museum lover, you will enjoy the **Musée des Beaux Arts** in the palace of Charles de Valois. It is one of France's most popular museums, with some wonderful old woodcarvings and paintings. (*Open all year except Tuesdays, tel: 03.80.74.52.70.*) The aperitif Kir (cassis and white wine) was named after Canon Kir, the city's mayor and wartime resistance leader. Food note: There are plenty of opportunities to purchase Dijon mustard and, if you visit in November, you can attend the superb gastronomic fair.

From Dijon begins the wine region of the prestigious Côte de Nuits. The wine estates date back to 10th-century abbeys whose monks first planted vineyards predominately with the Pinot Noir grapes. Much of the 3,000 hectares are enclosed behind stone walls and the vineyards are referred to as *Clos*. Chambertin, Clos de Vougeot, and Romanée Conti represent Burgundy's Grands Crus and are located here. Further up the slopes, 550 hectares producing fine Burgundies are referred to as Hautes-Côtes de Nuits.

Outside Dijon, for a greater dose of the countryside, leave the autoroute after Sombernon at the village of Pont de Pany, pass the large hotel on your right, cross the canal, and turn right on the D35, signposted Urcy and Nuits Saint Georges. This scenic little country road winds steeply up a rocky limestone escarpment past the Château Montclust and through rolling farmland to **Urcy**, a tight cluster of cottages set around a church. After passing through Quemigny Poisot, turn left for Chamboef and left again in the village for Gevrey Chambertin. Down the limestone escarpment you go through a rocky tunnel around a couple of precipitous bends and you're in the vineyards.

Turn right and follow the D122 into Gevrey Chambertin where you join the great wine and tourist route, **Route des Grands Crus**, winding you through the villages that produce the premier Burgundian wines. As you drive around, look for the Flemish-style colored tiles arranged in patterns that decorate the roofs of the region—a reminder of the time when the Dukes of Burgundy's duchy stretched into the Low Countries. There are very few large estates in this region, most of the land belonging to small farmers who live and make wine in the villages and go out to work in their vineyards. Fields are called *climats* and every *climat* has a name. Some *climats* produce better wines, which are identified by their own name; others are identified by the name of the village. This is fine for the larger centers such as Beaune and Pommard, but the little villages—searching for an identity—have incorporated the name of their best-known vineyard into the village name. Thus Gevrey became Gevrey Chambertin, Saint Georges became Nuits Saint Georges, and Vougeot became Clos de Vougeot. **Gevrey Chambertin** is one of the region's most delightful villages, with narrow streets lined with gray-stone houses and numerous vintners' signs inviting you in to sample their wares.

Arriving at **Morey-Saint-Denis**, park in the large car park before the village and walk along its narrow streets.

The vineyards of **Chambolle–Musigny** produce some spectacular wines and you can learn about them at the wine museum housed in the cellars of the **Château-Hôtel André Ziltener** (also a hotel). This informative tour (given in English, French, or German) includes a tasting of the four grades of wine produced in the area. Madame Ballois, who is in charge, is a charming hostess, extremely knowledgeable and proud of the fact that the six red wines they offer for tasting are all, impressively, *première* and *grands crus*. The price of the tour is quite reasonable, or free to guests of the hotel.

The hillsides of **Clos de Vougeot** were first planted by Cistercian monks in the 14th century and a stone wall was built to encircle the vineyards and protect them from raiders in the One Hundred Years' War. An organization called **Chevaliers du Tastevin**, now recognized worldwide, chose the 16th-century **Château de Vougeot** in 1944 as a base from which to publicize Burgundy wines. You can see the courtyard, the great pillared hall where banquets take place, and the impressive cellars and 12th-century wine presses.

Nuits Saint Georges is somewhat larger than the other towns along the route. A great deal of wine is blended here under the town's name. After Nuits Saint Georges the Route des Grands Crus continues along the N74 to end at Corgoloin. The Côte de Beaune begins virtually where the Côte de Nuits ends.

After the Route des Grands Crus the first great commune is **Aloxe Corton** whose vineyards were once owned by Charlemagne. Legend states that Aloxe Corton is known for both its red and white wines because, during the time that Charlemagne owned the vineyards, his wife claimed that red wine stained his white beard and so he ordered the production of white wine too. He is commemorated by the white wine Corton-Charlemagne.

Hôtel Dieu

Arriving in **Beaune**, do not follow signs for *Centre Ville* but stay on the ring road that circles the city's walls in a counterclockwise direction. Park in one of the car parks adjacent to the ring road and walk into the narrow old streets of the wine capital of Burgundy. Today the most important landowner in the region is the Hospices de Beaune, a charitable organization founded in 1443 by Nicolas Rolin, chancellor of the Duke of Burgundy. Every year they hold a wine auction at the Hôtel Dieu—it is one of the wine trade's most important events. Built as a hospital, the **Hôtel Dieu** is so elegantly decorated that it seems more like a palace. You will want to take a guided tour of this lovely building which is an exceptional example of medieval architecture whose rooms house an incredible collection of furnishings, art, tapestries, and the incredible exhibit, the *Last Judgement* by Rogier van der Weyden. (*Open all year, tel: 03.80.24.45.00, www.hospices-de-beaune.tm.fr.*)

You can also visit the **Musée du Vin de Bourgogne** in the Hôtel des Ducs de Bourgogne. (*Closed Tues, Dec to Apr, tel: 03.80.22.08.19.*) There are delightful shops, restaurants, and cafés aplenty. Wine lovers may want to visit one of the *négotiant-éleveurs* who buy wines of the same *appellation* from growers and blend and nurture them to produce an "elevated" superior wine. At the heart of the wine region, Beaune serves as a wonderful base from which to explore the region. The wine capital, it reigns over 5,000 hectares of the Côte de Beaune whose wines are as diverse in character as they are high in quality. Full bodied reds as well as rich and complex whites are produced by vineyards known the world over: Pommard, Meursault and Puligny-Montrachet. When following the *Route des Vins* don't overlook the 650 hectares of the Hautes-Côtes de Beaune which wind up the slopes and are recognized for their red and white Burgundies.

Leave Beaune on the A74 in the direction of Chagny. After a short distance take the D973 to **Pommard** where tasting is offered at the château on the outskirts, as well as at vintners in the crowded confines of the village. (*Tel: 03.80.22.12.59, www.chateaudepommard.com.*) From Pommard continue into **Meursault**, a larger village that offers tasting at small vintners and at the larger Domaine du Château de Meursault. (*Tel: 03.80.26.22.75.*)

From Meursault, the D973 brings you into Auxley Duresses. At the far end of the village turn right following the brown signs indicating **Haute Côte de Beaune**. This wine route takes you on a narrow country lane up through the steeply sloping village of **Saint Romain**, high above the vineyards and back down to vineyards in **Orches**, a village clinging to the limestone cliffs, through **Baubigny** and into the wine center of **La Rochepot**. On the approach to the charming village of La Rochepot, visible on the horizon is its intricate, fairy-tale castle with its multi-tiled roof in vibrant colors of yellow, olive, red, black, and ochres, which has stood on its rocky peak since the 13th century. You can also see the ruins of the original castle that occupied the site, built in the 11th century by Alexander of Burgundy.

During the 15th century, the **Château de la Rochepot** became the home of the Lords Régnier and Philippe Pot, both Knights of the Golden Fleece and counselors to the Dukes of Burgundy. At the end of the 19th century Colonel Sadi Carnot carefully restored the castle, which had been destroyed during the French Revolution. Today a visit to the château (complete with drawbridge) gives you a glimpse of what life was like for the several hundred lords, ladies, guards, servants, and soldiers who called La Rochepot home. A tour of the castle shows you the dining room, kitchen, guards' chambers, and watch wall. *(Open Apr to Nov, closed Tuesday, tel: 03.80.21.71.37.)*

A short drive from Rochepot brings you to the intersection of the N6, which when followed south will take you past the vineyards of Puligny-Montrachet and then deliver you to the very scenic and historical wine region of the Chalonnais and the Mâconnais. The Côte Chalonnais is a geographic extension of the Côte de Beaune with its four thousand hectares of grapes planted from Chagny in the north to just north of Tournus. Leading vineyards of the Chalonnaise are Rully, Mercurey, Givry, and Montagny.

With its narrow streets winding down to the banks of the Saône, **Tournus** was once a prominent fishing town and the curious horizontal stones that pierce many of the town roofs are testament to that history. Fishing nets were draped on poles that were suspended between the stones, left to dry in the sun. Today the **Saint Philibert Abbey** (oldest of the great Romanesque churches of Burgundy), the **Perrin-de-Puycousin Museum** with its collections of traditional costumes and Bresse furniture, and the art museum dedicated to the local painter Jean-Baptiste Greuze are worth a visit. Tournus is also the northern geographic marker for the region of the Mâconnais. This is the largest and southernmost of the Burgundy wine districts with over 6,500 planted hectares. Chardonnay and Gamay grapes yield great fruity whites and rich reds and are distributed under famous labels such as **Mâcon**, Mâcon-Villages, and Pouilly-Fuissé.

From Tournus, we suggest you make a loop east and then south for an adventure that will include both architectural history and wine. From Tournus traveling the D14, it is approximately a 12-kilometer scenic drive to the medieval-walled town of **Brancion**. With a history that goes back to the 10th century, it was once considered one of the most strategic strongholds in southern Burgundy. It is necessary to park outside town and then venture by foot to explore this village where time seems almost to have stood still. It is interesting to visit the church with its lovely frescoes and the ruins of the old castle.

Brancion is situated almost equally distant from Tournus and the lovely **Château de Cormatin**. Surrounded by gorgeous gardens and heralded as having some of the most magnificent Louis XIII apartments left in France with its wonderful furnishings and tapestries, it is also famous as the site for many international meetings hosting heads of state from all over the world. (*Open Apr 1 to Jul 13, Aug 16 to Nov 11, Tel: 03 85 50 16 55.*)

From Cormatin, follow the well-signed 13 kilometers south along the D981 to **Cluny** and its famous Benedictine abbey, Saint-Pierre and Saint-Paul. Founded in 910, its abbots were considered as powerful and influencial as the kings or pope for the role they played in the ecclesiastical reform movement that reached to over 2000 monastaries throughout Western Europe. The present abbaye was built in 1089, and although much of it was destroyed during the French Revolution, its ruins embrace the narrow streets of town and stand proud on the horizon.

From Cluny travel 5 kilometers south on the D980 and then take the scenic D17 east (that parallels the N79), a road that wends its way through the charming hillside villages of **Berzé le Châtel, La Croix Blanche** and then **Berzé le Ville**. Built on a rocky outcrop just below the village of Berze le Ville is a lovely 12th-century chapel, **Chapelle des Moines**. Commissioned by the abbot of Cluny, its first structure was destroyed by a storm but then rebuilt by Italians. Intimate with a Byzantine-influence architecture, it is especially worth visiting for the gorgeous paintings that cover its vaulted walls. Their intensity of color is remarkable due to the fact that they were covered up by stucco and not discovered or exposed until the 19th century.

From Berzé la Ville cross over and pick up N79 traveling southeast until you see signs for small country towns are synonomous with the world's finest wines–Pouilly, Fuissé and Saint-Véran. A maze of country roads cross back and forth and journey through the vineyards that embrace these charming wine villages of Mâconnais. There are numerous wineries where one can stop and sample the liquid gold of the region, but we especially liked our visit at the **Château de Fuissé**, located at the heart of the town of the same name. Operated by Jean-Jacques Vincent and family, a visit here includes a tour of the cellars, the vineyards, and sampling their vintages. They are also set up to ship wines worldwide. (*www.chateau-fuisse.fr, tel: 03.85.35.61.44.*)

After exploring the wine towns it is a short distance on to Mâcon travel. From here one can catch the TGV on to other destinations or pick up the autoroute south to Lyon–one of France's most regal and gastronomique centers. A large city, you need to be armed with patience and a good map to negotiate to its historic center.

To the northwest of Lyon is the magical medieval village of **Pérouges**. Settled by the Romans and sentimentally named for the village they left, Perugia, this is an enchanting, walled, medieval village with cobbled streets, a few craft shops, restaurants (one must sample the local tarte) and a hotel. This medieval village was once home to farmers, craftsmen and weavers and although not rich in architecture, it remains much as it was in the middle ages. To visit is like stepping back in time. In fact we have the owners of the Ostellerie du Vieux Pérouges to thank for its preservation. At a time when all but a handful of residents had abandoned the town for more modern conveniences and appreciation for what was historic and old was forgotten, the town was slated for destruction. But the Thibaut Family started a foundation to preserve and restore Pérouges.

Pérouges is recommended as either a perfect end to this wine country journey or a convenient stopover before continuing on to explore our French Alps itinerary.

Wine Country Alsace

Strasbourg

Molsheim

A352   A35

Haut-ottrott   Obernai

Ottrott   Barr

Mittelbergheim

Andlau   Itterswiller

Blienschwiller

Colroy
la Roche   Dambach-la-Ville

Dieffenthal

Haut Koenigsbourg   D35   Scherwiller

Bergheim   N59   Sélestat

Ribeauvillé

Col de Calvair   Hunawihr
D48   Riquewihr   Zellenberg

Kaysersberg   D10

Route des Crêtes

Kientzheim
Ammerschwihr

D417

*Col de la
Schlucht*   Munster   Turckheim   Colmar

Eguisheim

Husseren

Hattstatt   N83   A35

Pfaffenheim

Rouffach

Thann   Mulhouse

A36

GERMANY

Paris

Basel

SWITZERLAND

O Orientation
● Sightseeing
■ ■ ■ Itinerary route

131

Wine Country–Alsace

Alsace borders Germany—in fact, from the Franco-Prussian war to the end of World War I Alsace was part of Germany. After World War II the district began to market its white wines sold in distinctive long, thin, green or brown bottles. The vineyards are at the foot of the Vosges mountains on east-facing hills set back from the broad Rhine river valley. The hills are never particularly steep or spectacular but are laced by narrow roads that wind along the vineyards from one picturesque village to the next. Villages such as Riquewihr and Kaysersberg are picture-book perfect with their painted eaves and gables, narrow cobbled streets, archways, and window boxes brimming with colorful geraniums.

Riquewihr

Wine Country–Alsace

Recommended Pacing: Select a hotel in the wine region and use it as a base for your explorations of the area—two nights minimum. Finish your tour with a night or more in Strasbourg, a beautiful city.

In Alsace, the wines are known by the names of the vineyards or villages and are identified by the type of grape from which they are made: Riesling, Gewürtztraminer, Muscat, or Pinot Gris, and sometimes by the phrase *réserve exceptionelle,* which indicates a higher price and premier wine. The grapes are similar to those used for German wines but the majority are used to make dry wines, not dessert wines.

Just before Mulhouse, a sprawling industrial city, leave the autoroute (exit 6) and take the N83, following signposts for Thann, around the outskirts of Cernay (signposted Colmar) to **Rouffach**. Nestled at the foot of the vineyards, this is a delightful town that is known in the region for its Festival of Witches, held the evening of the third Saturday of

July, in recognition of the sorcerers held captive in the tower so many centuries ago. Rouffach also has a wonderful park dedicated to the preservation of storks. As recently as the 1950s there were just seven breeding pairs, and as a direct result of efforts such as the protective park in Rouffach, there are now more than 250 pairs that are known to migrate from France to the African shores. Babies born here are kept in protective custody for three years until they are strong enough to sustain the long, arduous journey.

Surprisingly, altering their natural cycle in youth does not seem to influence or negate their natural instinct to migrate when released after maturity.

Just north of Rouffach is **Pfaffenheim**, a tiny wine village, where you leave the busy N83 to weave through the narrow village streets and into the vineyards to join the **Route du Vin**, a signposted routing that follows a winding itinerary through the vineyards. You soon arrive at **Gueberschwihr**, a cluster of gaily painted houses where, as you reach the village square, intricate painted signs advertise wine tasting in cobbled courtyards.

From the square, turn right and drive 2 kilometers to Hattstat, and on to Obermorschwir where the narrow road climbs steeply to **Husseren les Châteaux**, a cluster of homes with its castle perched high above the village.

Plan on spending some time in **Eguisheim**, a trim little medieval walled town complete with dungeon, lovely old timbered houses, shops, and restaurants set along narrow cobbled lanes. From Eguisheim the road drops down to the busy N83, which quickly brings you into Colmar.

Colmar is the largest town along the wine road and an important center for wine trade. Beyond the suburbs lies a pedestrian zone—an interesting mix of French and German culture and architecture. Short streets wind round old buildings between the plazas and lead you to the town's old quarter, with its intricately carved and leaning houses, known as **Petite Venise** because a shallow canal weaves its way through the narrow streets. Enterprising students offer gondola rides along the waterways, reminiscent of Venice.

Although Colmar is an easy city to explore on foot, with many streets restricted to pedestrians only, another option for touring the heart of the old town is a fun ride on the colorful train that chatters along the cobbled streets and offers an interesting commentary of the city's highlights. There are numerous craft, antique, and boutique shops, and a full offering of restaurants. When sightseeing, be sure to visit the Dominican monastery, now the **Unterlinden Museum** with an excellent collection of portraits and an exhibition of crafts and customs. One room is a re-created Alsatian vintner's cellar complete with wine presses. (*Closed Tues, Nov to Mar, tel: 03.89.20.15.50.*)

Colmar is an intimate city and one you will want to explore but it can also be used as a base from which to explore Strasbourg. It is a short commute by train between the two cities, and Strasbourg, a truly large city, is not as overwhelming to negotiate when you arrive conveniently *sans auto* at its center.

Just west of Colmar is the charming Alsatian village of **Turckheim**. Park outside the town walls and then venture inside to explore a maze of cobbled streets that boast numerous shops and restaurants — a wonderful town.

From Turckheim, make a detour off the Route du Vin up the D417. As the vineyards wane, the valley narrows and pine trees decorate the heights as you drive the 15 kilometers to **Munster**, situated at the foot of the Vosges. Munster is famous for being the home of the celebrated cheese, rather than for its picturesque streets.

From Munster, the D417 climbs and twists through green Alpine fields dotted with farms. Climbing higher, you enter a vast pine and oak forest to emerge at the summit, **Col de la Schlucht**, which offers spectacular views across the wild slopes of the Vosges mountains. Turn right on **Route des Crêtes** (D61), a skyline road constructed by the French during World War I to ensure communications between the different valleys. Now the route presents a scenic trip and signposts lead you to several beautiful spots that you can walk to before coming to **Col de Calvair**, a tiny ski resort. At Col du Bonhomme, join the D415, which travels down the ever-widening valley to Kaysersberg.

Kaysersberg rivals its neighbors as being one of the most appealing towns in Alsace. Vineyards tumble down to the town from its ancient keep and 16th-century houses line narrow roads along the rushing River Weiss. **Albert Schweitzer** was born here and his house is open as a small museum. (*Open May to Oct.*)

Leave Kaysersberg on the narrow D28 in the direction of Ribeauvillé and pass **Kientzheim**, a picture-perfect little village encircled by a high wall and surrounded by vineyards. Ammerschwihr, another charming town, and Riquewihr, the finest walled town and a gem of Alsace, lie just a few kilometers farther on, one to the south and one to the north.

Turn south from Kientzheim to the lovely walled town of **Ammerschwihr**, worth a detour if only to seek out its Porte Haute Cigognes, one of the entry towers, where each year storks nest—it is from here that their young test their first flight.

Just to the north of Kientzheim, **Riquewihr,** one of the most beautiful villages in Alsace, is completely enclosed by tall, protective walls and encircled by vineyards. It is easy to understand why this picturesque spot is a magnet for visitors. This picture-book village is a pedestrian area, its narrow streets lined with half-timbered houses. Signs beckon you into cobbled courtyards to sample the vintners' produce, and cafés and restaurants spill onto the streets. The local museum is housed in the tall square stone-and-timber tower **Dolder Gate** and **Tour des Voleurs** (Thieves' Tower), which exhibits grisly instruments of torture. (*Open Jul and Aug, closed Oct to Easter, open weekends rest of year, tel: 03.89.49.08.40.*)

Just beyond Riquewihr is another charming, picturesque town, **Zellenberg**, worth a detour off the Route du Vin, if only to circle up through its medieval streets and back down—here you find nothing commercial, just a pretty village.

Nearby **Hunawihr** boasts a much-photographed fortified church sitting on a little hill among the vineyards beside the village and the **Center for the Reintroduction of Storks**. Just a few years ago the roofs of the picture-book villages of Alsace were topped with shaggy storks' nests. Alas, in recent years fewer and fewer storks have returned from their winter migration to Africa and the center is dedicated to their reintroduction into the area. Concentrated within the boundary of the park are seemingly hundreds of the birds who build their nests on the multitude of frameworks provided. Storks born in the park are protected and kept until the age of three to establish the instinct of the park being a migratory base to which to return, season after season.

It is wonderful that the storks are returning in greater numbers each season and it is truly captivating to travel the region and look up to see the nests and pairs of large white, long-legged birds atop many of the region's rooftops. (*Closed Nov 11 to Apr, tel: 03.89.73.72.62.*)

Rising behind the attractive town of **Ribeauvillé** are the three castles of Ribeaupierre, a much-photographed landmark of the region. The shady side streets with their beamed houses are quieter and contain some lovely buildings.

Continuing on the Route du Vin, just a few kilometers to the north is the charming town of **Bergheim**. Protected by its walls, Bergheim lies just off the main road and is a much quieter village than many along the wine route.

Haut Koenigsbourg

Continuing north from Bergheim, make a sharp left on the D1-bis at the medieval village of **Saint Hippolyte** and climb steeply up from the vineyards to **Haut Koenigsbourg**, the mighty fortress that sits high above the town. This massive castle was rather overzealously restored by Kaiser Wilhelm II in the early part of this century to reflect his concept of what a medieval fortress should look like, complete with massive walls, towering gates, a drawbridge, a keep, a bear pit, towers, a baronial great hall, and an armory. From the walls the view of vineyards tumbling to a sky-wide patchwork of fields that stretches to the Rhine river valley is superb. On especially clear days you can see the very distant outline of the Black Forest. (*Closed in Jan.*)

Leave the castle in the direction of Kintzheim and turn left on the D35 for **Chatenois**. Take the narrow entry into the town square and continue straight across the busy N59 on the D35 through **Scherwiller**, dominated by the ruined castles of Ortenbourg and Ramstein high on the hill above, through the vineyards to **Dieffenthal**, **Dambach la Ville**, where a bear clutching a flagon of wine between its paws decorates the fountain in front of the Renaissance town hall, and the wine village of **Blienschwiller** before arriving in the hillside village of Itterswiller.

Itterswiller has its attractive, timbered houses strung along the ridge facing south to the vineyards. This is a lovely village with lovely shops and lovely views.

Continuing north along the Route du Vin from Itterswiller, the road travels through a number of wine towns crowned by the ruins of their castles, **Château d'Haute Andlau**, **Château de Landsberg** above the larger wine town, **Barr**, and the **Château d'Ottrott** above the charming village of **Ottrott**. Between Andlau and Barr, it is worth the short detour off the wine road to drive up and through the village of **Mittelbergheim**, designated as one of France's Most Beautiful Villages. Although there are not many stores, Mittelbergheim boasts some of the region's best winemakers and many of their cellars are located along the village streets and are open to visitors.

From Ottrott, follow the road as it winds back toward the main road and the larger city of **Obernai**. If you like to shop, park on the main street through town and then investigate the maze of pedestrian streets with their enticing shops and restaurants.

Strasbourg, the *grande dame* of the region and one of France's most beautiful cities, is just a short distance northeast of Obernai on the border with Germany. Although, personally, I usually avoid large cities, Strasbourg is gorgeous and well worth the effort to navigate its miles of urban surround to penetrate its old quarter. Begin armed with a good map and take the time to chart a route before you begin the journey.

Set on the banks of the River Rhine where it meets the Ill, Strasbourg's city center is full of charm. The old quarter is an island banded by the River Ill, with the Place Kléber and the lacy pink-sandstone **Nôtre Dame Cathedral** at its core. It is filled with interesting little streets of shops, restaurants, and hotels and leads to the footbridges that span the River Ill. The nearby **Petite France** quarter, where craftsmen plied their trades in the 16th and 17th centuries, is full of old timbered houses, most notably the fine **Maison des Tanneurs** with its intricate wooden galleries. Many of the craftsmen's old workshops are now delightful restaurants.

From Strasbourg, you can cross into Germany's Black Forest, journey on into Switzerland, or travel a 350-kilometer drive (four hours) on the autoroute to Reims where you can join the Champagne wine route. It is also approximately a 300-kilometer drive (three and a half hours) from Strasbourg to the heart of the Burgundy region and Beaune, reputed to be the capital of the wine industry.

Old Strasbourg, Petite France

Wine Country–Alsace

Wine Country
Champagne

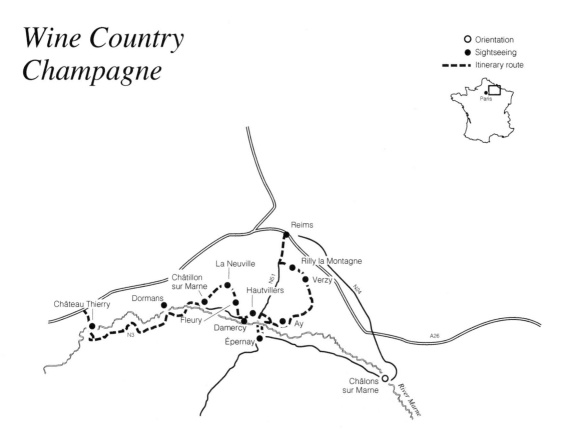

O Orientation
● Sightseeing
∎ ∎ ∎ ∎ Itinerary route

Paris

Reims

La Neuville

Rilly la Montagne

Châtillon sur Marne

Verzy

Hautvillers

N51

Château Thierry

Dormans

Fleury

Ay

N3

Damercy

Épernay

N24

A26

Châlons sur Marne

River Marne

Wine Country–Champagne

Champagne is a small wine district dedicated to the production of the effervescent liquid that we associate with happy occasions and celebrations. The name "champagne" can be used only for the wines produced by this region's vineyards. Its capital is Reims, a not-very-attractive city due to being almost razed in World War I, but many of its buildings and its fine old Gothic cathedral have been restored. Below the city is a honeycomb of champagne cellars. Nearby lies the most important town for champagne, Épernay, where the mighty mansions of the producers alternate with their *maisons* (the term for their offices, warehouses, cellars, and factories). The vineyards are south of Reims, along the valley of the Marne. It is not particularly beautiful countryside, just gentle slopes facing towards the sun, interspersed with workaday villages that offer opportunities for sampling, but few tourist facilities such as cafés, restaurants, or shops.

Épernay, Mercier Champagne Cellar

Recommended Pacing: Our Champagne itinerary covers a very small geographic area. We suggest you spend two or three nights in the region. Any of the hotels we recommend in the region would serve as a convenient base from which to explore and sample the bounty of Champagne.

Unlike wines from Burgundy, the quality of champagne is not derived solely from the area but also from the manufacturing process. It is the dose of sugar or "bead" that makes the bubbles, and the smaller the bead, the better the champagne. The essence of champagne is the blending of several different grapes; a branded wine, it is known by the maker and not by the vineyard. There are three distinct zones in the 55,000 acres in Champagne: the *Montagne de Reims*, the *Vallée de la Marne*, and *Côte des Blancs*. This itinerary visits the champagne houses in Reims and Épernay and drives round the Mountain of Reims and along the Valley of the Marne before returning you to Paris.

This journey begins in **Reims**, once the capital of France (4th to 9th centuries) and now one of the capitals of the Champagne district. The **Nôtre Dame Cathedral** dates from the 12th century and is where the kings of France used to be crowned (follow signs for *Centre Ville*). Begun in 1211, it is one of the oldest examples of Gothic architecture in France, and while it suffered heavy damage in World War I, it was beautifully restored in 1938. Traffic around the cathedral is terribly congested.

You may want to save your cellar tours until Épernay, but if you like to visit a house in each city, several invite you to come by without appointment. While the basic procedures and methods used to produce champagne are similar, the grand names for champagne all have their own history and interesting stories to tell. Tours are available in English and take about an hour. Except in July and August the houses are usually closed between 11:30 am and 2 pm.

Mumm, 34 Rue de Champ de Mar, offers a film, guided tour of the cellars, and tasting. (*Closed weekends in winter, tel: 03.26.49.59.70.*)

At **Piper-Hiedsieck**, 51 Blvd. Henry Vasnier, visitors tour the galleries in six-passenger cars that take you on a Disney-like tour of the cellars with giant dioramas of grapes and interesting explanations on the production of champagne from harvest to disgorging. (*Open Mar to Jan, tel: 03.26.84.43.44.*)

Pommery, 5 Place du Général Gourard, offers a film, guided tour of the cellars, and tasting. (*Closed Christmas to New Years, tel: 03.26.61.62.56.*)

Taittinger, 9 Place Saint-Nicaise, offers a film, guided tour of the cellars, and tasting. (*Open all year, tel: 03.26.85.84.33.*)

Leave Reims south in the direction of Épernay (N51). After leaving the suburbs and light industrial areas behind, when you're among the fields and vineyards, take the first left turn signposted **Route du Champagne**, which charts a very pleasant horseshoe-shaped drive around the **Montagne de Reims** to Épernay. Above, the vineyards end in

Faux de Verzy

woodlands and below, they cascade to the vast plain, the scene of so much fighting during World War I.

The first small village you come to on the D26 is **Villers Allerand**, which leads you to **Rilly la Montagne**, a larger village which offers the opportunity for a stroll and a drink in a café as well as the chance to sip champagne. As you drive along, look for the peculiar-looking tractors with their high bodies and wheels set at a width that enables them to pass through the rows of vines and meander down the little lanes.

As the route nears **Mailly Champagne** and **Verzy**, you pass some of the most superior vineyards for the production of champagne grapes. The picturesque windmill found between the two villages was used as an observation post during World War I.

The wine route rounds the mountain at Verzy where a short detour up into the woodlands brings you to **Faux de Verzy**, an unusual forest of gnarled, stunted, and twisted beech trees hundreds of years old. Return to Verzy and continue along the D26, turning south through **Villers Marmery**, **Trépail**, and **Ambonnay** to **Bouzy**, a community famous not only for its champagne grapes but also for its red wine. At Bouzy the wine route splits and our route follows signposts into nearby Épernay.

Traffic is much less of a problem in **Épernay** than Reims. While much of the damage has been repaired, there are still several scars from the severe bombing that Épernay suffered in World War I. Follow signposts for *Centre Ville* and particularly *Office de Tourisme,* which brings you to your destination in this sprawling town, the Rue de Champagne, a long street lined with the *maisons* and mansions of the premier champagne producers Möet et Chandon, Perrier Jouët, Charbaut, De Venoge Pol Roger, and Mercier.

Try to allow time to take both the Möet et Chandon and Mercier cellar tours. **Möet et Chandon**, founded in 1743, is across the street from the tourist office. They offer a very sophisticated tour of their visitors' center (where Napoleon's hat is displayed), a walk through one of the largest champagne cellars in the world, and an excellent explanation on how champagne is made. (*Open all year, tel: 03.26.51.20.00.*)

Just as the Rue de Champagne leaves behind its grand mansions, you come to **Mercier's** modern visitors' center where the world's largest wine cask sits center stage. Holding the equivalent of 200,000 bottles of champagne, it was made to advertise Mercier at the World Trade Fair in Paris in 1889 and proved as great an attraction as the Eiffel Tower. Houses that interrupted its progress to Paris had to be razed. Mercier's tour gives you an upbeat movie history of Mercier champagne, then whisks you down to the galleries in a glass-sided elevator past a diorama of the founders ballooning over their estate. An electric train weaves you through the vast cellars past some interesting carvings and boundless bottles of bubbly. (*Closed Tues and Wed, Nov to Mar, tel: 03.26.51.22.22.*)

Hautvillers

Leaving Épernay, follow signposts for Reims until you see the Route de Champagne signpost to both the left and right. Turn left to **Ay** and follow the route along the Vallée de la Marne to **Hautvillers**, the prettiest of Champagne's villages with its spic-and-span homes and broad swatch of cobbles decorating the center of its streets. It was in the village basilica that Dom Perignon performed his miracle and discovered how to make still wine sparkling by the *méthode champenoise*. He also introduced the use of cork stoppers (tied down to stop them from popping out as pressure built up in the bottles) and blended different wines from around the region to form a wine with a superior character than that produced by a single vineyard. The abbey is now owned by Möet et Chandon and contains a private museum. However, you can enjoy the lovely view of the valley from the abbey terrace.

From Hautvillers, descend through the vineyards to **Cumièrs**, a workaday village known for its red wine, and on to **Damery** with its pretty 12th- and 16th-century church. Climbing through vineyards, you have lovely views across the River Marne to the villages and vineyards strung along the opposite bank.

Pass through **Venteul** and **Arty** and on to the more attractive village of **Fleury**, which offers tasting in the large building decorated with murals. As you climb through pretty countryside to **Belval**, vineyards give way to fields. Passing through woodland, you come to **La Neuville aux Larris** with its enormous champagne bottle sitting next to the church, and return to the River Marne at **Châtillon-sur-Marne**. A huge statue overlooking the river proclaims this village as the birthplace of Pope Urban II.

At **Verneuil** cross the river and continue on the N3 into **Dormans**, which saw fierce fighting in World War I and was badly damaged. Set in a large green park, the **Chapelle de la Reconnaissance** (Chapel of Gratitude) commemorates those killed in the battles of the Marne in 1914 and 1918 and offers splendid views over the valley. You can quickly return to Épernay on the N3 or continue to Paris via **Château Thierry**, set on the River Marne against a lovely wooded backdrop. The English claimed the town as theirs in 1421 then Joan of Arc recaptured it for France. The gates through which she entered the city still stand—**Porte Saint Pierre**. Napoleon defended the city against Russian and Prussian troops in 1814.

Wine Country–Champagne

The French Alps

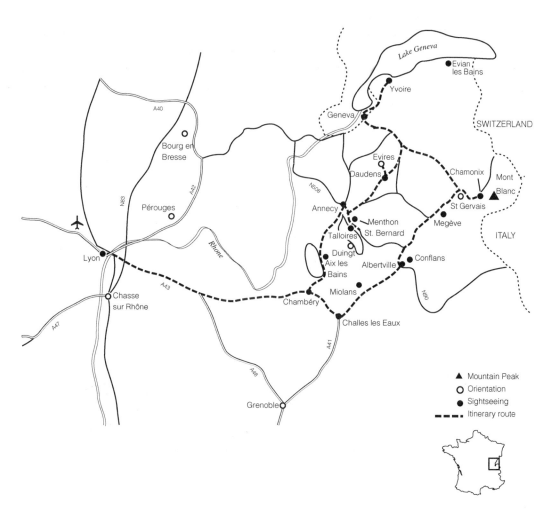

Lake Geneva

Evian
les Bains

Yvoire

Geneva

SWITZERLAND

Evires

Daudens

Chamonix

Mont
Blanc

A40

Bourg en
Bresse

N508

Annecy

St Gervais

Pérouges

Menthon
St. Bernard

Megève

N83

A42

Talloires

ITALY

Rhone

Duingt

Aix les
Bains

Albertville

Conflans

Lyon

Miolans

N90

Chasse
sur Rhône

A43

Chambéry

A47

Challes les Eaux

A41

A48

Grenoble

▲ Mountain Peak
○ Orientation
● Sightseeing
▪▪▪ Itinerary route

The French Alps

The French Alps encompasses a beautiful region tucked to the south of the shores of Lake Geneva with majestic peaks establishing a natural border between Italy, France, and Switzerland. This is a region of towering mountains, Alpine valleys, lakes, and rivers, a region that will be appreciated by all who share a love of nature and the mountains— both the sportsman and the photographer. It is a region to be enjoyed year round, but a chameleon with its dramatic changes in seasonal dress.

Mont Blanc, Chamonix

The French Alps

Recommended pacing: This itinerary assumes your travels will both begin and end in Geneva. However, it is important to note that if you are traveling along the Rhône Valley, it is also easy to make an itinerary loop of this region with Lyon as the originating city. If your travels begin in Geneva, you will most definitely want to spend a few nights here to enjoy this elegant city just across the Swiss border. With a beautiful waterfront setting, gardens, fountains, and bridges spanning the river that weaves through the city, Geneva is intimate in size. It is easy to walk and explore its many distinctive districts, from the elegant shopping streets and regal residential quarters to the cobbled streets of its old quarter. (For recommendations of places to stay in Geneva, either refer to our guide, *Switzerland: Charming Inns & Itineraries* or visit our website, *www.karenbrown.com.*) Once you leave Geneva, it is recommended that you select one place to stay for a minimum of two nights in one of the key mountain towns such as Chamonix or Megève, and then select a base for two nights for exploring the lake region of Annecy. Before returning to Geneva, we strongly recommend an overnight in medieval Yvoire, a little way beyond the city on the shores of Lake Geneva. If your trip originates in Lyon, again we would recommend two nights near Lake Annecy, two nights in the mountains near Mont Blanc, and then a night in Geneva as well as one night on its lake in the charming village of Yvoire.

From **Geneva**, travel a gorgeous, narrow valley shadowed by towering peaks in the direction of Chamonix and Mont Blanc. If you're in a rush you could take the autoroute, but the N205 parallels the autoroute and seems just as efficient and perhaps prettier as it travels through the villages. This area is absolutely gorgeous in spring and summer, with a dramatic backdrop of high snow-covered peaks that contrast with lush green pastures dotted with chalets, grazing cattle, and an abundance of wildflowers. The many ski lifts and gondolas that climb from the villages indicate that this is definitely a winter sport destination, but in other seasons parachutes color the skies and mountain trails, waterfalls, and mountain peaks beckon and challenge all abilities.

The resort town of **Chamonix** is nestled in a valley of the same name that stretches 20 kilometers between the towering Mont Blanc range to the south and the Aiguilles Rouges

Mountains to the north. Considered the ultimate winter and summer resort, Chamonix was home to the first Winter Olympics in 1924 and boasts the highest summit in Europe, the towering peak of **Mont Blanc**. Although of international renown and acclaim, Chamonix retains the ambiance of a small mountain town, especially in the pedestrian village of Chamonix Sud with its charming, weathered *chalets chamoniards* individualized by their elegantly painted façades, shopping arcades, an intimate town square, and the delightful Rue du Moulins.

From Chamonix, retrace your path traveling west and then turn south toward the charming Alpine village of **Megève**. Described as the "essence of rustic chic," the town was conceived in the 1920s to be France's version of Switzerland's St. Moritz. Ideally located for visiting many of the region's exclusive resorts (St. Gervais, Combloux, Les Contamines, and Chamonix), Megève boasts a number of gourmet restaurants, luxury boutique hotels, and gorgeous shops. At its core, a pedestrian zone preserves its character and minimizes the impact of crowds, who are forced to utilize one of the many parking garages on the perimeter.

In the shadow of Mont Blanc, all the Haute Savoie villages offer the sportsman both a winter and summer paradise. In winter you can enjoy: paragliding, hot springs, downhill skiing, cross-country skiing, helicopter skiing, snowmobiling, Turkish-bath saunas, ice-skating, curling, and Megève's casino. Summer attractions include: spa treatments, mountain biking, walking, tennis, golf, archery, paragliding, lake and river fishing, rafting, swimming, the summer luge, horse-back riding, mountaineering, and the tramway.

The French Alps

From Megève, it is a beautiful drive following the Arly River as it cuts a path through a rugged, narrow mountain canyon to the city of **Albertville**. Albertville, built on the valley floor after flood channels were dug to eliminate flooding, became the area's new commercial center. Its predecessor, the old walled town of Conflans, still remains, strategically positioned on the hillside above the city and the confluence of the Arly and Isère rivers. Dating back to Roman times, the town is fun to explore with its ancient fortifications, buildings, and cobbled streets.

A bustling city, Albertville was home to the 1992 Olympic Winter Games. The year marked the first Olympics since the reunification of Germany in 1990 and the breakup of the Soviet Union in 1991, and resulted in a record 2,174 athletes from 65 countries. This was also the last time the Winter Games were held in the same year as the Summer Games. Only 18 of the 57 events were held in Albertville itself, while nearby resorts hosted the rest.

Continuing south along the Isère, the beauty of the region wanes a bit past Albertville until the silhouette of castle ruins appears at **Miolans**. In the 10th century this impressive fortress was commissioned by the Miolans family on the site of an ancient settlement. It was later confiscated by the Dukes of Savoy who used the fortress as a prison. Over a period of 200 years it served to confine 192 prisoners, the most famous of whom was the Marquis de Sade, who managed to escape. The château overlooks the Combe de Savoie valley, a rich wine-growing region that extends from Miolans, dips south at Montmeilian, and then continues north to Calles les Eaux. The various varietals grown in the region include Pinot, Gamay, Mondeuse, Chardonnay, and Altesse.

Chambéry, the capital of the counts and dukes of Savoy during the 14th century, is located just south of the **Lac du Bourget**, in the heart of the French Alps. Dominated by the castle, the remarkable old town is preserved as a pedestrian area and has lovely old mansions, dramatic fountains, and intriguing alleys lined with cafés.

It is just a short drive on to the Lac du Bourget and **Aix les Bains,** its principal resort town, which is very touristy and full of sun worshipers. I much prefer the lovely **Lac**

d'Annecy to the northeast. Nestled on its northern shore is the beautiful city of **Annecy**, crowned by its silhouetted castle. The city enjoys a lovely old pedestrian district transected by waterways and gardens along the waterfront, a magnet in warm weather for sun seekers who blanket its lawn. Numerous boat excursions originate from its harbor to explore the lake and Alpine setting.

Château de Miolans

From Annecy, roads depart along both the west and east banks of Lac d'Annecy. The drive along the east bank is definitely the prettiest, with little villages whose homes and hotels cluster along the waterfront. Detour just off the riverfront to visit the ornate turreted château above **Menthon St. Bernard.** Far away from the workaday hustle, nestling in a vast park, the stone towers of Menthon St. Bernard's castle dominate the lake. A baronial residence, it has passed down to descendants of the same family since the 11th century.

Talloires, a lovely village with one of the prettiest settings along the lake, is found about a third of the way south from Annecy along the eastern shore. Nestled in a serene alcove on the lakeshore, this would be a lovely place to lunch at one of its terrace restaurants. From Talloires you can also enjoy views across the narrow stretch of lake to the decorative towers of Duingt.

If you are fond of pottery, travel northeast from Annecy following the N203 (in the direction of Chamonix and Thonon les Bains) and turn off at Daudens, following signs to **Evires**. After crossing the railroad tracks, turn right just before town to find the pottery workshop and museum, housed in an old farm, of master potter Jean Christophe Hermann, considered the best in the region. Founded in 1981, the museum enjoys a rich collection of over two million pieces. This is considered one of the finest collections of Savoyard pottery in the world. (*L'Atelier de Poterie. Visits by reservation only, tel: 04.50.62.01.90*)

Before circling back to Geneva, head to the lakeshore just to the northeast of the city, to the picturesque village of **Yvoire**. With its 700-year-old castle, ramparts, and tower gates, Yvoire is an enchanting medieval village situated on the French side of Lake Geneva. Cars are not permitted within the walls and so wandering the narrow cobbled streets and the paths along its shore and harbor is both peaceful and scenic. Although it is a convenient half-hour drive back to Geneva from Yvoire, you can also travel the distance by train or boat (one hour). Numerous lake excursions are offered from the port.

The French Alps

Paris
Hotel Descriptions

First Arrondissement

Hotel #1 Le Relais du Louvre
J Place Vendôme
K Jardin des Tuileries
L Palais du Louvre
M Palais Royal
N Forum

Second Arrondissement

Hotel #2 Le Stendhal Hôtel
Hotel #6 Le Relais Saint Honoré
Hotel #7 Le Horset Opéra

Third Arrondissement

Hotel #3 Pavillon de la Reine
S Musée Picasso

Fourth Arrondissement

Hotel #4 Hôtel de la Bretonnerie
Hotel #5 Hôtel du Jeu de Paume
O Centre George Pompidou
P Hôtel de Ville
Q Île de la Cité— Nôtre Dame & Sainte Chapelle
R Île Saint Louis
V Place des Vosges

Fifth Arrondissement

Hotel #8 Hotel Minerve
Hotel #9 Hôtel des Grandes Écoles
Hotel #10 Hôtel des Grands Hommes
Hotel #11 Hôtel du Panthéon
Hotel #12 Relais Saint Jacques
Y Panthéon

Sixth Arrondissement

Hotel #13 Victoria Palace Hôtel
Hotel #14 Saint Germain Left Bank Hôtel
Hotel #15 Relais Christine
Hotel #16 Hôtel d'Aubusson
Hotel #17 Au Manoir Saint Germain des Prés
Z Palais du Luxembourg

Seventh Arrondissement

Hotel #18 Hôtel Duc de St. Simon
AA Musée d'Orsay
BB Hôtel des Invalides
CC École Militaire
DD Tour Eiffel
HH Musée Auguste Rodin

Eighth Arrondissement

Hotel #19 Hôtel San Regis
Hotel #20 Hôtel Chambiges
D Grand Palais
E Petit Palais
F Place de la Concorde
G Sainte Marie Madeleine
H Gare Saint Lazare

Ninth Arrondissement

I Opéra

Tenth Arrondissement

T Gare du Nord
U Gare de l'Est

Twelfth Arrondissement

JJ Bois de Vincennes
W Gare de Lyon

Thirteenth Arrondissement

X Gare d'Austerlitz

Fifteenth Arrondissement

EE Gare Montparnasse

Sixteenth Arrondissement

A Trocadéro
B Palais de Chaillot
C Arc de Triomphe
II Musée Marmottan
KK Bois de Boulogne

Eighteenth Arrondissement

FF Sacré Coeur
GG Montmartre

Paris

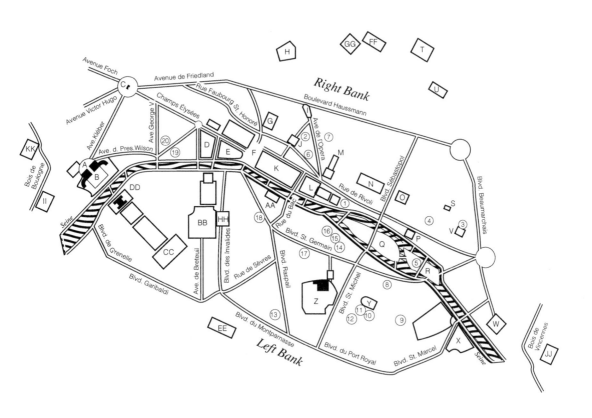

Paris Hotel Map

159

Paris

Paris, beautiful and sophisticated, lives up to her reputation. Sectioned off by *arrondissements*, there is not just one interesting area to visit, but many. Each arrondissement has its own character, flavor, and style. It is almost as if "Paris" were a name given to a group of clustering villages. Depending on the reason for your trip or the number of times you've been to Paris, each arrondissement will have its own appeal and attraction. We include descriptions of selected arrondissements. The arrondissements chosen are especially interesting and are the location for some some charming, boutique hotels. Avoid disappointment and make hotel reservations as far in advance as possible.

Place de la Concorde

Paris Hotel Descriptions

First & Second Arrondissements

The First and Second Arrondissements are ideal locations for "first-timers" in Paris. At the heart of the city, many of the major tourist attractions are situated here: the Place de la Concorde, Rue de Rivoli, the Madeleine elegant and expensive shops along the well-known Rue du Faubourg Saint Honoré, the Tuileries, and the Louvre. Find a hotel here and you will never have to deal with the Métro or taxi drivers. You can take romantic walks along the Seine or in the Tuileries Gardens. Excitement was born on the Champs Élysées, a wide boulevard that runs from the Place de la Concorde to the Arc de Triomphe at the Place de l'Étoile, officially known as the Place Charles de Gaulle.

The Madeleine

Tucked on a small side street practically in the shadow of the Louvre and close enough to enjoy the sounds of the church, Saint-Germain-l'Auxerrois, the Relais du Louvre is a lovely hotel, reasonably priced for its location and comfort. Set under old beams, rooms are pretty with their pastel-washed walls and floral fabrics. Guestrooms that open onto the central courtyard enjoy the quiet and those that overlook streets enjoy views out over the Louvre at the front or Nôtre Dame at the back. Guestrooms vary dramatically, so there is quite an offering in terms of selection. From the top penthouse suite with its spacious bedroom, full bath, large dining room with fireplace, kitchenette and private balcony; to room number two on the ground floor that opens on the central patio—each room has its own individuality and defining space. A personal favorite is one of just two rooms sharing the fifth floor, number 52, termed a Junior Suite that enjoys two sets of windows and views of Saint Chapelle. Since, with the exception of the lovely entry-salon (they have a computer with internet access set up for guest use), public areas are minimal, breakfast is served to the privacy of the guestroom. Bread delivery dictates how early one can request it but there is no restriction as to how late or lazy one wants to be. This is a lovely little hotel whose staff offers a warm and gracious reception who strive to offer an exceptional level of service.

LE RELAIS DU LOUVRE
Owner: Roger Thiery, Directeur: Sophie Aulnette
19, Rue des Prêtres-Saint-Germain-l'Auxerrois
75001 Paris, France
Tel: 01.40.41.96.42, Fax: 01.40.41.96.44
21 Rooms, Double: €150–€190
Breakfast not included: €12
Open: all year, Credit cards: all major
Located behind the Louvre, Métro: Louvre
www.karenbrown.com/lerelaisdulouvre.html

When Le Relais Saint Honoré caught my attention, I questioned how I could have previously passed and not noticed this charming hotel with its appealing façade that fronts the prestigious and historic Rue Saint Honoré and wraps around the corner onto the rue de la Sourdière. My momentary doubt regarding the thoroughness of my research skills was dispelled when I learned that it had only recently been renovated and opened as a small hotel after long existing as an abandoned shell of a building. In this charming and delightful hotel with a staff dedicated to making your visit a special one, travelers are now provided an intimate stay in proximity to one of Paris's most elite shopping districts, only a few blocks from the Seine and Tuileries. From the street, large windows afford a glimpse into the cozy living room that also serves as the lobby. Guestrooms are located on each of the six floors. On the ground floor beyond the entrance is a guestroom allowing for handicap access to the quiet side street. Under the beams of the sixth floor are a junior suite and a two-room apartment. Each of the remaining floors in between offers a comfortable front room with windows overlooking the bustle of the rue St. Honoré, an intimate central guestroom, and quiet back guestroom overlooking the side street. As the public area is limited to the entry living room, breakfast is delivered to the privacy of guestrooms.

LE RELAIS SAINT HONORÉ   ***New***
Owner: Paul Bogaert, Hôtelier: Marie-Pierre Peron
308 rue Saint Honoré, 75001 Paris, France
Tel: 01.42.96.06.06, Fax: 01.42.96.17.50
13 Rooms, Double: €196–€330, Breakfast not included: €12
Open: all year, Credit cards: all major
Located in the fashionable shopping district of the Rue Saint Honoré
Métro: Tuileries or Pyramides
www.karenbrown.com/honore.html

Located on a quiet, side street just a few blocks from the Opéra and in the other direction from the Seine, Le Horset Opéra enjoys an incredible location on Paris' Right Bank. I have long recommended hotels owned and managed by the Teil Family, two of which are nestled on the left bank, one is in the prestigious residential district of the 8th arrondissement, and am now pleased to recommend Le Horset Opéra. The Teil consistency in good taste is evident from the moment one passes through the door into a pretty sitting area opposite an inviting and intimate bar. Recently purchased and completely renovated, all 48 double and six single rooms are handsome in their décor with attractive wallpapers and fabrics that beautifully compliment those in the bedspreads and drapes. Although not overly spacious, the rooms are very comfortable in size—most with twin beds that convert to king (the six singles boast double beds) with modern bathrooms finished in either marble or tile, all with a tub/shower unit, sink, toilet and towel warmer. Rooms are equipped with direct dial phones, satellite TV, wireless internet access, and excellent lighting. Rooms are identified by numbers engraved on brass plaques with the symbolic coquille—the universal sign of welcome. A lavish breakfast buffet is included in the price of the room or a continental will graciously be served to your room for a small additional charge.

HORSET OPÉRA   New
Directors: Antoine et Stéphane Teil
18, rue d'Antin, 75002 Paris, France
Tel: 01.44.71.87.00, Fax: 01.42.66.55.54
54 Rooms, Double: €180–€260
Open: all year, Credit cards: all major
Located near the Air France-Orly Airport & Roissy-CDG Airport bus stops at Rue Scribe
Metro: Opéra
www.karenbrown.com/horset.html

The special allure of this charming hotel is not the fame of the author who lived and died here, but rather its intimate atmosphere, idyllic location, and value. It has also become a personal as well as reader favorite because of the incredible welcome and hospitality extended by the gracious staff! Located on the right bank on a small one-way street that runs parallel to the Rue St. Honoré just a few blocks from Place Vendôme, this delightful hotel is small enough for staff to personalize their attention to one's needs. The ten "classic" rooms, four of which have twin beds, are the most reasonable in price and the room we saw (room 41) was lovely—a twin-bedded room just off its own little hallway with a sweet rose and light-blue decor of ribbons and flowers that enjoys a quiet location overlooking the back courtyard. Room 43, an example of a "superior" room, is delightful in tones of yellows and blues and has two windows overlooking the narrow street. Room 24, a junior suite, is lovely as it overlooks the courtyard and is very quiet. The Stendhal Suite (room 52), located at the front, is decorated in red and black to honor his novel and its tub has Jacuzzi jets. Under the arched arcade of the cellar, tables are placed intimately for breakfast, a lavish buffet including baked goods, a hot beverage, juice, and a choice of three items (yogurt, egg, cereal, grapefruit, or ham). Breakfast is also served in the guestrooms. Amenities include room service, laundry service, TVs, two direct phone lines per room, computer connections, air conditioning, and mini-bars.

LE STENDHAL HÔTEL
Directeur: Virginie Gicquel
22, rue Danielle Casanova, 75002 Paris, France
Tel: 01.44.58.52.52, Fax: 01.44.58.52.00
21 Rooms, Double: €247–€383, Breakfast not included: €17
Open: all year, Credit cards: all major
Located near the Place Vendôme, Métro: Opéra, Pyramides & Tuileries
www.karenbrown.com/lestendhal.html

Third & Fourth Arrondissements

The highlight of the Third Arrondissement is the picturesque Place des Vosges and the focus of the Fourth Arrondissement is Paris's two quaint and charming islands, the Île Saint Louis and the Île de la Cité. The Place des Vosges is a tranquil park, shaded by trees and echoing with the sound of children at play, and a short walk away is the wonderful Musée Picasso. The Île Saint Louis is a charming island with many enticing antique and craft shops and neighborhood restaurants. The larger Île de la Cité is home to Paris's *grande dame*—the spectacular Nôtre Dame and the intricate and delicate Sainte Chapelle with its stunning display of stained glass. Crossing bridges in either direction, it is a short walk along the *quai* to the Latin Quarter or a pleasant stroll to the Louvre.

Fishing along the Seine

This charming hotel offers visitors to Paris a wonderful location on the beautiful square and park, the Place des Vosges. Built to accommodate the wedding of Louis XIII and Ann of Austria, the park was orignally inaugurated as the Place Royale. It became the heart of elegant Paris and some of its most notable residents were Madame de Sévigné and Victor Hugo who claimed the location inspired "Les Misérables." The park was renamed in 1800 as tribute to the people from the Vosges region who were the first to pay their taxes! The Pavillon de la Reine was named in honor of the Queen when it was converted to a hotel in 1985. Set back off the Place, fronted by its own flowered courtyard, the Pavillon de la Reine was built on the site of an older pavilion and was surprisingly coverted from a complex of different individual flats, all dating from different periods. The handsome 17th-century beams of the beautiful lobby are, remarkably, as old as the place itself. Trademarks of the Pavillon de la Reine are tasteful furnishings and, most importantly, pride and excellence of service. With every modern convenience, the hotel offers luxurious comfort and a warm decor of beamed ceilings, antiques, attractive reproductions, and beautiful art and paintings. Accommodations are expensive and offered as standard double rooms, two-level duplexes, and two-bedroom suites. The hotel has a lovely salon, and breakfast is served under the vaulted ceilings of the old cellar. To stay here is to enjoy the ambiance of old-world Paris.

PAVILLON DE LA REINE
Hoteliêr: Yves Monnin
28, Place des Vosges, 75003 Paris, France
Tel: 01.40.29.19.19, Fax: 01.40.29.19.20
56 Rooms, Double: €345–€790, Breakfast not included: €20 to €25
Open: all year, Credit cards: all major
Located on the Place des Vosges, Métro: Saint Paul
Chateaux & Hotels de France
www.karenbrown.com/reine.html

Located in a quaint, artistic neighborhood of Paris, popular with the gay community, La Bretonnerie offers comfortable and reasonable accommodation. The reception is on the ground floor and sits opposite an inviting sitting area. The rooms are found tucked along a maze of corridors, all attractive in their furnishings, and all with private bathrooms. Many of the rooms are set under heavy wooden beams, some cozy under low ceilings, ours was quite spacious with 13-foot-high ceilings at the back. A few rooms are two-level and offer a loft bedroom and sitting room below. Although it is not the largest, I like number 37, which enjoys its own balcony and cozy red décor; number 10, a bright corner room; and number 12 which is small but charming. In the basement under vaulted beams, heavy wooden tables are matched with high-backed chairs staging a medieval atmosphere for breakfast. The hotel has a great location within walking distance of the Place des Vosges, the Picasso Museum, the Pompidou Center, and Les Halles. The Bretonnerie is set on a quiet street and offers a comfortable and quiet night's sleep.

HÔTEL DE LA BRETONNERIE
Hoteliêr: Mr Philippe Bidal
22, Rue Sainte-Croix de la Bretonnerie
75004 Paris, France
Tel: 01.48.87.77.63, Fax: 01.42.77.26.78
29 Rooms, Double: €110–€180*
*Breakfast not included: €9.50
Open: all year, Credit cards: MC, VS
Located across the river from Nôtre Dame
Métro: Hôtel de Ville
www.karenbrown.com/hoteldelabretonnerie.html

To find the Hôtel du Jeu de Paume it is easier to locate the imposing deep-blue door than the small identifying brass plaque. Behind the large door, a long outdoor corridor with stone-tiled floor and heavy wooden timbers buffers the hotel from any street noise. Inside, the Jeu de Paume is an architectural wonder whose walls and vaulted ceilings are striped with beams. Dramatic in its furnishing, the decor is an artistic blend of tapestries, chrome, glass, and leather set against a backdrop of wood and plaster. The core of the hotel, converted from a 17th-century Jeu de Paume, is one large room divided up into a series of rooms: the entry, the living room warmed by a lovely fire, and the dining room whose tables are overpowered by the stunning end beams and soaring rafters. Be sure to take note of the large painting over the bureau whose canvas is reminiscent of the times of Louis XIII. A few guestrooms open onto the central room, while the majority of rooms are located in a side annex and open onto a courtyard and basic garden. Two junior suites have the luxury of two bathrooms and number 7 enjoys a private terrace. The Rue Saint-Louis-en-L'Île runs the length of this miniature island—right down it's center. To stay at the Hôtel du Jeu de Paume allows one to enjoy the beautiful Île Saint Louis and its enchanting residential neighborhood—one of Paris' treasures.

HÔTEL DU JEU DE PAUME
Hoteliêr: Elyane Prache
54, rue Saint -Louis-en-l'Île
75004 Paris, France
Tel: 01.43.26.14.18, Fax: 01.40.46.02.76
30 Rooms, Double: €230–€495*
*Breakfast not included: €18
Open: all year, Credit cards: all major
Located on the Île Saint Louis, Métro: Pont-Marie
www.karenbrown.com/hoteldujeudepaume.html

Fifth, Sixth & Seventh Arrondissements

The Fifth, Sixth, and Seventh Arrondissements together comprise the ever-popular Latin Quarter. Here you will find activity and companionship abounding. There are crêperies, sidewalk cafés, food stands, the Sorbonne and its students, antique shops and art galleries, and so many restaurants—all promising "favorites" to be discovered. At night many of the small streets are blocked off and the Latin Quarter takes on a very special ambiance. The Left Bank of the Latin Quarter is separated from the Right Bank by the Seine and the Île de la Cité. The grandeur of Nôtre Dame is overpowering when illuminated at night. Along the *quai* are many secondhand book stalls. The Musée d'Orsay in the grand old train station houses an exhibition of Paris' greatest collection of Impressionist art. With the Left Bank as a base, you can also conveniently tour the Luxembourg Gardens and Les Invalides, the wonderful Musée Auguste Rodin with his works housed in a lovely mansion as well as staged in a gorgeous garden, and view Paris from the Eiffel Tower. The Left Bank and Latin Quarter offer an endless wave of activity and several charming hotels.

Nôtre Dame and the Île de la Cité

Large green doors close off the cobbled walk leading to the three peach-colored buildings with white shutters and gray mansard roofs set around a lovely walled garden that comprise this delightful, extremely reasonably priced hotel. The adorable Mme Le Floch sets the mood and ambiance of the hotel and personally welcomes her many returning guests with a lingering warm handshake and an intimate greeting. The staff, described as "family" seems to take pride in embellishing the welcome that Mme Le Floch extends. The guestrooms are simple in their appointments and not exceptionally large but they are comfortable and spotlessly clean and enjoy the quiet of the off-street courtyard setting. We were able to see a wide range of rooms although the hotel was obviously full—as the staff was cleaning, they proudly showed off each room with its subtle differences. Decor is feminine, with pretty, soft-colored patterns for the wallpapers and spreads. The bathrooms are not luxurious in size but have hairdryers, towel warmers, and tub showers. Breakfast is served at the convenience of the guests, from early to late—weather permitting at tables set in the pretty garden courtyard.

HÔTEL DES GRANDES ÉCOLES
Hoteliêr: Madame Le Floch
75, rue du Cardinal Lemoine, 75005 Paris, France
Tel: 01.43.26.79.23, Fax: 01.43.25.28.15
51 Rooms, Double: €110–€135*
*Breakfast not included: €8
Open: all year, Credit cards: MC, VS
Located a few blocks from the Panthéon
Métro: Cardinal Lemoine & Monge
www.karenbrown.com/ecoles.html

The Hôtel des Grands Hommes enjoys a quiet location facing onto the Place du Panthéon—a haven in Paris. Set behind a lovely old door, the handsome lobby with its interior courtyard garden sets the mood of a regal town home with an intimate ambiance. A delicious French breakfast can be savored at small wooden tables paired with tapestry chairs set under the light-stone arches of the house's original cellar. The bedrooms are found up a spiral staircase (or elevator) and are beautiful in their newly refurbished decor. Attractive, traditional furnishings are set against pretty wallpapers and under fresh, white-painted beams. We were able to see only a sampling of rooms as the hotel was almost full, but of those room 22 was a wonderful triple room with a front corner location and 21 enjoyed a balcony and views of the Panthéon. The amenities and comforts seem to exceed the standards of a three-star rating and the air conditioning is welcome on those hot summer days. This is truly a delightful hotel, giving good value for its price, and the staff prides itself on personalized, refined service.

HÔTEL DES GRANDS HOMMES
Hoteliêr: Marie Jose Hery
17, Place du Panthéon, 75005 Paris, France
Tel: 01.46.34.19.60, Fax: 01.43.26.67.32
31 Rooms, Double: €147–€382*
*Breakfast not included: €12
Open: all year, Credit cards: all major
Located on the Place du Panthéon
Métro: Luxembourg
www.karenbrown.com/hommes.html

The Gaucheron family has proudly finished the major renovation of the Minerve Hôtel, conveniently located next door to the Familia. Gregarious Eric is often present and by example sets a high standard of service for his incredible team, while his parents are often there overseeing details of the two hotels. The Minerve's rooms are a little larger than their neighboring, sister property, the Familia's (recommended in our France Bed & Breakfast guide) and also feature exposed beams and stone walls wherever possible. Eric's fondness for tapestries, Persian rugs, and original frescoes is evident in both properties. The hotel enjoys a lovely large entry and sitting room distinguished by an attractive mural, lovely Persian rugs on the marble floor, antiques, grandfather clocks, and the view of a back central garden. Descend the circular stair to a handsome breakfast room embraced by the old stone walls. Guestrooms are found on each of the six floors from the handicapped-accessible rooms on the first floor to the cozy top-floor rooms under angled ceilings with lovely glimpses across to the spires of Nôtre Dame. I especially liked rooms 507, 304, and 307, all cozy in size but enjoying two balconies draped with geraniums, and 303, a quiet back room overlooking the interior courtyard, lovely in colors of blues and golds and with a beautiful hand-painted fresco of Chartres Cathedral. The Minerve is recommended as a simple hotel with clean rooms, an excellent location on the Left Bank, and a price that is an extremely good value for Paris.

MINERVE HÔTEL
Hoteliêr: Eric Gaucheron
13, rue des Écoles, 75005 Paris, France
Tel: 01.43.26.26.04, Fax: 01.44.07.01.96
54 Rooms, Double: €100–€132, Breakfast not included: €8
Open: all year, Credit cards: all major
Located between the Panthéon & Nôtre Dame, Métro: Cardinale Lemoine
www.karenbrown.com/minerve.html

This property is located next door to its sister hotel, the Hôtel des Grands Hommes, and enjoys the same professional management and service. Similar in feeling and décor, both 18th-century houses have been attractively converted and the Panthéon's 34 air-conditioned bedrooms are all tastefully decorated in period style. The lobby and entry of the du Panthéon is a little grander than its neighbor, with stone floors, heavy old beams, a lovely library; a side sitting room that doubles as a 24-hour, self-service bar; and, partitioned off by columns, a second seating area with a clustering of rose and cream chairs. Although there is no restaurant, the vaulted basement cellar has been converted to a breakfast room or you can enjoy morning coffee and croissants in the privacy of your room. On each floor, two guestrooms overlook the courtyard and four to six enjoy views of the Panthéon. There are a few rooms on the fifth floor with step-out terraces (too small for tables) for no extra charge. I made note to request room 60 on my next visit. This is decorated in soft grays and pinks and has surprising views across the Panthéon to Sacré Coeur. I also really liked room 22 that overlooks the Panthéon and room 23, a pretty side corner room with the benefit of windows on two sides. In fact, any room ending in "3" from the second through the sixth floor are all corner rooms. Like its sister property, this hotel is well priced for its level of comfort and, being on the Place du Panthéon, enjoys a quiet location at the heart of the city.

HÔTEL DU PANTHÉON
Hoteliêr: Pascal Solves
19, Place du Panthéon, 75005 Paris, France
Tel: 01.43.54.32.95, Fax: 01.43.26.64.65
36 Rooms, Double: €203–€243, Breakfast not included: €12
Open: all year, Credit cards: all major
Located on the Place du Panthéon, Métro: Luxembourg
www.karenbrown.com/hoteldupantheon

This elegant six-story hotel overlooks a lovely tree-lined street and is within easy walking distance of the Luxembourg Gardens and Palace. A number of the guestrooms also look across the rooftops of Paris to the spire of the Panthéon. Bedrooms are designated as either "privilege" (standard) or "prestige." Room 301, Valençay, is a twin room decorated in soft yellows and blues with a lovely peek at the Panthéon. There are eleven "prestige" rooms—these are large and enjoy a greater expanse of window than the standard rooms. We were able to see Room 502, Le Clos Luce, with its handsome four-poster and the very pretty Room 302, Cande. Street-front rooms look out through the leafy foliage of the trees lining the street and enjoy views of the rooftops and glimpses of the Panthéon. Front, second and fifth floor rooms enjoy step-out balconies. Back rooms on the courtyard overlook the faux-painted inner wall and ensure a quiet night's repose. Off the entry and reception area a small bar, furnished with red leather chairs and small tables intimately topped with individual lamps, is partitioned by a column to separate it from the yellow-and-white breakfast room. While guests can have a continental breakfast in their bedrooms, a more lavish buffet is offered in the breakfast nook from 7am to 11am. Also off the entry is an attractive sitting area that has the feel of a library with a full wall of shelves.

RELAIS SAINT JACQUES
Hoteliêr: M. Bonneau
3, rue de l'Abbé de l'Epée, 75005 Paris, France
Tel: 01.53.73.26.00, Fax: 01.43.26 17.81
23 Rooms, Double: €195–€475*
*Breakfast not included: €13
Open: all year, Credit cards: all major
Located near the Luxembourg gardens, RER: Line B
www.karenbrown.com/relaissaintjacques.html

This is yet another Teil family hotel in Paris. As is so typical of all of their hotels, handsome woods specially crafted in the Auvergne cover the walls and beautiful fabrics dress walls, beds, chairs, and windows. With a narrow street-side frontage, the building runs deep and hallways (especially with the purple carpets) tend to be dark. Guestrooms at the back enjoy the quiet of the courtyard, and double-paned windows block the noise from rooms overlooking the boulevard. Sixth-floor guestrooms are tucked under beams—if you are lucky, number 601 will be available as it is the only room with a terrace. Another favorite is room 302 with two sets of windows and views overlooking the church. In general, rooms vary by color scheme: rich creams enhanced with Provençal blue, soft pink, a striking amber, and rich red. A few bedrooms have a futon to accommodate a third person. Breakfast, included in the price of the room, is graciously served in the privacy of your room, or a more lavish self-service buffet can be enjoyed in a charming room or back garden courtyard. This hotel is situated on the Boulevard Saint Germain, conveniently located near shops, a variety of restaurants, the heart of the Latin Quarter and a choice of metro stations that makes getting around Paris so wonderfully easy.

AU MANOIR ST. GERMAIN DES PRÉS
Hoteliêr: Teil Family
153, Boulevard Saint Germain, 75006 Paris, France
Tel: 01.42.22.21.65, Fax: 01.45.48.22.25
32 Rooms, Double: €176–€280
Open: all year, Credit cards: all major
Located across from the cathedral of St. Germain des Prés
Métro: St. Germain des Prés
www.karenbrown.com/aumanoirsaintgermaindespres.html

Large brass letters contrast with the dramatic, heavy, deep-blue doors that enclose the entrance of the Hôtel d'Aubusson. The ambiance of the d'Aubusson is handsome rather than cozy or charming—almost spartan, the entry has just a few chairs placed against the cream stone walls. Through a glass partition in the hotel reception you can glimpse clusters of mahogany tables and chairs that accommodate guests in the bar, which is attractive and also uncluttered in its decor. Venture just round the corner from the bar, however, to the room that I was drawn to. Dramatic with its high-beamed ceilings and full-length windows draped in heavy tapestry fabric, the guest lounge is warm and inviting, with seating round a large open fire—one would almost wish for a cold day to justify an afternoon before the crackling logs. On warm days breakfast and drinks are offered in the pleasant courtyard. Authenticating the name of the hotel, a beautiful Aubusson covers the stone wall above the buffet in the breakfast room. Guestrooms circle the central corridor. The rooms in the back are in the original part of the hotel dating from the 17th century. They enjoy high-beamed ceilings and the quiet of the back corridor. Rooms at the front are in a newly constructed section that circles round to create the inner corridor. Although traditional in materials and decor, these rooms enjoy more modern amenities and ceiling heights more practical for this century.

HÔTEL D'AUBUSSON
Directeur: (Gérant) M. Pascal Gimel
33, Rue Dauphine, 75006 Paris, France
Tel: 01.43.29.43.43, Fax: 01.43.29.12.62
50 Rooms, Double: €270–€425*
*Breakfast not included: €23
Open: all year, Credit cards: all major
Located just a few blocks up from the Pont Neuf, Métro: Odéon
www.karenbrown.com/aubusson.html

The Relais Christine achieves an elegant countryside ambiance at the heart of Paris' Latin Quarter. A large, flowering courtyard buffers the hotel from any noise and a beautiful wood-paneled lobby ornamented with antiques, Oriental rugs, and distinguished portraits is your introduction to this delightful hotel. A converted monastery, this is a very handsome property and the majority of guests are repeat clientele who consider it their personal pied à terre. Fully air conditioned, there are 35 double rooms whose beds easily convert to twin beds. There are two-level and single-level accommodations, all individual in their decor, ranging from attractive contemporary to a dramatic Louis XIII. A few of the bedrooms overlook a small back street, but the majority open onto the garden or front courtyard. The Relais also has sixteen beautiful suites, of which four on the ground floor open directly onto a sheltered garden. The Relais Christine is distinguished by its excellent personalized service and elegant comfort. Located in historic vaults under 13th-century natural stone, you may wish to visit their spectacular underground spa—one of the most beautiful ones I have ever seen.

RELAIS CHRISTINE
Hoteliêr: Jean-Luc Chomat
3, rue Christine
75006 Paris, France
Tel: 01.40.51.60.80, Fax: 01.40.51.60.81
51 Rooms, Double: €395–€740*
*Breakfast not included: €25
Open: all year, Credit cards: all major
Located near Pont Neuf, Métro:Odéon
Chateaux & Hotels de France
www.karenbrown.com/relaischristine.html

The Saint Germain Left Bank Hôtel has a great location on a quiet street just off the Boulevard Saint Germain within comfortable walking distance of the Île de la Cité and the heart of the district with its narrow cobbled streets, many restaurants, and shops. The Saint Germain Left Bank also offers charming accommodation and very professional service. The entry is one of the most inviting in Paris with its handsome wood paneling, tapestries, paintings, and attractive furnishings. Set with tables, a cozy room tucked off the entry serves as an appealing spot for a breakfast of croissants, rolls, juice, and coffee, which can also be enjoyed in the privacy of your room. A small elevator conveniently accesses the thirty-one rooms evenly distributed on six levels. Windows of rooms at the back open up to views of distant Nôtre Dame and the panorama improves with each floor. One of the largest rooms, 604 is termed a suite and enjoys views of church spires as does the smaller, charming 504. Attractive in their decor, often set under exposed beams, the air-conditioned rooms are comfortable, with writing desks, built-in armoires, direct-dial phones, wireless internet access, and modern bathrooms.

SAINT GERMAIN LEFT BANK HÔTEL
Owner: Teil Family
Hoteliêr: Fanny Desquesnes
9, rue de l'Ancienne Comédie, 75006 Paris, France
Tel: 01.43.54.01.70, Fax: 01.43.26.17.14
31 Rooms, Double: €185–€220
Open: all year, Credit cards: all major
Located off the Boulevard Saint Germain, Métro: Odéon
www.karenbrown.com/stgermainleftbankhotel.html

The Victoria Palace is a lovely, elegant, four-star hotel whose special details, personalized service, and excellent value set it apart from its peers. Although the hotel has 62 rooms, the owner's presence and caring touches are ever apparent. From the moment you enter from the small side street off the Rue de Rennes, just two blocks from Gare de Montparnasse and the airline coach terminal, Philippe Schmitt's style of decor is very evident. He has a weakness for reds and heavy red damask covers the wall of the bar with its gold and green chairs, very reminiscent of the 19th-century look, and faux marble, which is a replica of the original. Throughout are handsome, commissioned copies of 17th-, 18th-, and 19th-century French and English paintings and drawings. The breakfast room is inviting with a series of botanical prints on the walls and floor-to-ceiling windows opening onto an inner courtyard. A lavish buffet of juices, meats, cheeses, eggs, sausages, bacon, yogurts, and fruits is set out for breakfast. Guestrooms are classed as either deluxe rooms or junior suites. Junior suites have a little more space, with a sitting area incorporated into the layout of the room. Some of the rooms at the front of the house have bay window terraces while those at the back enjoy the quiet of the inner courtyard overlook. Hallways are wide and grand and attractively adorned. There are also two very special, two-level duplexes, with an entry off each level, a sweeping stair connecting the living room with the bedroom, and intimate furnishings. These offer guests a wonderful feeling of having their own pied-à-terre in Paris.

VICTORIA PALACE HÔTEL
Hoteliêr: Philippe Schmitt, Directeur: Philippe Venet
6, rue Blaise Desgoffe, 75006 Paris, France
Tel: 01.45.49.70.00, Fax: 01.45.49.23.75
62 Rooms, Double: €307–€595, Breakfast not included: €18
Open: all year, Credit cards: all major
Located a few blocks from Gare Montparnasse, Métro: Montparnasse or Saint Placide
www.karenbrown.com/victoriapalace.html

On a small, quiet side street of the same name, the Hôtel Duc de Saint-Simon is just steps from the Boulevard Saint Germain and the pulse of the Left Bank. Guarded by handsome gates and buffered from the street by its own shaded courtyard, this charming hotel offers a very peaceful retreat. The decor throughout is sumptuous and elegant in its use of furnishings, fabrics, paintings and fixtures. Lavish flower arrangements are the perfect complement to the refined ambiance. Guestrooms are each individual in decor and vary from comfortable standard rooms to more spacious two-room suites. There are so many rooms to call favorites, but even so, there are a few that are very special. Off the central courtyard, at the top of a separate entry and stair is a lovely room, 42, with a pretty mix of patterns used in the decor and whose French windows open onto a private terrace. In the main house, 19, an appealing suite, overlooks the lushness and quiet of the back garden. If you are fortunate to enjoy repeated trips to Paris, you, as do so many of this hotel's loyal clientele, will soon establish your personal favorite. In the basement, against the exposed rough stone of the old coal and wine cellar, you find a breakfast room as well as an intimate bar where you can enjoy a beverage or light snack.

HÔTEL DUC DE SAINT-SIMON
Hoteliêr: M. Lindquist
Directeur: Mme Siggelko
14, rue de Saint-Simon, 75007 Paris, France
Tel: 01.44.39.20.20, Fax: 01.45.48.68.25
34 Rooms, Double: €220–€375*
*Breakfast not included: €15
Open: all year, Credit cards: all major
Located off the Blvd St. Germain, just up from the Seine
Métro: Rue du Bac
www.karenbrown.com/saintsimon.html

Eighth & Ninth Arrondissements

The Eighth Arrondissement, crowned by the Arc de Triomphe, graced by the Champs Élysées, and home to the Grand and Petit Palais, is a bustle of activity and sits next to the Ninth Arrondissement with the sophisticated Opéra. There are shops, sidewalk cafés, nightclubs, cinemas, and opportunities for endless people watching. It makes for a wonderful evening's entertainment to stroll the wide boulevard: people are always about and it is safe and well lit. It is also a lovely walk down the "Champs" to the Louvre. Also located in the Eighth is the Gare Saint Lazare, first built in 1837 as the main link between Paris and St. Germain en Laye. Trains from Gare Saint Lazare travel to Normandy and Great Britain via Dieppe.

Arc de Triomphe

The Teil family has moved to a different quarter of Paris—the very exclusive residential district of the Eighth Arrondissement. From this location it is an easy walk to the Champs Élysées or across the Seine to the Eiffel Tower. When making extensive renovations to their new property, they incorporated their now almost-trademark decor of beautiful woods from the Auvergne and gorgeous fabrics. The hotel boasts 34 rooms and suites that all benefit from soundproofing and air conditioning. The suites comfortably accommodate a family of four. The rooms are truly elegant and rival in comfort, luxury, and decor some of Paris' finest hotels. In addition to the guestrooms, public areas also offer a wonderful retreat. The lounge and library are inviting and the enclosed winter garden, set under the verandah, is intimate and a wonderful place to settle for a drink. I teased Monsieur Teil that he had planned to stop expanding with the opening of his last hotel, but he claims he needs a business for his lovely daughter, Laurence, who has now graduated from the prestigious school at Lausanne. Since his son is also about to graduate, I doubt this will be the last of the Teil hotel dynasty!

HÔTEL CHAMBIGES
Hoteliêr: Teil Family
8, rue Chambiges, 75008 Paris, France
Tel: 01.44.31.83.83, Fax: 01.40.70.95.51
34 Rooms, Double: €195–€330, 1 apartment: €427
Open: all year, Credit cards: all major
Located a few blocks from Avenue George V
Métro: Alma-Marceau
www.karenbrown.com/chambiges.html

Small, traditional, and intimate, the San Regis was once a fashionable townhouse. With exclusive boutiques and embassies as its sophisticated neighbors, the hotel maintains an air of simple yet authentic elegance. It is easy to pass this marvelous hotel by: a small sign is the only thing that advertises its presence. Beyond the small foyer you find a comfortable, ornately decorated lounge area and small dining room where you can enjoy a quiet drink and/or lunch and dinner. The bedrooms are large and handsomely furnished, and the bathrooms are very modern and thoughtfully stocked. Huge double doors buffer sounds from other rooms. The rooms that front the Rue Jean-Goujon are favored with a view across to the tip of the imposing Eiffel Tower, but courtyard rooms are sheltered from street noise. Every time I visit the San Regis I am more impressed than ever. The attention to detail is incredible and there is an obvious commitment to renovate guestroom decor on a alternating cycle. The hotel always appears as if it had just opened, with everything beautiful, perfect, and polished. But the hotel's greatest pride, and what instills the loyalty of its returning guests, is its staff—the team dedicated to making your stay incredible. It is easy to understand why the San Regis is a favorite of so many who would prefer to keep it their secret hideaway.

HÔTEL SAN REGIS
Hoteliêr: Maurice Georges
12, Rue Jean-Goujon, 75008 Paris, France
Tel: 01.44.95.16.16, Fax: 01.45.61.05.48
44 Rooms, Double: €425–€1,025*
*Breakfast not included: €22
Open: all year, Credit cards: all major
Located between the Seine & Champs Élysées
Métro: Franklin Roosevelt & Champs-Élysées Clémenceau
www.karenbrown.com/hotelsanregis.html

Tenth, Twelfth, Thirteenth & Fifteeth Arrondissements

If you plan to arrive in or depart from Paris by train, you will find yourself in one of these four arrondissements (with the exception of the Gare Saint Lazare in the eighth), which are located near the city's core. Train tracks do not cross the River Seine, so the train station you use will be determined by whether your outlying destination/point of origin is to the north, east, south, or west. Trains to eastern France, Germany, Switzerland, and Austria leave from the Gare de l'Est, whose original building, now termed the Western Wing, dates to 1850, in the Tenth Arrondissement. Also in the Tenth, the Gare du Nord was first built in 1864 and then expanded and rebuilt three more times. The Gare du Nord, as its name implies, services destinations to the north: Belgium, Holland, Northern Germany, and Scandinavia. In the Twelfth, trains from the Gare de Lyon travel to southern France, the Alps, Switzerland, Italy, and Greece. The Gare de Lyon was built to coincide with the Universal Exhibition of 1900 and recent modernizations allow it to service the pride of the French rail network, the TGV (Train à Grande Vitesse). A destination in its own right and considered an historical monument, Le Train Bleu is a wonderful restaurant within the station. Opened in 1901, with a Belle Époque interior, it boasts 40 paintings by 30 artists that depict city destinations. In the Thirteenth, trains from the Gare d'Austerlitz travel to points in the southwest: the southwest of France, Spain, and Portugal. This station was named for the famous battle won by Napoléon in Austria in 1805 against Austro-Russian armies. The Gare Montparnasse, in the Fifteenth, is one of the oldest stations, dating to 1840, and was completely rebuilt after World War II. It services Brittany, western France, and the TGV-Atlantique.

Sixteenth Arrondissement

The Sixteenth Arrondissement is Paris's elite residential district. It is a quiet area, characterized by stately, elegant apartment buildings, lovely shopping streets, and exclusive corner markets. The Rue de la Pompe and the Avenue Victor Hugo are two well-known avenues lined with beautiful and expensive shops. Also tucked away here is the Musée Marmottan, a personal favorite, with one of the most magnificent collections of Impressionist art housed in what was formerly a hunting lodge and then the private home of the Marmottans. In the Musée Marmottan one can view works of Degas, Manet, and Renoir and the world's largest collection of Monet. The Sixteenth Arrondissement is bordered on one side by the Bois de Boulogne, a scenic park where people walk, exercise their dogs, cycle, run, play soccer, and escape the frenzy of the city.

Eighteenth Arrondissement

This neighborhood of Paris, more usually and colloquially known as **Montmartre** rather than the Eighteenth Arrondissement, is an enchanting, artistic district. Climb the narrow streets and mount the steps to the **Sacré Coeur**, begun in 1875 under the genius of the architect Abadie who tragecally died before seeing its completion in 1914. The interior of the church contains one of the world's largest mosaics, depicting Christ with outstretched arms. It is worth the climb to the top of the dome from where you get a panoramic view of the city.

Countryside Places to Stay

Aïnhoa is justifiably considered one of Basque's most beautiful villages. The Hôtel Ithurria, once a country farm, offers unique tradition, charm, and character and is owned by a family who has perfected its welcome over three generations. The hotel has a first-class regional restaurant and the decor of the gorgeous dining room incorporates all that is cozy and welcoming from its original construction: heavy old beams, a large open fireplace, wonderful old tiled floors. Soft-colored patterned drapes hang at the paned windows and French doors, and tables are dressed with pretty linens and silver. A grandfather clock and lovely accent antiques complete a perfect picture. In the original home there are eight pretty, nicely appointed bedrooms with modern reproduction furnishings and renovated bathrooms. Room 4 is especially nice as it looks over the front garden and up to the mountains. At the back, built in the style of an old Basque farmhouse, is a wing of new rooms, all very similar in look to those in the main house but with the enhancement of air conditioning. Behind the inn stretches a pretty garden and beyond that you come to a lovely large pool and accompanying pool house with fitness room and sauna. *Directions:* From Biarritz take the D932 southeast 14 km to the outskirts of Cambo les Bains then turn southwest towards Esplette on the D918. After about 4 km take the left fork and drive along the D20 for about 5.5 km to Aïnhoa.

HÔTEL ITHURRIA
Hoteliêr: Isabal Family
Directeur: Stephane Isabal
64250 Aïnhoa, France
Tel: 05.59.29.92.11, Fax: 05.59.29.81.28
27 Rooms, Double: €105–€145*
*Breakfast not included: €10
Open: Easter to Nov 2, Credit cards: AX, VS
Châteaux & Hotels de France
Region: Basque, Michelin Map: 525
www.karenbrown.com/ithurria.html

Aix is an intriguing city to explore. The cobbled streets of the old quarter are lovely to wander around and at night the illuminated tree-lined Cours Mirabeau is enchanting—reminiscent of Paris with its many sidewalk cafés. It is just a 15-minute walk from the old quarter to the attractive Hôtel le Pigonnet, run very professionally by the Swellen family. A tree-lined road leads you away from the noise and traffic of the city center to this hotel. Set in its own 2-acre garden, the Hôtel le Pigonnet is surrounded by an abundance of flowers and towering ancient chestnut trees. It was from this garden that Paul Cézanne painted the Mountain of Sainte Victoire. The hotel also has a lovely large pool, most inviting on a hot summer day in Provence. Inside are cozy sitting rooms and a large airy restaurant whose tables are set on the back patio on balmy evenings to overlook the lush expanse of garden. The hotel's bedrooms, all with private bathroom, vary dramatically from elegant suites to attractive, standard hotel rooms. Le Pigonnet is not a country inn, but a lovely hotel with first-class accommodation and service that maintains a country ambiance and setting within the city of Aix en Provence. *Directions:* Take the No. 30, Pont de l'Arc, exit off the autoroute and turn north in the direction of the center of town. At the third light turn left—Le Pigonnet is 50 meters on the left.

HÔTEL LE PIGONNET
Hoteliêr: Swellen Family
5, Avenue du Pigonnet
13090 Aix en Provence, France
Tel: 04.42.59.02.90, Fax: 04.42.59.47.77
50 Rooms, Double: €180–€550*
*Breakfast not included: €15–€25
Open: all year, Credit cards: all major
Region: Provence, Michelin Map: 528
www.karenbrown.com/hotellepigonnet.html

This lovely little hotel is a gem at the heart of the old quarter of Aix, on the south side of Cours Mirabeau. Under new ownership, the hotel has a little entry salon, stairway, and the 13 small but comfortable guestrooms are tastefully decorated with the warm flavor and style of Provence. Walls are painted in a wash of muted colors, fabrics are reminiscent of Pierre Deux, simple furnishings are attractive with their hand-painted motifs, and there are lovely accents such as handsome prints and a wonderful terra-cotta pot filled with dried flowers. An old stairwell with a skylight casting a wealth of light in the hotel winds up from the reception to the various floors—be forewarned that the hotel does not have an elevator. The top-floor rooms are worth the climb as they are set under the old beams which lend a bit more character. All guestrooms have en suite bathrooms and are air conditioned. These rooms are definitely intimate in size—if you have lots of luggage or prefer spacious accommodation, while the price is definitely tempting, this hotel might not fit your needs. Parking is always difficult in Aix. If you are fortunate enough to find a place on one of the side streets, grab it and then the hotel can direct you to one of the long-term parking areas nearby. Be sure to lock your car and remove all belongings. *Directions:* Follow signs to city center, then travel along the Cours Mirabeau, turn right on Rue du 4 Septembre to Rue Roux Alphéran.

HÔTEL DES QUATRE DAUPHINS
Hoteliêr: Monsieur Lafont
54, Rue Roux Alphéran
13100 Aix en Provence, France
Tel: 04.42.38.16.39, Fax: 04.42.38.60.19
13 Rooms, Double: €65–€85*
*Breakfast not included: €9
Open: all year, Credit cards: MC, VS
Region: Provence, Michelin Map: 528
www.karenbrown.com/dauphins.html

This lovely property set on a hillside shaded by a clustering of trees is imbued with the air of an elegant home rather than a commercial hotel. The staff are all are eager to serve with a graciousness and warmth that reflect the great pride they take in their participation. The decor of this peach-washed building can only be described in superlatives as elegant, rich, beautiful, and yet surprisingly comfortable and welcoming. Sitting areas, both inside or outside on a garden terrace under the shade of trees or by the pool, are inviting and intimate. Guestrooms, all with private bathrooms, are found either in the original building, in newly constructed wings off the reception, or in little villas. Luxurious in size and appointments, no two rooms are decorated alike—wallpapers and fabrics range from a wonderful blend of cream and reds in an array of plaids, checks, and patterns to a more dramatic finish in splashes of golds and browns. Most rooms have either a shade-covered terrace or expanse of balcony and all enjoy the quiet of the setting. Breakfast is a grand affair under the personal supervision and flourish of Michel, who creates a mood of great fun. A motto popular with the staff boasts there are never problems, only solutions. *Directions:* Follow signs to city center and then to the Villa Gallici, traveling the road that circles the heart of Aix. At the Place Bellegarde, turn north on the Avenue Jules Isaac then left on Avenue de la Violette.

VILLA GALLICI
Hoteliêrs: Daniel Jouve, Gil Dez & Charles Montemarc
Avenue de la Violette
13100 Aix en Provence, France
Tel: 04.42.23.29.23, Fax: 04.42.96.30.45
22 Rooms, Double: €300–€660*
*Breakfast not included: €22 or €28
Meals for guests only, Closed: Jan
Credit cards: all major, Relais & Châteaux
Region: Provence, Michelin Map: 528
www.karenbrown.com/villagallici.html

Le Manoir les Minimes is a lovely 18th-century manor built on the site of a 13th-century convent, convenient to the wonderful town of Amboise with its intriguing streets and shops. The hotel has a spectacular location in the shadow of the château right on the river's edge, surrounded by acres of gardens and embraced by an old stone wall. Furnishings are elegant, with antiques and attractive color schemes. The salon is spacious and formal in a wash of warm yellow, while the dining room is light and pretty (you can opt to eat in the garden when weather permits). The hotel offers eleven guestrooms in the main building and four in the facing annex. All the rooms have large beds that can convert to twins. A first-floor room is easily accessed by those who have difficulty with stairs and is also the one truly handicapped-fitted room. At the top of the first stairway is the most spectacular room (10), a corner suite decorated in beiges and creams with magnificent views both of the flowing river and up to the crowning château. I also adored the end corner suite (14) decorated in handsome blues. There are several superior rooms on the second floor, which have glimpses of the Loire and are equipped with every modern convenience, while on the third floor are some great-value rooms. The rooms in the annex are spacious and very handsome in their decor. *Directions:* Located on the riverbank on the south side of the bridge in the shadow of the castle.

LE MANOIR LES MINIMES
Hoteliêrs: Patrice Longet & Eric Deforges
34, Quai Charles Guinot
37400 Amboise, France
Tel: 02.47.30.40.40, Fax: 02.47.30.40.77
15 Rooms, Double: €95–€240*
*Breakfast not included: €11.50– €16
Open: all year, Credit cards: all major
Region: Loire Valley, Michelin Map: 519
www.karenbrown.com/lesminimes.html

Located on the outskirts of Les Andelys, the Hôtel de la Chaîne d'Or looks up to the castle ruins and backs onto the Seine. Just an hour or so to the north of Paris, Les Andelys is convenient to Charles de Gaulle airport and Roissy and just a few kilometers from Giverny, Monet's home: a visit to Monet's home and the gardens that inspired his genius will prove a highlight of your trip. The hotel is managed by Sylvia and Gérard Millet who take pride in welcoming guests and oversee the restaurant. Of the ten bedrooms, six (1, 3, 5, 7, 10 and 11) overlook the river and enjoy views of the Seine and the constant, entertaining parade of barges. Room 10 is a spacious king-bedded room and room 1 is set with twins—both have water views. I especially like room 7, an end room, overlooking the water traffic, cozy in its soft decor of pink. The restaurant windows look over the Seine and across to a small island with an abandoned manor. It is an intimate place for lunch or dinner: the service is relaxed and comfortable and the menu offers an appealing selection of items. The Millets ask that overnight guests dine at the hotel. *Directions:* Take the D313 out of Vernon, a very scenic route, 26 km northwest to Les Andelys. La Chaîne d'Or is located in the old town, on the river's edge.

HÔTEL DE LA CHAÎNE D'OR
Hoteliêrs: Sylvia & Gérard Millet
27, Rue Grande, 27700 Andelys (Les), France
Tel: 02.32.54.00.31, Fax: 02.32.54.05.68
10 Rooms, Double: €75–€129*
*Breakfast not included: €12
Restaurant: closed Sun night & Mon & Tue lunch
Closed: Jan, Credit cards: all major
Region: Normandy, Michelin Map: 513
www.karenbrown.com/chaine.html

Those who know me, know I love to boast a truly new discovery! Aragon is a relatively undiscovered, medieval village that I'm certain will eventually be recognized as one of France's most beautiful. At the top of the cobbled streets is a delightful inn that opened just two months prior to our visit. The pastel-washed, newly constructed building with wrought-iron gates compliments the regional hillside village. The décor inside is Mediterranean with cheerful colors of yellows, blues, oranges, and greens. Terracotta tiles pattern the floors. The building steps down the hillside at the back, so the entry is actually on the top level, accessed from the parking area. Inside the entrance, one steps down into a cheerful dining room exposed on all sides by windows framing the surrounding hillsides. Also accessed from the parking area, with separate entrances, are two guestrooms. The remaining six are located on the lower level, accessed by an interior, central stairway. All the guestrooms are named for plants and flowers of the region and are reflected in the interiors with special touches, such as artwork matching the room's title (i.e., Poppy, Sunflower, Iris) and hand-painted headboards (by an aunt). This is a family affair. Mme. Galibert proudly showed us around. Her son is the chef. He lives here with his wife and their baby. *Directions:* From Carcassonne, travel D118 north 5 km to Villegailhenc, then the D935 northwest to Aragon.

LA BERGERIE
Owner: Fabien Galibert
Allée Pech Marie
11600 Aragon, France
Tel: 04.68.26.10.65, Fax: 04.68.77.02.23
8 Rooms, Double: €60–€90*
*Breakfast not included: €7
Closed: Jan 17 to Feb 9, Credit cards: MC, VS
Region: Languedoc, Michelin Map: 526
www.karenbrown.com/bergerie.html

With the River Rhône running through it, Arles is a beautiful city, rich with Roman and medieval monuments. Just 50 kilometers from the sea, Arles has long guarded a strategic location. It is also convenient to all of Provence and an ideal base for exploring the region. The Hôtel d'Arlatan is tucked away on a small street in the center of town near the Place du Forum, within easy walking distance of all the city's major sights. In the 12th, 15th, and 17th centuries the Hôtel d'Arlatan belonged to the Counts of Arlatan de Beaumont and served as their private home. It is now the pride of Monsieur and Madame Yves Desjardin who offer an ideal retreat with charming accommodation and service. This is a quaint hotel, ornamented with antiques and pretty fabrics. Many of the bedrooms look onto a quiet inner courtyard or garden or across the tiled rooftops of Arles. No two guestrooms are alike, each with its own special charm, perhaps a sheltered patio, a lovely old fireplace, a private deck; each unique trait making a selection all the more difficult. Although there is no restaurant, a delightful breakfast can be enjoyed on the patio or in the inviting salon with a portion of its floor covered by glass to expose the excavated aqueduct. *Directions:* Arles is 36 km south of Avignon off the N570. At Place Lamartin enter the ramparts on Rue Septembre, which becomes Rue du Sauvage.

HÔTEL D'ARLATAN
Hoteliêrs: M & Mme Yves Desjardin
26, Rue du Sauvage, 13631 Arles, France
Tel: 04.90.93.56.66, Fax: 04.90.49.68.45
48 Rooms, Double: €85–€243*
*Breakfast not included: €12
Open: all year, Credit cards: all major
Châteaux & Hotels de France
Region: Provence, Michelin Maps: 524, 528
www.karenbrown.com/hoteldarlatan.html

The Grand Hôtel Nord-Pinus has held court on the Place du Forum for generations. It is located at the heart of Arles and has been the chosen destination of many, most colorfully the grand matadors, bullfighters en route from Paris or Spain. With a decor of terra-cotta tiles, wrought iron, and splashes of color in bountiful flower arrangements, the Nord-Pinus has served as home to many artists and writers as well. The inviting and attractive restaurant, just off the entry, is a convenient place to dine on regional specialties. Guestrooms all have private bathrooms and vary from quite spacious to comfortable, with a decor of art deco to more traditional. Furnishings seem a bit worn, but somehow the worn look lends to the feeling of nostalgia and times past and is therefore forgiven. Choice rooms are number 4, a wonderful corner room that overlooks the plaza, and number 32, a suite, which is more modern in decor and a proven favorite of artists and photographers as it enjoys an expanse of window giving lots of light and views over the tiled rooftops of Arles. Smaller rooms such as number 7 are more reasonably priced, also nice in size, and almost always matched with a large bathroom. Breakfast is served behind arched columns on the first-floor landing or in the guestrooms. *Directions:* Travel the road that circles the heart of Arles and then follow signs to the hotel.

GRAND HÔTEL NORD-PINUS
Hoteliêr: Anne Igou
Place du Forum, 13200 Arles, France
Tel: 04.90.93.44.44, Fax: 04.90.93.34.00
25 Rooms, Double: €145–€285*
Apartment: €450
*Breakfast not included: €14 or €20
Open: all year, Credit cards: all major
Region: Provence, Michelin Maps: 524, 528
www.karenbrown.com/grandhotel.html

In the middle of the 17th century a Carmelite convent was erected in Arles by Mother Madeleine Saint Joseph. It was a residence for nuns until 1770 when the order was expelled in the midst of the French Revolution. The convent then became state property until it was purchased and transformed into a hotel in 1929. In this beautiful old convent, the Hôtel Jules César has earned a rating of four stars under the directorship of Monsieur Michel Albagnac. The hotel is situated next to and shares a courtyard with the Chapelle de la Charité, which belongs to the hotel and also dates from the 17th century. The restaurant, Lou Marquès, is air conditioned and lovely, known for its classic and Provençal cooking. Little tables and chairs are set in the cloister where breakfast and light, quick lunches are served in the winter, and on the terrace in summer. All bedrooms are air conditioned and spacious: room 72, with windows opening onto the garden, is an elegant, large room with two double beds. The pool is a welcome addition for those hot summer days in this region and now neighbors a beautiful Provençal garden. *Directions:* Arles is located 36 km south of Avignon traveling on the N570. The Jules César is on Boulevard des Lices, a main artery that borders the ramparts on the south.

HÔTEL JULES CÉSAR
Hoteliêr: Michel Albagnac
Boulevard des Lices, BP 116
13631 Arles, France
Tel: 04.90.52.52.52, Fax: 04.90.52.52.53
58 Rooms, Double: €158–€385*
*Breakfast not included: €20
Open: Dec 23 to beg-Nov, Credit cards: all major
Relais & Châteaux
Region: Provence, Michelin Maps: 524, 528
www.karenbrown.com/hoteljulescesar.html

I wanted to abort my travels, unpack bags, and settle in at the beautiful Château de Vault de Lugny. I arrived on a warm spring afternoon and the obvious contentment of guests who were relaxing at tables on the front lawn was enviable. Voices were subdued and did not break the lovely quiet of the setting—perhaps because the individual desires of each guest were well tended to. It was early afternoon, yet I noticed one guest lounging over a late breakfast, a few guests sleeping with books neglected on their laps, and a foursome playing a game of cards under the shade of a large central tree. The Château de Vault de Lugny is a handsome cream-stone building with white shuttered windows and weathered-tile roof secluded by a high wall, moat, and tall gates. There are 12 bedrooms in the château, all with lovely modern bathrooms. Lavish and regal in their decor, the larger rooms are very popular. The smaller standard rooms are also charming and a better value. Snacks are available at any hour, table d'hôte dinners are served at a handsome trestle table set before a massive open fireplace and a more traditional dining experience is also an option. An added bonus for guests is the chance to ride in a hot-air balloon. *Directions:* Traveling the A6 between Paris and Beaune, take the Avallon exit and follow the direction of Vézelay west to Pontaubert, then turn right after the church. The château is on the right, 550 meters from the village.

CHÂTEAU DE VAULT DE LUGNY
Hoteliêr: Elisabeth Matherat-Audan
11, Rue du Château, Pontaubert
89200 Avallon, France
Tel: 03.86.34.07.86, Fax: 03.86.34.16.36
14 Rooms, Double: €160–€480*
*Breakfast not included: €10, Restaurant: closed Wed
Open: mid-Apr to mid-Nov, Credit cards: all major
Châteaux & Hotels de France
Region: Burgundy, Michelin Map: 519
www.karenbrown.com/vaultdelugny.html

Avallon is a lovely town convenient to Paris and also the starting point for a very picturesque drive through the Cousin Valley. At the heart of this old market town, just off the Place Vauban, is a delightful old posting lodge with a soft-pink façade dressed with flags that has welcomed guests since 1701—previously by horse-drawn carriage and now by car. From an arched entryway the hotel runs down two sides of the length of a cobbled courtyard. Guestrooms at the front of the building above the reception area are attractive, modern yet traditional in decor, and conveniently reached by elevator. Those on the third floor enjoy the charm of exposed old beams. Running the length of the cobbled courtyard are some suites and apartments with their own private entries. The elegant restaurant, just off the entry, is long and narrow and again runs the length of the courtyard. This is a popular dining spot with locals as well as travelers. Breakfast can be delivered to the privacy of your bedroom or you can enjoy it in the intimate dining room whose tables look out to the courtyard where tables are also set in warm weather. At the back you find a few gardens as well as a parking area. If staying in a town with the convenience and interest of regional shops appeals to you, you will enjoy the comfort and luxury of La Poste—and the price is a good value. *Directions:* Exit the A6 and travel just 8 km west on the N6 to Avallon. The hotel is at the center of town.

HOSTELLERIE DE LA POSTE
Hoteliêr: Patrick Lefort, Directeur: Alain Gand
13, Place Vauban, 89200 Avallon, France
Tel: 03.86.34.16.16, Fax: 03.86.34.19.19
30 Rooms, Double: €114–€167*
*Breakfast not included: €11–€12,50
Restaurant: closed Sun evenings & Mon
Open: Mar to Nov 15, Credit cards: all major
Châteaux & Hotels de France
Region: Burgundy, Michelin Map: 519
www.karenbrown.com/delaposte.html

Hôtel d'Europe is a classically beautiful 16th-century mansion, formerly the home of the Marquis of Gravezon. The mansion was converted into a hotel in 1799 as it is within walking distance of the River Rhône, a prime location to attract travelers who in that period voyaged predominantly by boat. The hotel has been completely modernized using handsome furnishings that suit the mood and complement this grand home. The walls of the marble entry hall, once an open courtyard, and the walls of the upper levels are now hung with magnificent tapestries. The bedrooms, all different in character and size, are furnished in traditional pieces and antiques. Many of the rooms are quite spacious and comfortable for extended stays. Although within the city walls of Avignon, many of the rooms overlook the hotel's courtyard and afford a quiet night's rest. You can dine in elegant formality in the hotel's fine restaurant, La Vieille Fontaine, or under the trees in the courtyard on balmy Provençal nights. *Directions:* From the A7 take the Avignon Nord exit towards Avignon Centre Ville. Follow the Rhône to the ramparts. On the right, under the bridge of Avignon follow signs to Hotel d'Europe and the entrance of Porte de l'Oulle. Just inside the ramparts, the Place Crillon is on the left.

HÔTEL D'EUROPE
Hoteliêr: Christine Daire-Fabri
Directeur: Hendrick Daudeij
12, Place Crillon, 84000 Avignon, France
Tel: 04.90.14.76.76, Fax: 04.90.14.76.71
45 Rooms, Double: €145–€750*
*Breakfast not included: €23
Open: all year, Credit cards: all major
Region: Provence, Michelin Maps: 524, 528
www.karenbrown.com/hoteldeurope.html

La Mirande dates from the 14th century with various additions made to it in the 15th, 17th, and 18th centuries. It was the residence of Cardinal Armand de Pellegrue, nephew of Pope Clement V, and later a private residence for the mayor of Avignon. The Stein family came from Germany, fell in love with the property, and converted it to a luxury hotel with a desire to improve upon the four-star hotels they had experienced in their travels. They have exceeded their goals and created a superlative property. Every luxurious detail has been well thought out and implemented, seemingly without consideration of cost—only consideration of the guests and their comfort. A multitude of public rooms and the 20 guestrooms are beautifully appointed with rich fabrics and gorgeous antiques. The dining room has an absolutely stunning 15th-century French ceiling and needlepoint carpet, an Aubusson tapestry draping an entire wall, and is warmed by a large open fireplace in winter months. Dinner is served on the terrace patio on balmy summer nights. Overlooking the palace walls, La Mirande is spacious and luxurious, an oasis for its guests. It has even been said that, had the Pope ended up at La Mirande instead of across the street, he might never have returned to Rome. *Directions:* Exit off A7 at Avignon Nord, take the gate Porte de la Ligne into the walled city, and follow signs to La Mirande.

LA MIRANDE
Hoteliêr: Achim Stein
4, Place de la Mirande
84000 Avignon, France
Tel: 04.90.14.20.20, Fax: 04.90.86.26.85
20 Rooms, Double: €295–€475*
*Breakfast not included: €24
Open: all year, Credit cards: all major
Châteaux & Hotels de France
Region: Provence, Michelin Maps: 524, 528
www.karenbrown.com/lamirande.html

The cobblestoned town of Barbizon has attracted artists for many years, and the 19th-century timbered Hôtellerie du Bas-Bréau has had its share of famous guests. Robert Louis Stevenson wrote in "Forest Notes" about this hotel and it is often called "Stevenson's House." Famous painters who treasured this corner of the Forest of Fontainebleau include Millet, Corot, Sisley, and Monet. Some accommodations are in the main timbered house, but most are in a two-story building in the back garden. Each room is different in decor and has a bath. The restaurant is superb, drawing dinner guests from as far away as Paris. With unusually attractive flower arrangements on each table, the atmosphere of the dining room is elegant and romantic. Political leaders from Italy, Germany, Great Britain, Ireland, Greece, Luxembourg, Denmark, and the Netherlands selected the hotel as a conference location—you will understand their choice when you dine at Hôtellerie du Bas-Bréau where the menu features homegrown vegetables and herbs and specialties such as wild boar. The house wine list is incredible. *Directions:* From Paris take A6 south in the direction of Fontainebleau and exit at Barbizon. From the south on A6, exit at Fontainebleau. At the obelisk in Fontainebleau take the N7 in the direction of Paris and travel 8 km to Barbizon.

HÔTELLERIE DU BAS-BRÉAU
Hoteliêrs: Mme & M Jean Pierre Fava
Directeur: Tino Malchiodi
22, Rue Grande, 77630 Barbizon, France
Tel: 01.60.66.40.05, Fax: 01.60.69.22.89
12 Rooms, Double: €140–€502*
*Breakfast not included: €20
Open: all year, Credit cards: AX
Relais & Châteaux
Region: Île de France, Michelin Map: 513
www.karenbrown.com/dubasbreau.html

La Baule, a small town on the southern coast of Brittany, is popular for its wide stretch of sandy beach and for its chic casino. Most hotels in La Baule have been built in recent years to accommodate the many people who come here for their summer holidays. Happily, for those who prefer the nostalgic charm of yesteryear, the Castel Marie Louise not only has a prime position across from the beach, but also exudes charm and grandeur. As you look at the immense stone house with its steeply pitched roof and fantasy of perky gables and turreted towers, you assume it must have been built as a fancy hotel but, in fact—hard as it is to believe—this masterpiece was originally built as a private home. The hotel sits majestically in expansive, parklike grounds, with a velvety lawn sweeping down to the road and beyond to the promenade by the sea. Inside there is a formal, old-world ambiance. Guestrooms are all tastefully decorated and some have views out over the gardens to the water. The food, featuring regional specialties, is excellent and is served in a cheerful, sunny dining room with large windows, though in balmy weather many guests choose to eat outside overlooking the manicured English garden. For those who like to gamble, the casino is just a short walk down the road. *Directions:* Coming from Nantes on the N171, take the exit toward La Baule Ouest. The hotel is located in the center of town, facing the sea, near the casino.

CASTEL MARIE LOUISE
Hoteliêr: Arnaud Barnvens
1, Avenue Andrieu, 44500 Baule (La), France
Tel: 02.40.11.48.38, Fax: 02.40.11.48.35
31 Rooms, Double: €157–€540*
*Breakfast not included: €18
Restaurant: closed high season
Closed: mid-Nov to mid-Dec, Credit cards: all major
Relais & Châteaux
Region: Brittany, Michelin Map: 517
www.karenbrown.com/louise.html

This inn nestled at the base of the village of Les Baux de Provence occupies a quiet location among olive trees surrounded by the chalky, white-rock hillsides dotted with the green shrubbery of Provence. The soft sandstone color of its exterior, dressed with soft green shutters, white trim, and a rust tile roof, was artfully selected to blend rather than contrast with the warmth of its setting. The entry of the hotel is light and spacious, decorated with a mix of modern pieces and contemporary fabrics. Beams contrast with whitewashed walls and the floor is of terra-cotta tile. The lovely bedrooms are decorated with rustic oak furniture and dressed with Provençal prints and light colors. Some of the rooms have lovely hand-painted furniture. Bathrooms are spotless and modern and each room is equipped with color satellite TV, safe, mini-bar, and air conditioning. A few guestrooms open onto garden terraces with their own garden entry and a lovely suite enjoys its own private garden and terrace, and looks out to the olive trees. The pool with Jacuzzi offers a peaceful oasis, surrounded by a lush green lawn, and it is here that grilled meats and Provençal salads are served at lunchtime. After a day of sightseeing, you can relax on a comfortable lounger, looking out to the hills of Provence. We continue to receive only positive feedback from our readers who love this charming hotel. *Directions:* The entrance to Mas de l'Oulivie is located just off the D27.

※ ⚞ 💳 ☎ 🏠 ⅄ P 🍴 ⏝ ⋌ 🏛 ⚅ ☎ 🏃 👫 🐎 🍇

MAS DE L'OULIVIE
Hoteliêrs: Mme & M Emmanuel Achard
13520 Baux de Provence (Les), France
Tel: 04.90.54.35.78, Fax: 04.90.54.44.31
25 Rooms, Double: €120–€245*
2 apartments: €380–€410
*Breakfast not included: €11
Open: mid-Mar to mid-Nov, Credit cards: all major
Châteaux & Hotels de France
Region: Provence, Michelin Maps: 524, 528
www.karenbrown.com/masdeloulivie.html

Bayeux is renowned for being the home of the Bayeux Tapestry and it is also one of France's most picturesque towns. I include the Hôtel d'Argouges as Bayeux is a wonderful town to spend the night in and the d'Argouges is conveniently located on one of its main squares, sheltered behind tall gates. A large courtyard and stone, semi-circular staircase, dressed with an abundance of flowers, lead to the front entry of the hotel. French doors in the gracious salon-library open onto the quiet back garden and terrace. Looking out over the garden or front courtyard, many of the bedrooms have exposed beams, fabric-covered walls, and comfortable furniture as well as private shower or bath and phones. There are four suites with a small extra room for children and 27 is a dramatic, ground floor suite converted from what was the previous owner's private accommodation. Additional bedrooms are found in an adjacent home. Breakfast can be enjoyed in the privacy of your room, in the intimate breakfast salon, or on the back garden terrace overlooking the brightly colored flowers. A convenient haven for travelers visiting Bayeux, the Hôtel d'Argouges offers good value in lovely surroundings plus gracious hosts, Pierrette and Yves, who take great pride in their métier and are commited to making the property even more beautiful than ever. *Directions:* From Paris follow directions to Centre Ville and you will find yourself on Rue Saint Patrice.

HÔTEL D'ARGOUGES
Hoteliêrs: Pierrette & Yves Ropartz
21, Rue Saint Patrice, 14400 Bayeux, France
Tel: 02.31.92.88.86, Fax: 02.31.92.69.16
28 Rooms, Double: €82–€100*
*Breakfast not included: €8
Open: all year, Credit cards: all major
Region: Normandy, Michelin Map: 512
www.karenbrown.com/hoteldargouges.html

The Château de Sully affords the traveler a convenient base from which to explore Normandy. Just to the north of Bayeux at the end of a tree-lined drive, this beautiful 18th-century château is set on an expanse of green lawn with gorgeous gardens at the back—an elegant hotel. The dining room is lovely, with a color scheme of blues and beiges from table linens to drapes to china, and has an enclosed outdoor terrace overlooking the garden. Public rooms run the length of the château at the back and also enjoy beautiful garden views. The games room with its billiard table is a social place to settle, the bar with its intimate clustering of tables is most attractive, and the grand sitting room is very pretty. Of the 22 guestrooms 13 are found in the main château and the rest in the neighboring Petite Manoir. Although classification of rooms varies from standard to suite, the difference is not in the elegance, the comfort, or style of furnishings but rather in the size of room and location. There is only one suite, number 17, a romantic room draped in a handsome fabric of reds and greens. The annex rooms, which share the building with the fitness room and indoor pool, are more modern and a bit larger and two on the garden level enjoy their own terrace. *Directions:* Leave Bayeux on the D6 in the direction of Port en Bessin. The Château is just a few kilometers north of the city limits on the east side.

CHÂTEAU DE SULLY
Hoteliêrs: Inka & Antoine Brault
Route de Port en Bessin, Sully, 14400 Bayeux, France
Tel: 02.31.22.29.48, Fax: 02.31.22.64.77
22 Rooms, Double: €110–€190*
*Breakfast not included: €11.5
Restaurant: closed for lunch on Mon, Tues, Wed & Sat
Open: Mar to Nov, Credit cards: all major
Châteaux & Hotels de France
Region: Normandy, Michelin Map: 512
www.karenbrown.com/sully.html

Renovated from a wine-merchant's house, La Tonnellerie is located on a quiet street near the church in the country village of Tavers. Just 3 kilometers from the medieval city of Beaugency and only an hour-and-a-half's drive from Paris by the autoroute, the Hostellerie de la Tonnellerie is an ideal starting point for visiting the châteaux of the Loire Valley. The bedrooms and suites are invitingly decorated and each has its own immaculate bathroom. Two wings of the building border a central courtyard ablaze with flowers, next to the swimming pool. On the first floor of one wing La Tonnellerie's restaurant features regional specialties as well as nouvelle cuisine. The atmosphere of this lovely restored home, which a century ago housed coopers making barrels for wine merchants, is enhanced by antiques, floral arrangements, lovely watercolors, and decorative wallpapers. The decor is warm and inviting and the Pouey family's welcome very gracious. *Directions:* Exit from the A10 at Meung/Beaugency, 28 km southwest of Orléans. The hotel is 3 km southwest of Beaugency on the RN152 going towards Blois.

HOSTELLERIE DE LA TONNELLERIE
Hoteliêrs: Marie-Christine & Alain Pouey
12, Rue des Eaux-Bleues
Beaugency, 45190 Tavers, France
Tel: 02.38.44.68.15, Fax: 02.38.44.10.01
20 Rooms, Double: €150–€232
Closed: Dec 24 to Feb 28, Credit cards: all major
Châteaux & Hotels de France
Region: Loire Valley, Michelin Map: 519
www.karenbrown.com/latonnellerie.html

La Réserve, nestled along the edge of the sparkling blue sea in one of the most glamorous towns on the Riviera, radiates quiet sophistication and opulent charm. The impression of old-world grandeur is established by your first glance of the handsome, pastel-pink building whose entrance is flanked by tall, majestic palm trees. A high standard of excellence is set by the Delion family, professional hôteliers who also own the sensational Résidence de la Pinède in Saint Tropez and who have created a tranquil, homelike atmosphere in this world-class hotel. Madame Delion personally oversaw the decor and evidence of her impeccable taste and loving attention for detail is seen throughout in the hotel's understated elegance. Tones of delicate peach and creamy whites set the color scheme, while fine antiques and glorious displays of fresh flowers complete the feeling that you are in a hotel not owned by a large corporation, but run by owners who truly care. As might be expected, the spacious guestrooms are beautifully decorated. The dining room, a beautiful long room with a gorgeous parquet floor and framed on both sides by huge windows, is spectacular. Not only is the room stunning but, more important, the food and service are outstanding. On a lower-level terrace there is a lovely swimming pool overlooking the sea. *Directions:* Follow the main road through Beaulieu sur Mer to the lowest seaside level where you find the hotel.

HÔTEL LA RÉSERVE
Hoteliêr: Delion Family
5, Boulevard Général Leclerc
06310 Beaulieu sur Mer, France
Tel: 04.93.01.00.01, Fax: 04.93.01.28.99
40 Rooms, Double: €150–€1350*
*Breakfast not included: €27
Open: Mar 3 to Nov 7 & Christmas
Credit cards: all major
Relais & Châteaux, Region: Riviera, Michelin Map: 528
www.karenbrown.com/hotellareserve.html

In the heart of the lovely medieval town of Beaune, Le Cep offers charming and comfortable air-conditioned bedrooms decorated with elegance and taste. The Bernards' son returned to Beaune and settled in with his own family to take over management of Le Cep. He is charming and continues the high standard of welcome and service. The bedrooms vary in size and decor but are all handsome—highly polished wooden antique furnishings are accented by the beautiful, softly colored fabrics used for the curtains, bedspreads, and upholstery. With each visit these past few years we have been able to see the renovations of yet a few more rooms in the buildings that encircle the inner courtyard. Spacious and grand, these new suites can only be described as elegant and regal. In the bar and public areas, heavy-beamed ceilings, old gilt-framed portraits, and fresh-flower arrangements add character and elegance. The former wine cellar, a cozy room with a low, arched stone ceiling, is used as a breakfast room when the weather does not permit service outdoors in the pretty courtyard. While Beaune is a destination in itself, it is also a delightful base for touring the Burgundy wine region. Le Cep combines elegance and warmth in perfect proportions. *Directions:* Beaune is located at the heart of Burgundy, 45 km south of Dijon. Circle the town on the road that follows the ramparts. Turn left into the center of town on Rue Maufoux. Le Cep is on the right side of the road.

HÔTEL LE CEP
Hoteliêr: Nerino Bernard Family
27, Rue Maufoux, 21200 Beaune, France
Tel: 03.80.22.35.48, Fax: 03.80.22.76.80
62 Rooms, Double: €160–€500*
*Breakfast not included: €18
Open: all year, Credit cards: all major
Region: Burgundy, Michelin Map: 520
www.karenbrown.com/hotellecep.html

Countryside Places to Stay   209

Hôtel de la Poste is located on the old ring road that follows the ancient city walls of Beaune. With parts of it dating back to 1660, the hotel has in recent years undergone a complete renovation including the addition of double-paned windows and a lovely new flower garden for guests to enjoy. There are also five new deluxe guestrooms located in a quiet back wing that enjoy a separate entry, handsome furnishings, and sumptuous space. The lobby and bar have retained their old-world ambiance, but the bedrooms in the main building are a mix of traditional as well as contemporary in their decor. This is a lovely city hotel, centrally located for touring Burgundy, that is also large enough to cater to groups. The principal restaurant, very pretty in a decor of subdued elegance, has maintained its standard of excellence and some of France's finest Burgundies are a perfect accompaniment to the hotel's outstanding menu selections. A second restaurant, Le Bistro, located off the garden courtyard, is open for lunch and on pretty days meals can also be enjoyed in the garden. It is wonderful to stay in Beaune and just a few minutes' walk brings you to the heart of this charming old walled town and its delightful pedestrian streets. *Directions:* Beaune is located at the heart of Burgundy. Circle the town on the ring road to Boulevard Clemenceau.

HÔTEL DE LA POSTE
Hoteliêr: M. Martinet
5, Boulevard Clemenceau
21200 Beaune, France
Tel: 03.80.22.08.11, Fax: 03.80.24.19.71
36 Rooms, Double: €120–€300*
*Breakfast not included: €18
Open: all year, Credit cards: all major
Châteaux & Hotels de France
Region: Burgundy, Michelin Map: 520
www.karenbrown.com/hoteldelaposte.html

L'Auberge de l'Abbaye is a very pretty, half-timbered inn in the picturesque village of Le Bec Hellouin. The lovely old abbey, built along a stream and surrounded by half-timbered and thatched buildings, enjoys a peaceful pastoral setting far removed from any hustle and bustle. When we entered the cozy, low-ceilinged restaurant of the 18th-century inn, we were greeted by the sight and aroma of a large, freshly baked apple tart. We were told by the welcoming owner, Madame Conroux, that her restaurant is renowned all over the world for apple tarts. Calvados, a specialty of the region, is also featured here, with large bottles present on each table. The restaurant is full of old-world, country-French charm: lace curtains grace the windows, polished copper and faïence ornament the walls, country-style tables are set with care, and the low-beamed ceiling adds character. A narrow little staircase leads to the bedrooms, which are small, but I was pleased to see on a recent visit that they have been redecorated with light, pretty colors and that fresh new carpets dress the hallways. Each guestroom is accompanied by a basic but spotlessly clean bathroom. L'Auberge de l'Abbaye is the epitome of a simple, country-French restaurant with rooms. *Directions:* Located 42 km southwest of Rouen. Take the N138 from Rouen in the direction of Alençon to Maison Brulée. Just before Brionne turn right to Le Bec Hellouin.

L'AUBERGE DE L'ABBAYE
Owners: Catherine & Fabrice Conroux
27800 Bec Hellouin (Le), France
Tel: 02.32.44.86.02, Fax: 02.32.46.32.23
10 Rooms, Double: €70*
Apartment: €110
*Breakfast not included: €8
Closed: two weeks in Jan & Nov, Credit cards: all major
Region: Normandy, Michelin Map: 512
www.karenbrown.com/aubergedelabbaye.html

I was so glad the owners contacted me about his charming inn as it gave me reason to return and fall in love again with this delightful coastal town. In fact, Yves vacationed here as a child and decided to leave the world of business in Paris and settle here with his own family. In Biarritz, casinos and grand hotels line the central beach whose end lighthouse seems to take a respectful watch and old fishermen's cottages now house a number of terrace restaurants. The new owners offer travelers a warm welcome in an attractive home converted to an intimate three-star hotel, just blocks up from the old port. Just off the entry is a small, attractive sitting room with a fireplace whose mantel boasts a lovely print of a couple dancing at sunset and a wonderful display of lighthouses. The breakfast room is opposite. There is one guestroom on the main floor, with the rest on the second and third floors up a beautifully banistered winding staircase. The decor throughout is appealing in its simplicity—whites and beiges against the beauty of a few wood furnishings. The clean, simple rooms are not overly large but each has a direct-dial phone, television, curtained-off closet area, and private bath. *Directions:* Follow signs to Centre Ville and when near the beach on the Place Clemenceau, look for the Galleries Lafayette, which is just a block south of Rue Gambetta. There is parking in town or you can park on a nearby street.

MAISON GARNIER
Hoteliêr: Yves and Anne Gelot
29, Rue Gambetta, 64200 Biarritz, France
Tel: 05.59.01.60.70, Fax: 05.59.01.60.80
7 Rooms, Double: €95–€125*
*Breakfast not included: €9
Open: all year, Credit cards: all major
Region: Basque, Michelin Map: 525
www.karenbrown.com/maisongarnier.html

In Pays Basque, Alain Ducasse has created yet another oasis. Clustered on a hillside of a serene valley, he has commissioned Basque-style homes as counterpart to the original farmhouse that is heart of the complex. On 45 hectares, the property enjoys a sense of remoteness with sweeping views of surrounding farmland grazed by dairy cattle and horses, ringed by snow-capped peaks. To preserve this pristine setting, guests are met at the entrance with electric golf carts in exchange for their cars. Named after indigenous trees, each building is painted the red typical of the region with a rustic tile roof. Whether two-story duplex, luxury suite, or deluxe room, guestrooms enjoy shuttered windows that open to the beauty of the setting. The soft, natural colors selected for the fabrics compliment the handsome wood doors, beams, and terracotta tile floors. Breakfast on the garden terrace of the original home is well worth the journey from your cottage. Here you will also find the large pool, sauna, fitness rooms, and restaurant. Gorgeous, comfortable dining rooms are located in the original farmstead and impart old-world ambiance. I am impressed with Alain Ducasse's commitment to the region's architecture; as well as the local people, customs, and products. *Directions:* Bidarray is a small village located off D918, approximately a 30-minute drive from Bayonne. Ostape is located just outside Bidarray. Get detailed directions when making reservations.

OSTAPE
Owner: Alain Ducasse
Domaine Chahatoenia
64780 Bidarray, France
Tel: 05.59.37.91.91, Fax: 05.59.37.91.92
22 Rooms, Double: €220–€540*
5 Villas, *Breakfast not included: €15
Closed: Nov 7 to Apr, Credit cards: all major
Châteaux & Hotels de France
Region: Basque, Michelin Map: 525
www.karenbrown.com/ostape.html

The views from Domaine de Rochevilaine, perched at the end of a rocky promontory in Brittany, are stupendous, especially when the sun shines on the glistening sea or when the wind howls as the waves crash against the rocks below. The vast windows of the sitting room and the restaurant overlook a sky-wide expanse of open sea, giving the distinct sensation of being shipboard. Oriental carpets grace old polished hardwood floors and a roaring fire burns in the grate on cool days. The menu is superb, and the service is both attentive and gracious. Bedrooms are found either in the little, old stone cottages or in a new (though traditionally styled) wing of rooms near the luxurious indoor swimming pool (there's also a salt-water pool set into the rocks on the ocean's edge). All of the bedrooms enjoy dramatic sea views, and several have private terraces, handsome wood floors, and mellow paneling. The most dramatic room is The Admiral's Room, room 11, named for its 270-degree views. Our room with its expanse of view out to the sea was a wonderful place to linger and inspired me to write. The health center offers a gymnasium, massages, and saunas. *Directions:* The Domaine de Rochevilaine is at Pointe de Pen Lan, 5 km from Muzillac on the D5. Muzillac is located 25 km southeast of Vannes on the road between Vannes and Nantes.

DOMAINE DE ROCHEVILAINE
Hoteliêr: Bertrand Jaquet
Pointe de Pen Lan
Billiers, 56190 Muzillac, France
Tel: 02.97.41.61.61, Fax: 02.97.41.44.85
35 Rooms, Double: €126–€490*
*Breakfast not included: €18
Open: all year, Credit cards: all major
Relais & Châteaux
Region: Brittany, Michelin Map: 517
www.karenbrown.com/rochevilaine.html

In France, one often talks about passion—and this is the most appropriate term I can impart when describing the accommodations, the cuisine, and the dreams of Sabine and Hervé. Sweethearts from grammar school, they launched a dream by converting this handsome 18th-century Relais du Poste into an exceptional hotel, conveniently located on the approach to town. With a Mediterranean accent, the exterior is easy to spot. It is washed in warm ochre, and the windows are trimmed in white and paired with distinctive blue shutters. A lovely outdoor pool is on a terrace set just below the entrance. Inside, in style that displays subtle elegance, Sabine's talents are apparent throughout. Guestrooms are extremely comfortable, modern, and very restful in muted earth tones. The restaurant could not be prettier; especially in the evenings, when candlelight softly illuminates the pale, yellow walls and table linens. But it is Hervé's talents that will really excite. His choice of pairing the finest ingredients in creating his mastery and, with a sparkle in his eye, the creative and artful, almost playful, presentation is incredible and truly outstanding! Under the direction and example of Sabine and Hervé, it is the attentive, professional, and unpretentious service that makes a stay here memorable and the experience superlative. *Directions:* Located approximately 33 km west of Beziers, take the D11 west to Cabezac and then the D26 north in the direction of Bize-Minervois.

LA BASTIDE CABEZAC
Owners: Sabine & Hervé Dos Santos
18-20 Hameau de Cabezac
11120 Bize-Minervois, France
Tel: 04.68.46.66.10, Fax: 04.68.46.66.29
12 Rooms, Double: €75–€130*
*Breakfast not included: €10
Closed: Christmas, Credit cards: all major
Châteaux & Hotels de France
Region: Languedoc, Michelin Map: 527
www.karenbrown.com/cabezac.html

Bléré is a delightful little town that is perfectly located for exploring the châteaux of the Loire Valley and quiet enough that it is not mobbed by tourists. Facing the town's pedestrian center, Le Cheval Blanc has a contemporary façade that disguises the fact that this is a very old building, once an annex for the neighboring church. After the Revolution, the building was converted to a café-bar and remained so for almost two centuries. It was purchased by Micheline and Michel Blériot several years ago and they have converted the café into a most attractive restaurant with pretty wallpaper, wooden chairs, and tables dressed with crisp linens. For this simple country hotel, the restaurant is surprisingly elegant and the gourmet offering of the menu outstanding. An inner courtyard latticed with vines and set with white outdoor tables is a delightful spot for breakfast. Michel is the chef while Micheline looks after the front of the house. Upstairs, the bedrooms are very simply decorated, and all but one are small with either a tiny shower or bathroom. They are all spotlessly clean and provide very good value for money. *Directions:* Bléré is on the N76, 27 km east of Tours and 8 km west of Chenonceaux. The rear of the hotel faces Place Charles Bidault and the hotel's car park.

LE CHEVAL BLANC
Hoteliêrs: Micheline & Michel Blériot
5, Place Charles Bidault, Place de l'Église
37150 Bléré, France
Tel: 02.47.30.30.14, Fax: 02.47.23.52.80
12 Rooms, Double: €60–€96*
*Breakfast not included: €10
Restaurant: closed Sun night & Mon
Closed: Jan, Credit cards: all major
Region: Loire Valley, Michelin Map: 519
www.karenbrown.com/chevalblanc.html

Nestled back from the road that follows the bank of the Loire—a five minute walk to the Blois châteaux—the Côté Loire is hidden behind foliage of the tree that shades the square. Do not judge this hotel by its one star rating. It is an intimate, 7-room hotel that was just purchased by Thierry and Laurent. With their care and attention to detail, it will soon become one of Blois' most charming small hotels. The lovely, old stone and timbered walls have embraced guestrooms for over 400 years. It was originally built to accommodate the servants and horses of notable clientele who settled in at a more luxurious neighbor. Accessed by a beautiful, central stairway, the majority of guestrooms are still modest in their décor and cozy in size, in harmony with the original construction. Theirry and Laurent have concentrated on comfort and cleanliness, and sincerely want to offer value to their guests. It was wonderful to be able to see the charming décor achieved in room 2, the largest with a handsome, antique bed and shuttered windows that open onto the square. Family mementos and antiques already decorate the public areas. A cozy bar doubles as reception and a side room serves as the lovely restaurant. The limited menu changes every few days. The kitchen is just off the bar and the door is always open—Thierry and Laurent welcome the opportunity to engage with their guests. *Directions:* Travel the RN152 along the river through Blois to the Place de la Grève.

CÔTÉ LOIRE
Owners: Thierry Lode & Laurent Morin
2, place de la Gréve, 41000 Blois, France
Tel: 02.54.78.07.86, Fax: 02.54.56.87.33
7 Rooms, Double: €39–€65*
*Breakfast not included: €7,50
Closed: January, Credit cards: all major
Region: Loire Valley, Michelin Map: 519
www.karenbrown.com/coteloire.html

Set on the banks of Lake Geneva (Lake Léman), the 12th-century Château de Coudrée is a true castle, with a square tower-dungeon dating to the 6th century. Since the castle was constructed for defense, vulnerable exposure to the waterfront was avoided, so only one of the 19 guestrooms enjoys lake views. Room 1, a long, narrow bedroom with windows on both sides looking out to the water and the interior corridor, has gorgeous parquet floors under Renaissance beamed ceilings, handsome antiques, and comfortable sitting areas. Many of the guestrooms offer two-level accommodation with a sitting area or bedroom on the entry level and loft accommodation upstairs. However, one of my favorites, number 6, a large side room overlooking the gardens and pool, is all on one level. It is decorated in soft green and has a sitting area and a regal four-poster bed set under dramatically high ceilings. Another dramatic room—the dungeon (surprisingly, up in the square turret)—features a regally draped bed under an 18-meter ceiling. On the main level three extremely grand, large medieval chambers with magnificent fireplaces, old hand-painted beams, intricately carved paneling, and beautiful tiled floors now serve as two restaurants and a lovely bar. *Directions:* Located east of Geneva on the south shore of Lake Geneva. Travel the N5 and in the village of Bonnatrait watch for signs just past Sciez directing you to the lakeside and the short drive to the château.

CHÂTEAU DE COUDRÉE
Hoteliêr: Catherine Reale-Laden
Bonnatrait, 74140 Sciez-sur-Léman, France
Tel: 04.50.72.62.33, Fax: 04.50.72.57.28
19 Rooms, Double: €132–€330*
*Breakfast not included: €18
Closed: Nov, Credit cards: all major
Châteaux & Hotels de France
Region: French Alps, Michelin Map: 523
www.karenbrown.com/coudree.html

Tucked 10 kilometers farther up a quiet valley from the larger town of Brantôme, Bourdeilles has an idyllic setting. In this old village crowned by a castle, the Hostellerie des Griffons sits next to a narrow bridge and offers accommodation in a tranquil, picture-book setting. The outside shutters are a pretty blue and the new courtyard and beautiful garden terrace located between the river and the castle are quite attractive. This is a charming inn in an enchanting setting and it is nice to be able to recommend it unconditionally. Guaranteeing a peaceful night's sleep, many of the bedrooms nestle under old beams and overlook the quietly flowing river. I have many personal favorites: number 9 is a charming corner room set under romantic beams and eaves, number 6 is tucked under the angled beams and looks across to the mill, and number 4 is pretty in its decor of blue and enjoys the water view. The restaurant is intimate and inviting, with windows opening up to the soothing sound of cascading water. Tables are set on the lovely garden terrace on warm summer nights. The outdoor setting, between castle and river, is romantic and perfect for enjoying wonderful Périgord specialties. This is a delightful inn and a good value on the northern boundaries of the Dordogne. *Directions:* Bourdeilles is located 24 km northwest of Périgueux. From Périgueux take the N939 north to Brantôme and then travel 10 km west on the D78.

HOSTELLERIE DES GRIFFONS
Hoteliêrs: M & Mme Bernard Lebrun-Goldschmidt
Le Bourg, Bourdeilles, 24310 Brantôme, France
Tel: 05.53.45.45.35, Fax: 05.53.45.45.20
10 Rooms, Double: €85–€98*
*Breakfast not included: €9,20
Open: Apr 1 to Nov 5, Credit cards: all major
Châteaux & Hotels de France
Region: Dordogne, Michelin Map: 521
www.karenbrown.com/griffons.html

Brantôme, with its Benedictine abbey tucked into the cliffs, narrow streets lined with gray-stone houses, and ancient footbridge spanning the River Dronne beside Le Moulin de l'Abbaye, offers an enchanting setting. The hotel looks across the river to the town from its picturesque riverside location. Owner Régis Bulot is president of Relais & Châteaux hotels and you can be certain that he ensures that his hotel is a flagship for this prestigious organization. Dinner is a real treat—we found it no more expensive than at far inferior places and its wine list had many well-priced wines. Dinner, whether served outdoors on the terrace or in the elegant dining room, profits from the idyllic riverside setting. The lovely bedrooms are found in three buildings: the mill, an adjacent home, and a charming riverside house just two minutes' walk across the bridge and through the park. We particularly liked our village bedroom atop a broad flight of spiral stairs. It enjoys delightful decor, views across the rooftops through tiny windows, and a luxurious bathroom with an enormous circular tub. *Directions:* Brantôme is located 27 km northwest of Périgueux on the N939. The mill is at the edge of the village on the road to Bourdeilles.

LE MOULIN DE L'ABBAYE
Hoteliêr: Régis Bulot
Directeurs: Mme & M Bernard Dessum
1, Route de Bourdeilles, 24310 Brantôme, France
Tel: 05.53.05.80.22, Fax: 05.53.05.75.27
19 Rooms, Double: €190–€310*
*Breakfast not included: €19
Open: May 2 to Oct 23, Credit cards: all major
Relais & Châteaux
Region: Dordogne, Michelin Map: 521
www.karenbrown.com/moulindelabbaye.html

The Château de Brélidy is located in Brittany, in an area surrounded by quiet woods and fishing streams, yet just 20 kilometers from the northern coastline. This is a professionally run, château-hotel offering a full range of accommodation, from basic to luxurious, and a warm welcome to tourists and business travelers alike. Fifteen bedrooms are located in a beautifully reconstructed 16th-century wing of the castle, and although decorated with period-style furniture and tapestry-style fabrics, are modern and spotless. They all have private baths, TVs, and direct-dial phones. Guests are invited to relax in the castle's salon where tapestry chairs, a huge open fireplace, vases of fresh flowers, and *objets d'art* create a refined setting. A stay here is as comfortable as it is full of atmosphere, for although the castle dates from the 16th century, extensive and dedicated restorations have brought it to its current polished state of perfection. For travelers with smaller pocketbooks, modest bed-and-breakfast accommodation in four intimate attic rooms is available. These rooms each have private bath and toilet, are homey, comfortable, and spotlessly clean. *Directions:* From Saint Brieuc take the N12 in the direction of Brest to the D767 and exit for Lannion-Treguier. Take the D712 and D8 to Treguier, then the D15 to Brélidy.

CHÂTEAU DE BRÉLIDY
Hoteliêr: William Langlet
22140 Brélidy, France
Tel: 02.96.95.69.38, Fax: 02.96.95.18.03
15 Rooms, Double: €94–€140*
*Breakfast not included: €12
Open: Mar 1 to Jan 1, Credit cards: all major
Region: Brittany, Michelin Map: 517
www.karenbrown.com/chateaudebrelidy.html

The Château de Noirieux is exceptional. A beautiful wooded property set in the hills above Angers in the Loire Valley, it has gardens abounding with flowers, a lovely pool, tennis courts, and gorgeous river views. A charming couple, the Cômes, oversee the welcome and the exceptional kitchen. Upstairs in the château are the largest and most expensive rooms with elegant decor and views of the river. Number 1 is a corner room decorated in cascades of blue-and-cream fabric; the middle room, number 2 is decorated in a fabric of ribbons and roses in soft tones of blues and pinks; and number 3 is the smallest room but with a larger bathroom. Also in the château there are six rooms overlooking the inner courtyard, which are also lovely in decor but smaller and more moderate in price. Another ten rooms are located in the neighboring manor, all attractive and spacious. A bowl of nuts (noirieux), a basket of fruit, fresh flowers, and personalized toiletries welcome guests in each room. The ambiance in the restaurant, with its linens and drapes in soft hues of yellow, is very romantic. A pretty breakfast room, enclosed with full glass windows, is set just off the terrace. *Directions:* From the A11 from Paris exit at 14, from Angers exit at 14B, following directions to Briollay and Soucelles, on the D109.

CHÂTEAU DE NOIRIEUX
Hoteliêrs: Anja & Gerard Côme
26 Route du Moulin, Briollay 49125 (Angers), France
Tel: 02.41.42.50.05, Fax: 02.41.37.91.00
19 Rooms, Double: €175–€350*
*Breakfast not included: €20
Restaurant: seasonal closings
Closed: Feb 15 to Mar 24 & Oct 29 to Nov 30
Credit cards: all major, Relais & Châteaux
Region: Loire Valley, Michelin Map: 518
www.karenbrown.com/noirieux.html

The atmosphere of the Middle Ages prevails in the narrow, winding, cobblestoned streets leading to the Château Grimaldi, built in 1309 by Raynier Grimaldi, the ruler of Monaco. As the streets become narrower, passing under buildings that form an archway, you arrive at Le Cagnard, a hotel that has been in operation for over 40 years. Continuing the tradition of welcome perfected by the Barel family, their daughter and her husband, Madame and Monsieur Barel Laroche, are now the resident innkeepers. Dinner on the terrace, set under a full moon, or indoors, with the atmosphere of a medieval castle with candlelight flickering against age-old walls, is a romantic experience and the presentation of the food is exceptional. The elevator is charming, presenting biblical paintings changing with each floor. Guestrooms are located either in the main building with the restaurant or tucked off cobbled streets in neighboring buildings. Rooms have a medieval flavor to their decor and are comfortable, but not overly luxurious. A few prize rooms enjoy patios with wonderful views over the tiled rooftops out to the countryside. *Directions:* If you arrive by the A8, N7, or N98, follow the sign Centre Ville along J.F. Kennedy and Marchel Juin, then Haut de Cagnes-Château-Musée. At the entrance to the old city you'll pass an automatic car park called Le Planastel. Turn right and the hotel is 200 meters farther along this narrow road.

LE CAGNARD
Hoteliêrs: Mme & M Barel Laroche
Rue sous Barri, Haut de Cagnes
06800 Cagnes sur Mer, France
Tel: 04.93.20.73.21 & 22, Fax: 04.93.22.06.39
25 Rooms, Double: €150–€300*
*Breakfast not included: €16
Restaurant: closed Nov 1 to Dec 20
Open: all year, Credit cards: all major
Relais & Châteaux, Region: Riviera, Michelin Map: 528
www.karenbrown.com/lecagnard.html

This is an enchanting complex of thatched cottages nestled amongst beautiful English gardens. The front entry and reception are spacious and open to the second story. Stepping down off the entry, to one side is a bar whose windows look out to the pool and lawn and on the other is the cozy, narrow breakfast room. There are eight guestrooms on the ground floor with large shuttered windows opening onto a private garden terrace. The rooms are small and cozy, with two small chairs, the bed, and private bathroom. Upstairs, the four guestrooms are a little longer and feel a bit more spacious under vaulted ceilings. They also enjoy private balconies tucked into the thatched roofline. With the exception of room 42, which has an entry large enough to accommodate a twin bed, the rooms vary little with the exception of decor and color. There is also a duplex available in a separate building. The restaurant, which serves exceptional food, is found off the entry terrace and in warm weather the tables overflow to the garden terrace. You could strip this inn of its ambiance and charm and I would still recommend it as I don't remember when we have been made to feel more genuinely welcome and embraced by such warm and gracious service. This is a wonderful inn. *Directions:* From Pont Audemer travel south on the D810 in the direction of Bernay and then after 400 meters turn off to the east towards Campigny. From this point the hotel is well signed.

LE PETIT COQ AUX CHAMPS
Hoteliêrs: Fabienne Desmonts & Jean-Marie Huard
La Pommeraie Sud, Campigny
27500 Pont-Audemer, France
Tel: 02.32.41.04.19, Fax: 02.32.56.06.25
12 Rooms, Double: €130–€149*, 1 duplex: €164
*Breakfast not included: €10
Restaurant: seasonal closings
Closed: Jan 4 to Jan 23, Credit cards: all major
Region: Normandy, Michelin Map: 512
www.karenbrown.com/coqauxchamps.html

Les Rimains is a sensational tiny hotel, truly a gem. I can't imagine anyone not falling in love with its setting and romantic ambiance. As you drive into the pine-studded parking area, it is a bit confusing—what you see before you looks like a lovely private home. Nothing even hints at anything commercial, not even a "reception" sign. But don't be intimidated: just ring the bell and you will be warmly welcomed into an intimate foyer where you check in. There are only six guestrooms. Although not large, they are quite spacious and each has a superb view of the sea. The beautifully decorated rooms exude an air of refined, understated, quiet elegance. All the rooms are slightly different in decor but similar in mood, and all have some antique furnishings. Terraced below the hotel is a gorgeous garden, interspersed with romantic little nooks with lounge chairs and umbrellas. The view is absolutely stunning, with the bay spreading out below, dotted by boats and little islands. The cozy Les Rimains is an intimate hotel serving breakfast only. *Directions:* From the center of town, follow signs to Les Rimains.

LES RIMAINS
Hoteliêr: Olivier Roellinger
1, Rue Duguesclin, 35260 Cancale, France
Tel: 02.99.89.64.76, Fax: 02.99.89.88.47
6 Rooms, Double: €145–€240*
*Breakfast not included: €16
Closed: Jan to Apr, Credit cards: all major
Relais & Châteaux
Region: Brittany, Michelin Map: 517
www.karenbrown.com/rimains.html

Set in the quiet Loire Valley countryside, Le Fleuray is a lovely soft-peach manor, covered in Virginia Creeper with window boxes hanging heavy with geraniums. Large, well-kept gardens have lawns, a pond and an orchard. Dating from the 1800s, its English owners, Peter and Hazel, converted it into a charming country hotel and now run it in style with their son and daughter, Jordan and Cassie. The decor is pretty with floral and stripes both in the fabrics and wallpapers. White wicker and country-house-style furnishings complement the exterior color of the building. The 15 attractive bedrooms are named after local flowers with views over the gardens. Guestrooms with terraces overlooking the heated swimming pool are located in the converted barn, a wonderful option for families. The Newingtons offer a lovely breakfast and dinner, under the shade of trees on the garden terrace and in the cozy restaurant near a gorgeous stone fireplace. Both à la carte and fixed priced menus are offered while the wine list keeps faithfully to the Loire vineyards. Le Fleuray is an ideal base from which to explore the area's many castles, villages, and vineyards—all short and easy drives along quiet back roads. *Directions:* Take exit 18, Amboise/Château-Renault, off the A10, then travel south on the D31 to Autrèche, east on the D55 to Dame Marie les Bois, and south on the D74 to Fleuray.

LE FLEURAY
Hoteliêr: Newington Family
Fleuray, 37530 Cangey, France
Tel: 02.47.56.09.25, Fax: 02.47.56.93.97
15 Rooms, Double: €78–€120*
*Breakfast not included: €10,50
Closed: Early November, Credit cards: MC, VS
Region: Loire Valley, Michelin Map: 519
www.karenbrown.com/lefleuray.html

In 1997 two hotels in the medieval fortress of Carcassonne were completely renovated and became one under the name of the Hôtel de la Cité. The hotel offers luxury and refined service and it is also memorable to settle for an evening behind the massive walls of the fortress in this lovely hotel. Recessed into the walls near the Basilica Saint Nazaire, the hotel occupies the site of the ancient Episcopal palace and offers you elegant comfort in a medieval atmosphere. Enjoy a beverage in the cozy and intimate Library Bar. Evening dining is an elegant and memorable experience in the hotel's restaurant, La Barbacane, while the less formal brasserie, Chez Saskia, is a lovely spot for lunch or dinner. The hotel's bedrooms, many of which open up onto the ramparts and a large enclosed garden, vary in price according to size, decor, and view. They are all lovely and suite 108, opening onto the privacy of the gardens, is spectacular with gorgeous carved paneled walls and painted frieze. Ideally located for exploring this magnificent fortress—the hotel can arrange other activities if you want to add to your adventure: barge and bike trips, cooking classes, winetasting, etc. *Directions:* Although the city is closed to all but pedestrian traffic from 9 am to 6 pm, you can enter it by car (via Porte Narbonnaise), travel Rue Mayrevieille, Rue Porte d'Aude, and Rue Saint Louis to the hotel's private parking area between the castle walls.

HÔTEL DE LA CITÉ
Hoteliêr: M Jacques Hamburger
Place de l'Église, Cité Médiévale
11000 Carcassonne, France
Tel: 04.68.71.98.71, Fax: 04.68.71.50.15
61 Rooms, Double: €250–€1,250*
*Breakfast not included: €25
Closed: Jan 29 to Mar 2, Dec 2–31
Credit cards: all major
Region: Languedoc, Michelin Map: 526
www.karenbrown.com/hoteldelacite.html

Nestled in the valley just below the fortress of Carcassonne, Domaine d'Auriac offers proximity to the town and yet a tranquil setting away from its crowds. Marie Helen, who greeted us at reception, not only takes pleasure in the details of ensuring guests' comfort but also, during the off season, makes the drapes and comforters for the rooms that are being redecorated. Marie Helen's brother helps her manage the property, and her mother, Anne Marie, takes care of the family home. This is truly a hands-on family operation! In addition to the luxurious accommodation offered in the main building, the family has renovated a number of cottages, buildings that were once the bakery, the granary, and the stables, and created almost a little village of additional accommodation. The new units are spacious and often have a loft, separate sitting area, or separate unit. In the main house the elegant public rooms are inviting and the gentlemen's cigar room is club-like in ambiance with intimate groupings of tapestry-covered chairs set on old tiled floors. Settle here for more than just a few days in order to enjoy the sightseeing and the property itself with its tennis, swimming, golf, wonderful food, and very relaxing setting. *Directions:* From the A61 exit at Carcassonne Ouest, following signs for the city center and Centre Hospitalier. The Domaine is on the road that leads south from Carcassonne to St. Hilaire.

DOMAINE D'AURIAC
Hoteliêr: Rigaudis Family
Route de Saint Hilaire, BP 554
11000 Carcassonne, France
Tel: 04.68.25.72.22, Fax: 04.68.47.35.54
24 Rooms, Double: €150–€450*
*Breakfast not included: €19
Open: Feb 7 to Jan 3, Credit cards: AX, VS
Relais & Châteaux
Region: Languedoc, Michelin Map: 526
www.karenbrown.com/auriac.html

Château de la Caze is a fairy-tale 15th-century castle, majestically situated above the Tarn. With its heavy doors, turrets, and stone façade, it is a dramatic castle, yet intimate in size. It was not built as a fortress, but rather as a honeymoon home for Soubeyrane Alamand. She chose the idyllic and romantic location and commissioned the château in 1489. Now a hotel, its grand rooms with their vaulted ceilings, rough stone walls, and tiled and wood-planked floors are warmed by tapestries, Oriental rugs, dramatic antiques, paintings, copper, soft lighting, and log-burning fires. Each bedroom in the castle is like a king's bedchamber. Room 6, the honeymoon apartment of Soubeyrane, is the most spectacular room, with a large canopied bed and an entire wall of windows overlooking the Tarn and its canyon. Another room has a painted ceiling depicting the eight very beautiful sisters who later inherited the château. Just opposite the château, La Ferme offers six additional, attractive apartments. The restaurant enjoys spectacular views of the canyon. A very elegant property, the Lecroqs, by their presence (Monsieur in the kitchen, Madame at the reception, and their adorable children in the home) imparts to La Caze a familial ambiance. The welcome is genuine, the château is lovely-both as magnificent as the setting. *Directions:* La Malène is 42 km northeast of Millau traveling on N9 and D907. From La Malène travel northeast for 5.5 km on D907.

CHÂTEAU DE LA CAZE
Hoteliêrs: Mme & M Jean Paul Lecroq
La Caze, (La Malène) 48210 Sainte Enimie, France
Tel: 04.66.48.51.01, Fax: 04.66.48.55.75
16 Rooms, Double: €108–€260*
*Breakfast not included: €14
Restaurant: closed Wed & Thur for lunch in low season
Open: Apr 4 to Nov 11, Credit cards: all major
Châteaux & Hotels de France
Region: Tarn, Michelin Map: 527
www.karenbrown.com/chateaudelacaze.html

When Alain Ducasse (a world-renowned chef and owner of one of our favorite hotels in Moustiers Sainte Marie) asked us to visit his new hotel, L'Hostellerie de l'Abbaye de La Celle, we knew it would be a winner. We were already familiar with the property, which had been featured in our guide until it closed. Reopened in December 1999 under the talented guidance of Alain Ducasse and Bruno Clément, this charming inn is more beautiful than ever. Nestled next to a lovely 12th-century Benedictine convent in the sweet village of La Celle, L'Hostellerie de l'Abbaye de La Celle was built in the 1700s as a bourgeois home. It is not until you step through the gates that the true grandeur of the building and its gardens is revealed. The handsome mustard-yellow mansion with dark-green shutters faces onto its own 3-hectare park dotted with magnificent plane trees, chestnut trees, mulberry trees, and centuries-old cypresses. Lovingly tended beds of flowers and a stone swimming pool complete the picture of perfection. Inside is no disappointment. The lounges are tastefully decorated with fine antiques and the dining rooms exude charm. The spacious guestrooms have all been totally renovated with taste and refinement. A favorite one is the suite where Général de Gaulle stayed during his years as President. *Directions:* Exit the A8 at Brignoles. Go west on N7 and then south on D43 toward Toulon. La Celle is just off the D43, 3 km southwest of Brignoles.

L'HOSTELLERIE DE L'ABBAYE DE LA CELLE
Manager: Pascal Budor
Place du Général de Gaulle
83170 Celle-en-Provence (La), France
Tel: 04.98.05.14.14, Fax: 04.98.05.14.15
10 Rooms, Double: €205–€345*
*Breakfast not included: €19
Closed: Jan 16 to Feb 3, Credit cards: all major
Châteaux & Hotels de France
Region: Provence, Michelin Map: 528
www.karenbrown.com/abbayedelacelle.html

Le Mas Trilles is an enchanting complex of sun-washed, amber-colored stone and terracotta-tiled cottages nestled among fruit trees, bountiful flowers, and greenery that thrive in this Mediterranean climate. Located in a hamlet neighboring the picturesque village of Céret, this idyllic and serene setting has inspired the subject of many a canvas. Influenced by its neighbor, Spain, this region is known for its hospitality. Your gracious hosts, who exude the warmth of the region, fell in love with the area while on vacation. They purchased the complex, built in 1631, and spent five years in its meticulous renovation. Always with a sparkle of humor, Laszlo has a background in the Swiss hotel business and brings the professional level of service to new heights. Sweet and beautiful, Maya is an artist and her sculpture and paintings are displayed throughout. Guestrooms are elegant in their uncluttered simplicity. With good lighting, and modern beds and bathrooms, as the first priorities, Maya selected provincial fabrics, lovely carpets, antiques, and handsome furnishings to decorate the rooms. In colder months, breakfast is offered in cozy rooms warmed by a crackling fire; but I wish for you a sunny morning to enjoy your meal at tables set on the expansive lawn. *Directions:* From Perpignan travel 17 km south on A9. Take the Le Boulou exit, and travel west on D115 to Céret, and then to Amélie les Bains. Le Mas Trilles is past the bridge in Le Pont de Reynes.

LE MAS TRILLES
Owners: Marie-France (Maya) & Laszlo Bukk
Le Pont de Reynes, 66400 Céret, France
Tel: 04.68.87.38.37, Fax: 04.68.87.42.62
10 Rooms, Double: €105–€220
Closed: Oct 7 to Apr 9, Credit cards: MC, VS
Châteaux & Hotels de France
Region: Languedoc-Roussillon, Michelin Map: 527
www.karenbrown.com/mastrilles.html

This is an impressive, very beautiful 18th-century turreted château set in a park on the outskirts of Chagny. You reach the small reception area through a door off the back courtyard. The dining room, with its creaking floors and beautiful wood paneling, is absolutely gorgeous and off this in the turret round are a few tables set for breakfast. Upstairs in the main château are twelve bedrooms and one suite. The suite is located at the end of the hall with windows looking out to the park and a sitting room in the turret above the breakfast niche. The other rooms are about half the price and, while not as large, are comfortable and very good value. La Commanderie, a 12th-century building opposite the courtyard, houses eight guestrooms. Rooms 20 and 21 are enormous and grand, with high, beamed ceilings: 20 has twin beds against a tapestry backdrop and a spacious modern bathroom, while 21 has two queen beds and a bathroom tucked into the stone-walled tower. The remaining rooms are all spacious and lovely. Even if you are not staying in La Commanderie, climb to the first landing to see an impressive display of past visitors' shields. Set in the lawn is a large swimming pool. In season guests are asked to take at least lunch or dinner at the château. *Directions:* Bellecroix is on the southeast outskirts of Chagny. Leave Chagny on the N6 towards Châlon sur Saône and watch for a small road that turns off almost immediately to the east to Bellecroix.

HOSTELLERIE DU CHÂTEAU DE BELLECROIX
Hoteliêr: Mme Gautier
71150 Chagny, France
Tel: 03.85.87.13.86, Fax: 03.85.91.28.62
21 Rooms, Double: €84–€200*
*Breakfast not included: €17
Open: Feb 14 to Dec 20, Credit cards: all major
Châteaux & Hotels de France
Region: Burgundy, Michelin Map: 520
www.karenbrown.com/bellecroix.html

As I arrived unannounced on a busy Sunday morning, I was hesitant to bother staff by requesting a tour. However, I was impressed that my visit was accommodated with enthusiasm and warmth—a response totally in keeping with the management's sincerely positive and welcoming attitude. With an absolutely gorgeous setting on a terrace shaded by mature trees above a small flowing river, the Château des Comtes de Challes is a complex of three separate buildings, the oldest of which dates to the 13th century. The reception is found in the main château, off a handsome stone-floored entry guarded by a knight in armor and next to a very attractive and inviting bar/salon. Looking out to the beauty of the setting through large French windows is a lovely dining room whose tables are regally set on handsome parquet floors. There are 20 guestrooms in the château and 26 in the adjacent manor houses. At the time of our visit, the hotel had just been acquired by a local family who within a few months had completely and beautifully renovated the rooms in the main château. Guestrooms in L'Orangerie and Le Demeure du Parc, though as yet unrenovated, are clean, spacious, and less expensive. This is not the first hotel for the Treves Family. They are true professionals and they take great pride in the arts of service, welcome, and comfort. *Directions:* Challes Les Eaux is located 6 km east of Chambéry along the N6. The hotel is well signed to the north of the road.

CHÂTEAU DES COMTES DE CHALLES
Hoteliêr: Treves Family
247, Montée du Château
73190 Challes les Eaux, France
Tel: 04.79.72.72.72, Fax: 04.79.72.83.83
46 Rooms, Double: €80–€235*
*Breakfast not included: €12
Open: all year, Credit cards: all major
Châteaux & Hotels de France
Region: French Alps, Michelin Map: 523
www.karenbrown.com/challes.html

Chambolle-Musigny is a delightful village nestled amongst the vineyards in the heart of the Burgundy wine region. On one of the village's narrow streets, secluded behind a high wall, lies the Château-Hôtel André Ziltener, one of the region's most elegant properties (and a personal favorite) which was originally built as a hunting lodge for the Burgundy Parliment. Guests can relax in the grand drawing room where tall French windows look out to the garden. Breakfast is offered around the oval table in the dining room or at courtyard tables. For evening meals guests enjoy the atmosphere of the lovely wine bar where they can sample specialties and wines of the region. The bedrooms, whether designated as standard, junior suite, or apartment, are gorgeous in their decor and are furnished in an open and spacious manner, and have splendid marble bathrooms with every luxurious amenity. Although, it is hard to select a favorite, especially enchanting is Les Amoureuses, a gorgeous apartment decorated in soft yellow. I was impressed by the subtle elegance of this lovely château and its beautiful surrounding gardens. Included in your hotel tariff is an informative guided tour of the wine museum in the château's cellars and a sampling of the four grands crus of Chambolle. *Directions:* Chambolle-Musigny is between Gevrey Chambertin and Nuits Saint Georges on the D122, a country road that parallels the N74 which runs between Dijon and Beaune.

CHÂTEAU-HÔTEL ANDRÉ ZILTENER
Hoteliêr: Madame Dagmar Ziltener
Directrice: Doris Schwarz
Rue de la Fontaine, 21220 Chambolle-Musigny, France
Tel: 03.80.62.41.62, Fax: 03.80.62.83.75
10 Rooms, Double: €200–€350*
*Breakfast not included: €15
Open: Mar 1 to Dec 15, Credit cards: all major
Châteaux & Hotels de France
Region: Burgundy, Michelin Map: 520
www.karenbrown.com/andreziltener.html

The Auberge du Bois Prin, nestled above world-famous Chamonix, has a breathtaking setting—looking across the valley, face-to-face with Mont Blanc. A flower-banked lane leads up to the hotel, which looks like a private home—which actually it almost was. The owner's father was planning to live here, but friends told him the view was too precious not to share, so, instead, he opened a small hotel. Built of dark wood in the local chalet style, it is picture-perfect, with beautifully tended displays of colorful flowers and geraniums cascading from window boxes and adorning all the decks. There is a most intimate charm throughout the hotel and it is truly like being a guest in a private home. In the reception area there is no formal counter, just a discreet antique desk that is used for check-in, and in one corner a cozy nook with a fireplace and a few comfortable chairs. A large deck stretches in front of the hotel where guests dine in the sunshine with the majesty of the mountains seemingly at their fingertips. All the individually decorated bedrooms capture the view of Mont Blanc. Most have either a private terrace enclosed by shrubbery or balcony. The Auberge du Bois Prin is proud of its sauna and spa as well as its reputation for quality service. *Directions:* On the hillside above Chamonix. Follow signs from town center to Télécabine du Brévent and Les Moussoux.

AUBERGE DU BOIS PRIN
Hoteliêr: Denis Carrier
69 Chemin de l'Hermine, Les Moussoux
74400 Chamonix, France
Tel: 04.50.53.33.51, Fax: 04.50.53.48.75
11 Rooms, Double: €138–€236
Restaurant: closed Mon & Wed lunch
Closed: two weeks Apr & all of Nov
Credit cards: all major, Châteaux & Hotels de France
Region: French Alps, Michelin Map: 523
www.karenbrown.com/boisprin.html

Le Hameau Albert 1er is an attractive complex that includes the original soft-peach-washed three-story building that the Carrier family has operated as a hotel since 1903 and a cluster of rustic buildings set on an expanse of lawn and garden, referred to as The Farm. Built from heavy beams and timber, The Farm is a handsome contrast to the refinement of the main house. The reception is found in the main building where you will most likely be welcomed with a refreshing beverage and will be embraced by the warmth of the inviting and cozy entry, which, along with the adjoining lovely sitting areas, salons, and the intimate bar, gives you the impression of being in a private home. Stretching along the length of the building and bordered by an expanse of window are three lovely rooms that comprise the gourmet Michelin two-star restaurant, Albert 1er. Twenty-one guestrooms are found upstairs in the main house. A lovely indoor-outdoor pool bridges the gap between the country restaurant, La Maison Carrier, and the timbered building that houses The Farm's 12 guestrooms. There are also two chalets for two persons each and a larger chalet with a living room, two bedrooms, and loft accommodation, which can house up to six guests. Guestrooms are handsome, individually decorated, and enjoy private bathrooms. *Directions:* Take the Chamonix North exit and then take the second right to the arched entry to the hotel.

LE HAMEAU ALBERT 1ER
Hoteliêrs: Martine & Pierre Carrier
38, route du Bouchat
74402 Chamonix, France
Tel: 04.50.53.05.09, Fax: 04.50.55.95.48
33 Rooms, Double: €116–€1,000*
3 cottages, *Breakfast not included: €18
Closed: Nov 13 to Dec 1, Credit cards: all major
Relais & Châteaux
Region: French Alps, Michelin Map: 523
www.karenbrown.com/hameaualbert.html

Le Moulin du Roc is a small, picture-perfect 17th- and 18th-century stone mill hugging the bank of the River Dronne on the edge of the village of Champagnac de Bélair. Flower-filled gardens surround the mill and a little wooden bridge arches across the river to the swimming pool set amidst gardens on the opposite bank. The intimate dining room utilizes the weathered old beams and wooden parts and mechanisms of the original mill in its cozy decor. Preserving the traditions of fine gastronomy and employing established Périgord specialties, the restaurant has received many accolades. The bedrooms are intimate and exquisite. One particularly enchanting suite, the Seigle, bridges the river and offers a bedroom decorated in blue floral fabrics and an adjoining small bedroom with a single bed. The suite windows overlook the lazy River Dronne, the gardens, and the birch-lined pastures. On the first floor, Tournesol with its four-poster bed is especially romantic. If you want to economize, choose Blé, the least expensive guestroom. This is a small but charming four-poster corner room overlooking the river. Maryse and Alain maintain the excellent service extended to guests for so many years by their parents in this little piece of paradise. *Directions:* From Périgueux travel north on the D939 to Brantôme and on towards Angoulème. Take the D82 east to Champagnac de Bélair. The hotel is well signed from the town center.

LE MOULIN DU ROC
Hoteliêrs: Maryse & Alain Gardillou
24530 Champagnac de Bélair, France
Tel: 05.53.02.86.00, Fax: 05.53.54.21.31
13 Rooms, Double: €135–€240*
*Breakfast not included: €16
Restaurant: closed mid-week seasonally
Closed: Jan 1 to Mar 10, Credit cards: all major
Region: Dordogne, Michelin Map: 521
www.karenbrown.com/moulinduroc.html

Haute Provence is a region of France whose beauty is bounded by the snow-covered Alps, the fields of lavender and olive trees of Provence, and the blue waters of the Riviera. Villages of soft stone and sienna-tiled roofs cluster on hilltops and dot this picturesque landscape. Haute Provence serves as an ideal resting spot when traveling between the regions that border it. La Bonne Étape is an old coaching inn, a gray-stone manor house with a tiled roof—blending beautifully with and suited to the landscape. From its location it enjoys panoramic views over the surrounding hills. Dating from the 18th century, the hotel has eleven bedrooms and seven apartments, all attractively decorated. The restaurant is recognized for the quality of its cuisine. Pierre Gleize and his son, Jany, employ local ingredients such as honey, lavender, herbs, lemon, lamb, and rabbit to create masterpieces in the kitchen. Dine in front of a large stone fireplace and sample some of their specialties. Exceeding the praise for the cuisine are the superlatives guests use to describe the hospitality extended by your charming hosts, the Gleize family. *Directions:* Château Arnoux is situated 80 km north of Aix en Provence, halfway between Albertville and Nice on the N85.

LA BONNE ÉTAPE
Hoteliêrs: Jany & Pierre Gleize
Chemin du Lac, 04160 Château Arnoux, France
Tel: 04.92.64.00.09, Fax: 04.92.64.37.36
18 Rooms, Double: €165–€350*
*Breakfast not included: €18
Restaurant: closed Mon & Tues off season
Open: Feb 13 to Nov 26 & Dec 12 to Jan 3
Credit cards: all major, Relais & Châteaux
Region: Haute Provence, Michelin Map: 528
www.karenbrown.com/bonneetape.html

Wishing to offer our readers a property within walking distance of the valley's most beautiful châteaux, Chenonceaux, I recommended this hotel previously and now underscore it for the new generation of the Jeudi family. Guestrooms vary in size and price, with locations in wings and annexes of this old posting inn. The best values are the less expensive rooms. While the larger, recently remodeled "suites" are very comfortable, they are as costly as more luxurious properties with more ambiance. However, it is the convenience of the location, the assurance of a comfortable bed, and the excellent restaurant that are the main reasons to stay here. Mme. greets you at the reception with a warm, gracious welcome and is a perfect example of quality service. Monsieur is responsible for the excellent menu. Dining here is a memorable experience, either in the intimate room in a décor of soft-green and floral prints or in the larger, soft yellow dining room. A number of charming salons are available to guests in the main house. The numerous guestrooms are staggered throughout the five buildings; one building for each of the generations of family that have taken on the role of innkeepers. There are pretty courtyard gardens and an expanse of back garden that is very restful. *Directions:* Chenonceaux is located approximately 40 km east of Tours. The hotel is well posted in town.

HOSTELLERIE LE BON LABOUREUR
Owner: Jeudi Family
6, rue du Docteur Bretonneau
37150 Chenonceaux, France
Tel: 02.47.23.90.02, Fax: 02.47.23.82.01
24 Rooms, Double: €85–€185*
*Breakfast not included: €11
Closed: Nov 12 to Feb 06, Credit cards: AX, VS
Region: Loire Valley, Michelin Map: 519
www.karenbrown.com/laboureur.html

We simply could not resist stopping at Les Chalets de la Serraz, drawn by the hotel's stunning setting and its incredible display of flowers. A path, bordered on both sides by an amazing riot of colorful flowers, leads down a gentle slope to the hotel which is built like a large chalet with the ubiquitous pots of geraniums draping every window and balcony. From the hotel, the slope continues downward to a lovely glacier stream that runs through the valley. Although fully reconstructed, the building dates back to 1830, when it was an old farm. Today the heritage of the hotel is carefully maintained with a sophisticated, yet rustic, elegance within. Everything is fresh and pretty, and totally pleasing in every detail. The decor is most attractive, with lots of wood used throughout, beamed ceilings, polished floors, country-style antiques, pretty fabrics, and many accents such as cow bells and bouquets of fresh flowers. The dining room is especially attractive, with windows opening to the lovely valley and mountain view. When the weather is nice, you can enjoy the same view from a large terrace. There is a large swimming pool on a terrace below the hotel. For families or friends traveling together, there are individual wooden chalets tucked in the garden, which are just as cute as can be. *Directions:* From Annecy, take D909 east for 32 km. The hotel is on D909, 3 km east of La Clusaz.

LES CHALETS DE LA SERRAZ
Hoteliêrs: M & Mme Gallay
Route du Col des Aravis
74220 Clusaz (La), France
Tel: 04.50.02.48.29, Fax: 04.50.02.64.12
7 Rooms, Double: €90–€185, 3 cottages*
*Includes breakfast & dinner
Closed: May & Oct, Credit cards: all major
Châteaux & Hotels de France
Region: French Alps, Michelin Map: 523
www.karenbrown.com/laserraz.html

There's a magic to Collioure, and Casa Païral holds a key to this wonderful location at its heart. Tucked inside this lovely port town, on a small side street, the appealing stucco façade bathed in a color reminiscent of the Mediterranean sun will catch your eye. Entered from the arched stone-trimmed doorway, you find yourself in an oasis of tranquility. A complex of buildings stagger around the graveled courtyard, graced by a soothing fountain in the shade of a magnificent magnolia tree. The reception area is just off the tiled entrance, inside the original Maître house. Guestrooms are located up the winding stairs of the main house or up courtyard stairways of the more recently added buildings. We visited a number of rooms, all different in size and configuration, each with its own special charm. Room 26 is staggered on two levels; room 19 had two twin beds in a spacious large room with end windows. I especially liked room 22, a cozy corner room graced with its own small balcony and a double bed that overlooked the pool. The two junior suites share a large terrace. For breakfast, step down from the reception area into a room whose windows showcase the garden, where a buffet is set on a table dramatically curving around a centuries-old lime tree. *Directions:* From the north, take D114 off N114 to the heart of Collioure. At Carrefour du Crist, turn left, travel two blocks, and opposite the square, the narrow alley with Impasse des Palmiers is on the left.

CASA PAÏRAL
Innkeeper: Mme Alix Guiot
Impasse des Palmiers
66190 Collioure, France
Tel: 04.68.82.05.81, Fax: 04.68.82.52.10
28 Rooms, Double: €80–€185*
*Breakfast not included: €10
Open: Mar 26 - Nov 2, Credit cards: all major
Region: Languedoc-Roussillon, Michelin Map: 527
www.karenbrown.com/pairal.html

Relais des Trois Mas terraces up a hillside and is spread around a little cove and public beach, directly across the picturesque port. A brick passageway, walls adorned with beautiful tiles designed with motifs of impressionist paintings, weaves along the terraced gardens and past the pool and the three Mas (old farm buildings) that house the guestrooms and restaurant. Guestrooms are named for the many artists once attracted to this idyllic spot. Whether the Van Gogh room, a smaller room, or the Matisse, the grandest room of all; all the guestrooms enjoy the view across the water to the scenic port town. Priced for the magnificence of the setting; rooms are comparatively expensive. Matisse is magnificent—composed of one large room that accommodates a living room, writing area, bedroom, full length of window—its French doors open to a private garden equal in size to the room, and the view. On a budget, I would request a standard room; but do splurge for a private terrace or balcony. It is the view and setting you should take full advantage of as they are the reasons for staying here. Bathrooms are appropriately adorned with a tile relief that copies a painting of the room's namesake. The gourmet restaurant is located below the guestrooms and, whether you dine indoors or on the outdoor balcony, the views are as memorable as the cuisine. It is possible to walk to town, but the road is busy. Directions: Located on the edge of town, on the road to Port Vendres. *Directions:* Located on the edge of town, on the road to Port Vendres.

❄🚌☎🐴♈P🍴🖼≈🚶🍇

RELAIS DES TROIS MAS
Owner: Mme Juan
Route de Port-Vendres
66190 Collioure, France
Tel: 04.68.82.05.07, Fax: 04.68.82.38.08
23 Rooms, Double: €230–€440*
*Breakfast not included
Closed: Nov 15 to Dec 15, Credit cards: MC, VS
Region: Languedoc-Roussillon, Michelin Map: 527
www.karenbrown.com/troismas.html

I was enchanted by the Hostellerie le Maréchal and the gracious Bomo family that extends a warm and sincere welcome while exuding a fierce pride in their home, their "dream." The hotel itself is a clustering of four charming 15th-century buildings whose common walls have been opened up to accommodate an interconnecting passageway that jogs and weaves at a slant along the various levels. Hung heavy with geraniums, the front of the inn is set back off the road behind its own gates, and the half-timbered back of the inn sits on the edge of the meandering path of the River Lauch. The hotel enjoys a lovely, picturesque setting in a quarter referred to as Colmar's "Little Venice" and is within walking distance from the heart of town. Le Maréchal's 30 guestrooms are individual in their ornate and flowery decor, and priced according to size and whether they overlook the front courtyard or the river. My favorite rooms here are not always the lavishly decorated suites but some of the cozy, smaller rooms. Set under the old beams, staggered on different levels, there are numerous niches, alcoves, and loft areas that comprise the hotel's wonderful restaurant, À l'Echevin, and deciding at which romantic spot to dine might pose a greater problem than selecting from the incredible offering of its menu! *Directions:* Easy to find following the city's signs for the hotel, the hotel is also conveniently located 1 km from the train station.

HOSTELLERIE LE MARÉCHAL
Hoteliêrs: Roland & Alexander Bomo
4–6, Place des Six-Montagnes-Noires, "Petite Venice"
68000 Colmar, France
Tel: 03.89.41.60.32, Fax: 03.89.24.59.40
30 Rooms, Double: €95–€245*
*Breakfast not included: €12,50
Open: all year, Credit cards: all major
Châteaux & Hotels de France
Region: Alsace, Michelin Map: 516
www.karenbrown.com/lemarechal.html

Housed in one of Colmar's most historic buildings at the heart of the pedestrian district is La Maison des Têtes, its intricate façade ornamented with a multitude of heads (têtes). To reach the reception, pass under the archway and through a quiet cobbled courtyard. The hotel has 21 guestrooms, including a spacious apartment. Two very special rooms (104 and 204) overlook the Rue des Têtes and enjoy spectacular sitting areas enclosed by the two gorgeous mullioned bay windows. All the rooms, even those described as small, are lovely, extremely comfortable, and very attractive in their traditional decor. Most overlook the central courtyard and enjoy a magical silence at the heart of a bustling city. This lovely hotel is rich in woods, from the gorgeous, ornately carved wooden exterior to the beams and paneling of the interior. The restaurant is beautiful—large, but with tables set intimately on various levels against a backdrop of rich paneling and handsome mullioned windows. Breakfast is served in a lovely breakfast room, on the central terrace, or in your bedroom. This is an intimate-sized hotel whose owners are personally involved. Marc, a chef, also oversees the kitchen. He is not new to the business—his family had a large hotel in the north of Alsace. *Directions:* Located at the heart of the pedestrian district of Colmar. Rue des Têtes spokes off the Rue des Unterlinden across from the Place de la Mairie. Ask for a detailed map.

LA MAISON DES TÊTES
Hoteliêrs: Carmen & Marc Rohfritsch
19, Rue des Têtes, 68000 Colmar, France
Tel: 03.89.24.43.43, Fax: 03.89.24.58.34
21 Rooms, Double: €91–€235*
*Breakfast not included: €14
Open: all year, Credit cards: all major
Châteaux & Hotels de France
Region: Alsace, Michelin Map: 516
www.karenbrown.com/tetes.html

Down a private drive, Manoir d'Hautegente idyllically sits beneath shady trees in a garden bounded by stone walls, colorful flowers, and a rushing stream. The original core of this ivy-covered manor house was a forge for the local abbey and dates from the 13th century. The forge later became a mill and other sections were added with the distinctive arched windows and doors. The Hamelin family has lived here for over 300 years and the present generation is in place, as Patrick and his charming wife and adorable toddler, Batiste, have settled in and oversee the professional service and incredible welcome. The family also operates a second business, Conserves Artisanales, the production and sales of many regional gourmet offerings. In the evenings Patrick is in the dining room to discuss the different menu choices prepared by Chef Ludovic. Family antiques decorate the salons, halls, and bedrooms, including the tallest of grandfather clocks on the landing. With their high ceilings, fabric-covered walls, and coordinating drapes and bedspreads, the bedrooms vary greatly in size, but all enjoy river views. Bounded by a cornfield, the heated swimming pool is a perfect retreat on warm summer days. *Directions:* From Brive go towards Périgueux on the N89 and turn at Le Lardin in the direction of Montignac for 6 km to Condat. Turn east towards Coly on the D62. A sign before Coly directs you to the mill.

MANOIR D'HAUTEGENTE
Hoteliêrs: Patrick & Marie Josee Hamelin
Coly, 24120 Terrasson, France
Tel: 05.53.51.68.03, Fax: 05.53.50.38.52
17 Rooms, Double: €85–€215*
*Breakfast not included: €13,50
Restaurant: closed for lunch Mon, Tues, Wed
Open: Easter to All Saints, Credit cards: all major
Châteaux & Hotels de France
Region: Dordogne, Michelin Maps: 521, 522
www.karenbrown.com/hautegente.html

I am fortunate to have experienced some of the world's finest hotels and yet every once in a while there is one that captures my heart—as did Le Moulin de Connelles. The setting is magical. This fairy-tale teal-blue and cream timbered 19th-century grain mill, topped by a medley of dormer windows and chimneys, straddles a river on the banks of its own island. Green lawn and geraniums add dramatic color. However, it is the warmth of welcome and comfort of accommodation that capture the soul. Karine is truly charm personified and juggles everything with finesse, embracing the business and, more importantly, the guests with graciousness and warmth. Guestrooms are found up a winding staircase. We settled into a suite (4) with windows on two sides and views overlooking the river and the pool. Room 2 on the first floor and room 9, a junior suite with balcony just above, are both located right over the water. All the bedrooms are lovely, even number 11, the smallest, tucked under the eaves with hillside views and a small balcony nestled in the roofline up against the turret. A favorite, number 1 is the largest, with windows on both sides and a dramatic bath with the Jacuzzi sunk into the turret round. There are many sightseeing destinations nearby and lots of activities on the property. *Directions:* We definitely recommend that you print the directions from their website, but basically, leave the A13 at exit 19 from the north or exit 18 from the south.

LE MOULIN DE CONNELLES
Hoteliêr: Karine Petiteau
Départementale 19, 27430 Connelles, France
Tel: 02.32.59.53.33, Fax: 02.32.59.21.83
13 Rooms, Double: €120–€245*
*Breakfast not included: €14
Open: all year, Credit cards: all major
Châteaux & Hotels de France
Region: Normandy, Michelin Maps: 512, 513
www.karenbrown.com/connelles.html

The medieval village of Conques overlooks the Dourdou Gorge. Off the beaten track, the village is glorious in the gentle light of evening or in the mist of early morning. Conques' pride is an 11th-century abbey, directly across from a lovely hotel, the Sainte Foy. The shuttered windows of our room opened to church steeples and we woke to the melodious sound of bells. The decor of the air-conditioned bedrooms is simple and oftentimes a bit dark. The dining rooms are a bit more attractive with tables topped with crisp linen, country-French furniture, flagstone floors, ancient stone walls, and low-beamed ceilings. In summer you can dine in the sheltered courtyard or on the rooftop terrace which overlooks the abbey. You can order à la carte or select from a well chosen and well priced three- or four-course fixed menu. The restaurant offers a number of regional dishes. The wine list contains a wide selection of fine French wines. On a recent visit, I was concerned to find the attention to detail lacking—no fresh flowers or fresh linens or cloths. To be honest, the property looked a little worn. However, the location is so outstanding, that I include it and look forward to my next visit. *Directions:* From Rodez take the D901 northwest for 37 km towards Decazeville and Figeac to Conques. Although, located at the heart of the pedestrian zone, you can drive directly into the village and park in front of the hotel to unload luggage and check in.

GRAND HÔTEL SAINTE FOY
Hoteliêr: Marie France Garcenot
12320 Conques, France
Tel: 05.65.69.84.03, Fax: 05.65.72.81.04
17 Rooms, Double: €115–€207*
*Breakfast not included: €13,50
Open: Easter to Nov 1, Credit cards: all major
Region: Lot, Michelin Maps: 522, 526
www.karenbrown.com/saintefoy.html

The Hostellerie de l'Abbaye, a small country hotel whose chef is also the owner, sits on a cobblestoned street just a block from the entrance of Conques. While we know they have welcomed numerous Karen Brown travelers, a photo of their most famous guest, Prince Charles, is proudly displayed at the front desk. On a recent visit the young owner, Monsieur Etourneaud, personally showed us around with much enthusiasm. Conques was one of the main stopping places on the old pilgrimage route to Santiago de Compostela in Spain (known as the Way of Saint James), and, as such, has been host to travelers for many years. While you are in Conques, if you are on a budget, the Hostellerie de l'Abbaye makes a good choice for a hotel. New modern chairs and fabrics contrast with the ancient beams and the antiques that have long graced the public rooms. Guestrooms are clean and neat, and the bathrooms are modern. All rooms are spick-and-span and carry rates appropriate for a moderately priced hotel. The restaurant is charming and the menu reflects the talents of the personable chef. *Directions:* Conques is a small village located 38 km northwest of Rodez, 57 km southwest of Aurillac. The Hostellerie de l'Abbaye is just off the main cobbled square.

HOSTELLERIE DE L'ABBAYE
Hoteliêr: M Etourneaud
Rue Charlemagne, 12320 Conques, France
Tel: 05.65.72.80.30, Fax: 05.65.72.82.84
8 Rooms, Double: €76–€98*
*Breakfast not included: €11
Open: all year, Credit cards: all major
Region: Lot, Michelin Maps: 522, 526
www.karenbrown.com/delabbaye.html

Centuries removed from its original function—this was once a water mill—and the source of its past is responsible for much of its unique charm as an inn: weathered beams, thick stone walls, intimate rooms, and a water setting. Nestled on the river bank, the property stretches along the water's edge, from the parking area and lovely shaded pool to the inn and restaurant. It was a holiday weekend and I arrived too late to view the private rooms. However, if the public rooms are any indication of the charm and comfort offered here, Le Moulin de CambeLong is definitely the region's "choice" place to stay. Entered from a path bordering the river, a stairway leads up to a large, open area cozy under the old beams. Furnishings are clustered on tile floors dressed with oriental carpets, creating intimate areas. One can settle in front of the fireplace or at a trestle table with an attractive backdrop of pretty wallpapers and a handsome, old grandfather clock, while looking out windows framing the river below and surrounding pastures. Step down from here to the dining room, an inviting room whose elegantly set tables are paired with tall, fabric-covered chairs and floor-to-ceiling windows, draped in attractive fabrics, overlook the pool, garden, and river. The ambiance alone would warrant a stay; but so would the menu. Under the talented charge of Hervé, whose mastery is acclaimed, dining here is incredible. *Directions:* Located just below Conques, on the D901, to the south.

LE MOULIN DE CAMBELONG
Owners: Dominique & Hervé Busset
12320 Conques, France
Tel: 05.65.72.84.77, Fax: 05.65.72.83.91
10 Rooms, Double: €100–€170*
*Breakfast not included: €15
Closed: Nov 15 to Feb 15, Credit cards: all major
Châteaux & Hotels de France
Region: Lot, Michelin Maps: 522, 526
www.karenbrown.com/cambelong.html

Vieux Cordes is an enchanting, medieval hilltop village with the Hôtel du Grand Écuyer located at its center. Once the home and hunting lodge of Raymond VII, Comte de Toulouse, this grand hotel, which seems to improve with age, was completely redecorated with beautiful fabrics in 1999. Found along the upstairs hallway whose floors creak and slant, the bedrooms are very impressive in their decor. Decorated with period furnishings, a few of the rooms boast magnificent four-poster beds and some even enjoy large fireplaces. The bedroom windows, set in thick stone walls, open onto glorious vistas of the surrounding countryside. The reputation of the hotel's restaurant reflects the expertise of Monsieur Yves Thuriès, under whose direction and guidance selections from the menu are further enhanced by artful and creative presentation. His specialty is desserts and they are divine in presentation as well as taste. If you want to try your own talent in the kitchen, purchase a copy of his book, "La Nouvelle Patisserie". Vieux Cordes is a gem—a medieval village that proves to be a highlight of many a trip and the Hôtel du Grand Écuyer is the extra lure that makes Cordes an ideal stopover for any itinerary. The Thuriès family has renovated the Hostellerie du Vieux Cordes, a simpler hotel at the top of this charming village. *Directions:* Cordes is 25 km northwest of Albi on D600.

HÔTEL DU GRAND ÉCUYER
Hoteliêr: Yves Thuriès, Directeur: Mme Colette Thuriès
79, Grand Rue Raimond VII
81170 Cordes-sur-Ciel, France
Tel: 05.63.53.79.50, Fax: 05.63.53.79.51
13 Rooms, Double: €105–€230*
*Breakfast not included: €13
Open: Apr 1 to Oct 15, Credit cards: all major
Châteaux & Hotels de France
Region: Tarn, Michelin Map: 526
www.karenbrown.com/grandecuyer.html

Les Roches Fleuries is nestled in a green meadow high on a mountainside with a breathtaking view across the valley to the dramatic peaks of Mont Blanc. Like most of the buildings that dot the countryside, the hotel is like a large chalet, wrapped around with decks and balconies which in summer are one solid mass of brilliant red geraniums. The country theme continues inside, with walls paneled in light pine, rustic-style furnishings, and Provençal-print fabrics used throughout. There is a fresh, uncluttered, sunny ambiance, with light streaming in through large windows. The dining room is especially gorgeous: it has a wall of windows (draped in a beautiful blue Provençal-print fabric) capturing a stunning panorama of the mountains. There is a second, less formal dining room, La Boite aux Fromages, in an adorable rustic chalet next to the main part of the hotel. The bedrooms are decorated in light pine accented by pretty country-print fabrics and are grouped in four categories based on size and color scheme. Suites come in two categories—either with or without mezzanine. The hills beckon and walking seems to be the favorite pastime, but there is also a pool in the garden behind the hotel as well as exercise equipment, Turkish baths, and a Jacuzzi. *Directions:* From Geneva take the A40 west to the Sallanches exit. From Chamonix, travel the RN205 to Sallanches. Just beyond Sallanches, look for a road up the mountain to Cordon.

LES ROCHES FLEURIES
Hoteliêrs: Jocelyne & Gerard Picot
Cordon, 74700 Sallanches, France
Tel: 04.50.58.06.71, Fax: 04.50.47.82.30
25 Rooms, Double: €125–€250*
*Breakfast not included: €14,50
Open: Dec 20 to Apr 10 & May 10 to Sep 25
Credit cards: all major
Châteaux & Hotels de France
Region: French Alps, Michelin Map: 523
www.karenbrown.com/lesrochesfleuries.html

Perched on a hill in the middle of a lovely valley in Provence is the charming medieval village of Crillon le Brave—truly one of France's jewels. It is comprised of only a cluster of weathered stone houses and a picturesque church. Just below the church, terraced down the hillside, is the deluxe Hostellerie de Crillon le Brave. This small hotel exudes an aura of elegance, yet there is nothing stuffy or intimidating about staying here. The well-trained staff is friendly and the ambiance delightful. Restoration has been accomplished beautifully, maintaining all the wonderful wood and stone textures which are accented delightfully by the bold colors of Provençal-print fabric. Fine country antiques are used throughout. The guestrooms are decorated in the same style and most have magnificent views of the countryside. The hillside location lends itself well to romance—the gourmet dining room is located in a medieval-looking, vaulted-ceilinged room with a massive fireplace, which opens onto a splendid terrace where meals are usually served. An intimate bistro, open only at dinner, offers lighter fare. From the terrace, a path leads down to a lower garden where a swimming pool invites you to linger on comfortable lounge chairs and soak in the view. *Directions:* In Carpentras follow signs toward Mount Ventoux and Bédoin on the D974. Travel 10 km northeast and just before Bédoin, turn left to Crillon le Brave.

HOSTELLERIE DE CRILLON LE BRAVE
Hoteliêrs: Peter Chittick & Craig Miller
Place de l'Eglise, 84410 Crillon le Brave, France
Tel: 04.90.65.61.61, Fax: 04.90.65.62.86
32 Rooms, Double: €155–€560*
*Breakfast not included: €20
Lunch weekends only, Bistro: dinner only, closed Tues
Open: Mar to Jan 1, Credit cards: all major
Relais & Châteaux
Region: Provence, Michelin Maps: 524, 528
www.karenbrown.com/crillonlebrave.html

Le Fort de l'Océan is a charming small hotel perched on the rocks at the tip of a peninsula, overlooking the windswept, rocky coast. Nearby is the quaint port of Croisic, filled with colorful fishing boats and attractive buildings. Tucked inside the stern-looking façade of the fort you discover a deluxe, beautifully furnished, absolutely delightful small hotel. The hotel is positively captivating—a small, chunky, two-story, superbly renovated, 17th-century fortress enhanced by dormer windows, jaunty chimneys, steep slate roof, and dark-green trim. A stone wall around the property encloses a perfectly maintained garden with lush lawns, beds of fragrant flowers, tall pines, and a sheltered swimming pool. Just above the pool is a deck where guests relax on comfortable wooden lounge chairs. The dining room, which is especially famous for its excellent seafood, exudes a quiet, understated elegance with light streaming in through large windows, pretty pictures hung on white walls, a large chandelier in the center of the room, fresh flowers, and tables set with fine linens. Some of the bedrooms are in the main building, others in an adjacent wing. All are luxurious and tastefully decorated with fine furnishings and beautiful fabrics, and display quality in every detail. With each room comes a private garage and bikes for exploring the splendid coastline. *Directions:* From Le Croisic, go around the harbor and continue on to Pointe du Croisic.

❄ ✎ 💳 ⌶ P ⫟ ⊘ 🏊 🖼 ⚓ 🎿 🚶 🏇 ⛵

LE FORT DE L'OCÉAN
Hoteliêr: Valérie Criaud
Côte Sauvage, La Pointe du Croisic
44490 Croisic (Le), France
Tel: 02.40.15.77.77, Fax: 02.40.15.77.80
9 Rooms, Double: €150–€260*
*Breakfast not included: €14
Restaurant: open mid-Feb to mid-Nov & Christmas
Open: all year, Credit cards: all major
Châteaux & Hotels de France, Region: Brittany
Michelin Map: 517, www.karenbrown.com/ocean.html

Philippe and Andonis have settled in a little world of paradise and generously share it with guests. Their lovely hotel is situated at the top of a hill, by a little church (worth a visit to see its gorgeous ceilings), next to the château of Cuq Toulza. As the name implies, it terraces down the hillside so that each level enjoys gorgeous views of the surrounding countryside—a setting reminiscent of Tuscany. The inn is small and intimate, with just seven bedrooms, six in the main house, all tastefully and beautifully decorated, with shuttered windows peeking out through thick stone walls and bathrooms that effectively and efficiently maximize the available space. I adored our top-floor corner room, Le Chat Bleu, which afforded a wonderful view of countryside looking from the bed out through the half windows and was decorated with a beautiful antique chest and side table. I also loved the White Room, fresh and pretty with white linens and lovely pine furnishings, set under old exposed beams. A duplex unit with a living room on the first level and an almost "bird's nest" bedroom on the second level is located next to the pool. Do dine here—our meal was truly outstanding and the setting, as the sun sank and the moon rose, glorious. The Cuq en Terrasses is magic. *Directions:* From Toulouse take the N126 towards Castres for about 35 km east to Cuq Toulza then take the D45 towards Revel for a few kilometers south to Cuq le Château.

HÔTEL CUQ EN TERRASSES
Hoteliêrs: Philippe Gallice & Andonis Vassalos
Cuq le Château, 81470 Cuq Toulza, France
Tel: 05.63.82.54.00, Fax: 05.63.82.54.11
7 Rooms, Double: €95–€150*
*Breakfast not included: €12
Daily market menu: €33
Open: Mar 25 to Oct 30, Credit cards: all major
Region: Tarn, Michelin Map: 526
www.karenbrown.com/cuqenterrasses.html

I love to drive the back country roads that weave through the vineyards of Burgundy and cut a path through the quiet stone villages. I followed a sequence of signs to an unfamiliar hotel—and I was rewarded with a delightful discovery. Newly constructed in the architectural style of a Burgundian farm complex, the Manassès is set on the hillside and overlooks the surrounding vineyards. The reception off the entry of the main building is just an informal desk overlooking the spacious public room where tables are set for breakfast. A handsome grandfather clock and antique bureau add richness to the spartan decor. On the second floor, down hallways with beams cleverly exposed to give an old-world look, seven guestrooms are simply furnished with a bed, desk, and chair, yet are freshly modern and very appealing in their newly refurbished decor. Three of the rooms look out to the vineyards while four overlook the central car park. A new building, also bordering the courtyard, houses five gorgeous guestrooms that are spacious, elegantly decorated and an incredible value. The Chaley family are also vintners and are happy to have you sample their wines. A quiet spot, the Manassès is well priced and convenient for exploring the wine region. *Directions:* Located approximately halfway between Dijon and Beaune. Turn east off the N74 onto D25/D35 at Nuits St. Georges, then after just a few kilometers at Villars-Fontaine follow signage to Le Manassès.

HÔTEL LE MANASSÈS
Hoteliêrs: Yves, Françoise, Éric, & Cécile Chaley
Curtil-Vergy
21220 Gevrey-Chambertin, France
Tel: 03.80.61.43.81, Fax: 03.80.61.42.79
12 Rooms, Double: €75–€100*
*Breakfast not included: €10
Open: Mar to Dec, Credit cards: all major
Region: Burgundy, Michelin Map: 520
www.karenbrown.com/manasses.html

Dinan is a magnificent old city of timbered houses and cobbled streets that rise from its old port to the fortification above. With its multitude of shops, galleries, restaurants, and sidewalk cafés, Dinan is fun to explore. In search of a hotel that would allow more than an afternoon visit, I was thrilled to happen upon the comfortable and charming d'Avaugour. Set on the main road within steps of the heart of the cobbled old quarter, this is a small, city, three-star hotel with character. You enter off the street into an attractive lobby with a sitting area and exposed beams. A modern bar is accessed off the entry or through another entrance off the street. With lots of plans and dreams, Monsieur Caron, who has been director of some of Paris's finest hotels, has modernized and revamped bathrooms and redecorated guestrooms. One of the hotel's greatest features is its wonderful garden, which extends out back. Here guests can enjoy breakfast on the terrace, wander the paths, and enjoy unobstructed views of Dinan's castle and a panoramic outlook over the countryside. *Directions:* On the road that circles the heart of the old town, on the south side, just up from the château.

L'HÔTEL D'AVAUGOUR
Hoteliêr: Nicolas Caron
1, Place du Champ, 22100 Dinan, France
Tel: 02.96.39.07.49, Fax: 02.96.85.43.04
24 Rooms, Double: €120–€250*
*Breakfast not included: €11
Closed: mid-Nov to mid-Feb, Credit cards: MC, VS
Region: Brittany, Michelin Map: 517
www.karenbrown.com/davaugour.html

This pretty château-in-miniature enjoys an idyllic setting above the River Rance and looking out to sea. Your first impression of the home is of its gorgeous gardens and profusion of flowers lining the entry drive and it is not until you are actually inside the hotel that you can quite appreciate the spectacular setting and water views. This intimate, whitewashed, two-story manor with gray-slate roof and single distinctive turret is owned and run fastidiously by Madame Jasselin. Feminine touches abound, as does her attention to detail. The entry is very inviting with its family antiques—a gorgeous Breton grandfather clock, a handsome armoire, and a dramatic, enormous copper tub filled with silk flowers. Off the entry breakfast tables set in the conservatory take full advantage of the view of sea. The salon is a comfortable place to settle, with pretty fabrics framing large picture windows and games placed on tables for anyone to enjoy. There is also a small bar area set with leather chairs. In warm weather, guests enjoy both breakfast and afternoon tea at tables on the garden terrace. Guestrooms, all but two of which enjoy a glimpse of the water, vary from simple, basic accommodation to spectacular large rooms such as 1 and 5 with banks of window and unobstructed sea views. *Directions:* From Dinard travel south on the D114 in the direction of La Richardais and then find the small road that travels northeast (the D5) to La Jouvente and the hotel.

MANOIR DE LA RANCE
Hoteliêr: Mme Jasselin
Château de Jouvente
Dinard, 35730 Pleurtuit, France
Tel: 02.99.88.53.76, Fax: 02.99.88.63.03
9 Rooms, Double: €100–€230*
*Breakfast not included: €10
Open: Mar 15 to Jan 5, Credit cards: MC, VS
Châteaux & Hotels de France
Region: Brittany, Michelin Map: 517
www.karenbrown.com/manoirdelarance.html

The River Dordogne makes a panoramic journey through a rich valley studded with castles. The ancient village of Domme has for centuries stood guard high above the river and commands a magnificent panorama. The town itself is enchanting, with ramparts dating from the 13th century and narrow streets that wind through its old quarter and past a lovely 14th-century Hôtel de Ville. Visitors come to Domme for its spectacular views of the Dordogne river valley and the best vantage point is from the shaded terrace of the Hôtel de l'Esplanade, located on the outside edge of the village. Staying at this hotel enables you to savor the village long after the tour buses have departed. The Gillards extend a warm and friendly greeting and René Gillard is both your host and chef—in either of the two dining rooms, charmingly country in their decor, he'll suggest some excellent regional specialties. Bedrooms in the main building of the hotel are found down narrow, ornately decorated hallways, and a few open onto unobstructed, million-dollar views of the Dordogne. Other guestrooms of the hotel are found in annexes down cobbled streets in neighboring buildings in the village. Most annex accommodations are housed behind old stone walls and, although attractively decorated and comfortable, are not luxurious. *Directions:* Domme is located 75 km southeast of Périgueux. From Sarlat take the D45 for 12 km to Domme.

HÔTEL DE L'ESPLANADE
Hoteliêrs: René Gillard & Family
24250 Domme, France
Tel: 05.53.28.31.41, Fax: 05.53.28.49.92
25 Rooms, Double: €80–€148*
*Breakfast not included: €12
Restaurant: closed Mon & Tues off season
Open: Mar 1 to Nov 11, Credit cards: all major
Châteaux & Hotels de France
Region: Dordogne, Michelin Maps: 522, 526
www.karenbrown.com/esplanade.html

At first glance this hotel appears as a typical French roadside restaurant with natural-wood shutters and flowerboxes overflowing with a profusion of red, pink, and white geraniums. The wonderful surprise is that behind a simple exterior lies a sophisticated hotel and gourmet restaurant run by Philippe Zeiger and Pascal Fouassier. New owners, they carry on the tradition of excellence and service as established by the Péradel family who owned the property for more than thirty years. In a convival surrounding, Philippe and Pascal are a team who share their passion for cuisine and hospitality. Bedrooms are located in quiet wings that stretch behind the hotel. The smaller, less expensive, rooms are decorated in what is described as rustic. Larger rooms are more county house-style in their decor. Sixteen plainer rooms are found in a modern house in the village. Philippe Zeiger presides in the kitchen and his appealing cuisine ensures that the restaurant attracts a great many local patrons. The menu, which changes with each season, boasts many regional specialties to compliment some of the regions's and the world's finest wines. *Directions:* From Reims take the N44 south to Châlons en Champagne and then the N3 east in the direction of Metz for 8 km.

AUX ARMES DE CHAMPAGNE
Hôteliers: Pascal Fouassier & Philipps Zeiger
31, Avenue du Luxembourg
51460 Épine (L'), France
Tel: 03.26.69.30.30, Fax: 03.26.69.30.26
37 Rooms, Double: €85–€305*
*Breakfast not included: €14
Closed: Jan 3 to Feb 11, Credit cards: all major
Châteaux & Hotels de France
Region: Champagne, Michelin Map: 513
www.karenbrown.com/auxarmes.html

The 17th-century Château d'Etoges is built on an island surrounded first by an expanse of water and then an expanse of green lawns and fountains of natural water sprays. An arched bridge crosses over to its dramatic courtyard banded on one side by an impressive arched corridor. Inside, the ambiance is inviting and comfortable. This château was used as a home for many years before being converted to a hotel. Just off the entry is a small salon and then round the corner is a small, ornate dining room decorated in lots of pink. I preferred the adjoining dining room, a larger room with a big open fire and soft-yellow walls playing beautifully with the soft-yellow linens and the light that streams in from the large windows. The range of guestrooms is dramatic and the decor in some is a bit whimsical, so inquire about available accommodation to ensure a room to your liking. I loved the smallest rooms in the house, Arcades #1 and #2: compact and charming, with windows that look out to the side greenery and moat. La Tour has a large blue and cream bathroom and a bedroom in the turret with the bed set back in an alcove. Two of the more creative rooms are Byzantine, with its two beds separated by a massive pool table, and Jaune, all in yellow from the coat hangers to the closet chair. Boats and bikes are available to guests. *Directions:* Follow the D51 south from Reims through Épernay, then just past Montmort take the D33 east for a short distance to Etoges.

LE CHÂTEAU D'ETOGES
Hoteliêr: Anne Filliette-Neuville
51270 Etoges, France
Tel: 03.26.59.30.08, Fax: 03.26.59.35.57
20 Rooms, Double: €80–€260*
*Breakfast not included: €12
Closed: Jan 22 to Feb 16, Credit cards: all major
Châteaux & Hotels de France
Region: Champagne, Michelin Map: 513
www.karenbrown.com/etoges.html

Set high in the hills above the cosmopolitan lakeside city of Evian, La Verniaz et Ses Chalets, once a Savoyard farmstead, is a beautiful cluster of cottages and attractive central courtyard set behind a stone-wall entry. Beautifully landscaped trees shade courtyard tables and flowers add color everywhere. Bedrooms are found in La Closerie (the former stables), the Hotel Principal, and in five individual chalets that enjoy their own entrance and supreme privacy. It was a hot summer day at the time of our visit and guests were lunching at courtyard tables, but the summer dining room with its pretty pink cloths was ready for cooler evening temperatures. In winter the cozy Rotisserie is romantic and so inviting that one might wish for chilly weather year round! We were able to see a number of guestrooms and I loved number 18, a standard room in La Closerie, which overlooked the entry courtyard and turret round. Also in the old stables, the one apartment is spectacular, with a lovely salon, a side bedroom and private bath, and a large master bedroom whose windows open onto a balcony and views across the hills to the distant water. This is a lovely property with the bonus of an ever-present, caring family that oversees its operation. *Directions:* Take Route 24 towards Thollon and then 124 to Neuvecelle-Eglise. Signs for La Verniaz are numerous from the east side of town.

LA VERNIAZ ET SES CHALETS
Hoteliêr: Verdier Family
Neuvecelle-Eglise
74500 Evian les Bains, France
Tel: 04.50.75.04.90, Fax: 04.50.70.78.92
32 Rooms, Double: €130–€250, 1 apt, 5 chalets*
*Breakfast not included: €15
Closed: mid-Nov to mid-Feb, Credit cards: all major
Relais & Châteaux
Region: French Alps, Michelin Map: 523
www.karenbrown.com/verniaz.html

The town of Les Eyzies de Tayac, where the skull of a Cro-Magnon man was unearthed, is considered the prehistoric capital of the Dorgogne. The town's museum is dedicated to the unearthed treasures and on the outskirts of town, open to the public, are two of the region's prehistoric caves (Les Combarelles and Font de Gaum—for additional information, see page 53). As a result, many people choose to use Les Eyzies as a base from which to explore the region and the town boasts quite a few hotels. With a picturesque setting on the banks of the Vézère, the Hôtel du Centenaire's attractive complex of ivy-covered buildings offers the town's most luxurious accommodation. People are drawn to Les Eyzies for the mysteries of old, but enjoy the comfort and appeal of the hotel's spacious, modern guestrooms and suites. The dramatic atrium dining room is elegant and the menu—incorporating the delicacies of the region: foie gras, cèpes, truffles—is superb under the mastery of chef Roland Mazère. The Hôtel du Centenaire is a member of the prestigious Relais & Châteaux group and is a full-service hotel, so if you want to take a day off from sightseeing, settling at the side of the pool is a welcome option. *Directions:* Les Eyzies de Tayac is located 45 km southeast of Périgueux. From Périgueux it is a pretty direct route but the road number changes often. First travel the N2089 to the D710 to the D45, which becomes the D47 to Les Eyzies.

HÔTEL DU CENTENAIRE
Hoteliêr: Mazère-Scholly Family
24620 Eyzies de Tayac (Les), France
Tel: 05.53.06.68.68, Fax: 05.53.06.92.41
19 Rooms, Double: €140–€260*
*Breakfast not included: €20
Restaurant: closed Tues & Wed lunch
Closed: Nov to beg-April, Credit cards: all major
Relais & Châteaux
Region: Dordogne, Michelin Map: 521
www.karenbrown.com/centenaire.html

For more than a thousand years this majestic château has soaked up the sun and looked across the beautiful blue water of the Mediterranean. Rising 400 meters above sea level, the medieval village of Èze looks down upon Cap Ferrat and Nice. You can happily spend an entire afternoon on the secluded hotel terrace overlooking the pool and the stunning coastline vistas and in the sparkle of evening lights, the coastal cities seem to dance along the waterfront. The hotel's bedchambers open onto views of the Riviera or surrounding hillsides. Housed within the old stone walls of this medieval village, the rooms are not especially large, but are tastefully appointed and enjoy modern conveniences. Enjoy a drink in the bar just off the pool while studying the day's menu selections. For lunch or dinner, a meal at the Château de la Chèvre d'Or is a wonderful experience, a combination of marvelous cuisine and incredible views. The restaurant is popular with the local community and the many celebrities who have homes on the Riviera, so reservations are a must. Attentive service, superb cuisine, beautiful views, and a serene, medieval atmosphere make the Château de la Chèvre d'Or a hotel to which you will eagerly return. *Directions:* Èze Village is located on the Moyenne Corniche, the N7, between Nice and Monaco (13 km east of Nice). Exit the A8, at La Turbie.

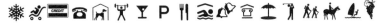

CHÂTEAU DE LA CHÈVRE D'OR
Hoteliêr: Therese Blay
Rue du Barri, 06360 Èze Village, France
Tel: 04.92.10.66.66, Fax: 04.93.41.06.72
32 Rooms, Double: €270–€2,640*
*Breakfast not included: €28
Open: Mar to Nov, Credit cards: all major
Relais & Châteaux
Region: Riviera, Michelin Map: 528
www.karenbrown.com/chevredor.html

Owners the Stein Group entirely redecorated Prince William of Sweden's former château, making this magnificent residence and hotel even finer. The Château Eza is located in the medieval village of Èze, perched 400 meters above the coastline of the Riviera. The hotel's bedrooms are found in a cluster of buildings that front onto Èze's narrow, winding, cobblestoned streets. Most have a private entry and blend in beautifully as part of the village scene. Although limited in comfort and light because of the old medieval walls, accommodation is extremely luxurious. Each room enjoys spectacular views and most have wood-burning fireplaces and private terraces, with views extending out over the rooftops of the village. The Château Eza has a renowned restaurant with views and service to equal the excellent cuisine. A multi-level lounge-bar with hanging ocean-view terraces is a delightful and informal spot for afternoon tea or a light meal. The Château Eza is a wonderful final splurge before leaving France—the airport at Nice is just 20 minutes away. As Èze is closed to cars, look for the reception at the base of the village: the two donkeys, les bagagistes, stabled out front. *Directions:* Èze Village is on the Moyenne Corniche, the N7, between Nice and Monaco. Exit the A8, at La Turbie exit number 57.

CHÂTEAU EZA
Hoteliêr: The Stein Group
Directeur: Chaline Stephan
06360 Èze Village, France
Tel: 04.93.41.12.24, Fax: 04.93.41.16.64
10 Rooms, Double: €150–€920*
*Breakfast not included: €22
Open: all year, Credit cards: all major
Châteaux & Hotels de France
Region: Riviera, Michelin Map: 528
www.karenbrown.com/chateaueza.html

The Château de Fère is delightful and just an hour from Charles de Gaulle airport. Set in parklike grounds, there are actually two castles. One built in 1206 by Robert de Dreux is now in ruins and serves as a background to the second, the 16th-century Château de Fère. The owner, Richard Bliah, is an architect, and he has remodeled and decorated his hotel in a style that he finds pleasing, with fabric-covered walls and matching draperies and bedspreads. He is diligent about redecorating and constantly improving accommodation. Room 10 at the top of the main staircase is spacious, enjoys views out through two large picture windows and a decadently luxurious bath, and is quite handsome, decorated in colors of gold, steel-blue, olive, and rust. The newest suite, Balneide (33) is spectacular—a large, pool-size Jacuzzi is set in a surround of hand-painted tiles and the bedroom is lovely, with a separate sitting area. The restaurants look out to the wooded grounds through tall windows, and display elegant linens, silver, and crystal. Ask for a seat in the pine-paneled restaurant or in the more whimsical main restaurant with its animal murals. A magnificent menu and an excellent wine list are offered, with the estate's champagne being a specialty. *Directions:* From Paris take A4 and exit at Château Thierry following directions to Soissons, then take D310 north to Fère en Tardenois. The château is located 3 kilometers outside town on D967.

CHÂTEAU DE FÈRE
Hoteliêr: Jo-Andréa Finck
02130 Fère en Tardenois, France
Tel: 03.23.82.21.13, Fax: 03.23.82.37.81
25 Rooms, Double: €150–€400*
*Breakfast not included: €18
Closed: Jan 2 to Feb 10, Credit cards: all major
Châteaux & Hotels de France
Region: Champagne, Michelin Map: 513
www.karenbrown.com/chateaudefere.html

Many editions ago I recommended the Château de Fleurville for the experience of a "vrai" (real) château at a reasonable price. After the quality slipped over the years, I was pleased to learn the property had come into the enthusiastic hands of a new owner. Leaving the corporate life behind, Pascal has conscientiously renovated the château to a higher level of quality never previously realized in over 400 years of existence. One accesses this intimate and pretty turreted château off either side of a circular staircase to an entry that both descends to the reception and climbs up to many of the guestrooms. Rays of light filter through the central stained-glass window creating a dance of colors on the walls. Most of the guestrooms are located in the château with décor appropriate to its theme and outfitted with all the modern conveniences. Five smaller rooms in a more modern décor are found at the top of the stairs accessed off the side garden, close to the pool and enjoying a shared outdoor terrace. Dining here is a memorable experience with a menu that Pascal says focuses on the "sauveur" with good meats and fresh fish prepared to accentuate their distinctive tastes. Dine either in the regal ambiance of the interior dining room or at tables set on the outdoor terrace with its tables separated from the lawn by a band of flowering roses, lavender and begonias—a truly beautiful setting. *Directions:* Take exit 27 off A6 at Tournus, then travel N6 south to Fleurville.

❄ ⚡ 💳 ☎ Υ P ⑪ 🏊 ⋏ 🖼 ⅃ ☎ 🏌

CHÂTEAU DE FLEURVILLE   New
Owner: Pascal Lehmann
71260 Fleurville, France
Tel: 03.85.27.91.30, Fax: 03.85.27.91.29
14 Rooms, Double: €60–€208*
*Breakfast not included: €10–€13
Open: Feb 5 to Nov 16, Credit cards: MC, VS
Châteaux & Hotels de France
Region: Burgundy, Michelin Map: 520
www.karenbrown.com/fleurville.html

La Régalido, converted from an ancient oil mill, is a lovely Provençal hotel, with its cream-stone façade, sienna-tiled roof, and shuttered windows peeking out through an ivy-covered exterior. Running the length of this hotel is a beautiful garden bordered by brilliantly colored roses. In the entry, lovely paintings and copper pieces adorn the walls, and plump sofas and chairs cluster before a large open fireplace. An arched doorway frames the dining room, which opens onto a verandah and the rose garden. The restaurant, with its tapestry-covered chairs placed around elegantly set tables, is renowned for its regional cuisine and its wine cellar. Monsieur Michel spends much of his day tending to the kitchen and is often seen bustling about the hotel, dressed in his chef's attire, but is never too busy to pause for a greeting. His wife's domain is the garden—the French say that she has a green hand instead of just a green thumb, and it shows. The bedrooms of La Régalido are very pretty in their decor and luxurious in size and comfort. About half of the rooms have terraces that look out over the tile rooftops of Fontvieille. This continues to be one of the hotels about which our readers rave. I am certain the accolades are a direct reflection of the owners and their gracious hospitality. *Directions:* From Avignon take N570 south in the direction of Arles. Ten kilometers before Arles turn southeast on the D33 to Fontvieille.

LA RÉGALIDO
Hoteliêrs: Mme & M Jean-Pierre Michel
Rue Frédéric Mistral, 13990 Fontvieille, France
Tel: 04.90.54.60.22, Fax: 04.90.54.64.29
15 Rooms, Double: €139–€290*
*Breakfast not included: €16
Restaurant: closed Mon, Tues & Sat lunch & Mon dinner
Closed: beg-Jan to end-Feb, Credit cards: all major
Relais & Châteaux
Region: Provence, Michelin Maps: 524, 528
www.karenbrown.com/laregalido.html

Pass quickly through the village of Forcalquier and continue on to a lovely knoll just outside of town and the Auberge Charembeau. As the name implies, the hotel is on a charming site, surrounded by large walnut trees, poppy fields, gardens, and lawns. André and Sandra Berger (who live here with their four sons) converted an 18th-century stone farmhouse into a lovely inn. Sandra, who has excellent taste, decorated the spacious guestrooms with Provençal fabrics, antique furniture, and handmade tiles on the floors and in the bathrooms. Many rooms have high, beamed ceilings. There is a newer section featuring rooms with kitchenettes, which are ideal for guests on extended stays. This newer wing, built in the same style, blends harmoniously with the original farmhouse. Throughout, the bedrooms have lovely views to the distant Luberon Mountains. The hotel also has a new heated swimming pool and a sun terrace surrounded by poppy fields. There is no restaurant, but André has a list of the best restaurants nearby—a list he constantly checks for quality. Auberge Charembeau offers very good accommodations at a most reasonable price. Rates are kept low so that happy guests keep returning, knowing they receive quality and value. *Directions:* From Apt take N100 east to Forcalquier. Then continue on N100 toward Niozelles. Charembeau is on your right about 2.5 km beyond Forcalquier.

AUBERGE CHAREMBEAU
Hoteliêrs: Sandra & André Berger
04300 Forcalquier, France
Tel: 04.92.70.91.70, Fax: 04.92.70.91.83
24 Rooms, Double: €56–€114*
*Breakfast not included: €8,50
Closed: mid-Nov to mid-Feb, Credit cards: all major
Region: Provence, Michelin Map: 528
www.karenbrown.com/charembeau.html

Madame Hubert, your charming hostess at the Manoir du Stang, describes her property as not really a small hotel or inn at all, but rather a comfortable family home where they receive guests. Set behind a moat and an arched gateway with a tower, this is certainly not an ordinary house, but rather a very dramatic home that affords regal accommodations. At the front of the handsome manor there are beautifully maintained, French-style gardens, while at the back you find a small lake and extensive woods. In all, there are over 100 acres to this impressive estate. Inside, beautiful original wood paneling enhances antique furnishings, all adding to the atmosphere of a private château. The hotel offers 24 bedrooms equipped with all modern comforts and furnished with period pieces in keeping with the mood of the lovely 16th-century building. The Louis XIV dining room is handsomely appointed, with tables set before a large fireplace. Waitresses adorned in costumes of the southern coast of Brittany provide service and lend an air of festivity to the meals. Although tucked into a forest setting, the hotel is just a short drive from the sea. *Directions:* From Quimper take D783 toward Concarneau. After 13 km, before you come to La Forêt-Fouesnant, the entrance to the hotel is on your right.

MANOIR DU STANG
Hoteliêrs: M & Mme Guy Hubert
29940 Forêt-Fouesnant (La), France
Tel & Fax: 02.98.56.97.37
24 Rooms, Double: €77–€185*
*Breakfast not included: €9
Restaurant: closed Sep to Jun, Dinner: €29
Closed: Oct to Apr, Credit cards: none
Châteaux & Hotels de France
Region: Brittany, Michelin Map: 517
www.karenbrown.com/stang.html

For twenty years Marie-Christine and Claude Combes have welcomed guests as friends to their family home, the Château de Garrevaques, recommended in our guide to French bed & breakfasts. One of our favorite properties to recommend because the welcome is so genuine, the accommodation regal, and the history of their home that has passed down for seventeen generations is so incredible, we are thrilled to introduce Le Pavillon du Château. Sharing the park of five hectares, Le Pavillon offers luxurious accommodation in what were the stables that serviced the château. Fifteen beautiful suites enjoy modern appointments, lavish bathrooms and are intimately decorated with family furnishings. The ambiance is grand with a lovely large atrium, living room, salon, and guests have the choice of two restaurants. Le Grenier du Pastel spills over onto the garden terrace and offers a lighter fare and more casual service, while La Cave, as the name implies is embraced by the stone walls of the cellar and offers a menu of fine, regional cuisine. Tennis courts, a large pool set out in the open fields, and a full service spa give guests every excuse to linger; although the location is also ideal for visiting Toulouse, Albi and the walled city of Carcassonne. *Directions:* From Toulouse take the D2/D622 about 45 km to Revel. In Revel, at the traffic lights, turn onto the D1 and then opposite the Gendarmerie, take the D79F to Garrevaques.

LE PAVILLON DU CHÂTEAU
Owners: Marie-Christine & Claude Combes
Château de Garrevaques
81700 Garrevaques, France
Tel: 05.63.75.04.54, Fax: 05.63.70.26.44
15 Rooms, Double: €100–€320*
*Breakfast not included: €15
Open: all year, Credit cards: AX, VS
Châteaux & Hotels de France
Region: Tarn, Michelin Map: 526
www.karenbrown.com/lepavillon.html

Once a Cistercian abbey, the Château de Gilly is surrounded by an expanse of grounds transected by a web of moats, with origins going back to the 6th century. At the heart of Burgundy, the château guards a location near Château du Clos de Vougeot, home of the Chevaliers de Tastevin. You can drive up over one arm of a moat to the entry, which was magnificently constructed to blend with two wings of the fortification that date back to the 17th century. Beautifully renovated, the interior of the château is rich in furnishings and comfort. Hung between dramatic beams, handsome tapestries drape the old stone walls. Lofty corridors, dramatic with vaulted ceilings and tile and stone floors lead to ground-floor bedchambers, and narrow, steep stairways wind up to rooms tucked under the heavy old eaves and beams. For complete privacy and ultimate luxury, request the Pavillion, set on its own overlooking the manicured gardens. Under the old stone arch of the cellar, an intimate bistro now offers winetasting paired with an incredible lunch menu. Wine is graciously offered at market price. Descend to an underground passageway that leads to the magnificent dining room. Dressed in deep-red fabrics, candlelight, crystal, silver, and heavy tapestries, the restaurant is very elegant. *Directions:* Go 22 km north of Beaune on N74. Just before Vougeot, watch for a small road and sign on the right, directing you east to Gilly les Citeaux and the château.

CHÂTEAU DE GILLY
Hoteliêr: Traversac Family, Directeur: Stéphane Dufour
Gilly les Citeaux
21640 Gilly (Vougeot), France
Tel: 03.80.62.89.98, Fax: 03.80.62.82.34
48 Rooms, Double: €150–€690*
*Breakfast not included: €23
Closed: Jan 1 to 15, Credit cards: all major
Grandes Etapes Francaises
Region: Burgundy, Michelin Map: 520
www.karenbrown.com/chateaudegilly.html

La Bastide was opened in recent years right at the heart of the medieval village of Gordes, and from the distance appears to be terraced into the hillside, with its striking pool set against the old stone walls. You enter off the street into a lovely and elegant reception area. Guestrooms overlook either the valley or the village street but double-glazed windows block out any noise and in the evening there is very little traffic. Rooms overlooking the valley are priced at a premium, but some of the smaller rooms on the village side are extremely good value. All the rooms are very similar in decor with an attractive rust-and-brown fabric used throughout and some rooms are equipped with king beds (rare to find in Europe). From the entry and living room you can enjoy views from tables set narrowly on an outstretched arm of the medieval wall—an ideal spot for enjoying an evening drink. Views look out spectacularly across the valley and down to the hotel's pool. From the terrace you can descend down a circular stone staircase to the pool and sauna and fitness room. One guestroom is located on the lower level, opening onto the lawn that stretches to the pool and enjoying lounge chairs and tables set just outside its door. Guests enjoy a delightful terrace restaurant with memorable views overlooking the valley and surrounding mountains. *Directions:* As you enter the village, La Bastide is the first hotel on the right.

LA BASTIDE DE GORDES & SPA
Hoteliêr: Jacques Mazet
Le Village, 84220 Gordes, France
Tel: 04.90.72.12.12, Fax: 04.90.72.05.20
45 Rooms, Double: €140–€598*
*Breakfast not included: €23
Open: all year, Credit cards: all major
Châteaux & Hotels de France
Region: Provence, Michelin Maps: 524, 528
www.karenbrown.com/bastidegordes.html

Grignan is a lovely village with stone houses and a maze of twisting, cobbled streets leading up the hill to the immense, Renaissance-style Château de Grignan. At the lower edge of town, facing a stone-pillared rotunda, is the tiny Le Clair de la Plume, a lovely hotel with great charm. Your heart will be won as you walk through the green wrought-iron gate into the delightful enclosed courtyard. The fragrance of roses and lavender fills the air and several nooks with trellises draped with greenery shade intimate eating areas. Facing this idyllic scene is a storybook-pretty house painted a pastel pink and accented by pastel-blue shutters. The oldest part of the building is the romantic kitchen, which dates back to the time when monks lived here. Breakfast is served in this cozy room with arched ceilings, tiled floor, and an immense open fireplace. There is no restaurant, but in the afternoon an English-style tea is offered, featuring pastry and lavender-honey ice cream. The individually decorated, attractive bedrooms are located upstairs. The house previously belonged to the Canadian Ambassador and it continues to offer the warmth of a private home. This ambiance is in great part due to your outstanding young host, Jean-Luc Valadeau, who runs this intimate hotel with great skill, and cares for each guest as a personal friend. *Directions:* From the A7, take the Montélimar sud exit and continue on D941 toward Nyons until you reach Grignan.

LE CLAIR DE LA PLUME
Hoteliêr: Jean-Luc Valadeau
Place du Mail, 26230 Grignan, France
Tel: 04.75.91.81.30, Fax: 04.75.91.81.31
10 Rooms, Double: €90–€165*
*Breakfast not included: €12
Open: all year, Credit cards: all major
Châteaux & Hotels de France
Region: Provence, Michelin Maps: 524, 528
www.karenbrown.com/leclairdelaplume.html

This lovely complex of salmon-wash buildings with tile roofs, nestled on a lawn and embraced by lovely, landscaped gardens, has long earned praise for its restaurant. As the name implies, *Frères* (brothers), share the kitchen. The main building houses a number of intimate, beautiful dining areas. Off the reception is a charming room referred to as the Verandah, another is called the Chapelle, and the largest, with windows on all sides, is named the Rotunda. On a beautiful day, guests have a choice of tables set under the shade of trees on the back patio that steps down to the garden. A tranquil setting, refined personal service, and the excellent menu are major attributes with the gracious warmth of the family behind it. Expanded by marriage, the team now includes sister-in-laws, who graciously share the task of welcoming guests. In a building below the restaurant complex, there are eight guestrooms on the first and second floors (an additional wing of five rooms has yet to be completed), each floor offering an end room with a separate sitting area. Guestrooms are attractive, spacious, comfortable, and modern. They possess handsome tiled bathrooms, high-beamed ceilings, and wood floors. Each has a name that sets the theme of the décor, as in the Clair de Lune with its celestial painted ceiling. Rooms enjoy either a terrace or a balcony overlooking the pool. *Directions:* Travel east from Bidart on D355 and, just past the A63, turn south on the Rue de l'Eglise.

L'HOSTELLERIE DES FRÈRES IBARBOURE
Owners: Philippe & Martin Ibarboure (The Brothers!)
Chemin de Ttalienea
64210 Guéthary (Bidart), France
Tel: 05.59.47.58.30, Fax: 05.59.54.75.65
8 Rooms, Double: €130–€230*
*Breakfast not included: €13
Closed: Nov 15 to Dec 5, Jan 1 to Jan 15
Credit cards: all major
Region: Basque, Michelin Map: 525
www.karenbrown.com/ibarboure.html

The Château de Locguénolé, isolated by acres of woodland, presents an imposing picture as it sits high above the River Blavet with lawns sloping down to the water's edge. This magnificent château has been the family home of the de la Sablière family since 1600 and today Madame de la Sablière and her son Bruno run it as an elegant Relais & Châteaux hotel. Family antiques abound in the four elegant salons. Down the grand curving staircase is the restaurant where Chef Jean-Bernard Pautrat presents a wonderful menu complemented by an excellent wine list. The principal bedrooms are grand, lofty, and high-ceilinged, overlooking a panorama of lawn, forest, and river. It is hard to beat the luxury offered by room 2, a decadent suite, and rooms 4 and 1, large rooms with massive bay windows. The attic rooms with their low beamed ceilings are delightful, but Bruno assured me that Americans prefer the cozy, comfortable rooms in the adjacent manor. With its close proximity to the coast, Château de Locguénolé offers exceptional accommodation and a lovely spot for exploring Brittany's coastline as well as visiting its historic hinterland. *Directions:* Hennebont is 10 km east of Lorient on N165. On the approach to Lorient, take the Port Louis exit from D781 for 2.5 km and then travel south away from Hennebont to the château.

CHÂTEAU DE LOCGUÉNOLÉ
Hoteliêrs: Mme & Bruno de la Sablière
Route de Port Louis
56700 Hennebont, France
Tel: 02.97.76.76.76, Fax: 02.97.76.82.35
22 Rooms, Double: €120–€295*
*Breakfast not included: €17-€23
Restaurant: closed Mon
Open: Feb 11 to Jan 3, Credit cards: MC, VS
Relais & Châteaux, Region: Brittany, Michelin Map: 517
www.karenbrown.com/locguenole.html

Narrow cobbled streets lined with ancient houses wind up from the picturesque sheltered harbor in Honfleur and just a short stroll from the bustle of Saint Catherine's Square is the Hôtel l'Écrin. Set behind tall gates, this was once a grand home and it retains that feel today. Now a complex of buildings set off its enclosed courtyard, the decor in the main home is flamboyant, to say the least—red velvet and gilt lavishly applied; the fanciest French furniture; a multitude of paintings; an assortment of decorations including stuffed birds, a larger-than-life-size painted statue of a Nubian slave, and two enormous wooden Thai elephants. The same lavish taste extends to the bedrooms in the main house where several large high-ceilinged rooms are decorated ornately. Buildings on either side of the courtyard and nestled in the back garden offer additional, less ornate bedrooms. The Blais family also purchased a neighboring building and completely remodeled it to provide five luxurious rooms that share a lovely sitting room in a building called L'Ecrin Village. Under the direction of Jean Claude, who is ever-present, the staff is friendly and helpful. Honfleur is one of France's most picturesque port towns and the Hôtel l'Écrin is quiet, convenient, and moderately priced. *Directions:* From Paris (180 km) take the A13 in the direction of Caen via Rouen. Exit A13 at Beuzeville, travel north on D22, then west on D180 to Honfleur. The hotel is signed.

HÔTEL L'ÉCRIN
Hoteliêr: M Jean Luc Blais
Directeur: Jean Claude
19, Rue Eugéne Boudin
14600 Honfleur, France
Tel: 02.31.14.43.45, Fax: 02.31.89.24.41
28 Rooms, Double: €90–€170*
*Breakfast not included: €11 or €16
Open: all year, Credit cards: all major
Region: Normandy, Michelin Map: 512
www.karenbrown.com/hotellecrin.html

Set on the coastal hills just outside the picturesque port town of Honfleur, La Ferme Saint Siméon is a lovely, 17th-century Normandy complex of timbered and shingled buildings with flower boxes adorning every window. Although a fire a few years ago mandated extensive renovations, the wonderful ambiance of old has been preserved—the transition from old to new is seamless, and La Ferme Saint Siméon is even more beautiful than ever. In the garden where painters such as Monet, Boudin, and Jongkind set up their easels, 17 rooms have been added. Of these new rooms, three are suites and, like the other rooms, all are individually styled and handsomely decorated with fine antiques. The intimate decor of the restaurant is beautifully accented by a beamed ceiling, bountiful flower arrangements and elegant place settings. The chef uses only high-quality, fresh produce, for which the region is famous, to create exquisite dishes. Reservations for this superb hotel and the exceptional restaurant are a must. La Ferme offers a convenient and luxurious base from which to explore enchanting Honfleur. The D-Day beaches and Giverny are both just an hour's drive away. *Directions:* From Paris (200 km) take Autoroute A13 in the direction of Caen to exit 3 signpost Honfleur. La Ferme is just beyond the town on the coastal road (D5130), going towards Deauville.

LA FERME SAINT SIMÉON
Hoteliêr: Bruno Boelen Family
Rue Adolphe-Marais, 14600 Honfleur, France
Tel: 02.31.81.78.00, Fax: 02.31.89.48.48
29 Rooms, Double: €220–€850*
*Breakfast not included: €20
Open: all year, Credit cards: all major
Relais & Châteaux
Region: Normandy, Michelin Map: 512
www.karenbrown.com/lafermesaint.html

Le Manoir du Butin is nestled against the forest just off the road on the left as you leave Honfleur in the direction of Deauville. It is a lovely, small, intimate home of three stories with stone detailing the exterior of the first floor and gray-blue timbers dramatically etching the top two. Views are across the lawn and west to ocean and sand unmarred by the towering chimney and factory stacks near Honfleur. Beautiful tiles warm the entry and to the right curtains open onto a gorgeous salon warmed by a large open fireplace. Tables in the dining room are dressed with soft yellows and are arranged to maximize the enjoyment of the view across the expanse of lawn to the sea. There are nine guestrooms in the house but since it was a holiday when I visited, I saw just a sampling of them—two of the small suites. On the second floor at the front of the house, room 7 offers a queen bed set opposite the view and chairs placed in front of the French doors and balcony. In a decor of creams, this room was very appealing and restful and the marble bathroom with tub and shower spoke of luxury. On the first floor the larger room 2, in creams and reds, enjoys the same orientation out to the sea but has no balcony. Breakfast is served either in the dining room or in the privacy of your room. *Directions:* Leave Honfleur traveling west on the D513 in the direction of Deauville. The manor is beyond La Ferme St. Simeon, on the south side of the road.

LE MANOIR DU BUTIN
Hoteliêr: Véronique Heulot
Phare du Butin, 14600 Honfleur, France
Tel: 02.31.81.63.00, Fax: 02.31.89.59.23
9 Rooms, Double: €120–€350*
*Breakfast not included: €10
Restaurant: closed Wed, Thur & Fri lunch
Closed: Nov 14 to Dec 2 & Jan 10 to Jan 27
Credit cards: all major, Châteaux & Hotels de France
Region: Normandy, Michelin Map: 512
www.karenbrown.com/dubutin.html

For those who want to experience a French beach town in a beautiful setting, I would recommend Les Hortensias du Lac. Hossegor, just north of the more famous resorts of Biarritz and St. Jean de Luz, has a wonderful relaxed atmosphere of people enjoying the outdoors. Les Hortensias is idyllically located outside town, only 300 meters from the sea, on a hillside looking through towering pines to a lake. The main building faces directly onto the lake and here you find the reception and a very pleasing and restful guest living room with a clustering of off-white sofas set on beige and white throw rugs in front of large picture windows, which frame a beautiful water view. Below the living room, with an equally lovely view, is the breakfast room where a lavish breakfast buffet is left out until the decadent hour of noon—just one of many ways Frederic ensures his guests a relaxing and enjoyable stay. While a few guestrooms are located in the main building, most are found in a group of two-story cottages. The rooms are all nicely furnished, and vary most dramatically as to whether or not they enjoy a lake view. I would definitely request a water view (cottage rooms 20 to 25 and 30 to 35) as it is the setting that makes this place so special. *Directions:* Leave the A63 at exit 8, following signs to the city center. In town follow signs for Les Hortensias du Lac, on the west side of the lake, to the north of the town center.

LES HORTENSIAS DU LAC
Hoteliêr: Frederic Hubert
1578, Avenue du Tour du Lac
40150 Hossegor, France
Tel: 05.58.43.99.00, Fax: 05.58.43.42.81
25 Rooms, Double: €115–€225*
*Breakfast not included: €18
Open: Mar 31 to Nov 4, Credit cards: all major
Châteaux & Hotels de France
Region: Basque, Michelin Map: 525
www.karenbrown.com/lac.html

Located in the beautiful region of the Maçonnaise, the Château d'Igé is superlative in every respect, as evidenced by 90% of the guests returning to its high level of accommodation, cuisine, service, setting and welcome. Once home to the Counts of Mâcon, this intimate salmon-hued château dates back to the 13th century. It was converted over three decades ago to a hotel and restaurant. Françoise continues the tradition and high standards set before her adding her own warmth and caring. The guestrooms are found off the hallways that extend off the stone-turreted stairs or the side wings and entrances. All are lovely in décor and extremely comfortable in appointments. The most very private and regal accommodation is found in the Tour du Parc. Dining is a memorable experience with an exceptional menu whether you settle in one of the regal dining rooms, whose tables are set on old stone floors against the fortified walls under heavy old beams warmed by a large open fireplace, or at tables set on the terrace bathed in the soft glow of the evening lights on a warm evening. The grounds that embrace the château are magical with an incredible abundance of flowers distinguishing pathways that lead to a multitude of romantic garden niches and escapes. *Directions:* From Lyon, take A6 north, exit Mâcon sud, then take N79 toward Moulins, Tontceau. Exit la Roche Vineuse and then travel towards la Roche Vineuse, Verzé and then on to Igé.

CHÂTEAU D'IGÉ   New
Hôtelier: Françoise & Pasqual Lehman
71960 Igé, France
Tel: 03.85.33.33.99, Fax: 03.85.33.41.41
8 Rooms, Double: €93–€210*
*Breakfast not included
Open: Mar 1 to Nov 30, Credit cards: all major
Châteaux & Hotels de France
Region: Burgundy, Michelin Map: 520
www.karenbrown.com/ige.html

The Hôtel Arnold is a simple country hotel in the village of Itterswiller, nestled on the hillside amongst the vineyards, a wonderful base from which to explore Alsace. The accommodation and restaurant are in three separate buildings. The color wash of these handsomely timbered buildings varies from soft yellow to burnt red, and all have windowboxes hanging heavy with a profusion of red geraniums. Most bedrooms are located in the main building, referred to as Hôtel Arnold, set just off the road on the edge of the village. All the guestrooms, which used to be simple in their decor, are beautifully decorated with Alsatian fabrics and carved furnishings. Most of the guestrooms enjoy their own deck and lovely, unobstructed views of the vineyards below. Completely renovated in 2005, there are also six very pretty rooms plus a top floor, three bedroom apartment in a delightful little home, La Reserve, next to Weinstube Arnold, the hotel's restaurant. Weinstube Arnold, set under lovely old beams with pretty cloths and decorative flower arrangements adorning the tables, is an appealing place to dine on regional specialties and to sample the estate's wines. Arnold's also has a delightful gift shop. *Directions:* From the A4, Paris-Strasbourg, take A35/A352 towards Colmar to Exit 13. Continue in the direction of Mittlebergheim/Epfig following signs for Epfig (N422). In Epfig, turn right at the first road sign, Itterswiller.

HÔTEL ARNOLD
Hoteliêrs: M & Mme Simon
98, Route du Vin
67140 Itterswiller, France
Tel: 03.88.85.50.58, Fax: 03.88.85.55.54
29 Rooms, Double: €84–€120*
*Breakfast not included: €12
Restaurant: closed Sun evenings & Mon
Open: all year, Credit cards: all major
Region: Alsace, Michelin Map: 516
www.karenbrown.com/hotelarnold.html

Le Phébus is nestled high on a hill in the Luberon, warmed by the brilliant sunshine of Provence. It is a charming, honey-colored stone building made to appear as if each stone were selected and hand-placed without mortar. The original building dates from the time of the Templar Knights and shelters beautifully decorated rooms of understated elegance, with one room flowing into the next. There is a gracious dining room with fresh flowers, beamed ceiling, high-backed, tapestry-upholstered chairs, and oil paintings. However, on balmy days, most guests prefer to eat outside on the stunning terrace, which captures sweeping views of the valley, vineyards, and quaint towns nestled in the hills. To add yet another ingredient of perfection, the chef, Xavier Mathieu, is noted for his innovative cuisine. Active guests can enjoy the tennis court and the swimming pool romantically snuggled on a level just below the dining terrace. The bedrooms, brightly furnished with Provençal-fabric bedspreads and drapes, are decorator-perfect. Most have balconies and some even have a private pool. The concierge helps guests plan trips to all the nearby areas of interest: hilltowns, antiques fairs, abbeys, and museums. *Directions:* From Avignon, take N100 toward Apt. At Coustellet, take D2 toward Gordes. Continue past the foot of Gordes on D2 toward St. Saturnin d'Apt. Turn left off the D2 at Joucas and follow signs to the hotel, up the hill on your right.

HOSTELLERIE LE PHÉBUS
Hoteliêr: Xavier Mathieu
84220 Joucas, France
Tel: 04.90.05.78.83, Fax: 04.90.05.73.61
26 Rooms, Double: €145–€605*
*Breakfast not included: €14–€20
Open: Mar to Nov, Credit cards: all major
Relais & Châteaux
Region: Provence, Michelin Maps: 524, 528
www.karenbrown.com/lephebus.html

Le Mas des Herbes Blanches sits high in the hills close to Joucas, a perfectly preserved jewel of a village perched on a hillside in the Luberon area of Provence. This light-beige stone building fits perfectly with those found in the marvelous nearby hilltowns of Lacoste, Bonnieux, and Gordes, You enter through a stone archway into an intimate courtyard where flowers and the sweet melody of a little fountain set the mood of romance. Inside, the lobby is bright and inviting, with everything done in lovely pastels—nothing dark or heavy looking. Even the wooden beams on the ceiling are light. This decor blends beautifully with the happy, colorful Provençal fabrics. The dining room has views in three directions, looking to the countryside and distant mountains over the pool and adjacent woods and vineyards. The honey stone is everywhere, reflecting the Provençal sunshine with artistic brilliance. The bedrooms are large and bright, some with light-wood furniture and Provençal prints, others with blue walls and painted furniture. All have balconies or terraces. The complex consists of a main building, dining room, and pool, and an adjacent building containing apartments for longer stays. All areas are separated by flowers, plantings, and gardens. *Directions:* From Avignon, take N100 toward Apt. At Coustellet, take D2 toward Gordes, continuing past the foot of Gordes toward St. Saturnin d'Apt. Turn left off the D2 at Joucas and follow signs.

LE MAS DES HERBES BLANCHES
Directeur: Evelyne Juillard
84220 Joucas, France
Tel: 04.90.05.79.79, Fax: 04.90.05.71.96
19 Rooms, Double: €175–€460*
*Breakfast not included: €21
Closed: Jan to Mar 10, Credit cards: all major
Relais & Châteaux
Region: Provence, Michelin Map: 528
www.karenbrown.com/blanches.html

At the heart of the charming timbered village of Kientzheim, L'Abbaye d'Alspach is like a village within a village—the hotel rambles through three different buildings, with guestrooms accessed across old wooden bridges, down creaking timbered hallways, or up old stone stairwells. This is a charming, family-run hotel where you are assured the traditional Alsatian warm welcome. The reception is located off the interior cobbled courtyard through a door in the distinctive tower. The entry salon is very inviting, with antiques set on old tiles under dark, heavy beams. Guestrooms are found off the tower or in a wing of rooms on the other side of the old wooden bridge. We saw number 14, one of the more expensive rooms, at the top of the old stone staircase—it was very commodious, with small windows overlooking the rooftops of town. In the building on the other side of the courtyard, number 16, a middle-priced room, was very appealing, with windows on both sides giving natural cross-ventilation in summer. The family has also recently added a new building which houses five exceptional suites and a fitness center. Number 1, a family suite, is gorgeous in rich fabrics and has an entry salon with steps up to a twin bedroom and bath and then a stairway up to a loft, double bedroom, and second bath. *Directions:* From the N83 between Colmar and Strasbourg, 10 km north of Colmar turn west at Houssen and drive about 6 km to Kientzheim.

L'ABBAYE D'ALSPACH
Hoteliêr: Philippe Schwartz Family
2 & 4 Rue Foch, Kientzheim
68240 Kaysersberg, France
Tel: 03.89.47.16.00, Fax: 03.89.78.29.73
34 Rooms, Double: €66–€135*
*Breakfast not included: €9,60
Closed: Jan 6 to Mar 15, Credit cards: all major
Châteaux & Hotels de France
Region: Alsace, Michelin Map: 516
www.karenbrown.com/alspach.html

Perched above the flowing River Dordogne and backed by formal French gardens and acres of parkland, the Château de la Treyne has been renovated and returned to its earlier state of grandeur. A fairy-tale fortress, the château will enchant you with its presence, its grace, its regal accommodation, and excellent restaurant. Inside, heavy wood doors, wood paneling, and beams contrast handsomely with white stone walls and the rich, muted colors of age-worn tapestries. Public rooms are furnished dramatically with antiques and warmed by log-burning fires. The resident dog usually lounges lazily in front of one of those crackling fires, adding a touch of homeyness to this elegant ambiance. In summer, tables are set on a terrace with magnificent views that plunge down to the Dordogne. On brisk nights a fire is lit in the beautiful Louis XIII dining room, the tables are set elegantly with silver, china, and crystal, and a pianist plays the grand piano softly. Up the broad stone staircase the château's bedrooms are all luxuriously appointed and furnished. Individual in their decor, size, and location, the bedrooms have windows opening onto either dramatic river views or the lovely grounds. If the Château de la Treyne is full, ask about its sister château hotel just 10 minutes away. *Directions:* From Souillac on the N20 take D43 for 6 km west towards Lacave and Rocamadour. Cross the Dordogne and the gates to the château are on the right.

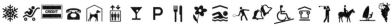

CHÂTEAU DE LA TREYNE
Hoteliêr: Mme Michèle Gombert-Devals
Directeur: Philippe Bappel
Lacave, 46200 Souillac, France
Tel: 05.65.27.60.60, Fax: 05.65.27.60.70
16 Rooms, Double: €180–€360*
*Breakfast not included: €18
Restaurant: closed Tues, Wed & Thur lunch
Closed: mid-Nov to Easter, Credit cards: all major
Relais & Châteaux, Region: Dordogne, Michelin Map: 522
www.karenbrown.com/latreyne.html

Housed within the walls of four beautiful Renaissance houses in Vieux Lyon that once belonged to the Lord of Burgundy, Claude de Beaumont, this hotel is unique in Europe and has been described as an architectural masterpiece. The decor of the Cour des Loges perserves the Italian spirit, dressed with the majesty of contemporary artwork and light flows though the nine interior courtyard domes with dramatic, suspended gardens. A beautiful jewel, the Cour des Loges is a stunning contrast of modern and old. The restaurants of the hotel, Les Loges, offer gastronomic menus. Effort has been made in recent years to ensure guests' comfort. Double windows buffer city noises, automatic shutters block out the light, televisions offer CNN, and bathrooms are ultra-modern. Accommodations are surprisingly varied in size and appointments, from a small duplex tucked under beamed ceilings, to a junior suite overlooking gardens, or an apartment in a more classical layout and priced accordingly. In some cases the bathrooms are located on a terraced level in the room—not for the modest. *Directions:* From A6 going south exit at Vieux Lyon (after the Fourvière tunnel). Follow the Quai Fulchiron to where it becomes the Quai Romain Rolland. At the bridge turn left on Rue Octavio-Mey, then first left on Rue de l'Angile. At the end of the street on the right is a welcome (accueil) garage where a special code is needed to open the barrier so you can drive to the hotel.

COUR DES LOGES
Hoteliêr: Georges-Eric Tischker
6, Rue du Boeuf, Vieux Lyon
69005 Lyon, France
Tel: 04.72.77.44.44, Fax: 04.72.40.93.61
62 Rooms, Double: €230–€590*
*Breakfast not included: €22
Open: all year, Credit cards: all major
Region: Rhône Valley, Michelin Maps: 523, 524
www.karenbrown.com/courdesloges.html

The Basilique de Fourvière dominates the wonderful old quarter of Vieux Lyon. Set just in its shadow is the Villa Florentine, whose seemingly perched location affords it an unrivaled setting and dramatic, sweeping vistas of the city. With an exterior wash of soft yellow-cream and salmon, its feeling is reminiscent of Italy. Inside, the Florentine's decor is very traditional and grand, with a stunning contrast of modern furnishings and appointments against old beams and walls. High ceilings, chandeliers, and a marble floor grace the entry off which is a lovely pool, which seems to extend out to the vista's edge. One can enjoy an aperitif at tables set on the sweeping expanse of patio. The hotel has a fine dining room on the landing off the reception for winter months, while in the summer guests sit at tables on the verandah and terrace, enjoying gorgeous views. Guestrooms are all attractive with modern furnishings and traditional fabrics—though rooms on the sixth floor have the added charm of wonderful wooden floors under lovely beams. Rooms 4, 7, and 8 have particularly breathtaking views. They have also recently added nine new rooms, suites and a fitness center! The hotel's multilingual staff is very professional, and if you are traveling by train, they will arrange to have you met at the station. *Directions:* Follow signs for Vieux Lyon Centre Ville and then Saint Paul to the Montée Saint Barthélémy.

VILLA FLORENTINE
Hoteliêr: Giorgi
25–27 Montée Saint Barthélémy
69005 Lyon, France
Tel: 04.72.56.56.56, Fax: 04.72.40.90.56
28 Rooms, Double: €230–€800*
*Breakfast not included: €16
Open: all year, Credit cards: all major
Relais & Châteaux
Region: Rhône Valley, Michelin Maps: 523, 524
www.karenbrown.com/florentine.html

Located just 100 kilometers to the northeast of Paris, but a world away in a village of Norman timbered houses and cobbled streets, is a dear inn owned by the very charming Madame Brun. It has an absolutely storybook timbered exterior of old beams set into salmon-pink stucco, a decorative wrought-iron sign of a unicorn, and an inscription indicating that it has been an inn since 1610. You enter into a cozy hallway with a large old trunk set on the sienna and cream tiles, all under old beams. You will want to linger over breakfast as the breakfast room is so cozy and intimate with its large open fireplace, handsome copper pieces, and wonderful corner grandmother clock. Opposite is a salon where you can sit on red velvet sofas or grab a stool at the bar. In warm weather it is also lovely to sit at tables nestled in the shade of the back garden. While three of the guestrooms are found in a cottage off the garden, most (16) are up a creaking staircase with a marvelous heavy old banister. Guestrooms are a bit dated in decor but they are clean and bright, enjoy private baths, and for the price are appealingly spacious. I especially liked rooms 5 and 6: both were large, had a sitting area, and overlooked the activity of the front street and old central market. *Directions:* From the N14 between Paris and Rouen, exit approximately 24 km to the southeast of Rouen on the D321 and drive east for 12 km to Lyons-La-Forêt.

 P

LA LICORNE
Hoteliêr: Mme Brun
27, Place Benserade
27480 Lyons-La-Forêt, France
Tel: 02.32.49.62.02, Fax: 02.32.49.80.09
19 Rooms, Double: €68–€130*
*Breakfast not included: €10
Restaurant: closed Nov 15 to Jan 25
Closed: Dec 20 to Jan 25, Credit cards: all major
Region: Ile de France, Michelin Map: 513
www.karenbrown.com/licorne.html

This ancient Relais de la Poste excels in its traditional role as provider of a comfortable night's lodging and good food. The hotel is first and foremost a family operation—the Coussau family is ever present, setting a wonderful example of welcome and hospitality and displaying an impressive attention to detail both from a service and a cleanliness standpoint. Located just off the road but backing onto its own tranquil acreage of gardens, woods, swimming pool, and tennis courts, the hotel has a peaceful setting. This long and narrow two-story building is especially attractive because of its handsome shuttered, paned windows and balconies draped with red geraniums. As soon as we entered we were met by numerous staff who took our bags, waived the fanfare of check-in, and showed us directly to our room so we could rest. They offered a simple welcome and smile, which went a long way after a long, tiring journey. Our room, overlooking the side garden, was comfortable, modern in decor, with traditional furnishings, and had a luxurious, recently remodeled bathroom. Dinner was an enjoyable experience—we chose the menu dégustation, an excellent and reasonably priced selection of the chef's specialties. Service was attentive and formal but not overbearing and the setting, looking out through large windows, was very attractive. *Directions:* Magescq sits at the junction of the N10 and the D16, to the northwest of Dax. The hotel is well signed.

RELAIS DE LA POSTE
Hoteliêrs: Jean & Jacques Coussau
24, Avenue de Maremne, 40140 Magescq, France
Tel: 05.58.47.70.25, Fax: 05.58.47.76.17
17 Rooms, Double: €137–€350*
*Breakfast not included: €18
Restaurant: closed Mon eve & Tues
Closed: Nov 12 to Dec 20, Mon & Tues, Oct to May
Credit cards: all major, Relais & Châteaux
Region: Basque, Michelin Map: 525
www.karenbrown.com/relaisdelaposte.html

Enter through an arched doorway into the interior courtyard of this lovely hotel and you are embraced by the tranquillity and beauty of the setting. This was once a religious school for girls and you can almost hear echoes of their laughter in the hallways and gardens. Set across the lawn from the entrance is a beautiful chapel and guestrooms are found in the various buildings that enclose the complex. We toured rooms in each building and they all had their own charm and attributes. I loved the privacy of number 7 with its own entrance at the top of the stairs and cozy bedroom tucked under the vaulted ceiling and beams. Number 6 with its king bed is exceptionally large and enjoys an outlook to the back garden, while number 3 is lovely with a king bed and large jetted tub and French doors opening to the splendor of the surrounding gardens. The colors and patterns selected for fabrics and furnishings are very pretty and the rooms all enjoy modern appointments and comforts. Each building has both accommodations and public rooms for guests, who can also relax in the beautifully landscaped grounds and the delightful pool. Breakfast can be taken in one's room, on the lovely garden terrace, or in the cozy breakfast room with its wonderful open fireplace. This is a charming hotel in a charming village in the beautiful Dordogne. *Directions:* Martel is located on the N140 about 15 km to the northeast of Souillac and about 24 km north of Rocamadour.

HÔTEL LE RELAIS SAINTE ANNE
Owners: M. Neuenschwander, M. Kurt & M. Bettler
Hoteliêr: M. Peter Bettler
Rue Pourtanel, 46600 Martel, France
Tel: 05.65.37.40.56, Fax: 05.65.37.42.82
16 Rooms, Double: €70–€245*
*Breakfast not included: €12– €15
Open: Mar 15 to Nov 15, Credit cards: AX, VS
Châteaux & Hotels de France
Region: Dordogne, Michelin Map: 522
www.karenbrown.com/relaissainteanne.html

Le Fer à Cheval abounds with romantic charm. A feeling of intimacy and genuine hospitality prevails, untainted by any hint of ostentatious grandeur. Throughout, you find walls and ceilings paneled with wood gleaming with the patina of age, fine oil paintings, grandfather clocks ticking in every room, cozy fireplaces, fabulous country antiques, and gorgeous Provençal fabrics. Isabelle Sibuet, who is extraordinarily gifted, has decorated all the rooms and, what is truly astounding, has sewn the innumerable pillows, curtains, bed coverings, and tablecloths. The bedrooms exude the same quality and country charm, with antiques, pine paneling, and puffy down comforters on the beds. Nestled in the garden at the back of the hotel is a swimming pool and, next to it, a terrace, a favorite spot to dine on warm evenings. However, you must not miss the dining room: it is a dream, with low, paneled ceiling, paneled walls, a large fireplace, lovely linens, and soft candlelight. Best of all, the food is fantastic. Le Fer à Cheval offers exceptional quality displayed in every detail of this ever-so-charming hotel. *Directions:* From Chamonix take A40 west to the Sallanches exit. From Sallanches take N212 south for 13 km to Megève. Le Fer à Cheval is located on the edge of town as if you were heading toward Sallanches. Watch for a small sign that directs you back up a small, angled side street.

LE FER À CHEVAL
Hoteliêrs: Isabelle & Marc Sibuet
36, Route du Crêt d'Arbois
74120 Megève, France
Tel: 04.50.21.30.39, Fax: 04.50.93.07.60
50 Rooms, Double: €300–€708*
*Includes breakfast & dinner
Open: Dec 15 to Apr 15 & Jun 15 to Sep 15
Credit cards: all major
Region: French Alps, Michelin Map: 523
www.karenbrown.com/leferacheval.html

Jocelyne and Jean-Louis Sibuet are masters in the hotel business, owning several premier hotels in the lovely mountain village of Megève—but for sheer drama, none can surpass Les Fermes de Marie. This is definitely no ordinary hotel, but rather a cluster of antique chalets put together to look like a typical Haute-Savoie village. The owner, Jean-Louis Sibuet, spent five years combing the countryside for marvelous old farmhouses, which he brought back and reconstructed in a two-acre park and meadow on the outskirts of Megève. While Jean-Louis was busy searching for buildings, his talented wife, Jocelyne, was scouting the region for antique artifacts and furniture. When the houses were in place, Jocelyne added her magic decorating touch. Every room is filled with antiques and many whimsical accessories such as cute paintings of geese and contented cows. The bedrooms are each individually furnished, but have the same country-cozy charm. There is an abundance of paneled walls, open-beamed ceilings, and pretty fabrics throughout. Although the hotel has a rustic ambiance, its top-notch amenities appeal to the most sophisticated traveler, with excellent bathrooms, a health and beauty-care center, and an indoor swimming pool. *Directions:* From Chamonix take A40 west to the Sallanches exit. From Sallanches take N212 south 13 km to Megève. Les Fermes is located just outside town, in the direction of Praz sur Arly.

LES FERMES DE MARIE
Hoteliêrs: Jocelyne & Jean-Louis Sibuet
Chemin de Riante Colline
74120 Megève, France
Tel: 04.50.93.03.10, Fax: 04.50.93.09.84
71 Rooms, Double: €190–€834*
*Breakfast not included: €17, Includes spa use
Open: Jun to mid-Oct & mid-Dec to mid-Apr
Credit cards: all major
Region: French Alps, Michelin Map: 523
www.karenbrown.com/lesfermesmarie.html

Hôtel Mont-Blanc is in the heart of Megève's pedestrian zone, facing onto the square in front of the church. The exterior looks similar to many chalet-style hotels but once you are inside, enchantment begins. The decor blends the ambiance of an elegant chalet with that of a private English club. You enter into a cozy lounge with polished wood floors and ceiling and walls completely paneled in gorgeous antique pine. The focal point of the room is a large fireplace with bookshelves on either side, flanked by comfortable sofas. The color scheme is where the "clubby" look comes in: rich "racing-green" drapes are tied back with crimson sashes, the chairs are slip-covered in greens and reds, and the handsome wing-back chairs are done in green-and-red plaid. Antiques abound—a beautiful writing desk, handsome oil paintings, beautiful chests of drawers, grandfather clocks, to name only a few. In the breakfast room the mood changes from slightly formal to definitely country-cozy, with wooden carved chairs and Provençal-print fabrics. The guestrooms continue the charming rustic ambiance. Each has its own personality, but all are similar in style with an abundant use of pretty country-print fabrics and lots of mellow woods. *Directions:* From Chamonix take A40 west to the Sallanches exit. From Sallanches take N212 south for 13 km to Megève. The hotel is in the center of town. Ask the hotel at the time of making your reservations where to park.

HÔTEL MONT-BLANC
Hoteliêrs: Jocelyne & Jean-Louis Sibuet
Place de l'Eglise, 74120 Megève, France
Tel: 04.50.21.20.02, Fax: 04.50.21.45.28
40 Rooms, Double: €182–€626*
*Breakfast not included: €17
Closed: May 1 to Jun 10, Credit cards: all major
Region: French Alps, Michelin Map: 523
www.karenbrown.com/montblanc.html

With an ideal location in the heart of the Luberon Regional Nature Park, La Bastide de Marie, a renovated 18th-century farmhouse surrounded by 15 acres of vineyards, is the most beautiful property of the entire region. It offers 14 absolutely gorgeous air-conditioned bedrooms made chic and comfortable with antiques, wrought-iron beds, rich fabrics, and fine furnishings, all remodeled to preserve authenticity. Decoration is typically Provençal, mixing the colors and lights of the south. In the grounds you find a heated swimming pool and an old fishpond transformed into a two-level pool with a little fountain. The owners really want you to feel at home and, in fact, sometimes you just help yourself to what you need. Guests stay on a half-board basis (breakfast and lunch or dinner), and also enjoy afternoon tea. Dining is a special experience here, with many home-produced fresh ingredients. You have the opportunity to taste all the property's different wines as well as visiting the wineries and cellars and participating in the grape harvest. La Bastide de Marie opens its doors to a world where the good life reigns and you long to stay for a long while. *Directions:* From Avignon follow the N100 towards Apt then at les Beaumettes take the road for Ménerbes on your right (D103) for 6 km, following the sign for Bonnieux (still on the D103). Once you have passed the dolmen, drive 150 meters and La Bastide de Marie is on your right.

※ ▣ ⚞ 🏧 🏠 🏡 ⛾ P 🍴 🚫 🏊 🖼 🏃 🚶 🍇

LA BASTIDE DE MARIE
Innkeepers: Jocelyne & Jean-Louis Sibuet
Route de Bonnieux, Quartier de la Verrerie
Ménerbes, France
Tel: 04.90.72.30.20, Fax: 04.90.72.54.20
14 Rooms, Double: €415–€715*
*Includes breakfast & lunch or dinner and tea break
Open: mid-March to mid-Nov, Credit cards: all major
Region: Provence, Michelin Map: 528
www.karenbrown.com/marie.html

There is an enchantment about this beautiful castle high above Mercuès and the Lot Valley. Once you have seen it, you will not be able to take your eyes away or to drive through the valley without stopping—it appears to beckon you. Here you can live like royalty with all the modern conveniences. The château has been restored and decorated in keeping with formal tradition. Accommodation is dramatic and memorable: the 30 guestrooms are magnificent—the furnishings are handsome and the windows open to some splendid valley views. Unique and priced accordingly, room 19 (in a turret) has windows on all sides and a glassed-in ceiling that opens up to the beams. Enjoy a marvelous dinner in the elegantly beautiful restaurant. The Vigouroux family owns vineyards which produce sumptuous wines bottled under the Château de Haute Serre and Château de Mercuès label and they have built some large cellars under the gardens with a connecting underground passage to the château to store their produced and acquired wines. *Directions:* Located 6 km from Cahors. Take D911 from Cahors to Mercuès and then turn right at the second light in the village of Mercuès.

CHÂTEAU DE MERCUÈS
Hoteliêr: Georges Vigouroux
Directeur: Bernard Denegre
Mercuès, 46090 Cahors, France
Tel: 05.65.20.00.01, Fax: 05.65.20.05.72
30 Rooms, Double: €180–€400*
*Breakfast not included: €20 in room, €23 buffet
Open: Apr 1 to Oct 31, Credit cards: all major
Relais & Châteaux
Region: Lot, Michelin Map: 526
www.karenbrown.com/mercues.html

In one of Burgundy's most elegant wine villages, Les Magnolias is a handsome 18th-century complex that once served as a private home. Your host, Monsieur Delarue, is charming, and the home reflects both his French and English origins. At the time of our spring visit, the cream stone building hung heavy with roses. Tall trees frame the entry and teal-blue shutters adorn the windows and also serve to close out the heat during the hot summer months. The largest building in the complex accommodates charming but simple guestrooms, sweet in the fabrics selected and comfortable with good mattresses and large square pillows. Room 1 is a spacious king-bedded room on the entry level, and especially pretty are room 3 on the second floor, decorated in a soft cream and rose, and room 6 under the eaves, decorated with a small blue print. Guests enjoy an intimate sitting room just off the entry. Across the graveled courtyard, a smaller building houses a few more rooms and one lovely garden suite. Breakfast is enjoyed in the privacy of one's guestroom or at tables set in the yard behind the entry gates. Les Magnolias is a stately country home and has the atmosphere of a private residence. Thoughtful touches such as fresh flowers in the bedroom and posies in the bathroom are appreciated. *Directions:* Leave the A6 at Beaune and follow signs to Châlon sur Saône or Lyon on the N74 then wind through the vineyards on the D973 to Meursault.

HÔTEL LES MAGNOLIAS
Owner: M. Delarue, Manager: Therese Bato
8, Rue Pierre Joigneaux
21190 Meursault, France
Tel: 03.80.21.23.23, Fax: 03.80.21.29.10
12 Rooms, Double: €89–€165*
*Breakfast not included: €9
Open: Mar 15 to Dec 1, Credit cards: all major
Region: Burgundy, Michelin Map: 520
www.karenbrown.com/lesmagnolias.html

La Ferme Lamy, a sprawling farm complex on the outskirts of Sarlat, was renovated and converted to a wonderful 12-room hotel. Park to the side of the inn and walk past the pool fronted by roses, whose water seems to cascade over the edge, to the entry of the hotel. To one side of the entry is a very attractive salon with chairs set in front of a large, open fireplace and intimate tables set for breakfast. On the other side, a door opens to the gorgeous country kitchen, where the scent of baking breads draws many a guest to the heart of the home. Upstairs, our room 11, as well as room 12, were very spacious under an A-frame pitched roof with exposed beams. The decor in our room was quite pretty with country prints, a beautiful old armoire, and a handsome antique table in addition to a table set with two chairs by the window. I also liked rooms 9 and 10, in a separate building, both air-conditioned and lovely with their country decor and old beams. Five smaller rooms are equipped with loft beds and open onto a terrace with tables set just outside their doors. Under new ownership, I look forward to meeting the Duneau family on my next trip and welcome feedback from our readers. *Directions:* Halfway between the towns of Les Eyzies and Sarlat. Take the D47 to the C3. At Benives watch for signs directing you to the right to La Ferme Lamy.

LA FERME LAMY
Owners: Christine, Pauline & Michel Duneau
24220 Meyrals, France
Tel: 05.53.29.62.46, Fax: 05.53.59.61.41
12 Rooms, Double: €105–€200*
*Breakfast not included: €10
Open: all year, Credit cards: all major
Châteaux & Hotels de France
Region: Dordogne, Michelin Maps: 521, 526
www.karenbrown.com/fermelamy.html

Overpowered by the walls of the towering Jonte Canyon, the picturesque houses of Meyrueis huddle along the banks of the River Jonte. From this quaint village you take a farm road to the enchanting Château d'Ayres. A long wooded road winds through the grounds and, hidden behind a high stone wall, the château has managed to preserve and protect its special beauty and peace. Built in the 12th century as a Benedictine monastery, burned and ravaged over the years, it was at one time owned by an ancestor of the Rockefellers. In the late 1970s the property was sold to Jean-François de Montjou, under whose meticulous care and incredible devotion the hotel is managed today. A dramatic wide stone stairway sweeps up to the handsome bedchambers. Rooms vary in their size and bathroom appointments, which is reflected in their price, but all enjoy the quiet of the park setting. The decor throughout the château is lavished with personal belongings and is well worn, comfortable, and homey. Instead of having one large formal room, tables are intimately set in a few small cozy niches in rooms that serve as the restaurant. Works of culinary art are created in the kitchen daily. The Château d'Ayres is a lovely and attractive hotel and, if time allows, spend an extra night simply for the luxury of lounging at the pool. *Directions:* From Millau take N9 for 7 km to Aguessac; turn right on D907. At Le Rozier cross the bridge, still on the D907, direction Meyreuis.

CHÂTEAU D'AYRES
Hoteliêrs: Jean-François & Helene de Montjou
48150 Meyrueis, France
Tel: 04.66.45.60.10, Fax: 04.66.45.62.26
27 Rooms, Double: €92–€163*
*Breakfast not included: €13
Open: all year, Credit cards: all major
Châteaux & Hotels de France
Region: Tarn, Michelin Map: 527
www.karenbrown.com/chateaudayres.html

Relais la Métairie is a charming country hotel nestled in one of the most irresistible regions of France, the Dordogne. La Métairie is an attractive soft-yellow-stone manor set on a grassy plateau. Views from its tranquil hillside location are of the surrounding farmland and down over the Cingle de Trémolat, a scenic loop of the River Dordogne. The bedrooms and one apartment are tastefully appointed and benefit from the serenity of the rural setting. The bar is airy, decorated with white wicker furniture. The restaurant is intimate and very attractive with tapestry-covered chairs, and a handsome fireplace awaits you in the lounge. The owners hail from Switzerland where they also run an inn in the Bernese Oberland. They are becoming more and more committed to France, however, as they have also purchased the beautiful property La Grande Bastide in St. Paul de Vence, and while they do see the need to spend time at all three properties, they consider La Métairie their jewel. Relais la Métairie is found on a country road that winds along the hillside up from and between Mauzac and Trémolat. Without a very detailed map, it is difficult to find. However, it is worth the effort, as this is a lovely country inn with an idyllic, peaceful setting. *Directions:* From Trémolat travel west on the D31 as it hugs the river and then at Mauzac follow signs for Cingle de Trémolat, turning up to Millac and on to La Métairie.

RELAIS LA MÉTAIRIE
Hoteliêrs: Heinz & Rita Johner
Millac, 24150 Mauzac, France
Tel: 05.53.22.50.47, Fax: 05.53.22.52.93
11 Rooms, Double: €110–€230*
*Breakfast not included: €15
Open: Apr 1 to Oct 31, Credit cards: all major
Châteaux & Hotels de France
Region: Dordogne, Michelin Map: 525 526
www.karenbrown.com/lametairie.html

A glimpse of the dramatic Château de la Bretesche with its clustering turrets will draw you through the gates but it is the luxury of accommodation at the neighboring hotel that will tempt you to settle. The hotel is distanced from the château by the encircling waters of La Bière and elegantly housed in what were once the château's stables and farm buildings. Its 200-hectare grounds back onto its own golf course, which weaves through the lush and beautiful national park. Off the handsome, stone-tiled entry a very attractive bar is cleverly incorporated into the former stables, with individual groupings of tables in each stall and old wood, troughs, and implements attractively featured in the decor. Tables are set in the gourmet restaurant facing floor-to-ceiling windows, which afford views of the water. The friendly clubhouse just across the courtyard offers a more casual ambiance and lighter fare at lunchtime. The hotel has four categories of guestrooms in the principal building and less expensive rooms in the Résidence wing. The hotel has a wonderful tranquil setting, is convenient to the rugged beaches of Brittany yet removed from the often harsh winds, and offers an ideal spot in which to break your more traditional sightseeing to play golf or tennis or lounge by the pool. *Directions:* Halfway between La Roche Bernard and Pontchâteau on the E60, turn north at Missillac. The hotel is just off the autoroute on D2.

HÔTEL DE LA BRETESCHE
Hoteliêr: Christophe Delahaye
44780 Missillac, France
Tel: 02.51.76.86.96, Fax: 02.40.66.99.47
31 Rooms, Double: €150–€430*
*Breakfast not included: €18,50
Closed: Jan 20 to Mar 8, Credit cards: all major
Relais & Châteaux
Region: Brittany, Michelin Map: 517
www.karenbrown.com/delabretesche.html

A sign identifying Mittelbergheim as one of France's most beautiful villages tempted us off the Route du Vin to travel the narrow streets of this delightful village. We kept our eyes open for a hotel to recommend and spotted an attractive hanging sign on a handsome building with exterior stenciling on a corner of the main street. We climbed the steps to the hotel to learn that every room was taken by Germans who had crossed the border for a long holiday weekend but Madame graciously let us peek into occupied rooms to appreciate the hotel's style and ambiance. Fifteen original rooms are found up a circular stone stairway designed by the same man responsible for Strasbourg Cathedral — it is incredible to note the date etched into the stone, 1615 — a passage of time that is hard to comprehend. Rooms are comfortable and decorated in pretty colors and while they aren't overly luxurious, they are well priced and the location in this charming village is a delight. Four new rooms have been added at the very top of the stair. Under the eaves and beams these are lovely, new and enjoy views over the town rooftops. Long before the family added guestrooms, the name Gilg was recognized for its outstanding restaurant. Entered off the front reception, two lovely rooms set under old beams offer an intimate and charming ambiance along with some of the region's finest wines to complement the menu. *Directions:* From the N422 between Selestat and Obernai, just south of Barr, take the D62 less than 1 km east to Mittelbergheim.

HÔTEL GILG
Hoteliêr: Gilg Family
67140 Mittelbergheim, France
Tel: 03.88.08.91.37, Fax: 03.88.08.45.17
19 Rooms, Double: €50–€85*
*Breakfast not included: €7
Closed: Jun 25 to Jul 11 & Jan 7 to 30
Credit cards: all major
Region: Alsace, Michelin Map: 516
www.karenbrown.com/gilg.html

On a recent visit I was thrilled to find Les Moulins du Duc closed for renovation as, just a few years ago, I sadly had to pull it from our guide when it no longer met our standards. I don't honestly know what made me take the time to detour back to see the mill as, at the time, I wasn't aware of the change of ownership. This charming 16th-century complex of mills and little cottages beside a peaceful lake and rushing stream is absolutely picture-perfect and I am delighted to once again be able to recommend it. The new owners are young and charming and were hard at work painting and redecorating when I visited. The largest mill is reflected in the pond that fronts it and also sits right up against the river at its side. It houses an attractive reception area, cozy sitting rooms (one of which incorporates the grinding machinery), and a charming dining room overlooking the rushing water of the millstream. The interior is romantic and intimate under the old exposed beams of the working mill. The guestrooms are dispersed amongst the various buildings and vary in price according to size and comfort of amenities. *Directions:* Moëlan sur Mer is located 7 km south of Riec sur Bélon on the D24. The mill is on the outskirts of town nestled on the tip of the inlet. On the Michelin map the location is actually noted by the symbol of a small box within a box (indicating a remote hotel) on a small, unmarked road that winds north to the D783.

LES MOULINS DU DUC
Hoteliêr: Thierry Quilfen
Route des Moulins
29350 Moëlan sur Mer, France
Tel: 02.98.96.52.52, Fax: 02.98.96.52.53
26 Rooms, Double: €94–€146*
*Breakfast not included: €13
Restaurant: closed seasonally for lunch & Sun dinner
Closed: Nov 30 to Mar 1, Credit cards: all major
Region: Brittany, Michelin Map: 517
www.karenbrown.com/moulinsduduc.html

Haute Provence is a beautiful region of rugged terrain and villages of warm sandstone buildings and tiled roofs, nestled between the Riviera, the Alps, and Provence. The Bastide du Calalou was built in the shadow of Moissac to match the village architecturally and blend beautifully into the landscape. Monsieur and Madame Vandevyver keep the property clean, the public areas fresh, the garden immaculately groomed, and the terrace swept. The Vandevyvers extend a gracious welcome and their staff is accommodating. The bedrooms are freshly decorated, simple with antique furnishings in their decor, and have very comfortable beds and modern bathrooms. The rooms look out over the swimming pool to spectacular valley views or open onto a private terrace. You can dine either in the glass-enclosed restaurant, a smaller, more intimate dining room, or on the garden terrace. During high season, May through mid-September, the Vandevyvers request that guests stay at Le Calalou on a demi-pension basis. Off season, take advantage of the hotel's proximity to the village of Tourtour, "village dans le ciel", and discover its many charming restaurants along medieval streets.

Directions: Moissac Bellevue is about 86 km from Aix. From Aix take the A8 to Saint Maximin and follow the D560 northeast through Barjols to Salernes where you take the D31 north to Aups and D9 to Moissac Bellevue.

BASTIDE DU CALALOU
Hoteliêrs: Mme & M Vandevyver
83630 Moissac Bellevue, France
Tel: 04.94.70.17.91, Fax: 04.94.70.50.11
33 Rooms, Double: €77–€230*
*Breakfast not included: €13
Open: Apr 1 to Nov 1, Credit cards: all major
Châteaux & Hotels de France
Region: Haute Provence, Michelin Map: 528
www.karenbrown.com/bastideducalalou.html

Le Clos is a centrally located, well-priced hotel from which to explore Burgundy. A sister hotel to Le Parc (a property we recommend in our France Bed & Breakfast guide), Le Clos offers three-star accommodation in a beautifully converted old farmstead near Beaune. Stone walls and the buildings themselves enclose the complex and embrace the central graveled courtyard with its old wine press, farming implements, and old well. The main entry is gorgeous—a welcoming reception sits opposite an intimate salon and adjoining bar, all set under beams on a flooring of old stone before a large open fireplace. Breakfast is served in a very pretty room off the entry or on the quiet back terrace. There are 24 guestrooms, of which 19 are standard rooms and 5 are suites. We saw a multitude of rooms that can accommodate every need and found them all reasonably priced for their comfort and ambiance. Rooms 1 and 2 on the ground floor and rooms 11 and 12 on the second floor, for example, are set behind a common door, enjoy a private entry, and would prove ideal for a family or friends traveling together who want privacy. Room 23 is the largest, a two-story room with sitting area and a bedroom loft. All the rooms are individual in decor and handsomely decorated in fabrics specially commissioned in London. *Directions:* Just southeast of Beaune.

LE CLOS
Hoteliêrs: Christine & Alain Oudot
Montagny les Beaune, 21200 Beaune, France
Tel: 03.80.25.97.98, Fax: 03.80.25.94.70
24 Rooms, Double: €65–€105*
*Breakfast not included: €9
Open: Jan 20 to Nov 20, Credit cards: MC, VS
Region: Burgundy, Michelin Map: 520
www.karenbrown.com/leclos.html

A small lane winds through a dense forest and then, in a clearing standing in magnificent splendor, is the stunning Château d'Artigny. The château exudes a storybook-perfect quality with its steeply pitched mansard roof accented by dormer windows, white stone façade, two rows of ornate marble columns, and a wing on each end of the building with stone sculptures accenting the eaves. Inside, the grandeur continues, with soaring ceilings, gilt furniture, elaborate chandeliers, marble floors, and Oriental carpets. A sweeping staircase leads to the upper floor where you find an oval room that will make you smile. A dome, richly adorned with frescoes, forms the ceiling and below it, circling the room, is a gallery where life-sized paintings of beautifully dressed people (who are obviously enjoying a lavish party) gaze down upon you. Also in the room is a painting of François Coty (of perfume fame), who built the château in the style of the 18th century, using the Palace of Versailles as his model for the interior decor. The accommodations are luxuriously decorated in a formal, elegant style. There are also guestrooms in the gatehouse and seven bedrooms (less formal, with more of a country feel) in the Moulin d'Artigny, on the bank of the River Indre which runs below the hotel. The property has a beautiful swimming pool nestled in the forest, tennis courts and a putting green. *Directions:* From Montbazon take D17 toward Azay le Rideau and follow signs.

CHÂTEAU D'ARTIGNY
Hoteliêr: M Puvilland
37250 Montbazon, France
Tel: 02.47.34.30.30, Fax: 02.47.34.30.39
65 Rooms, Double: €160–€410*
*Breakfast not included: €21
Open: all year, Credit cards: all major
Grandes Etapes Francaises
Region: Loire Valley, Michelin Maps: 518, 519
www.karenbrown.com/dartigny.html

Domaine de la Tortinière, built in 1861, has a most impressive exterior, an inviting interior, and charming hosts, Xavier and his wife Anne. Xavier explained that his mother (recently retired) did not want a hotel with a stiff, formal atmosphere, but rather the feeling of a home with a blend of contemporary and traditional decor with modern and antique furniture. In the drawing room old paneling painted in soft yellows combines with modern sofas and tables and traditional chairs to create a very comfortable room. Bedrooms continue in the same vein with a pleasing blend of traditional and contemporary, and are found in the main château, the adjacent pavilion, a little cottage by the entrance to the property and the recently converted manor where Xavier's grandparents used to live—the accommodation is spectacular and absolutely gorgeous in the decor as selected by Anne. In autumn the surrounding woodlands are a carpet of cyclamens, while in summer the heated swimming pool and tennis courts are great attractions for guests. The Domaine de la Tortinière remains a favorite in terms of accommodation, welcome, and charm and its dining room is exceptional. Seasonally, cooking courses are offered that serve as an introduction to regional cuisine and provide the opportunity to dine with the owners. *Directions:* The château is located just off N10, on D287 leading to Ballan-Miré, 2 km north of Montbazon, 10 km south of Tours.

DOMAINE DE LA TORTINIÈRE
Hoteliêrs: Anne & Xavier Olivereau
Les Gués de Veigné, 37250 Montbazon, France
Tel: 02.47.34.35.00, Fax: 02.47.65.95.70
30 Rooms, Double: €145–€300*
*Breakfast not included: €15
Open: Mar 1 to Dec 20, Credit cards: MC, VS
Region: Loire Valley, Michelin Maps: 518, 519
www.karenbrown.com/latortiniere.html

An intimate, romantic castle from the age of Napoleon III, the Château de Puy Robert is set in its own beautiful park, just 2 kilometers from the famous prehistoric Lascaux caves. This pretty cream-colored stone castle with its turrets and gray roof houses 15 guestrooms. The rest of the rooms are found in a nearby annex, La Gentilhommière. The bedrooms in the main château are more intimate, particularly those that have a turret incorporated into their living space. Those in the annex are spacious and enjoy either a terrace or patio that overlooks the grounds and the lovely pool. The Parveaux family also owns the fabulous Château de Castel Novel, and their years as professional hôteliers show in the way they run this hotel. Guestrooms are all well appointed, many are decorated in pastel florals, and all enjoy the quiet of the setting. The large dining room prides itself on local cuisine—some of the finest France has to offer. The grounds are immaculate, geraniums overflow from terra-cotta pots, pink impatiens fill the borders, the lawn is mowed to perfection, and well-kept tables and chairs invite you to repose in the leafy shade. *Directions:* From the town of Montignac follow D65, which leads directly to the gates of the château.

CHÂTEAU DE PUY ROBERT
Owner: Albert Parveaux, Innkeepers: M & Mme Petrel
Route de Valojoulx, 24290 Montignac, France
Tel: 05.53.51.92.13, Fax: 05.53.51.80.11
38 Rooms, Double: €90–€280*
*Breakfast not included: €15
*Half board compulsory in Jul & Aug, €262–€453 p.p.
Restaurant: closed midweek for lunch
Open: May 1 to Oct 15, Credit cards: all major
Relais & Châteaux, Region: Dordogne, Michelin Map: 521
www.karenbrown.com/puyrobert.html

Isabelle and Vincent purchased La Roseraie, wanting to settle with their children, work in their own home, and start a business with a goal to offer reasonably priced, comfortable accommodation in one of the Dordogne's prime destinations, the village of Montignac, famous for Lascaux II. Distanced from the river by an expanse of beautiful rose gardens and pool, this is a lovely stone building. A gracious and attractive couple, the Nourrissons impart a high standard of service, cuisine, and comfort along with their experience and professionalism. On the entry level is a reception area, a small sitting area, a breakfast room, and the impressive restaurant. On most summer nights, tables are set under the stars. Climb the stairway to the two floors of guestrooms, each named after a different species of rose. Throughout, the furnishings are simple and comfortable, with pretty fabrics and colors for the décor. There is a full range of room sizes, and the largest rooms are equipped with multiple beds to accommodate families. The most incredible unit is located in a 13th-century building across the square with two stories of open space, exposed beams, brick and stone walls. As with the larger rooms in the inn, in high season, this is reserved for larger parties. Off season, when available to couples, it is like having your own pied à terre in Montignac. *Directions:* Located 26 km north of Sarlat, traveling the D704. La Roseraie is well signed and easy to spot on the river bank.

LA ROSERAIE
Owners: Vincent & Isabelle Nourrisson
Place d'Armes, 24290 Montignac, France
Tel: 05.53.50.53.92, Fax: 05.53.51.02.23
14 Rooms, Double: €75–€160*
*Breakfast not included: €11
Closed: Nov to Easter, Credit cards: all major
Châteaux & Hotels de France
Region: Dordogne, Michelin Map: 521
www.karenbrown.com/roseraie.html

The Château de Montreuil, across from the Roman Citadel in the charming fortified town of Montreuil, is beautiful with soft-yellow walls accented by turquoise green shutters and topped by a red-tiled roof. Set behind its own wisteria-hung wall within the town, the château has meticulous grounds and gardens. The reception area is intimate and cozy with beautiful old beams and leads to a lovely bar area. The dining room is very elegant, with cream linen and crystal set against a backdrop of soft gray and blue, handsome copper pieces, and silk flower arrangements giving splashes of color. Off the dining room, a glassed-in salon overlooking the gardens opens onto a terrace where breakfast is offered in warm weather. In the main château, first-floor rooms are more traditional in decor, with beams and old parquet and tile floors. Favorites are number 1 with a lovely old wood canopy, weathered brick floors, a large bathroom under a dramatic copper ceiling, and views of the front grounds; and number 3 overlooking the back garden, a lovely corner room with old wood paneling, twin beds, and a separate sleeping alcove off the bathroom. Second-floor rooms are refurbished, but retain an "old" atmosphere. There are three new, exceptionally lovely cottages and one superior room that share a courtyard behind the enclosed walls. *Directions:* At the heart of Montreuil, opposite the Roman Citadel.

CHÂTEAU DE MONTREUIL
Hoteliêrs: Lindsay & Christian Germain
4, Chaussée des Capucins
62170 Montreuil sur Mer, France
Tel: 03.21.81.53.04, Fax: 03.21.81.36.43
20 Rooms, Double: €200–€280*
*Breakfast not included: €18
Restaurant: closed Mon, Oct to May, Open: Feb to Dec
Credit cards: all major, Relais & Châteaux
Region: Pas-de-Calais, Michelin Map: 511
www.karenbrown.com/montreuil.html

This superlative property, recently totally rebuilt to incorporate all the modern comforts such as air conditioning, is ideally located on a small street tucked off the D122 and separated from the N74 by an expanse of vineyard. Guestrooms are well designed and insulated from one another, bathrooms are modern, and the welcome and service, under the direction of Sébastien Pilat, are exemplary. The hotel is set behind its own stone wall and tucked into its own expanse of garden. The breakfast room is located just off the reception and a cozy salon/bar is set off the other side, with intimate sitting areas arranged on old tiles in front of a large open fire. Beyond the salon is a lovely restaurant whose tables enjoy views of the outdoor terrace, terraced pool, and surrounding scenery. Of the guestrooms, number 2 is a lovely standard room in a wash of beige, and number 1 is an apartment at the top of the first landing, tucked in the corner with windows on two sides overlooking the vineyards and front courtyard, handsomely furnished with a four-poster bed, another double bed, and a decor of rich reds and golds. I loved number 5, another apartment tucked under beams with windows set in thick walls and a decor of warm amber and golds. *Directions:* Drive approximately 15 km south from Dijon on the N74 and then turn off to Morey-Saint-Denis—the hotel is visible from the N74 and is well signed.

CASTEL DE TRÈS GIRARD
Directeur: Sébastien Pilat
7, Rue de Très Girard
21220 Morey-Saint-Denis, France
Tel: 03.80.34.33.09, Fax: 03.80.51.81.92
8 Rooms, Double: €90–€180*
*Breakfast not included: €12
Closed: Feb 15 to Mar 1, Credit cards: all major
Châteaux & Hotels de France
Region: Burgundy, Michelin Map: 520
www.karenbrown.com/tresgirard.html

One of our favorite destinations in France has drawn one of the country's finest chefs, Alain Ducasse, to offer fine dining matched with fine accommodation. Just outside the pilgrimage village of Moustiers, the 17th-century La Bastide is set in extensive grounds boasting a lovely pool and pasture of grazing horses. Twelve rooms, five of which are situated in three cottages on the estate, enable even more guests to enjoy the wonderful experience of La Bastide. It is truly hard to select a favorite—Chambre Blanche is feminine and very European with its four-poster bed set across from two large windows and a painting of a lady in a peignoir; Chambre Coquelicot is cheerful in a decor of red provincial prints; and Suite Olive is rich and inviting in a warm color scheme of creams, yellows, and olive. In addition to the accommodation and the renowned cuisine, guests can also enjoy truffle hunts, pottery and painting classes, and can have an insight into the evening menu by accompanying chef Eric Santalucia to the local markets. Just off the first-floor landing, whose wall niches display an array of antique cooking implements, is a maze of rooms set for dinner. From a room reminiscent of a library to a cozy little romantic alcove, the selection is both attractive and varied, and the food guaranteed to please. Dinner is also served in the garden on balmy evenings. *Directions:* From the D952 follow signs to the hotel, located on a small lane.

LA BASTIDE DE MOUSTIERS
Hoteliêr: Alain Ducasse, Directeur: Dominique Potier
Chemin de Quinson
04360 Moustiers Sainte Marie, France
Tel: 04.92.70.47.47, Fax: 04.92.70.47.48
12 Rooms, Double: €155–€325*
*Breakfast not included: €19
Closed: end-Nov to mid-Dec, Credit cards: all major
Châteaux & Hotels de France
Region: Provence, Michelin Map: 528
www.karenbrown.com/moustiers.html

A lovely painted relief of grapevines along the top edge of the building and its pretty soft-pink-washed façade dressed with shutters lured me into the bar-reception of Le Relais. Not having discovered it on previous research trips, I questioned how recently it had opened, only to learn that it has existed for almost 50 years and that the present owner herself was born in the hotel! The main entrance to the hotel is just off the street and through the bar. The bar is popular with local residents, filled with conversation and smoke. Off the bar is a charming, simple country restaurant offering meals "en pension", with wooden tables set with Provençal cloths and faïence vases laden with flowers. Guestrooms are quite simple, very basic in decor, but fresh and clean, enjoying modern baths and proper lighting. Serviced by an elevator, the guestrooms are also equipped with direct-dial phones, alarm clocks, color televisions with British stations, and individual mini-bars. This is a hotel that can offer a central location with parking for a very reasonable price. A keyed back entrance is available for guests who do not want to come and go through the more public areas. *Directions:* Located at the heart of the village, on the square by the bridge.

HÔTEL LE RELAIS
Hoteliêrs: Pierre & Martine Eisenlohr
04360 Moustiers Sainte Marie, France
Tel: 04.92.74.66.10, Fax: 04.92.74.60.47
18 Rooms, Double: €55–€99*
*Breakfast not included: €10
Restaurant: closed Thur off season
Closed: Nov, Dec & Jan, Credit cards: all major
Region: Provence, Michelin Map: 528
www.karenbrown.com/hotellerelais.html

Noizay is a quiet town on the north side of the River Loire to the west of Amboise. The Château de Noizay, a lovely hotel tucked into the hillside, played a role in a turbulent period of French history. It was here in 1560 that Castelnau was held prisoner by the Duc de Nemours after a bloody assault in the town. Castelnau was then taken to Amboise where heads were guillotined and then speared and displayed on the balcony of that château. It was the massacre that marked the defeat of the Calvinists. The Château de Noizay entered a new era as a luxury hotel. Fourteen rooms, at the top of the grand central stairway, have been decorated with attractive fabrics and period furniture and each is accompanied by a modern bathroom. From the smallest third-floor rooms tucked under the eaves looking out through small circular windows, to the more dramatic and spacious second-floor bedchambers, accommodations are commodious and quiet. Off the entry, an elegant dining room decorated in a warm yellow and soft blue promises gastronomic cuisine and the wine selection comes from an impressive cellar. Five luxurious suites (air conditioned) are found in the adjacent building, the Clock House. The grounds of the château include a lovely forested park, formal garden, pool, and tennis courts. *Directions:* Cross the River Loire to the north from Amboise, then travel west on N152 for about 10 km. Turn north on D78 to Noizay.

CHÂTEAU DE NOIZAY
Hoteliêr: François Mollard
Route de Chançay, 37210 Noizay, France
Tel: 02.47.52.11.01, Fax: 02.47.52.04.64
19 Rooms, Double: €135–€270*
*Breakfast not included: €18
Open: mid-Mar to mid-Jan, Credit cards: all major
Relais & Châteaux
Region: Loire Valley, Michelin Map: 519
www.karenbrown.com/chateaudenoizay.html

After spending the day visiting the elegant châteaux of the Loire Valley, there is nothing more inviting than retiring to your own château in the evening, and we have yet to find a château-hotel that we enjoy more than Domaine des Hauts de Loire. Built as a grand hunting lodge in the 19th century for the Count de Rostaing, the ivy-covered château is framed by tall trees and reflected in a tranquil lake where swans glide lazily by. To complete the attractive picture are acres of woodland with inviting forest paths, tennis courts, and a swimming pool. The beautiful salon sets a mood of quiet elegance and it is here that guests gather for drinks and peruse the tempting dinner menu. The restaurant is gorgeous, with soft-pastel linens, silver candlesticks, china, and silver dressing every table. During our stay we were very impressed by the professional, friendly staff and attentions of Madame and Monsieur Bonnigal. Whether you secure a room in the château (what was once the library is exquisite in its furnishing with a gorgeous fireplace and tapestry) or the adjacent timbered wing (although, termed a standard room, 20 is lovely with its own private terrace), each luxurious room accompanied by a spacious modern bathroom is delightful. Reader feedback only reaffirms the superlatives we lavish on this magnificent château. *Directions:* Onzain is located northeast of Tours traveling 44 km on N152. From Onzain follow signs for Mesland and Herbault for 3 km to the hotel.

DOMAINE DES HAUTS DE LOIRE
Hoteliêrs: Marie-Noëlle & Pierre-Alain Bonnigal
41150 Onzain, France
Tel: 02.54.20.72.57, Fax: 02.54.20.77.32
35 Rooms, Double: €110–€430*
*Breakfast not included: €20
Closed: Dec to mid-Feb, Credit cards: all major
Relais & Châteaux
Region: Loire Valley, Michelin Map: 519
www.karenbrown.com/deshautsdeloire.html

Just recently converted from a private home, Hôtel À La Ferme is a dream. The charming hand-painted farm scene depicted together with the hotel name on the entry gate will draw you into the heart of this enchanting complex of blue timbered buildings, old weathered tobacco barns, and newer additions nestled on a lush lawn and gorgeous gardens. Three generations of the Hellmann family have welcomed dinner guests to their auberge, À L'Aigle D'Or, located just down the lane in the heart of this quiet Alsatian village. Following in the family's hospitable footststeps, now Jean Philippe, a third generation Hellmann, along with his wife, Brigitte, offer wonderful accommodations at Hôtel À La Ferme. Three guestrooms are found above the attractive sitting room and breakfast room of the main farmhouse (one standard, one suite, and one single) and four suites are located in the newly built addition. I fell in love with the single which is very comfortable with a double bed set on pine floors and upstairs corner windows draped in local woven Alsatian fabric framing the lush grounds. In the same high standard set by their restaurant, breakfast is a buffet feast with assorted meats, seafood, cheeses, homemade pastries, and an array of fruits from the bounty of the garden. *Directions:* From Strasbourg, head for Colmar on the A35/E25. Take exit 7, towards Ernstein Fegersheim, then the D288 to Osthouse.

HÔTEL À LA FERME   New
Owners: Brigitte et Philippe Hellmann
10, rue du Château
67150 Osthouse, France
Tel: 03.90.29.92.50, Fax: 03.90.29.92.51
7 Rooms, Double: €80–€130*
*Breakfast not included: €13
Open: all year, Credit cards: MC, VS
Region: Burgundy, Michelin Map: 516
www.karenbrown.com/ferme.html

Set on a cobbled street in the charming village of Ottrott, the 250-year-old L'Ami Fritz outshines all the neighboring grander hotels with its warmth, value, and charm, and the personal attention of the owners. Chef Fritz himself welcomed us when we arrived, even though he was dressed in chef's attire and the lunch hour was fast approaching. The hotel has a lovely, elegant restaurant dressed in pinks and salmons with a gorgeous scene in wood inlay at one end and a painting of the weinstube at the other. Downstairs in the oldest part of the building, the weinstube is my favorite room—enjoy a meal here at tables set before a large open fire. Upstairs, the inviting breakfast room is dressed in red checks. Of the guestrooms I loved 101 to 105 on the first floor and 201 to 205 on the second floor. These rooms are all appealing and quite charming, decorated in large blue checks with a complementing French-country motif. Room 228, under beams and overlooking the foliage of the treetops that shade the terrace, is very charming in its red decor. If traveling with one child, you might request number 110, an appealing room, also decorated in reds, with a single separated from a double bed by a wood partition screen. This is easily now one of our favorite hotels in all of Alsace. *Directions:* From Obernai follow the D214 for 4 km in the direction of Ottrott and then, once in the village, continue on following signs to the château.

L'AMI FRITZ
Hoteliêr: Patrick Fritz
8, Rue du Château, Le Haut
67530 Ottrott, France
Tel: 03.88.95.80.81, Fax: 03.88.95.84.85
22 Rooms, Double: €69–€99*
*Breakfast not included: €12
Closed: Jan, Credit cards: all major
Region: Alsace, Michelin Map: 516
www.karenbrown.com/lamifritz.html

For connoisseurs of fine wines, a visit to France without visiting the Médoc would be unthinkable. This region produces superb wines and beautiful landscape—endless vineyards etched with vibrant red roses and sumptuous châteaux attesting that wine production is indeed a most lucrative business. The Château Cordeillan-Bages is located in the heart of the most beautiful part of the Médoc, and even if you are not in the least interested in wine, you cannot help being captivated by the beauty and warmth of this small hotel. Perfectly tended flower gardens and a lush lawn front the hotel, while rows of meticulously groomed grapevines stretch to each side. This classic 17th-century beauty has a fairy-tale perfection, with stone walls of beautiful creamy yellow, a gently sloping roof, and round turrets. From the moment you step inside, you are surrounded by an aura of being a guest in a private home. Recently redecorated, the decor now imbues the ambiance of an Italianate manor. This is a luxurious property and reflects excellent taste and understated elegance throughout. As an added bonus, the staff is extremely gracious and the meals served in the beautiful dining room are excellent. *Directions:* From Bordeaux take D1 to Castelnau-de-Médoc. Continue north on N215 to St. Laurent and then turn east on D206 to Pauillac.

CHÂTEAU CORDEILLAN-BAGES
Hoteliêr: Marx Thierry
L'École du Bordeaux, Route des Châteaux
33250 Pauillac, France
Tel: 05.56.59.24.24, Fax: 05.56.59.01.89
29 Rooms, Double: €142–€446*
*Breakfast not included: €22, Michelin Map: 521
Restaurant: closed Mon and Tues & Sat lunch
Closed: Dec 10 to Feb 13, Credit cards: all major
Relais & Châteaux, Region: Bordeaux-Médoc
www.karenbrown.com/cordeillanbages.html

Set in the countryside northeast of Lyon, Pérouges is a wonderful medieval village settled by Italians in Roman times and sentimentally named for their hometown of Perugia. Although, it eventually became a "ghost town", the cobbled streets and old stone and timbered buildings now draw tourists from all over the world. The Thibaut family's ancestors were among the six who remained and partnered an association with the government to bring the village back to life. Enter the arched gateway to the town square, Place du Tilleul, and the beautiful timbered façade hung with wisteria and geraniums will easily catch your eye. Guestrooms are located in four separate buildings in the village. Facing the square, Le Manoir de St. Georges (five 4-star rooms) is easy to identify as its door is set under a carving of the saint himself and is set off its own garden and back terrace. Behind the privacy of its own stone wall, the Le Manoir houses ten 4-star rooms. On neighboring side streets are Le Pavillon (10 rooms) catering to corporate clients and Les Saisons (three rooms representing three seasons—no winter in Perouges). All guestrooms feature family antiques. Le Manoir and St. Georges, especially handsome in furnishings, enjoy the quiet privacy afforded by thick stone walls. *Directions:* Take Exit 7 off A42, Pérouges-Meximieux, and follow signs to Cité de Pérouges. Located in the pedestrian zone but you can drive into the city to check in.

OSTELLERIE DU VIEUX PÉROUGES   *New*
Owners: Christophe Thibaut,
  Laurence & Laurent Delord
Place du Tilleul, 01800 Pérouges, France
Tel: 04.74.61.00.88, Fax: 04.74.34.77.90
28 Rooms, Double: €110–€220*
*Breakfast not included: €14
Open: all year, Credit cards: all major
Region: Ain, Michelin Maps: 523, 524
www.karenbrown.com/perouges.html

Even O'Neill gave up a high-powered career to purchase his aunt's 15th-century manor-house hotel. His deep love for his home shows in every aspect of his solicitous management. All the rooms have been renovated and redecorated under Even's direction, ushering in a new era of freshness and elegant style to the ancient medieval surroundings. In spite of the thick stone walls and huge walk-in fireplaces, the feeling throughout is light, airy, and very comfortable. Under the eaves are several lovely bedrooms with modern bathrooms. Pleasing floral fabrics, paintings, and antiques lend a luxurious, yet personalized atmosphere. We particularly liked our large paneled bedroom but, for a deluxe room, found the bathroom rather small due to the physical limitations of a renovated 15th-century manor. The two cottage-style bedrooms in the carriage house are smaller and cozier than those in the manor and perfect for families. The library with its tall bookcases is a delightful, elegant room. Carol assists Even with the hotel but is also occupied raising their four sons. *Directions:* From Plancoët, take D768 towards Lamballe for 2 km. Go left on D28 for 7 km to the village of Pléven. Go through the village to the Manoir de Vaumadeuc on the right.

MANOIR DE VAUMADEUC
Hoteliêrs: Carol & Even O'Neill
Pléven, 22130 Plancoët, France
Tel: 02.96.84.46.17, Fax: 02.96.84.40.16
14 Rooms, Double: €90–€240*
*Breakfast not included: €10
Dinner by reservation for groups of ten or more
Open: Easter to Nov 1, Credit cards: all major
Region: Brittany, Michelin Map: 517
www.karenbrown.com/vaumadeuc.html

A reader wrote to tell us that we absolutely must include Les Hospitaliers in our book. He was absolutely right—Les Hospitaliers is a gem, set in one of France's romantic, picture-perfect little villages nestled in the hills of northern Provence. Although this charming hotel is of fairly new construction, you would never know it because the old and new are blended so harmoniously. Simple furnishings provide a homey, comfortable, uncontrived ambiance. While the rooms are extremely attractive, at Les Hospitaliers the view is king—rightly so, because the setting is breathtaking—and all rooms are positioned to take advantage of the scenery. The most stunning vista is from the terrace, which stretches to the old walls of the village. From this perch there is almost a 360-degree view of the valley bound by wooded green hills. On a lower terrace sits a large swimming pool lined with mosaics and decked with old Roman stones. When the weather is mild, most guests dine outside, while on chilly days, meals are served in a handsome dining room with stone walls, beamed ceiling, and casement windows. Wherever you dine, the food is delicious, with plenty of produce from the garden and wines from the huge wine cellar. *Directions:* Exit the A7 at Montélimar Sud or Nord. Follow white signs toward Dieulefit. Le Poët-Laval is about 8 km after passing La Bégude de Mazenc—the hotel is in the perched medieval village on the hill on the left.

LES HOSPITALIERS
Hoteliêr: Bernard Morin
26160 Poët Laval (Le), France
Tel: 04.75.46.22.32, Fax: 04.75.46.49.99
22 Rooms, Double: €72–€160*
*Breakfast not included: €15
Open: Mar 15 to Nov 15, Credit cards: all major
Region: Provence-Drôme, Michelin Map: 524
www.karenbrown.com/hospitaliers.html

La Ferme d'Augustin is tucked into the rolling, tree-studded hills between the colorful old port of Saint Tropez and Ramatuelle, a romantic medieval hilltown. The owners carefully preserved its rustic ambiance when they renovated this lovely old farm and converted it into a hotel. The guestrooms are clustered about the property in various farmhouses connected by fragrant, flower-lined paths. Ivy, wisteria, and climbing roses soften the exterior of the typical stone buildings with heavy, red-tiled roofs that dot the parklike grounds. The first building you encounter houses the reception area, lounges, and dining room. The lounges are attractively decorated with yellow slipcovered chairs and sofas, a few accents of antique furniture, and bouquets of fresh flowers. Just off the main lounge is a cozy nook whose focus is a fireplace flanked by benches softened with red-and-yellow provincial-print cushions. The dining room is in a glass-enclosed veranda overlooking the forest. There is a large swimming pool snuggled on a terrace shaded by a towering row of cypress trees and brightened by beds of colorful flowers. *Directions:* In Saint Tropez, follow signs first to the center of town, then Parking des Lices, and then Route de Tahiti. The hotel is on Route de Tahiti, a dead-end road that ends at Tahiti Beach.

HÔTEL LA FERME D'AUGUSTIN
Hoteliêr: Mme Jacqueline Vallet
Route de Tahiti, 83350 Ramatuelle, France
Tel: 04.94.55.97.00, Fax: 04.94.97.59.76
46 Rooms, Double: €100–€560*
*Breakfast not included: €14
Meals for guests only
Open: Apr 7 to Oct 20, Credit cards: all major
Châteaux & Hotels de France
Region: Riviera, Michelin Map: 528
www.karenbrown.com/fermedaugustin.html

Your heart will be captivated at first sight of Les Moulins de Ramatuelle, a romantic, 200-year-old stone building draped with ivy and accented by pretty white shutters, enhanced by a stunning garden featuring an herb garden and a lush carpet of lawn enclosed by towering cypresses. Beds of fragrant flowers, formal hedges, and manicured trees complete the picture. Inside, the gorgeous, ivy-bedecked dining room has enormous windows looking out onto the garden on one side and vineyards on the other and a canvas roof that glides back on balmy evenings so that you are dining under the stars. A soothing color scheme of soft whites, creams, and beiges radiates understated elegance and refinement. Best of all, the food is superb. The owner of this tiny inn, Christophe Leroy, is well known as one of the finest chefs in Saint Tropez and now owns several restaurants in town as well as catering to the rich and famous on their estates and yachts. For the few lucky guests who can linger after a gourmet dinner, this friendly, intimate inn offers five delightful bedrooms. These are not large, but offer all the amenities of a luxury hotel and exude gentle good taste with a decor in quiet pastels and an appealing, fresh, uncluttered look. In winter, Christophe runs a property in Avoriaz, the Hôtel des Dromonts. *Directions:* From Saint Tropez, take the D93 toward Ramatuelle. Soon after leaving town, the hotel is signposted on the right.

LES MOULINS DE RAMATUELLE
Hoteliêr: Christophe Leroy
83350 Ramatuelle, France
Tel: 04.94.97.17.22, Fax: 04.94.97.11.46
5 Rooms, Double: €222–€289*
*Breakfast not included: €14,50
Open: Mar to Nov, Credit cards: all major
Region: Riviera, Michelin Map: 528
www.karenbrown.com/ramatuelle.html

The Château de Maulmont offers lovely accommodation inside a historic building, with a welcoming and friendly atmosphere, established by the Bosmans. The red-and-gray-brick façade with steep gold and red turrets give the château a dramatic appearance. There are 19 guestrooms, standard ones being small but still very comfortable and charming in their limited decor. We stayed in the turret round in a "character" room with windows looking out to the park and a bathroom with a view of the terrace and countryside. To the right of the château's entry is a lovely, intimate bar from which a stair winds down to a fitness room and enclosed pool, while off the bar is a gorgeous wood-paneled conference room with many stained-glassed windows. The Bosmans are constantly making improvements and have completed the renovation of a two-story extension adding some luxurious new guest accommodation. In the gastronomic restaurant, Le Maulmont, you can enjoy fine French cuisine prepared by chef Stephane Roesch; while the second restaurant, La Taverne de Tempier, serves a more simple traditional cuisine. In the courtyard there is an aromatic herb garden used by the chef to flavor and decorate his dishes. The main dining room is very beautiful, with handsome wood paneling and fireplaces, and for a before-dinner drink you can settle into the bar. *Directions:* From Vichy take D1093 south for 14 km to Randan; travel east on D59 for 5 km to Maulmont.

CHÂTEAU DE MAULMONT — Cover Painting
Hoteliêrs: Mary & Theo Bosman
St. Priest Bramefant, 63310 Randan, France
Tel: 04.70.59.03.45, Fax: 04.70.59.11.88
19 Rooms, Double: €80–€220*
*Breakfast not included: €11
Closed: Jan 1 to Feb 13, Credit cards: all major
Châteaux & Hotels de France
Region: Auvergne, Michelin Map: 522
www.karenbrown.com/maulmont.html

Chateau Les Crayères has long been considered one of the finest hotels and restaurants. Set on the edge of the city, this elegant building was originally the town home for Mme Pommery and, like Monet at Giverny, she created the surrounding 7 hectares of park to buffer her from the city. Behind private gates off a main road in Reims, a circular drive delivers you to the entry of this elegant and refined hotel. Off the entry and reception a sweeping staircase climbs to the bedrooms, which even in the "standard" category can only be described as luxurious—a haven unto themselves. We were able to see a suite, an absolutely gorgeous back corner room with furniture set on old parquet floors and windows dressed in fabrics of blues and yellows framing the serenity of the back garden. Fresh flowers, a basket of fruit, and champagne awaited the fortunate guests. A standard room, number 18, in a beautiful decor of reds and creams, was delightfully intimate. Downstairs, public rooms are numerous and beautifully appointed and service is discreet but attentive. Under the brilliant direction of Chef Didier Elena, there are several dining rooms in which guests can experience his talents. Outdoors, set under the canopy of individual umbrellas, tables overflow onto the terrace. This is an exceptional property. *Directions:* Take the St. Rémi exit (25) off the A4, cross the river on Ave. du Champagne, veer right on Ave. Giraud to the intersection of Blvd Vasnier.

CHATEAU LES CRAYÈRES
Hoteliêr: Gardinier Family, Directeur: Fabrice Mercier
64, Boulevard Henry Vasnier
51100 Reims, France
Tel: 03.26.82.80.80, Fax: 03.26.82.65.52
*20 Rooms, Double: €280–€490**
**Breakfast not included: €26*
Open: Jan 15 to Dec 22, Credit cards: all major
Relais & Châteaux
Region: Champagne, Michelin Maps: 513, 514
www.karenbrown.com/crayeres.html

Set on a corner just below the hospital at the edge of town, this charming inn is easy to spot with its lower portion colored in a wash of soft yellow and the top a mix of sienna and rough timber. An arched doorway beckons you into the reception of this centuries-old home whose exposed walls of stone are dramatically softened by handsome fabrics hanging at the windows. The salon, a cozy place to settle with chairs set round the open fireplace, was once the forge and a pot hangs above the old well. The breakfast room—once the old cellar—has tables set with cheerful linens. A wide rope tethered to the wall eases the climb up the circular stair to the bedrooms and rough-hewn doors set in hallways of old plaster and timbered beams guard the guestrooms. Anselme II is a lovely, spacious room on the first floor whose twin beds are decked in rich fabrics of rusts, golds, and yellows, and harvest patterns of corn and wheat. Another flight up, Ulrich V is a delightful corner room with red-check print at the numerous windows and a handsome print of beiges and greens on the bed and in the fabric canopy over the bed. Beams, wainscoting, and lots of sunlight make this a true favorite. Located on the Route du Vin, Ribeauvillé is a charming town and makes for an ideal base from which to explore the region. *Directions:* Ribeauvillé is located 19 km north of Colmar via N83 and D106. In town follow signs to the church and then turn just before the church at the signs for the hospital.

HOSTELLERIE DES SEIGNEURS DE RIBEAUPIERRE
Hoteliêrs: Marie Madeleine & Marie Cecile Barth
11, Rue du Château
68150 Ribeauvillé, France
Tel: 03.89.73.70.31, Fax: 03.89.73.71.21
10 Rooms, Double: €118–€168
Open: Mar 1 to Dec 23, Credit cards: all major
Region: Alsace, Michelin Map: 516
www.karenbrown.com/ribeaupierre.html

The village of Riquewihr is encircled by a tall wall and surrounded by vineyards. Within the walls the narrow pedestrian streets are lined with ancient brick-and-timber houses built to produce wine on the ground floor while the family lived upstairs. Riquewihr is an idyllic little town and the Hôtel l'Oriel is ideally situated for exploring the Alsace wine region. On a narrow side street, the hotel occupies a 450-year-old building. Guests enjoy several public rooms: a large breakfast room, a small sitting area, and an inviting wine salon and bar in the cellar. Steep stairs and narrow corridors lead to the guestrooms, which overlook either the narrow street or a tiny central courtyard (it's not a place for large suitcases). Bedrooms are all very nicely decorated and outfitted with TV and phone. Three rooms have just been renovated in a building across the passage. They are spacious, beautifully appointed, and offer incredible value. Serge and Sylviane are a charming couple and wonderful hosts. They are happy to recommend restaurants in the village. *Directions:* Riquewihr is just south of Ribeauvillé. At the entrance to the town turn right, park in the first available parking space beneath the wall, and walk back to the first entrance through the wall. The hotel is on your right after 50 meters. The Wendels will provide you with a map so that you can drive your car to the hotel to unload luggage before parking it in a car park.

HÔTEL L'ORIEL
Hoteliêrs: Serge & Sylviane Wendel
3, Rue des Ecuries Seigneuriales
68340 Riquewihr, France
Tel: 03.89.49.03.13, Fax: 03.89.47.92.87
25 Rooms, Double: €65–€95*
*Breakfast not included: €9,50
Open: all year, Credit cards: all major
Region: Alsace, Michelin Map: 516
www.karenbrown.com/hotelloriel.html

The Domaine de la Rhue is exceptional, offering comfort and elegance in a beautiful country setting. Just an hour by footpath from the pilgrimage site of Rocamadour, the Domaine de la Rhue offers accommodation in converted stables in the shadow of its regal, ivy-clad château. The caring owners, Christine and Eric Jooris, first opted to farm the land but the soil was too poor so they decided to offer accommodation within the stone walls of the stables which they gutted, retaining the old character by preserving the weathered beams and implements. There are guestrooms in the main stable and a few in an outlying building, elegant in their simplicity, with fresh whitewashed plaster and rough beams complemented by fine wood furnishings and rich, muted fabrics. Two of the rooms in the stable enjoy their own entrance off the garden and a garden sitting area. Tucked off its own garden entrance, I adore room 9 with its loft beams and cozy decor in red checks. Also, what was once their private apartment is now a spacious, gorgeous guestroom, handsome with its wood furnishing and elegant soft white decor. The main room at the center of the inn sits behind large glass doors and is very inviting with various groupings of chairs set on old stone floors and warmed by a large open fireplace. *Directions:* From Rocamadour take the D673 for Brive, then continue towards Brive on the N140. After 1 km, turn left on a small road to Domaine de la Rhue.

DOMAINE DE LA RHUE
Hoteliêrs: Christine & Eric Jooris
46500 Rocamadour, France
Tel: 05.65.33.71.50, Fax: 05.65.33.72.48
14 Rooms, Double: €70–€130*
*Breakfast not included: €7,50
Hot air balloon rides of the canyon: €150 per person
Open: Apr 7 to Oct 19, Credit cards: MC, VS
Region: Dordogne, Michelin Map: 522
www.karenbrown.com/domainedelarhue.html

La Roche-Bernard is designated as one of France's towns with special character and L'Auberge Bretonne happily lives up to this same reputation of special charm. The hotel, made up of three old houses just brimming with character, is as pretty as a picture. The ones on the ends are painted white with blue trim, while the building in the middle is especially enticing—a stone two-story house with steep roof, gabled windows, and door and window trim painted blue. In summer, window boxes overflowing with geraniums add the final touch of perfection and color. L'Auberge Bretonne is best known as a restaurant—justifiably so since Jacques Thorel is a renowned chef and his talent in the kitchen attracts guests from far and near. The tables are set in intimate, small rooms so that there is no air of a large commercial establishment, but rather a homelike atmosphere. The rooms are clustered around a central patio where instead of flowers, vegetables used in the preparation of the meals are grown. Luckily for guests who love to linger over dinner and then climb the stairs for a sound night's slumber, the inn has eight lovely guestrooms. No two are alike, but all are most attractively furnished in a pleasing, fresh, and uncluttered style. *Directions:* Take N165 northwest from Nantes for 70 km to La Roche-Bernard. L'Auberge Bretonne is on Rue Saint James, facing the Place du Guesclin as you come into town.

L'AUBERGE BRETONNE
Hoteliêr: Jacques Thorel
2, Place du Guesclin
56130 Roche-Bernard (La), France
Tel: 02.99.90.60.28, Fax: 02.99.90.85.00
8 Rooms, Double: €130–€280*
*Breakfast not included: €17
Restaurant: closed Mon & Thur, Wed & Fri lunch
Closed: Nov 15 to Jan 15, Credit cards: all major
Relais & Châteaux, Region: Brittany, Michelin Map: 517
www.karenbrown.com/bretonne.html

Located only a short drive east of Tours, Les Hautes Roches is a small, deluxe Relais & Châteaux hotel on the road that traces the River Loire between Tours and Amboise. The name should include the word "château" since the hotel closely resembles so many of the other lovely petits châteaux that dot the landscape in the Loire Valley. The hotel snuggles into the hillside: out of the 15 guestrooms, 12 are actually built into the cellars that have been used for hundreds of years, not only for the storage of wines, but also for living quarters. Don't worry though—these rooms are far from being humble, dark accommodations. Instead, once you step inside you discover attractively decorated bedrooms with every modern comfort. It took the owner of the property, Philippe Mollard, who poured his heart into the project, almost two years to convert the abandoned manor into the deluxe hotel you see today. Originally the home of a wealthy vintner who produced fine Vouvray wines, the building dates to the 18th century, but the cellars' history goes back beyond the days when they sheltered refugees of the Wars of Religion to long ago when they were inhabited by monks. Les Hautes Roches is also renowned as a restaurant and has a beautiful dining room. Another bonus is a swimming pool on the terrace. *Directions:* From Tours take the N152 toward Amboise. You will see Les Hautes Roches perched on a hill on the left side of the road.

LES HAUTES ROCHES
Hoteliêr: Didier Edon
85, Quai de la Loire
37210 Rochecorbon, France
Tel: 02.47.52.88.88, Fax: 02.47.52.81.30
15 Rooms, Double: €135–€265*
*Breakfast not included: €18
Closed: Jan to mid-Mar, Credit cards: all major
Relais & Châteaux
Region: Loire Valley, Michelin Map: 519
www.karenbrown.com/roches.html

We were feeling rather chagrined (especially being the experienced travelers we claim to be!) when we arrived at the coast without a reservation, not knowing that it was the grand holiday weekend to launch the summer—everyone was at the beach. Luckily, we found a hotel in Rouen with one last room and were thrilled when we realized the location was on a quaint pedestrian street just a few blocks from the heart of the historic center, old quarter, and marketplace. With just 18 rooms, the hotel is intimate and offers personal service. The front is undistinguished but glass doors open to inviting sitting areas on either side of the reception, with a backdrop of cozy beams and stucco, and a glimpse down a back corridor revealed an attractive breakfast room. The hotel has a small elevator servicing four floors, but our room was tucked under the eaves on the fifth floor up a final flight of stairs. It was small but cozy and comfortable, with good lighting, a TV, a private bath, and skylights that opened to views across the rooftops of Rouen, taking in the magnificently lit cathedral spire. Breakfast was a generous buffet of breads, meats, cheeses, juices, yogurts, and cereal. Our only disappointment was that, like ourselves, the plumbing found it difficult to reach the fifth floor. *Directions:* Follow signs to the Rive Droite and Rouen Centre—the Dandy is well signed. The hotel is on a pedestrian street but you can park temporarily in front to unload and register.

HÔTEL DANDY
Hoteliêr: Mme Michelle Renouard
93, Rue Cauchoise, 76000 Rouen, France
Tel: 02.35.07.32.00, Fax: 02.35.15.48.82
18 Rooms, Double: €88–€101*
*Breakfast not included: €10
.Closed: Dec 26 to 30, Credit cards: all major
Region: Normandy, Michelin Maps: 512, 513
www.karenbrown.com/dandy.html

During the Middle Ages the Château d'Isenbourg was the cherished home of the prince bishops of Strasbourg and was more recently owned by wealthy winegrowers. On the hillside above the town of Rouffach, the château is still surrounded by its own vineyards. There are forty-one bedrooms, nine of which are modern additions that overlook either the vineyards, the wide plain of Alsace, or the castle park. The guestrooms are classified and priced as classic, traditional, deluxe, and superior. In the last three categories the rooms are attractive, the differences being in size of room, luxury of bathroom, location, and view. Room 3 (traditional) is a very handsome room on the ground floor in a decor of reds that overlooks the park; room 17 (deluxe) is a beautiful, spacious corner room with an expanse of window overlooking the front garden; room 2, (also deluxe) quite spacious, enjoys an expanse of terrace and overlooks the pool; and room 12 (superior) is a pretty twin-bedded room in shades of blue that looks out over the town. Classic rooms, located in the Pavillon, are smaller, more basic in decor, and are not air conditioned. You can savor a delicious meal and fine Alsatian wines appropriately in the vaulted 14th-century wine cellar or on the enclosed panoramic terrace. *Directions:* Travel 15 kilometers south from Colmar on the N83 in the direction of Cernay. Exit at Rouffach Nord. The Château d'Isenbourg is well signed.

CHÂTEAU D'ISENBOURG
Directeur: Bernard Urbain
68250 Rouffach, France
Tel: 03.89.78.58.50, Fax: 03.89.78.53.70
41 Rooms, Double: €110–€515*
*Breakfast not included: €23
Restaurant: closed Wed & Sat lunch
Open: all year, Credit cards: all major
Grandes Etapes Francaises
Region: Alsace, Michelin Map: 516
www.karenbrown.com/disenbourg.html

Beyond the ruins of a medieval arched gateway, the Hôtel de la Pélissaria nestles at the foot of the village of Saint Cirq Lapopie, which cascades down the hillside high above the River Lot. This delightful inn is enhanced by its owner, Madame Matuchet. Fresh and simple in its decor, the inn has whitewashed walls contrasting handsomely with dark-wood beams and sienna-tile floors. Thick stone walls and shuttered windows frame the idyllic scene of the village and the river. I definitely prefer the guest rooms that are located in the main complex that steps down the hillside as they are more intimate and charming in their décor, although the rooms in the annex across the street are described as more spacious. The attractive Marie-Françoise is wonderful with her guests and enjoys sharing her home. Although she no longer has a restaurant, there are several small restaurants within walking distance and she is very pleased to offer recommendations. Saint Cirq Lapopie is truly one of France's most picturesque villages: with only a handful of year-round residents, this hamlet of steep, narrow, winding cobbled streets, sun-warmed tile roofs, mixture of timber and stone façades, and garden niches is a postcard-perfect scene. It is wonderful to find an inn that so perfectly complements the beauty of this hamlet. *Directions:* Saint Cirq Lapopie is located 33 km east of Cahors (D653 and D662).

HÔTEL DE LA PÉLISSARIA
Hoteliêr: Marie-Françoise Matuchet
Saint Cirq Lapopie
46330 Cabrerets, France
Tel: 05.65.31.25.14, Fax: 05.65.30.25.52
10 Rooms, Double: €90–€133*
*Breakfast not included: €8,60
Open: Apr 1 to Nov 2, Credit cards: MC, VS
Region: Lot, Michelin Map: 526
www.karenbrown.com/pelissaria.html

The wine town of Saint Emilion was dressed with banners, filled with music and laughter, and visited by all the dignitaries of the region on a warm day in late September to begin the vendange—the grape harvest. The day was captivating and we fell in love with the town. Crowning a hillside with vistas that stretch out to the surrounding vineyards, medieval Saint Emilion has traditionally been considered the capital of the Bordeaux wine region. The Hostellerie Plaisance opens onto the square, in the shade of the church, and over the centuries its walls have echoed the church bells commemorating the start of the grape harvest. Staying here, you couldn't be more central to the activity and the town's events. The hotel's guestrooms are modern in their comfort and decor and many enjoy views extending out over vineyards and tiled rooftops. The dining room is lovely and extremely popular, with tables set against windows whose views appear to plunge over the valley. Service is gracious and accommodating. Offered only in summer and autumn are an additional seven rooms located in "The House" at the city center, priced around €250. The Plaisance is a lovely property and Saint Emilion is the most charming town of the Bordeaux wine region. *Directions:* St. Emilion is located 39 km east of Bordeaux. Take N89 east to Libourne and then travel on D936 in the direction of Bergerac. St. Emilion is signposted to the north off D936.

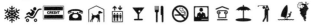

HOSTELLERIE PLAISANCE
Hoteliêrs: Gerard & Chantal Perse
Directeur: Philippe Etchebest
Place du Clocher, 33330 Saint Emilion, France
Tel: 05.57.55.07.55, Fax: 05.57.74.41.11
14 Rooms, Double: €150–€435*
*Breakfast not included: €20
Closed: Jan, Credit cards: all major
Relais & Châteaux
Region: Bordeaux, Michelin Maps: 521, 525
www.karenbrown.com/plaisance.html

St. Girons is a pretty town at the junction of the Lez and Salat rivers, near one of France's most beautiful villages, Saint Lozier, and convenient to the castle town of Foix, the Grotto of Niaux and the Gorges du Ribaouto. Near the heart of town and the rivers that transect it, the Hôtel Eychenne offers the traveler a warm welcome, a comfortable night's rest, and a restaurant renowned for some of the best food in the region. The reception, surrounded by paneling retrieved from a 16th-century château, is a gorgeous introduction to the hotel and from here you pass through to a sitting area and then through glass-paneled doors to an intimate bar. Around the corner is the formal dining room, very attractive with its wallpapering, wainscoting, and display of antique plates. Two arms of the hotel band the garden and the 35 guestrooms and 2 suites overlook either the town streets or the inner courtyard. The rooms are comfortable and hotel-standard in appearance. A section of the shaded garden is set with tables for summer lunch, dinner, and afternoon tea and at its end is a wonderful large pool with a children's play area next to it. Through their daughter, who lives in the United States, the Bordeau family has a real bond with Americans and extend a very genuine, warm welcome. *Directions:* Saint Girons is located south of Toulouse about halfway between Saint Gaudens to the west and Foix to the east on the D117. The hotel is well signed in town.

HÔTEL EYCHENNE
Hoteliêr: Family Bordeau
8, Avenue Paul-Laffont
09200 Saint Girons, France
Tel: 05.61.04.04.50, Fax: 05.61.96.07.20
37 Rooms, Double: €62–€185*
*Breakfast not included: €9,20
Open: Mar 15 to Nov 15, Credit cards: all major
Châteaux & Hotels de France
Region: Pyrénées, Michelin Map: 526
www.karenbrown.com/eychenne.html

Saint Jean Cap Ferrat is an engaging and picturesque port village on one of France's most exclusive residential peninsulas just a few kilometers from Nice and Monaco. Nestled above the harbor, overlooking a maze of yachts, sits La Voile d'Or, a hotel that is larger than those we usually recommend but, having looked at many of Saint Jean Cap Ferrat's hotels, we found this to be the very nicest, and, although expensive, good value for money. La Voile d'Or is a member of Concorde Hotels and offers the warm welcome, polished service, and elegant decor that we expect of members of this prestigious group. We particularly enjoyed the airy restaurant with its wonderful cuisine. The activity and scenes of the Mediterranean village are framed by floor-to-ceiling glass windows—the marina with its many yachts and fishing boats as a visual backdrop, simply serves as part of the hotel's decor. Soft Provençal pastels and countryside furnishings create a relaxed atmosphere. A gorgeous pool on a peninsula below the hotel and restaurant is surrounded on three sides by the sparkling blue water of the Mediterranean. *Directions:* Just west of Nice, take the Avenue Semeria off the N98 in the direction of Saint Jean Cap Ferrat. Signposts will direct you to the port where a one-way street will take you up to the La Voile d'Or located just above the marina.

LA VOILE D'OR
Hoteliêrs: Jean & Isabelle Lorenzi
06230 Saint Jean Cap Ferrat, France
Tel: 04.93.01.13.13, Fax: 04.93.76.11.17
45 Rooms, Double: €409–€815
Open: Mar to Oct, Credit cards: all major
Region: Riviera, Michelin Map: 528
www.karenbrown.com/voiledor.html

While strolling through the quaint pedestrian area of Saint Jean de Luz, we just happened to spot La Devinière, a small inn that looked so enticing that we just couldn't resist peeking inside. The exterior is painted white, with cute red shutters accented by bright red geraniums in window boxes. There is a recessed entryway laced with green ivy with an extra marvelous whimsical touch—where the "real" ivy ends, an artist has painted a delicate trail of ivy continuing around the arched entrance. What a pleasant surprise to walk through the double French doors and discover that the hotel is as pretty inside as out! You come first into a small parlor doubling as a reception area and just beyond is a charming lounge filled with country antiques. A wall of bookshelves, a grand piano, a fireplace, and leather sofas make the room as cozy as can be. Another surprise is that the hotel has its own cute little tearoom, L'Heure du Thé, opening off the reception area (it also has a separate door opening out to the street). Tea, of course, is served here, but this room also doubles as a breakfast room each morning. For a deluxe hotel choice in Saint Jean de Luz, the Hôtel Parc Victoria just can't be surpassed, but if your budget dictates less expensive accommodation, La Devinière makes an excellent alternative choice. *Directions:* Located on the Rue Loquin, a pedestrian street that runs perpendicular to the beach, behind the casino.

LA DEVINIÈRE
Hoteliêr: M. Carrere
5, Rue Loquin
64500 Saint Jean de Luz, France
Tel: 05.59.26.05.51, Fax: 05.59.51.26.38
11 Rooms, Double: €120–€150*
*Breakfast not included: €10
Open: all year, Credit cards: none
Region: Basque, Michelin Map: 525
www.karenbrown.com/deviniere.html

This stately gingerbread Victorian (Napoleon III if you're French) home sits in a manicured garden in a lovely residential suburb of the picturesque seaside town of Saint Jean de Luz. Roger Larralde purchased the home and converted it into a jewel of a hotel and extends a very gracious and warm welcome. The entrance hall with its displays of 1930s glassware leads to the spacious living room graced by delicate Victorian furniture. Here guests help themselves to drinks from the honor bar and contemplate the menu offered by the restaurant found just across the garden. Surrounded by lush landscape, windows in the restaurant afford tables a wonderful sense of being outdoors—on summer days and nights meals can actually be enjoyed at tables on the pool terrace. Don't miss the romantic little pavilion, game room (termed Pavillon des Chats because of the whimsical collection. The bedrooms are all decorated with beautiful antiques, many from the art deco period, and complemented by lovely fabrics and immaculate marble bathrooms. If you are looking for a romantic hideaway, ask for one of the six luxurious cottage suites on the grounds. From the front gate it is just a five-minute walk to the beach and a twenty-minute stroll into town—a tremendous advantage in summer when the narrow streets are clogged with cars. *Directions:* Leave the A63 at Saint Jean de Luz Nord; turn right at the fourth light, signposted Quartier du Lac. The hotel is on the right.

HÔTEL PARC VICTORIA
Hoteliêr: Roger Larralde, Directeur: Richard Perodeau
5 Rue Cepé, 64500 Saint Jean de Luz, France
Tel: 05.59.26.78.78, Fax: 05.59.26.78.08
18 Rooms, Double: €185–€635*
*Breakfast not included: €18
Restaurant: closed Tues in low season
Open: Mar 15 to Nov 15, Credit cards: all major
Relais & Châteaux
Region: Basque, Michelin Map: 525
www.karenbrown.com/parcvictoria.html

We felt privileged to be given a personal tour of this lovely old roadside hotel by the owner/chef himself. The hotel's restaurant, considered one of the best in Basque, was quite full and, knowing that Firmin Arrambide must be very tired after orchestrating the kitchen, I felt his gracious welcome was all the more a statement of his genuine warmth, hospitality, and love of his hotel. Set off the main square of St. Jean Pied de Port, this three-story, deep-salmon-colored building is hung heavy with cascading geraniums. The restaurant is quite elegant and overflows to tables on the outside terrace—a popular place to settle in fine weather. Guestrooms are named for flowers of the region and the colors and prints in their decor play on the theme names. We saw one of the standard bedrooms, which was spacious and had a large marbled bathroom—both rooms very modern in their comforts—and one of the smallest rooms, which I thought was still very comfortable in size, whose shuttered windows looked up over the rooftops of the village. Set below in the garden is a gorgeous swimming pool surrounded by a shaded lawn. Two large suites were recently incorporated into the old building next to the pool. Hôtel les Pyrénées is a member of the very prestigious Relais & Châteaux group and offers superb service. *Directions:* From Biarritz, travel the D032 (the D918 after Itxassou) about 50 km southeast to St. Jean Pied du Port.

HÔTEL LES PYRÉNÉES
Hoteliêr: Firmin Arrambide Family
19, Place du Général de Gaulle
64220 Saint Jean Pied de Port, France
Tel: 05.59.37.01.01, Fax: 05.59.37.18.97
20 Rooms, Double: €95–€250*
*Breakfast not included: €15
Closed: Nov 20 to Dec 20, Jan 5 to 28
Credit cards: all major, Relais & Châteaux
Region: Basque, Michelin Map: 525
www.karenbrown.com/pyrenees.html

The La Mare aux Oiseaux is so enchanting—in a whimsical, fairy-tale way—that it brings a whole new dimension to the word "adorable." It is located in the Brière National Park (a nature-lovers' paradise of tiny islands surrounded by marshlands) on the Île de Fédrun, reached by a causeway from Saint Joachim. The inn is a sweet cottage laced by climbing pink roses and enhanced by pretty light-blue shutters, blue doors, and a thick thatched roof. Inside, the romance continues. The dining room just oozes charm with its low, beamed ceiling, creamy-white thick walls, yellow draperies, fresh flowers on the tables, and a grandfather clock ticking gently in the corner. A cheerful color scheme of yellow and blue is used for both the fabrics and the dinnerware. The La Mare aux Oiseaux was primarily a restaurant with rooms and the charming owner/chef, Eric Guérin, spent several years cooking in famous Paris restaurants before moving here and opening his own. The very pleasant bedrooms, decorated with excellent taste by Eric Guérin and his mother, have modern, tiled bathrooms and are furnished in a refreshingly simple, pretty, uncluttered style. The price of the rooms is a great value for such quality and charm. *Directions:* From Saint Joachim, follow signs to Île de Fédrun. The hotel is well marked on the right-hand side of the road.

CREDIT P ¶

LA MARE AUX OISEAUX
Hoteliêr: Eric Guérin
162 Île de Fédrun
44720 Saint Joachim–Île de Fédrun, France
Tel: 02.40.88.53.01, Fax: 02.40.91.67.44
11 Rooms, Double: €80–€150*
*Breakfast not included: €9 or €11
Restaurant: open daily (except Mon lunch)
Open: all year, Credit cards: all major
Region: Brittany, Michelin Map: 517
www.karenbrown.com/aubergeduparc.html

La Chapelle Saint Martin is a small gray-washed manor resting on a velvet green lawn. Although there is very little exterior ornamentation (even the shutters are painted to blend with the façade), the interior decor is very ornate and detailed. Colorfully patterned wallpapers, complementing carpets, paintings hung in heavy gilt frames, lavish chandeliers, tapestries, and miniature statues decorate the rooms of the hotel. Known for its restaurant, La Chapelle Saint Martin serves meals in three elegant, small dining rooms. The setting and service are formal, with lovely porcelain, crystal, china, and silver used to enhance the presentation of owner, Chef Gilles Dudognon's masterful creations. La Chapelle Saint Martin is only a few minutes from Limoges, a city famous for its porcelain. Although many guests venture from Limoges for dinner, the manor does have rooms to accommodate overnight guests. The bedrooms are decorated with the same flavor as the restaurant and public rooms. Very spacious, the bedrooms all have private baths and look out onto the hotel gardens and greenery. The surrounding farmland and two ponds complete the storybook atmosphere of La Chapelle Saint Martin. *Directions:* From Limoges take the N141 in the direction of Angoulême to the D35 signposted Saint Martin du Fault. The hotel is 4 km after the Limoges airport.

LA CHAPELLE SAINT MARTIN
Hoteliêr: Gilles Dudognon
Saint Martin du Fault, Saint Martin
87510 Nieul, France
Tel: 05.55.75.80.17, Fax: 05.55.75.89.50
13 Rooms, Double: €95–€260*
*Breakfast not included: €14
Restaurant: closed Mon, Hotel closed: Feb
Credit cards: AX, VS, Relais & Châteaux
Region: Limousin, Michelin Map: 521
www.karenbrown.com/lachapelle.html

La Colombe d'Or is located opposite the main square at the gates to the fortified town of Saint Paul de Vence. The hotel is attractive and elegant in its rustic ambiance: antiques, worn over the years to a warm patina, are placed on terra-cotta floors set under rough wooden beams before open fireplaces, walls are washed white and contrasted by heavy wooden doors. Throw pillows, wall hangings, and flower arrangements introduce colors of rusts, oranges, browns, and beiges. The hotel also boasts a fantastic collection of art. In the past, a number of now-famous painters paid for their meals with their talents—and now the walls are hung like a gallery and the reputation of the inn dictates that the value of the art complements the cuisine. The restaurant of La Colombe d'Or is both excellent and attractive. Dine either in the intimacy of a room warmed by a cozy fire or on the patio whose walls are draped with ivy at tables set under the shade of cream-colored umbrellas. In the evening, stars and candles illuminate the very romantic setting. After a day of sightseeing, return to La Colombe d'Or and enjoy its refreshing pool set against a backdrop of aging stone wall and greenery. *Directions:* Saint Paul is 20 km northwest of Nice. From the Autoroute A8, either from Cannes or Nice, exit at Cagnes sur Mer and then travel north on D6 and D7.

HÔTEL LA COLOMBE D'OR
Hoteliêrs: Mme & M Roux
Place de Gaulle
06570 Saint Paul de Vence, France
Tel: 04.93.32.80.02, Fax: 04.93.32.77.78
26 Rooms, Double: €220–€330*
*Breakfast not included: €15
Open: Dec 20 to Nov 2, Credit cards: all major
Region: Riviera, Michelin Map: 528
www.karenbrown.com/lacolombedor.html

Perched on a hillside just above the road, La Grande Bastide captures an enchanting view of Saint Paul de Vence, just a few minutes' drive away. When it was purchased in the mid-1990s two years were spent in renovations and nothing was spared to make this a hotel of outstanding quality—especially for the moderate price. Although not rated as deluxe, this small hotel would certainly make any guest happy. Everything is fresh and pretty, and of excellent quality. You enter into a cheerful lounge area painted a deep yellow, setting off a collection of original art. This lounge opens onto a balcony overlooking a large swimming pool. Each guestroom is very pretty and individually decorated. The bathrooms are outstanding, each large and handsomely tiled. The owners of this hotel are Heinz and Rita Johner, who also own La Métairie in Millac, in the Dordogne, which we recommend—they divide their time between the two properties as well as a hotel in Switzerland. It is their warmth of welcome that makes this small hotel truly special and the fact that they successfully strive to make everyone feel like a guest in a private home. *Directions:* From the A8, exit at Cagnes sur Mer and travel north on D6 and D7. Before you come to the village of Saint Paul, watch for a sign to La Grande Bastide, which is located on a hill above the left side of the road.

LA GRANDE BASTIDE
Hoteliêrs: Heinz & Rita Johner
Route de la Colle
06570 Saint Paul de Vence, France
Tel: 04.93.32.50.30, Fax: 04.93.32.50.59
14 Rooms, Double: €150–€285*
*Breakfast not included: €16
Open: Feb 20 to Jan 15, Credit cards: all major
Châteaux & Hotels de France
Region: Riviera, Michelin Map: 528
www.karenbrown.com/grandebastide.html

Le Hameau is an old farm complex set on the hillside just outside the walled town of Saint Paul de Vence. The whitewashed buildings, tiled roofs aged by years of sun, shuttered windows, arched entryways, heavy doors, and exposed beams all create a rustic and attractive setting. The bedrooms of this inn are found in four buildings clustered together amidst fruit trees and flower gardens. Each building has its own character and name: L'Oranger, L'Olivier, Le Pigeonnier, and La Treille. Three of the largest bedrooms have a small room for an infant and a balcony (3 have twin beds and room 2 has a double bed). Room 11, with antique twin beds and a lovely view onto the garden, was my favorite. Le Hameau does not have a restaurant, but a delicious country breakfast can be enjoyed in the garden or in the privacy of your room. A lovely pool with magnificent views of the valley, the sea, and the Riviera is an inviting spot. Le Hameau is highly recommended as a wonderful inn and a great value. Its setting affords magnificent views from its guestrooms across the village to the beautful waters of the Riviera. *Directions:* Located 20 km northwest of Nice, from A8, either from Cannes or Nice, exit at Cagnes sur Mer and travel north on D6 and D7.

HÔTEL LE HAMEAU
Manager: Fabienne Gueguen
528, Route de la Colle
06570 Saint Paul de Vence, France
Tel: 04.93.32.80.24, Fax: 04.93.32.55.75
17 Rooms, Double: €105–€130*
*Breakfast not included €12,50 or €14
Open: Feb 17 to Nov 17 & Dec 22 to Jan
Credit cards: all major
Region: Riviera, Michelin Map: 528
www.karenbrown.com/hotellehameau.html

High atop a hill, set against the blue Riviera sky between Cannes and Monaco, the medieval town of Saint Paul de Vence is bounded by tall ramparts. Its narrow streets are lined with little houses and at its very heart you find Hôtel le Saint-Paul. The charming mood is set as soon as you enter the hotel and see the cozy lounge—appealingly decorated in a French country-Provençal theme. Because the hotel is built within the shell of a 16th-century home, the majority of rooms are not large, but each room is tastefully decorated with new fabrics and antique furnishings and offers every amenity. There are four luxurious suites, one of which, painted with charming frescoes, enjoys a large terrace overlooking the valley and, for the truly romantic, another suite has two luxurious bathrooms overlooking the fountain and a gorgeous view of the valley. For complete privacy or comfortable accommodation for four, request the top deluxe suite. The restaurant has beautiful murals, an interior fountain, and serves gourmet meals on the sheltered, flower-decked terrace in the summer. This is truly one of our favorite hotels! *Directions:* Located 20 km northwest of Nice. Exit the A8 at Cagnes sur Mer and go north on the D6 and D7.

HÔTEL LE SAINT-PAUL
General Manager: Giuseppe Artolli
86, Rue Grande
06570 Saint Paul de Vence, France
Tel: 04.93.32.65.25, Fax: 04.93.32.52.94
19 Rooms, Double: €190–€560*
*Breakfast not included: €22
Open: all year, Credit cards: all major
Relais & Châteaux
Region: Riviera, Michelin Map: 528
www.karenbrown.com/lesaintpaul.html

The Château des Alpilles has been renovated by the Bon family to its former state of grandeur with high ornate ceilings, decorative wallpapers, and tall windows draped with heavy fabrics. The public rooms are attractively decorated with period pieces. Upstairs, tiled hallways hung with tapestries lead to the lovely bedrooms. Large armoires, beds, desks, and chairs are arranged easily in the spacious rooms, each with private bath, and make for a very comfortable stay. The corner rooms are especially nice, with four large shuttered windows overlooking the shaded gardens, which are planted with a multitude of exotic species of trees. In addition to the rooms in the main house, La Chapelle is a charming, three-room house set in the grounds, and an adjacent farmhouse accommodates four suites and a family apartment. In summer for a midday meal a barbecue of lamb, beef, pork, or fish and large seafood salads are offered poolside. The Château des Alpilles now also has a more formal restaurant offering a fixed-price menu featuring refined Provençal specialties. The château is attentively managed by Françoise Bon and her daughter, Catherine Rollin. *Directions:* From Avignon travel south on N570 and N571 to Saint Rémy. Leave town to the west on D31.

CHÂTEAU DES ALPILLES
Hoteliêrs: Mmes Françoise Bon & Catherine Rollin
Route D31
13210 Saint Rémy de Provence, France
Tel: 04.90.92.03.33, Fax: 04.90.92.45.17
20 Rooms, Double: €170–€370*
*Breakfast not included: €17
Open: Feb 17 to Nov 13 & Dec 23 to Jan 7
Credit cards: all major, Châteaux & Hotels de France
Region: Provence, Michelin Maps: 524, 528
www.karenbrown.com/desalpilles.html

Fairy-tale in its setting and the luxury of its decor, the Château d'Esclimont is a memorable and convenient choice (only 65 kilometers from Paris) for either a beginning or an end to your countryside travels. Not inexpensive, but well priced for what it offers, the Château d'Esclimont is spectacular. Hidden off a small country road, its private drive winds through handsome gates to expose a stunning château framed by trees and reflected in a beautiful lake graced with swans. Turrets, moats, stone bridges, towers, and sculptured façades create a fanciful world of its regal past. Thirty rooms are located in the main château, all decorated regally with beautifully coordinating fabrics and handsome furnishings. Whether tucked into turret rounds or under the eaves of the third floor looking out through dormer windows, guestrooms are spacious and equipped with private baths. Also very attractive in their decor and setting, another 22 rooms are found in the Dungeon, the Pavilion des Trophées, and the Trianon—all stately buildings separated from the château by the moat. The Château d'Esclimont has a number of elegant rooms for dining and meetings. Although the hotel often hosts small tours and conferences, guests receive individual attention and excellent service. *Directions:* From Paris take A10 towards Chartres. Exit A10 at Ablis, then take N10 to Essars where you turn towards Prunay (D101) for 6 km to Saint Symphorien.

CHÂTEAU D'ESCLIMONT
Hoteliêr: Traversac Family
28700 Saint Symphorien-le-Château, France
Tel: 02.37.31.15.15, Fax: 02.37.31.57.91
52 Rooms, Double: €140–€1,280*
*Breakfast not included: €24
Open: all year, Credit cards: all major
Grandes Etapes Francaises
Region: Île de France, Michelin Map: 513
www.karenbrown.com/esclimont.html

Opt to stay at the Résidence de la Pinède for absolute luxury and pampering within walking distance of the quaint town of Saint Tropez. There is an aura of grandeur and elegance from the moment you step through the doors into this exquisite, lavish hotel. The Delion family also owns another hotel, La Reserve in Beaulieu. Both properties are very deluxe yet both exude the genuine feeling of welcome found in hotels where the family personally cares about the guest and oversees the details of management. La Pinède's terrific location cannot be appreciated from the street—it is only when you step inside the beautifully decorated lounge and look through to the glass doors beyond, that the perfection of location is revealed. The hotel nestles right at the water's edge and a stunning terrace with tables romantically set beneath towering pines stretches right to the hotel's own private white-sand beach. Next to the terrace is a gorgeous swimming pool where the rim of the pool plays tricks with the eye and the water magically seems to blend in with the sea. As would be expected, the bedrooms, like the rest of the hotel, are decorator-perfect in every detail. Many have their own spacious balconies looking out to sea where the awesome yachts of the rich and famous pass by. The hotel's restaurant is so outstanding that it has earned a coveted Michelin star. *Directions:* As you approach Saint Tropez from the N98, the hotel is on your left just before town.

❄ ✈ 💳 ☎ 🏠 🛏 ♨ ⛵ 🐕 🅿 🍴 ⛵ 🤿 ⛷ ⚓ 🏹 🏇 ⚓ 🍇

RÉSIDENCE DE LA PINÈDE
Hoteliêr: Delion Family
Plage de la Bouillabaisse
83990 Saint Tropez, France
Tel: 04.94.55.91.00, Fax: 04.94.97.73.64
39 Rooms, Double: €580–€865*
*Breakfast not included: €23
Open: Apr to Oct, Credit cards: all major
Relais & Châteaux
Region: Riviera, Michelin Map: 528
www.karenbrown.com/lapinede.html

It is great fun to spend the night right in the heart Saint Tropez to enjoy its magic after the hordes of tourists depart, and it once again assumes its mantle of a sleepy little village. Of course, the enormous yachts moored in the harbor quickly remind you that Saint Tropez is now the playground of the rich and famous. An excellent choice of accommodation is Le Yaca, whose history goes back to 1722 when it was originally built as a private home. During the Impressionist period, it was a favorite meeting place for many famous painters. Since that time it was "home" to numerous Hollywood celebrities including Tyrone Power, Rita Hayworth, Greta Garbo, and Orson Wells. Today, Le Yaca maintains its romantic heritage. The mood is one of understated elegance and refinement from the moment you step into the alluring lounge with its creamy-yellow walls and chairs upholstered in a pretty paisley fabric. A staircase with marble banister leads up to doors opening to a charming "secret" garden enclosed by high walls draped in greenery. The centerpiece of the garden is its pool, which is dominated by a tall palm tree. From the street you can't see much of the house, but from the back you can enjoy its charm—an intimate, small villa, almost totally draped with lacy ivy, through which peek crisp white shutters. *Directions:* Located in the center of the village, just a few blocks above the church.

LE YACA
Hoteliêrs: Laetitia & Francois Huret
1, Boulevard d'Aumale
83992 Saint Tropez, France
Tel: 04.94.55.81.00, Fax: 04.94.97.58.50
28 Rooms, Double: €395–€555*
*Breakfast not included: €22
Open: Apr to Oct, Credit cards: all major
Region: Riviera, Michelin Map: 528
www.karenbrown.com/leyaca.html

The Hôtel de la Plage is quite different in ambiance from what one generally expects of a Relais & Châteaux hotel. Instead of being a formal, super-sophisticated, grand hotel, it appears to be more like an old-fashioned, friendly, low-key resort—the kind of place that families return to year after year. Since it opened its doors in the 1920s, it has been a favorite destination for many vacationers. The style of the hotel blends in perfectly with the houses seen along this part of the Brittany coast—a white building with a dark-gray roof punctuated by dormer windows. Inside, the furnishings are mostly contemporary in feel in the public rooms with leather chairs and sofas and walls adorned with nautical prints. The restaurant is renowned for its excellent regional cuisine prepared with the local fishermen's catch of the day. The dining room is one of the highlights of the hotel—totally glassed-in on three sides, it has a delightful greenhouse quality. Not only is it filled with sunlight, but it also seems as if you are sitting almost right on the beach. And, speaking of beaches, the beach setting is what makes the Hôtel de la Plage so extraordinary. In front of the hotel is a huge, white beach that at low tide is awesome in its expanse. Enhancing this stunning beach are fabulous sand dunes interspersed with tall, windblown grass. *Directions:* Follow hotel signs from the center of Sainte-Anne-la-Palud.

HÔTEL DE LA PLAGE
Hoteliêrs: Anne & Jean Milliau Le Coz
29550 Sainte-Anne-la-Palud, France
Tel: 02.98.92.50.12, Fax: 02.98.92.56.54
30 Rooms, Double: €166–€292*
*Breakfast not included: €16
Restaurant: closed Tues lunch in low season
Closed: mid-Nov to Apr, Credit cards: all major
Relais & Châteaux
Region: Brittany, Michelin Map: 517
www.karenbrown.com/plage.html

Lucille and Jacques Bon welcome you to their 17th-century farmstead in the Camargue. Jacques' family were farmers who worked the rice fields of this windswept land with its stretches of marsh and wild horses, and he is passionate about the region. The Bons' home is covered with vines, shaded by trellises of grapes and wisteria, and decorated by tiled planters overflowing with geraniums. How fortunate that they have restored a wing of their 17th-century mas (farmhouse) into a luxurious inn. The guestrooms have rough, exposed, pine beams, and lovely old doors and windows incorporated into their new construction. The decor in their home marries old wood furniture with crisp white linens, giving a handsome, fresh look. Extremely gracious, Lucille is pretty and welcoming and Jacques is a handsome, friendly bull farmer with a large white mustache, tall and lean, hardened by years of work and riding. Cowboy, the family dog, is always by their side. Meals are served at just a few intimate tables in a large country kitchen in front of an open fireplace under 19th-century beams, or in summer on the garden terrace. Because the restaurant is very popular, reservations for either lunch or dinner are compulsory! Days are for swimming, horse riding, mountain biking, or visiting the rodeo with the magnificent Camargue bulls and horses. *Directions:* Leave Arles in the direction of Salin de Giraud (D36) for 25 km. Turn left 3 km after Sambuc.

LE MAS DE PEINT
Hoteliêrs: Lucille & Jacques Bon
Sambuc (Le), 13200 Arles, France
Tel: 04.90.97.20.62, Fax: 04.90.97.22.20
11 Rooms, Double: €205–€381*
*Breakfast not included: €20
Restaurant: closed Wed
Open: Mar 6 to Nov 23 & Dec 20 to Jan 10
Credit cards: all major, Châteaux & Hotels de France
Region: Provence, Michelin Maps: 524, 528
www.karenbrown.com/lemasdepeint.html

Set in the rolling foothills of the Pyrénées, in a picture-book village near the Spanish border, the Hôtel Arraya captures the tradition and rustic flavor of this Basque region. Long ago the hotel was founded to provide lodgings for pilgrims on the road to Santiago de Compostela. Today it accommodates guests who have fallen in love with this dear inn and return time and again. The Hôtel Arraya is decorated with an abundance of 17th-century Basque antiques and is a comfortable and hospitable village hotel. The entry, lobby, and breakfast nook are charming: cozy blue-and-white gingham cushions pad the wooden chairs, which are set around a lovely collection of antique tables. The restaurant offers regional Basque specialties to tempt you: ravioles de xangurro, agneau aux pochas, foie de canard frais, poêlé aux cèpes, fromages des Montagnes and pastiza, a delicious Basque almond cake filled with cream or black cherry preserve. The bedrooms are all individual in decor and size, and are attractive with their whitewashed walls, exposed beams, and pretty fabrics. The hotel has been in the Fagoagas' family for many generations and guests are welcomed as friends in the traditional way, round the zizailua (bench) near the fire. *Directions:* Exit the Autoroute A6 at Saint Jean de Luz (Nord, Exit 3). Follow directions to Saint Pée sur Nivelle on N10. After 5 km turn right to the village of Ascain and then take the Col de Saint Ignace to Sare.

HÔTEL ARRAYA
Hoteliêr: Jean Baptiste Fagoaga
Sare, 64310 Ascain, France
Tel: 05.59.54.20.46, Fax: 05.59.54.27.04
19 Rooms, Double: €62–€120*
*Breakfast not included: €9
Open: Apr 1 to mid-Nov, Credit cards: AX, VS
Châteaux & Hotels de France
Region: Basque, Michelin Map: 525
www.karenbrown.com/hotelarraya.html

Sitting on the edge of a Normandy village in a beautiful, lush region of farmland, only 1 kilometer from the sea, Le Relais des Dalles is a charming and intimate roadside inn dressed with window boxes overflowing with red geraniums, its timbered side entrance nestled and framed by a magnificent English garden. The Marciniaks settled in the village almost twenty years ago when the inn was just a restaurant, then six years ago they converted what were side dining rooms into four charming guestrooms, which are as superlative as their menu. The dining room, specializing in local seafood, is cozy, with elegantly dressed tables set under low, dark beams before a large open fire. In addition to à-la-carte choices, the inn offers a wonderful selection in its reasonably priced set menus. The bedrooms, all with private entrances off the lovely side garden, are individually decorated and enjoy the comforts of a little sitting area, private bath, direct-dial phone, and TV. The pretty rooms are comfortable in size, not overly spacious, but intimate and romantic. Elise is tucked under the beams and Théodore, the biggest, has a large Jacuzzi tub. Breakfast is served either in the restaurant or the garden. *Directions:* Take the Boug Achard exit off the A13, heading for Fécamp on the D313, and after crossing the Pont de Brotonne, follow the D940. In Louvetot, take a left on the D33 and then the D926. After Ypreville Biville, take the D17 to Valmont and then Sassetot-le-Mauconduit.

LE RELAIS DES DALLES
Hoteliêrs: M & Mme Marciniak
76540 Sassetot-le-Mauconduit, France
Tel: 02.35.27.41.83, Fax: 02.35.27.13.91
4 Rooms, Double: €68–€130*
*Breakfast not included: €10
Restaurant: closed Mon & Tues off season
Closed: Dec 16 to Jan 10 and one week in Feb
Credit cards: all major
Region: Pas-de-Calais, Michelin Map: 511
www.karenbrown.com/dalles.html

The Hôtel Anne d'Anjou is located within walking distance of this colorful town's historic center and of the 14th-century château perched high on the hill. Originally built in the 18th century as a private mansion, the building still displays many vestiges of its glorious past. One of the most dramatic of these is a handsome wrought-iron staircase forming a gallery at each level and crowned above by a trompe l'oeil ceiling—designated historic monuments. The hotel is owned by Jean-René and Mary Lyn Camus, who run it with grace and professionalism, aiming to create an environment where guests feel welcome and at home. When they bought the property it had already been converted into a hotel, but since then they have made many improvements, including upgrading the decor and adding tiled bathrooms. The five guestrooms on the first floor upstairs have retained their original Louis XVI furnishings. The other bedrooms have new furniture and decor, but still reflect the Empire style. Although the interior is very inviting, my favorite spot is the delightful inner courtyard, a magical place for a drink in the evening when you have a splendid view of the château glowing in the rays of the setting sun. At the end of the courtyard there is an adorable, tiny, 16th-century wine merchant's cellar, which has been converted to a wonderful restaurant, Les Ménestrels. *Directions:* Located on the south bank of the River Loire, at the east end of Saumur.

HÔTEL ANNE D'ANJOU
Hoteliêrs: Mary Lyn & Jean-René Camus
32–33 Quai Mayaud, 49400 Saumur, France
Tel: 02.41.67.30.30, Fax: 02.41.67.51.00
45 Rooms, Double: €89–€170*
*Breakfast not included: €10
Open: all year, Credit cards: all major
Châteaux & Hotels de France
Region: Loire Valley, Michelin Map: 518
www.karenbrown.com/annedanjou.html

Entirely surrounded by deep forests, Le Hameau de Barboron is less than 12 kilometers from the many activities and fine restaurants of medieval Beaune. Originating in the 16th century as a monastery, the property later became a farm and then a hunting lodge. Guests can still enjoy the thrill of and participate in a boar hunt. In 1994 Le Hameau de Barboron opened its doors as a small inn with the bedrooms housed in a group of sand-colored stone buildings that used to store grain. Since then the number of rooms has increased to twelve and they have earned a three-star status. Some of the rooms (with lofts in the rafters) accommodate families, others are cozy, and all have elegant modern country-style furnishings, beamed ceilings, and views of the tranquil forest in the distance. They all have beautiful modern blue-and-white-tiled bathrooms. Some have parquet floors with a hunting horn motif. Next to the reception area is a great room filled with trestle tables, graced with a high, beamed ceiling and a large fireplace, and lined with hunting trophies. Odile and her father also cater to hunting parties and conferences. *Directions:* From Beaune, head northwest for 8 km to Savigny-les-Beaune. Follow the signs through the town for Le Hameau, leaving town toward the hills. The road narrows to an unpaved, one-lane road. Press on for 3.2 km past farms and through forest to Le Hameau, centered in a large clearing.

LE HAMEAU DE BARBORON
Hoteliêr: Odile Nominé
Manager: Oliver
21420 Savigny-les-Beaune, France
Tel: 03.80.21.58.35, Fax: 03.80.26.10.59
12 Rooms, Double: €100–€200*
*Breakfast not included: €15
Open: all year, Credit cards: MC, VS
Region: Burgundy, Michelin Map: 520
www.karenbrown.com/barboron.html

Séguret is an absolute jewel—a picture-postcard-perfect village that is officially designated as one of France's most beautiful. If you fancy staying right in the heart of town, La Table du Comtat is definitely the choice for you. As you wind your way up the narrow, cobbled streets, passing by the many quaint stone houses accented by blue shutters, you end up at the picturesque Church of Saint Denis. Just beyond the church, snuggled at the very top of Séguret, you find La Table du Comtat. One of the most outstanding features of the hotel is its superb setting: perched high on the hill, the hotel captures an incredible, sweeping view out over endless fields of grapes that form a patchwork design of greenery stretching endlessly to the hills beyond. The hotel is well known for its restaurant, which is not only beautiful, but also serves excellent food. In addition to the inside dining room, there is a terrace where guests can eat when the weather is warm. The hotel exudes a quiet, refined elegance, an ambiance created by a background of pastel colors enhanced by antiques. Provence can be very hot in the summer, so an extra bonus of La Table du Comtat is its swimming pool where guests can relax after a day of sightseeing. *Directions:* From the A7 (Lyon to Aix en Provence) exit at Orange and continue on the N977 toward Vaison La Romaine. At the Séguret crossroads, turn right on the D88 to Séguret. The hotel is at the top of the village.

LA TABLE DU COMTAT
Hoteliêr: Franck Gomez
84110 Séguret, France
Tel: 04.90.46.91.49, Fax: 04.90.46.94.27
8 Rooms, Double: €80–€110*
*Breakfast not included: €14
Closed: Feb 2 to Mar 8, Nov 20 to Dec 6
Credit cards: all major
Region: Provence, Michelin Map: 528
www.karenbrown.com/comtat.html

Le Chaufourg is truly a dream—absolute perfection. Georges Dambier has created an exquisite work of art from what was originally a rustic 18th-century farmhouse that has been in his family "forever." The task of renovation was formidable, but all the ingredients were there: the house, built of beautiful soft-yellow stone, already had charm and its location on a bend of the Isle river is idyllic. Although strategically located in the heart of the Dordogne and conveniently near access roads to all the major sites of interest, once within the gates leading to the romantic front courtyard, one feels insulated from the real world. The exterior of the house is like a fairy-tale cottage with its white-shuttered doors and windows laced with ivy and surrounded by masses of colorful flower gardens. Inside, the magic continues. Each guestroom is entirely different, yet each has the same mood of quiet, country elegance, with natural stucco walls of warm honey-beige, stunning antiques, and tones of soft whites and creams. You find nothing stiff or intimidating—just the elegant harmony of country comfort created by an artist. Georges and his cousin, Agnes, add the final ingredient—the warmth of genuine hospitality. Another plus—romantically staged with intimate settings and candlelight, superb meals are served in his exquisite restaurant. *Directions:* From Périgueux take N89 southwest in the direction of Bordeaux for about 32 km to Sourzac (about 3 km before Mussidan).

LE CHAUFOURG EN PÉRIGORD
Owners: Georges & Agnes Dambier
24400 Sourzac, France
Tel: 05.53.81.01.56, Fax: 05.53.82.94.87
9 Rooms, Double: €160–€375*
*Breakfast not included: €16 , Minimum Stay Required
Open: all year, winter by reservation
Credit cards: all major
Châteaux & Hotels de France
Region: Dordogne, Michelin Map: 521
www.karenbrown.com/sourzac.html

Strasbourg is one of our favorite cities, and the charming Hôtel Cardinal de Rohan sits just around the corner from its magnificent cathedral on a quiet pedestrian street. Under new ownership, the hotel has benefited from noticeable improvements and upgrades. On the ground floor are the foyer and a traditional salon, hung with tapestries, where breakfast is served. The bedrooms are comfortable in size, hotel-like in layout and appointments, and are decorated in either traditional or a more country decor with pine paneling. All rooms rented to international guests are air conditioned and have bath-shower, phone, radio, television, and mini-bar. The bathrooms are lovely and the bedrooms have more queen and king beds "to please our American guests." Breakfast is the only meal served but the staff is delighted to make recommendations for nearby restaurants, which run the gamut from regional to gourmet cuisine. The location is ideal for exploring Strasbourg on foot. The narrow streets are a maze, winding in the shadow of leaning, timbered buildings and in the shade of lacy trees growing beside the river. *Directions:* From any direction take the Place de l'Etoile exit and then follow signposts for the cathedral. This will bring you to Place Gutenberg and the underground parking facility (a private garage available for guests staying multiple nights). Facing the cathedral, turn right—the hotel is 100 meters on the right.

HÔTEL CARDINAL DE ROHAN
Hoteliêr: Claude Hafajen
17–19, Rue du Maroquin, Strasbourg Cedex B.P. 39
67000 Strasbourg, France
Tel: 03.88.32.85.11, Fax: 03.88.75.65.37
36 Rooms, Double: €99–€129*
*Breakfast not included: €10
Open: all year, Credit cards: all major
Châteaux & Hotels de France
Region: Alsace, Michelin Map: 516
www.karenbrown.com/hoteldesrohan.html

In a city with many fine hotels to choose from, I always find myself prejudiced by a property that distinguishes itself as a member of the Romantik chain of hotels. Not only does the Beaucour offer the very professional, yet personalized level of service associated with the chain, its location is excellent and the accommodation is extremely comfortable and well priced. Flags adorn the street-front exterior, and the reception is set back behind the arched entry. I stayed at the Beaucour when traveling on my own and was pleased to be able to just walk across the bridge to the heart of the old district. Convenient and safe, the location also eliminated the need for public transportation. For fine regional dining, be sure to ask about the hotel owner's restaurants, the Maison Kammerzell and L'Alsace à Table, located nearby. A breakfast buffet is offered in the public dining room, or you can opt for the luxury of having a continental breakfast delivered to your guestroom. The rooms are newly furnished and the use of country pines and provincial fabrics is quite attractive. Bathrooms are lovely and modern in their appointments and the plush towels and robes are luxurious. The guest register reflects the greatest praise a hotel can receive—a long list of returning clientele. *Directions:* From the highways, take the Place de l'Etoile exit and follow signs to Parking Austerlitz. Rue des Bouchers is just across the Ill, south of the Cathedral.

ROMANTIK HÔTEL BEAUCOUR
Hoteliêr: Guy Pierre Baumann
5, Rue des Bouchers
67000 Strasbourg, France
Tel: (03) 88.76.72.00, Fax: (03) 88.76.72.60
49 Rooms, Double: €92–€174*
*Breakfast not included: €11
Open: all year, Credit cards: all major
Region: Alsace, Michelin Map: 516
www.karenbrown.com/beaucour.html

Convenient to the airport and with a professional, charming, English-speaking staff, the Château de l'Ile offers all modern comforts within a restored Alsatian château sitting in its own pretty park. Guestrooms, restaurants, and conference rooms are all ingeniously installed behind a façade that replicates an Alsatian village—peaked roofs and pastel-wash stucco set with timbered beams complement the intricate structure of the original castle. As with all Grandes Étapes hotels, guestrooms are categorized as "tradition", "superior", "deluxe" or "suite". The tradition rooms are lovely, found in the new wing along a long marble-floored corridor with Oriental runners. I found these to be very attractive and an exceptional value. Rooms classified as superior are located a floor above, off a carpeted hallway, and are a little larger in terms of room and bath. The prestige and suite rooms are all located in the château, and each has its own character, style, and special ambiance—they are all luxurious and extremely attractive. A dramatic apartment, referred to as "The American Suite", has a grand entry, sauna, living room, dining room, office, large bedroom, and an enormous bathroom. Dining is exceptional here, both in the Bavarian-style stube and the cozy, elegant, intimate dining room. *Directions:* Driving into Strasbourg on the A35, take exit 7, signed Lingolsheim and Entzheim (airport); then follow signs to the hotel in the village of Ostwald.

CHÂTEAU DE L'ILE
Hoteliêr: Pierre Traversac, Directeur: Olivier Voarick
4, Quai Heydt
67540 Strasbourg-Ostwald, France
Tel: 03.88.66.85.00, Fax: 03.88.66.85.49
62 Rooms, Double: €180–€700*
*Breakfast not included: €22
Open: all year, Credit cards: all major
Grandes Etapes Francaises
Region: Alsace, Michelin Map: 516
www.karenbrown.com/delile.html

Le Cottage is nestled near the shore of Lake Annecy in Talloires, a beautiful lakefront village. An attractive hotel, Le Cottage offers comfortable accommodations and a warm welcome, and is professionally managed by Christine and Jean Claude Bise. At Le Cottage, Jean Claude is definitely and most impressively ever-present and actively involved, doing everything at an enthusiastic and accelerated pace. Accommodation is offered in three separate clustering cottages (Le Cottage, Bourdière, and the Santa Maria) in more than 20 different categories: room with lake view, room with garden view, room with terrace, room with balcony, etc. All the rooms we saw were lovely in their appointments and a few had exceptional water views. The best lake-view rooms are found in Le Cottage and Santa Maria (my favorite was number 56, a pretty corner room under the eaves with windows on two sides overlooking the gorgeous water). The reception, a guest salon and bar, a charming restaurant with tables overflowing to a shaded outdoor terrace, and a pool are located at Le Cottage, which has the most elegant public rooms and antiques. *Directions:* From Annecy follow the D909 along the east side of the lake and at Menton St. Bernard take the right fork as it splits to become the D909A. Take the road off the D909A signed to the village of Talloires.

LE COTTAGE
Hoteliêrs: Christine & Jean Claude Bise
Lac d'Annecy, 74290 Talloires, France
Tel: 04.50.60.71.10, Fax: 04.50.60.77.51
35 Rooms, Double: €100–€280*
*Breakfast not included: €15
Open: end of Apr to mid-Oct, Credit cards: all major
Châteaux & Hotels de France
Region: French Alps, Michelin Map: 523
www.karenbrown.com/lecottage.html

La Bastide Rose, snuggled in a curve of the River Sorgues, has an enchanting, fairy-tale setting on an idyllic little island formed by a canal that loops from the river. Having lain derelict for many years, the property was in ruins when Poppy Salinger discovered it but she could visualize its enormous potential. Madame Salinger (widow of Pierre Salinger) had traveled throughout the world and dreamed of creating an intimate hotel incorporating the best features of places where she had stayed. She is continually making improvements: the extensive landscaping and pool have been completed and the five individually decorated guestrooms and two suites are proving immensely popular. Each bedroom is personally decorated by Poppy with its own eclectic theme. Although there is a style to fit every taste, the same high quality of amenities is found throughout: air conditioning, fine linens, down pillows, proper lighting, the best mattresses, televisions, telephones, and top-notch bathrooms. This hotel is so personal that we pondered whether to put it in our bed and breakfast book—like a bed and breakfast, this is Poppy Salinger's home, filled with her personal memorabilia and furnishings, where she pampers guests as friends. On the other hand, the amenities offered seem to classify the property as a hotel. By any name, this is a special place to stay! *Directions:* Located just west of Isle sur la Sorgues. Fax for detailed instructions.

LA BASTIDE ROSE
Hoteliêr: Nicole "Poppy" Salinger
99, Chemin des Croupieres
84250 Thor (Le), France
Tel: 04.90.02.14.33, Fax: 04.90.02.19.38
7 Rooms, Double: €120–€365*, 1 cottage: €1600 weekly
*Breakfast not included: €15, Dinner w/24 hours' notice
Open: all year, Credit cards: MC, VS
Châteaux & Hotels de France
Region: Provence, Michelin Maps: 524, 528
www.karenbrown.com/bastiderose.html

Nestled in the countryside not far from the Normandy coast is a beautiful hotel in a 20-hectare park that incredibly is of new construction and not converted from an ancient Norman farm as its character, beauty, and ambiance suggest. This lovely timbered farmstead is built round and opens onto a central courtyard. The reception shares the front wing with an intimate, cozy bar/salon on one side and a charming restaurant on the other. Rich warm colors have been chosen for the fabrics and dramatically hung on the timbered walls are paintings of actresses who have captured the world's heart (the owner is film director Claude Lelouch). Guestrooms run along either side of the courtyard: standard rooms are found on the first floor of one wing, junior suites are found on the second floor, and two-tiered triplex suites are mirrored on the other side. Standard rooms are lovely, spacious, and enjoy outdoor terraces and all the modern comforts. The Pavilion, a charming little house located just at the entrance to the hotel, enjoys its own kitchenette, enclosed patio, fireplace, sitting room, and two bedrooms—an incredible value. *Directions:* From the A13 between Caen and Paris, exit at Pont l'Évêque towards Trouville/Deauville. Just before the coast, at a roundabout, take the D27 for Tourgéville. Pass through a second round about and then take the first left, the D275, and when it splits go left on the D278. The next right is Chemin de l'Orgueil.

HOSTELLERIE DE TOURGÉVILLE
Hoteliêr: Claude Lelouch
Directeur: Wilhelm Stoppacher
Chemin de l'Orgueil, Tourgéville
14800 Deauville, France
Tel: 02.31.14.48.68, Fax: 02.31.14.48.69
25 Rooms, Double: €125–€330*
*Breakfast not included: €17
Closed: Feb 1 to Feb 23, Credit cards: MC, AX
Region: Normandy, Michelin Map: 512
www.karenbrown.com/tourgeville.html

Tours, in the heart of the Loire Valley, is an excellent place to stay and is just 55 minutes away from Paris by super-fast train. Once here you can either rent a car or bikes, use local trains, or take conducted tours to visit the famous châteaux along the river. If you want the joy of staying in the countryside combined with the convenience of the city, the Château Belmont makes an outstanding choice. It is such a lovely estate with secluded, beautiful, parklike grounds, secreted right in town. You approach through a gate and drive up a wooded lane to the extremely pretty, 18th-century cream-colored stone mansion. When you enter, there is a little parlor to your right with a frescoed ceiling of angels and clouds looking down on chairs slipcovered in a variety of sweet floral prints. Just beyond is a stunning breakfast room where the morning sun streams in through three walls of glass, enhanced by Victorian-looking, lacy, ornate grillwork. The individually decorated guestrooms are all lovely and offer excellent value. The grounds of the Château Belmont are sensational—you stroll along a path that meanders by romantic ponds dotted with ducks, small streams, woodlands, a greenhouse, lovely gardens, a tiny vineyard, lush lawns, a swimming pool, and even a gazebo. Many guests are lured to the Château Belmont just for its outstanding food. *Directions:* The hotel can send you directions if arriving by car. By train, just take a cab.

JEAN BARDET–CHÂTEAU BELMONT
Hoteliêrs: Sophie & Jean Bardet
57, Rue Groison, 37100 Tours, France
Tel: 02.47.41.41.11, Fax: 02.47.51.68.72
21 Rooms, Double: €150–€420*
*Breakfast not included: €22
Restaurant: closed Sun night to Tues noon
Open: all year, Credit cards: all major
Relais & Châteaux
Region: Loire Valley, Michelin Maps: 518, 519
www.karenbrown.com/belmont.html

Tours is in the center of the Loire Valley, which makes it a good base for exploring the region. It has the added advantage of being on the main rail route to Paris—less than an hour away by express train. For those taking advantage of this mode of transportation, the Hotel de l'Univers is a most convenient location since it is only a block from the train station and in a very pretty part of the city. The hotel, the oldest in Tours, dating back to 1846, is built of stone and accented by a green awning and a row of wrought-iron lamps. It has 85 rather commercial-looking guestrooms, each with built-in side tables, reading lights above the bed, a sitting area, and tiled bathroom. There is no need to splurge on a suite since the regular rooms are certainly adequate. Just beyond the reception foyer there is large lounge with beige-colored leather sofas placed around the perimeter and at the end of the room, a sweeping staircase leading to an upper mezzanine floor. There is a really fun, whimsical touch to this room since a continuation of a "real" balcony has been cleverly duplicated in a painted balcony that wraps around the walls. Looking down from this balcony are the standing figures of some of the illustrious guests who stayed at Hotel de l'Univers over the years, such as Katherine Hepburn, Ernest Hemingway, and Maurice Chevalier. *Directions:* One block west of the train station, on the south side of the street.

HOTEL DE L'UNIVERS
Hoteliêr: Phillippe Tiger
5, Boulevard Heurteloup
37000 Tours, France
Tel: 02.47.05.37.12, Fax: 02.47.61.51.80
85 Rooms, Double: €193–€398*
*Breakfast not included: €17
Open: all year, Credit cards: all major
Region: Loire Valley, Michelin Maps: 518, 519
www.karenbrown.com/univers.html

I had not expected to be so totally captivated by the Manoir de Lan-Kerellec, as the photos I had seen did not capture the hotel's exceptional charm, delightful decor, and—best of all—its spectacular setting. It sits on a wooded bluff with magnificent, sweeping views out over towering pines to the blue waters of a bay, which is dotted with many small rocky islands and countless boats. The 19th-century manor, typical of this part of Brittany, is a sturdy, buff-colored, stone building accented by white shutters and steep slate roof. Inside, a nautical look prevails and in the dining room there is a huge model sailboat suspended from a domed ceiling built in the shape of a boat's hull. Although the house is old, it is not in the least dark or dreary. The reception area and adjacent bar are enclosed with glass, giving plenty of light and a cheerful greenhouse effect. An exceptionally pretty small parlor has plate-glass windows opening to the bay, fine antique furniture, an Oriental carpet, and lovely floral draperies in rich shades of rose. Just below the hotel there is a large terrace with tables and chairs. All the guestrooms, individually decorated in the style of a country manor, not only have views of the bay, but feature fine antiques and lovely fabrics, which add a homelike, refined, gentle elegance. *Directions:* From the center of Trébeurden follow Port Plage and Manoir de Lan-Kerellec signs.

MANOIR DE LAN-KERELLEC
Hoteliêrs: Luce & Gilles Daubé
22560 Trébeurden, France
Tel: 02.96.15.00.00, Fax: 02.96.23.66.88
19 Rooms, Double: €100–€470*
*Breakfast not included: €17
Restaurant: closed Mon & Tues noon
Open: mid-Mar to mid-Nov, Credit cards: all major
Relais & Châteaux
Region: Brittany, Michelin Map: 517
www.karenbrown.com/kerellec.html

Set on a headland, with garden paths weaving down to a small crescent of golden sand, this large lovely home, Ti Al-Lannec, was opened as a hotel in 1978 by Danielle and Gerard Jouanny. The Jouannys offer a warm welcome rarely found in hotels, so it feels more like staying with friends at the seaside than in a hotel. Each bedroom has a different pretty wallpaper with coordinating drapes and bedspread. Family accommodations have two bedrooms, one for parents and one with bunk beds for children. My favorites were those with salon en verandah meaning that each has a small sitting area with doors opening to a tiny balcony so that whatever the weather you can enjoy the fantastic view of sand, ocean, and rocky promontories. The large windows of the restaurant share the same glorious view. The sitting rooms have thoughtfully been equipped with jigsaw puzzles, books, and games to accommodate the interests of the guests and the unpredictable moods of the weather. In the basement is L'Espace Bleu Marine, a complete health center where you can pamper yourself with massages and wraps, work out in the gymnasium, and relax in the solarium, sauna, and large Jacuzzi set in a gazebo overlooking the beach. Children enjoy the outdoor play equipment and giant chess set. *Directions:* From Rennes take N12 to Guigamp and follow signposts for Lannion for 9 km to Trébeurden.

TI AL-LANNEC
Hoteliêr: Famille Jouanny
14, Allée de Mezo Guen
22560 Trébeurden, France
Tel: 02.96.15.01.01, Fax: 02.96.23.62.14
33 Rooms, Double: €152–€349*
*Breakfast not included: €14
Open: Mar 1 to Nov 11, Credit cards: all major
Region: Brittany, Michelin Map: 517
www.karenbrown.com/tiallannec.html

Nestled on a picturesque bend of the Dordogne, referred to as the Cingle de Trémolat, is the sleepy, tobacco-growing village of Trémolat. Tucked away on a quiet street this charming hotel opens up on one side to farmland and has a pretty back garden with a small stream. The Giraudel-Déstord family has lived in this ancient, ivy-covered farm complex for 400 years, and the tradition of welcome and excellence of service seems only to improve with time. Bernard Giraudel-Déstord represents the current generation and he is often about overseeing details in the kitchen and guest quarters. The bedrooms are located in various ivy-draped buildings about the property whose tranquil views open onto the freshness of the countryside. Each room has an individual theme for its decor and everything matches, down to the smallest detail. A favorite is decorated in large red-and-white checks on the duvets, the pillows, the curtains, and the canopy on the four-poster bed. The main restaurant is in the barn and the tables are cleverly positioned within each of the stalls. Off the cigar lounge, at back, a smaller room is very cozy for winter dining. The ambiance in either restaurant is romantic and the menu is excellent, offering a tempting selection of regional specialties. *Directions:* Trémolat is located 54 km south of Périgueux. From Périgueux travel south on N139 and at Le Bugue travel southwest on D31 to Trémolat.

❋ ⚲ 📷 🏠 Ⴤ P ⴼ ⚓ ⚘ ☎ ⵣ ⴾⴾ 🐎 ⚓ ⵣ

LE VIEUX LOGIS ET SES LOGIS DES CHAMPS
Hoteliêr: Frédéric Nouhaud
Owner: Bernard Giraudel-Déstord
24510 Trémolat, France
Tel: 05.53.22.80.06, Fax: 05.53.22.84.89
25 Rooms, Double: €163–€335*
*Breakfast not included: €12 or €18
Restaurant: closed for lunch off season
Open: all year, Credit cards: all major
Relais & Châteaux, Region: Dordogne, Michelin Map: 526
www.karenbrown.com/champs.html

In the middle of a beautiful valley, with mountains towering as high as 1,500 meters on either side, the medieval town of Trigance clings to a rocky spur. The Château de Trigance is found within the walls and ruins of the ancient castle that crowns the village. The restorations and extent of the work involved to prepare this 11th-century fortress as a hotel are fully appreciated after seeing the "before" and "after" photographs. At present there are ten rooms tucked behind the ancient fortress's thick stone walls. The accommodation is definitely not luxurious and often a bit austere with beds butted right up against the ancient stone walls, but the setting and atmosphere are unique, with an authentic medieval flavor. You can even reserve a large room in the round tower that overlooks the village. The restaurant is renowned for its fine cuisine. Madame and Monsieur Thomas are in charge of the hotel in its magnificent setting under the warm blue skies of Haute Provence and their personalities enhance the character and attraction of this hillside accommodation. Park on the outskirts of this walled town and Monsieur Thomas or his charming son, Guillaume, will meet you. The location of the château is a perfect starting point for touring the spectacular Gorges du Verdon: Pack a picnic and spend a day driving along the canyon at your leisure. *Directions:* From Draguignan take D955 signposted Castellance for 45 km (north) to the hotel.

CHÂTEAU DE TRIGANCE
Hoteliêr: Jean-Claude Thomas Family
83840 Trigance, France
Tel: 04.94.76.91.18, Fax: 04.94.85.68.99
10 Rooms, Double: €115–€190*
*Breakfast not included: €14
Open: Mar 22 to Nov 1, Credit cards: all major
Châteaux & Hotels de France
Region: Haute Provence, Michelin Map: 528
www.karenbrown.com/trigance.html

It is always a delight to happen on what I consider an undiscovered gem. The lovely framed entry of La Maison des Chanoines is off a narrow cobbled street that winds up to the crowning château of the beautiful village of Turenne. Madame and Monsieur Cheyroux, as a team, have poured their heart and creativity into the renovation of this very special 16th-century inn. Its gourmet restaurant is set behind a thick, stone archway and tables are intimately set under the arched stone walls and ceiling of the cellar. Fresh flowers, beautiful copper candlesticks, handsome ceramic jugs, and beautiful china accompany each course. The selection on the menu and wine list is excellent and based on local and regional specialties. With just 16 place settings in the restaurant, it is wise to book ahead. In lovely weather, additional tables are available outside on the terrace. The guestrooms are also limited in number, with some in the main building and others across the road. The original rooms are accessed off a small street that winds up behind the restaurant entrance. Guestrooms are a fabulous value, comfortable, simple, and quite charming. Thick-set windows are draped with attractive curtains, beds are comfortable, lighting is good, and bathrooms are spotless and modern. *Directions:* Turenne is located 15 km south of Brive. Take the N20 south to exit 52 in the direction of Noailles and travel approximately ten minutes on to Turenne.

LA MAISON DES CHANOINES
Hoteliêrs: Mme & M Cheyroux
Route de L'Eglise, 19500 Turenne, France
Tel & Fax: 05.55.85.93.43
6 Rooms, Double: €65–€90*, 1 House: €650 weekly
*Breakfast not included: €9
Restaurant: closed midweek at lunch
Open: Easter to Nov 1, Credit cards: MC, VS
Region: Limousin, Michelin Map: 522
www.karenbrown.com/chanoines.html

Reveling in the fanciful experience of staying in a romantic château, we often forget that we are truly in someone's home. Château d'Urtubie has from its origin belonged to the de Coral family. As Laurent, a 5th generation of the château, toured us through the magnificent rooms with their grand, historical furnishings, which (amazingly) are all original to the home; he brought the personal element into perspective. One of the elegant salons was where he and his cousins watched television—the TV room to them! Carved into one of the mantels reads an old Basque welcome, Biltzen, Berotzen, Bozten (reunite, warm and make people happy), still the sincere intent of your hosts. They have converted rooms for guests and open their home to public tours in order to share their heritage. The grand salon is available to guests and a cozy side room, often warmed by a wood fire, serves as the breakfast room. There are over 6 hectares of gardens, forest, a park with tennis courts, and a pool. Enter off the graveled courtyard and climb the old stairs that wind up in the turret. The bedchambers are priced according to their varying size. I adored Louis XVI, a spacious, regal front corner room decorated in a rich fabric of reds and creams. Although dinner is not offered, Ferme Kalia, offering excellent Basque cuisine, is two blocks from the château. *Directions:* From A63 take St. Jean de Luz exit south, following signs to Urrugne on the left. The Château is just off N10.

CHÂTEAU D'URTUBIE   **New**
Owners: Laurent & Odile de Coral
South of St. Jean de Luz, RN 10
64122 Urrugne, France
Tel: 05.59.54.31.15, Fax: 05.59.54.62.51
10 Rooms, Double: €65–€135*
*Breakfast not included: €10
Closed: Nov 16 to Mar 15, Credit cards: all major
Châteaux & Hotels de France
Region: Basque, Michelin Map: 525
www.karenbrown.com/urtubie.html

As we drove through the glorious countryside of Provence with fields of grapes on both sides of the road stretching into the distance, we came upon the Domaine de la Ponche. At first sight, our hearts were won completely and we were relieved to discover this jewel of a hotel is as lovely inside as it is out. Dating back to 1629, the house still retains many of its early features, including one of its original round chubby towers with peaked roof. The mansion had been abandoned for many years and was in total disrepair when purchased by your gracious hosts, Madeleine Frauenknecht, Ruth Spahn, and Jean-Pierre Onimus. Together they have done a superb job in the restoration. The exterior of the manor is pastel cream with a blush of pink, given a fairy-tale look by pretty blue shutters and a lacing of ivy. Tall cypress trees frame the property, which includes a small vineyard and a beautifully tended garden where the swimming pool nestles. Next to the house, so close to the vineyards that you feel you could reach out and touch the grapes, intimate dining tables are set under a romantic, wisteria-draped trellis. Inside, the house has been decorated in a tasteful, understated style. There is nothing fussy or trendy, just large, uncluttered rooms accented by some magnificent antiques and lovely fabrics. *Directions:* Take the D8 from Bollene to Vacqueyras, then a few kilometers before you come to Vacqueyras, turn right at a sign to the hotel.

DOMAINE DE LA PONCHE
Hoteliêrs: Mme Frauenknecht, Mme Spahn & M Onimus
84190 Vacqueyras, France
Tel: 04.90.65.85.21, Fax: 04.90.65.85.23
6 Rooms, Double: €130–€200
Restaurant: closed off season
Open: Mar 1 to Nov 15, Credit cards: MC, VS
Region: Provence, Michelin Maps: 524, 528
www.karenbrown.com/laponche.html

A beautiful drive winds up to this lovely, gray-turreted château and the first impression is captivating. The Château de Castel Novel offers refined service and accommodation and, to top it off, the cuisine is superb. This is the country of such delicacies as foie gras, truffles, veal, and a delightful variety of mushrooms. The talented chef, who served his apprenticeship in the region and at some of France's finest restaurants, offers you a wonderful menu. Air-conditioned throughout, the bedrooms are attractive—I found, as they were shown to me, that each one became my "favorite." One is impressive, if you like to sleep in a turret; another has a pair of magnificent, spiraling-wood four-poster beds; and yet another has twin beds, two balconies, and a lovely view. The Parveaux family has added ten attic rooms in an annex, Le Cottage du Château. These rooms are furnished less luxuriously and do not offer the same wonderful ambiance, but are offered at a reduced rate. Built in the 14th and 15th centuries, the Château de Castel Novel is set in a garden of 15 acres with a swimming pool, tennis courts, and a practice area of three holes for golfers. In July and August, the hotel requires that guests stay on a demi-pension or bed & breakfast basis. *Directions:* Travel 10 km to the northwest from Brive la Gaillarde on D901, in the direction of Objat. Just as you enter Varetz, turn left on D152, where the hotel is signposted.

CHATEAU DE CASTEL NOVEL
Hoteliêrs: Mme & M Albert Parveaux
19240 Varetz, France
Tel: 05.55.85.00.01, Fax: 05.55.85.09.03
37 Rooms, Double: €110–€310*
*Breakfast not included: €15
Restaurant: closed midweek at lunch
Open: all year, Credit cards: all major
Relais & Châteaux
Region: Dordogne, Michelin Map: 522
www.karenbrown.com/castelnovel.html

If you are looking for reasonably priced accommodations in a stunning setting, with charming ambiance, absolute tranquillity, and great food, look no further than the romantic 16th-century mill, Le Moulin Fleuri. For a budget hotel, it is a real treasure. Strategically positioned for exploring the châteaux of the Loire, this charming old mill snuggles right at the edge of the River Indre, with its terrace (where breakfast and drinks are served in warm weather) extending to the very edge of the water. The scene is one of idyllic bliss with the green river running by, beautiful trees draped over the embankment, colorful flowers, and a picture-perfect stone bridge arched over the river. Le Moulin Fleuri is most famous as a restaurant. The dining room is very inviting, with a low, beamed ceiling, tables beautifully set with fine linens, watercolors on the walls, and at the end of the room a window that looks like a painting as it captures the lovely scene of the river. However, there are also nine simple, moderately sized bedrooms, six of which look out over the river. They are not luxurious, but most pleasant, with windows draped in pretty floral fabric and very good bathrooms (no bathtubs)—and everything is spotless! Another bonus of Le Moulin Fleuri is that it is a family operation, ensuring personal attention. *Directions:* Take the N10 south from Tours. Before Montbazon, turn right on D87 toward Monts. Go 2.2 kilometers and turn left, following signs.

LE MOULIN FLEURI
Hoteliêrs: Martine & Alain Chaplin
Route du Ripault, Veigné, 37250 Montbazon, France
Tel: 02.47.26.01.12, Fax: 02.47.34.04.71
9 Rooms, Double: €69–€105*, 1 Apartment: €103
*Breakfast not included: €9 or €12
Restaurant: closed Mon
Closed: Feb, Credit cards: all major
Châteaux & Hotels de France
Region: Loire Valley, Michelin Map: 519
www.karenbrown.com/moulinfleuri.html

Vence is a quaint little town of narrow streets, intriguing passageways, and tempting craft and specialty shops. Look for the largest tree in Vence and there you will find L'Auberge des Seigneurs. This is a delightful inn, located on a quiet side street at the center of Vence. The inn is charming in its decor and country ambiance—heavy old beams are exposed in the ceilings and walls are whitewashed. Copper plates, pans, and bed warmers adorn the walls, Provençal fabrics cover the tables, and lovely antiques decorate every nook and cranny. Wooden doors, rich in their patina, a large stone fireplace, and striking flower arrangements complete a scene in the restaurant and salon that is intimate and cozy. In the evenings the restaurant comes alive, mellow with the soft flicker of candlelight. Diners talk in hushed conversation at clustered tables and Madame Rodi orchestrates excellent and gracious service, tossing salads tableside, pouring wine, and tending chickens grilled on the open fire. Up a creaking stairway are ten delightful, small rooms. These inexpensive bedrooms, comfortable and simply decorated with pretty country prints, are a true bargain. *Directions:* From Nice travel southwest on N98 to Cros de Cagnes and then travel north on D36 to Vence. Vence is located 22 km to the northwest of Nice.

L'AUBERGE DES SEIGNEURS ET DU LION D'OR
Hoteliêr: Daniele Rodi
Place du Frêne, 06140 Vence, France
Tel: 04.93.58.04.24, Fax: 04.93.24.08.01
10 Rooms, Double: €70–€90*
*Breakfast not included: €10
Restaurant: closed Mon-Thu lunch
Closed: beg-Nov to mid-Mar, Credit cards: all major
Region: Riviera, Michelin Map: 528
www.karenbrown.com/desseigneurs.html

Hôtel le Pontot, a fortified house with a walled flower garden, sits amongst the winding medieval streets of the walled hilltop town of Vézelay. Charles Thum, the American owner, leaves the running of the hotel to the personable Christian Abadie, but he is usually on hand to help unilingual English-speaking guests with their reservations and questions. On warm days guests breakfast off Limoges china, with silver service, at little tables set in the garden; in inclement weather breakfast is served in the elegant blue salon. Curving stone steps lead up to the bedrooms and the comfortable lounge. The traditionally decorated bedrooms are furnished with antiques and have small modern bathrooms. We especially enjoyed the bedroom that contains Monet's easel, and the spacious suite with its blue silk coronet draperies above twin beds. For complete privacy request the suite in the former kitchen: its stone floor, huge fireplace, and old utensils give a rustic feel and you can scramble up above the oven to the extra little bed where the servants once slept. There are some delightful restaurants in the village and guests often dine with Marc Meneau in nearby Saint Père sous Vézelay. *Directions:* Vézelay is located 15 km west of Avallon on D957. From the town's main square turn up the hill towards the Basilica and park in the first carport on your left. The hotel is on the left.

RÉSIDENCE HÔTEL LE PONTOT
Hoteliêr: Charles Thum
Directeur: Christian Abadie
Place du Pontot, 89450 Vézelay, France
Tel: 03.86.33.24.40, Fax: 03.86.33.30.05
10 Rooms, Double: €105–€160*
*Breakfast not included: €12
Open: May 1 to Oct 15, Credit cards: MC, VS
Region: Burgundy, Michelin Map: 519
www.karenbrown.com/hotellepontot.html

Le Prieuré was built as an archbishop's palace in 1322 and became a priory in 1333—now it's a charming hotel at the heart of this inviting medieval village. Ivy clings to its warm stone exterior, green shutters dress its windows, and sun-baked tiles adorn the roof. The hotel has expanded and changed over the years and now has 26 rooms and 10 suites, many of which have lovely terraces, housed in a modern annex. The annex, which might at first disappoint as it doesn't boast the character of old, does enjoy all the welcome, modern comforts. Air conditioning has been incorporated throughout—an appreciated luxury in the hot Provençal summers. Le Prieuré is decorated with beautiful antiques, which add charm and beauty to the ambiance and setting. When blessed with the balmy weather of Provence, dine on the terrace surrounded by foliage and soft lighting in the subtle elegance of a summer night. François is your gracious host and his presence lends a personal and special touch to the very competent and professional service. *Directions:* Leave Avignon towards Nîmes and immediately after crossing the River Rhône turn right towards Bagnols sur Cèze on D980 for about 2 km. The hotel is in the heart of the village, next to the church.

LE PRIEURÉ
Hoteliêr: François Mille
7, Place du Chapître
30400 Villeneuve les Avignon, France
Tel: 04.90.15.90.15, Fax: 04.90.25.45.39
36 Rooms, Double: €98–€300*
*Breakfast not included: €17, Restaurant: closed Wed
Open: mid-Mar to Nov, Credit cards: all major
Relais & Châteaux, Region: Provence
Michelin Maps: 524, 528
www.karenbrown.com/leprieure.html

Terraced down the hillside with the original domaine as its focal point and center, the Domaine de Rochebois, with its soft, pale stone and gray roof, is elegant and very luxurious. You enter the reception through automatic glass doors and receive a welcome both professional and gracious. An elegant staircase winds up to ten of the pavilion guestrooms. Extremely spacious and handsome in their decor, the rooms look across the pool to the surrounding property and expansive golf course. Smaller rooms in the pavilion are less expensive but still quite comfortable in size with magnificently appointed bathrooms. The tiled-floor rooms in the side annex are more Italian-Mediterranean in their style and decor, also quite lovely with private balconies and priced according to view. There are four duplexes in the annex that enjoy a first-floor living room, a loft bedroom, and an expanse of private outdoor terrace. Breakfast is served either in a lovely breakfast room off the glassed-in corridor connecting the two buildings or in the guestroom. The Domaine de Rochebois has some wonderful dining options and it is often welcome to settle in and not drive somewhere for dinner after a long day of sightseeing. *Directions:* Located on the D703, 6 km south of Sarlat.

DOMAINE DE ROCHEBOIS
Hoteliêr: L. Van de Walle, Directeur: Anne Hillebrand
Route de Montfort, Vitrac
24200 Sarlat, France
Tel: 05.53.31.52.52, Fax: 05.53.29.36.88
40 Rooms, Double: €145–€420*
*Breakfast not included: €15
Open: end-Apr to end of Oct, Credit cards: all major
Châteaux & Hotels de France
Region: Dordogne, Michelin Maps: 522, 526
www.karenbrown.com/rochebois.html

Although wonderfully convenient if you have just crossed the English Channel or the Belgian border, this lovely seaside hotel is a destination in its own right. The entrance off the street is nondescript but the back of the building stretches along the boardwalk and borders a wide expanse of white-sand beach and ocean. Inside, you are immediately embraced by the mood and colors of the sea. Floors of cream tile and walls washed in a warm beige, decorated with nautical ornamentation and seashells, are reminiscent of the ocean. Fabrics reflect the blues and greens of the glistening waters. The entry steps down to a sitting area then to the bar and adjoining brasserie-restaurant, all open to the bank of windows magnificently framing the beach panorama. A renowned chef, Alain Delpierre takes pride in a menu that boasts the bounty of the sea. As well as an outdoor terrace restaurant, you'll also find a more formal restaurant upstairs, again with magnificent views. There are just eighteen fresh and pretty guestrooms, fourteen of which overlook the ocean. Although all the rooms are cozy in size, those classified as superior enjoy a little more space and a bathroom with a separate toilet. I thought number 12, a standard room, was charming with its cream and white seashell print dressing the bed. *Directions:* Wimereux is a beach town and most streets lead to the water. On the north side of town, wind your way to the waterfront, watching for signs that will direct you to the Atlantic.

HÔTEL L'ATLANTIC
Hoteliêrs: M & Mme Alain Delpierre
Digue de Mer, 62930 Wimereux, France
Tel: 03.21.32.41.01, Fax: 03.21.87.46.17
18 Rooms, Double: €70–€117*
*Breakfast not included: €10
Restaurant: closed Sun evening
Closed: Feb, Credit cards: all major
Region: Pas-de-Calais, Michelin Map: 511
www.karenbrown.com/wimereux.html

Nestled on the shore of Lake Geneva, the tiny walled medieval village of Yvoire is positively captivating—almost too quaint to be real. Its allure is even more enchanting in summer when every available bit of land is a flower garden and every house draped with red geraniums. Making everything perfect, there is a gem of a small hotel here—the 200-year-old Hôtel du Port, which absolutely oozes charm with a stone façade almost totally covered with ivy, brown shutters, and red geraniums spilling out of window boxes. It is just next to the dock where ferries flit in and out all day, making their circuit around the lake. The main focus of the hotel is its restaurant, which has a summer dining terrace stretching to the edge of the water. Although the majority of guests come just for lunch, for a lucky few there are seven sweet bedrooms available. If you want to splurge, request one of the five with a romantic balcony overlooking the lake (an elevator takes you to the upper floors). The moderately sized, spotlessly clean guestrooms are simple and attractive, with built-in wooden furniture and matching drapes and bedspreads. Each has a modern bathroom, air conditioning, telephone, TV, and mini-bar. As in so many of our favorite hotels, the gracious owners, Jeannine and Jean-François Kung, are also the managers, always keeping an eye out to be sure the hotel is impeccable in every way. *Directions:* Yvoire is on the south shore of Lake Geneva, 30 km east of Geneva.

❄ ⚓ 💳 ☎ ♿ ♈ P ⚏ 🚭 ⚡ 🏛 🔔 ☎ ⚓ 🚶 🏃 🐎 ⚡ 🍇

HÔTEL DU PORT
Hoteliêrs: Jeannine & Jean-François Kung
74140 Yvoire, France
Tel: 04.50.72.80.17, Fax: 04.50.72.90.71
7 Rooms, Double: €110–€190*
*Breakfast not included: €10
Open: Feb to Nov, Credit cards: all major
Region: French Alps, Michelin Map: 523
www.karenbrown.com/hotelduport.html

380

Index

Index

Notes

KAREN BROWN wrote her first travel guide in 1976. Her personalized travel series has grown to 17 titles, which Karen and her small staff work diligently to keep updated. Karen, her husband, Rick, and their children, Alexandra and Richard, live in a small town on the coast south of San Francisco. They settled here when they opened Seal Cove Inn. Karen travels frequently, but when home, she enjoys welcoming Karen Brown readers.

CLARE BROWN was a travel consultant for many years, specializing in planning itineraries to Europe using charming small hotels in the countryside. The focus of her job remains unchanged, but now her expertise is available to a larger audience—the readers of her daughter Karen's country inn guides. When Clare and her husband, Bill, are not traveling, they live either in Hillsborough, California, or at their home in Vail, Colorado.

JUNE EVELEIGH BROWN'S love of travel was inspired by the *National Geographic* magazines that she read as a girl in her dentist's office—so far she has visited over 40 countries. June hails from Sheffield, England and lived in Zambia and Canada before moving to northern California where she lives in San Mateo with her husband, Tony, their daughter Clare, their two German Shepherds, and a Siamese cat.

MARIE COLLINS KSSTENTINI, a contributing editor, is French and joined the Karen Brown team when she worked for a few years in California. She has settled on the Riviera with her beautiful daughters, Jessie and Chloé.

JANN POLLARD, the artist responsible for the beautiful painting on the cover of this guide, has studied art since childhood, and is well known for her outstanding impressionistic-style watercolors, which she has exhibited in numerous juried shows, winning many awards. Fine-art giclée prints of the cover paintings are also available at www.karenbrown.com.

BARBARA MACLURCAN TAPP, the talented artist who produces all of the hotel sketches and delightful illustrations in this guide, was raised in Sydney, Australia where she studied interior design. Although Barbara continues with architectural rendering and watercolor painting, she devotes much of her time to illustrating the Karen Brown guides. Barbara lives in Kensington, California, with her husband, Richard, and is Mum to Jono, Alex and Georgia.

Karen Brown Presents Her Own Special Hideaways

Karen Brown's Seal Cove Inn

Spectacularly set amongst wildflowers and bordered by cypress trees, Seal Cove Inn (Karen's second home) looks out to the distant ocean. Each room has a fireplace, cozy sitting area, and a view of the sea. Located on the coast, 35 minutes south of San Francisco.

Seal Cove Inn, Moss Beach, California
toll free telephone: (800) 995-9987
www.sealcoveinn.com

Karen Brown's Dolphin Cove Inn

Hugging a steep hillside overlooking the sparkling deep-blue bay of Manzanillo, Dolphin Cove Inn offers guests outstanding value. Each room has either a terrace or a balcony, and a breathtaking view of the sea. Located on the Pacific Coast of Mexico.

Dolphin Cove Inn, Manzanillo, Mexico
toll free telephone: (888) 497-4138
www.dolphincoveinn.com